London 2009

A Selection
of **Restaurants** & **Hotels**

Commitments

"*This volume was created at the turn of the century and will last at least as long.*"

This foreword to the very first edition of the MICHELIN Guide, written in 1900, has become famous over the years and the Guide has lived up to the prediction. It is read across the world and the key to its popularity is the consistency of its commitment to its readers, which is based on the following promises.

→ Anonymous inspections

Our inspectors make regular and anonymous visits to hotels and restaurants to gauge the quality of products and services offered to an ordinary customer. They settle their own bill and may then introduce themselves and ask for more information about the establishment. Our readers' comments are also a valuable source of information, which we can then follow up with another visit of our own.

→ Independence

Our choice of establishments is a completely independent one, made for the benefit of our readers alone. The decisions to be taken are discussed around the table by the inspectors and the editor. The most important awards are decided at a European level. Inclusion in the Guide is completely free of charge.

→ Selection & choice

The Guide offers a selection of the best hotels and restaurants in every category of comfort and price. This is only possible because all the inspectors rigorously apply the same methods.

→ Annual updates

All the practical information, the classifications and awards are revised and updated every single year to give the most reliable information possible.

Consistency: The criteria for the classifications are the same in every country covered by the Michelin Guide.

→ And our aim...

...to do everything possible to make travel, holidays and eating out a pleasure, as part of Michelin's ongoing commitment to improving travel and mobility.

Dear reader

We are delighted to introduce the third edition of the Michelin Guide for London.

This collection of City Guides began with the publication of our New York Guide in 2005. San Francisco, London, Paris, Los Angeles, Las Vegas and Tokyo followed, with Hong Kong being the most recent addition.

We make this guide for you and value your opinions, so let us know what you think about this guide and about the restaurants we have recommended.

All the restaurants within this guide have been chosen first and foremost for the quality of their cooking. You'll find comprehensive information on over 450 dining establishments within these pages and they range from gastropubs and neighbourhood brasseries to internationally renowned restaurants. The diverse and varied selection also bears testament to the rich and buoyant dining scene in London, with the city now enjoying a worldwide reputation for the quality and range of its restaurants.

You'll see that Michelin Stars are not our only awards – look out also for the Bib Gourmands. These are restaurants where the cooking is still carefully prepared but in a simpler style and, priced at under £28 for three courses, they represent excellent value for money.

As well as the restaurants, our team of independent inspectors has also chosen 50 hotels. These carefully selected hotels represent the best that London has to offer, from the luxurious and international to the small and intimate. All have been chosen for their individuality and personality.

Consult the Michelin Guide at www.viamichelin.com
and write to us at themichelinguide-gbirl@uk.michelin.com

Contents

Commitments	2
Dear reader	3
How to use this guide	6
A culinary history of London	8
Practical London	10

● Where to **eat**

Alphabetical list of restaurants	409
Starred restaurants • Rising Stars	14
Bib Gourmand	16
Restaurants by cuisine type	17
Restaurants with outside dining	23
Restaurants open late	24
Restaurants open on Sunday	26

CENTRAL LONDON — 29

▶ Mayfair • Soho • St James's	32
▶ Strand • Covent Garden	92
▶ Belgravia • Victoria	102
▶ Regent's Park • Marylebone	122
▶ Bloomsbury • Hatton Garden • Holborn	142
▶ Bayswater • Maida Vale	158
▶ City of London • Clerkenwell • Finsbury • Southwark	172
▶ Chelsea • Earl's Court • Hyde Park • Knightsbridge • South Kensington	210
▶ Kensington • North Kensington • Notting Hill	248

GREATER LONDON — 265

▶ **North-West** — 268
Archway • Belsize Park • Camden Town • Child's Hill • Crouch End • Euston • Hampstead • Highgate • Kensal Green • Kilburn • Primrose Hill • Queen's Park • Swiss Cottage • Tufnell Park • West Hampstead • Willesden Green

▶ **North-East** — 286
Barnsbury • Bow • Canonbury • Hackney • Hoxton • Islington • Mile End • Shoreditch • Stoke Newington • Stroud Green • Tottenham

▶ **South-East** — 304
Blackheath • Canary Wharf • Elephant & Castle • Forest Hill • Greenwich • Herne Hill • Kennington • Limehouse • Spitalfields • Wapping • West Dulwich • Whitechapel

▶ **South-West** — 316
Acton • Balham • Barnes • Brixton • Chiswick • Clapham • Ealing • East Sheen • Fulham • Hammersmith • Kew • Putney • Richmond • Southfields • Teddington • Tooting • Twickenham • Wandsworth • Wimbledon

Where to **stay**

Alphabetical list of hotels — 357

Maps **& plans**

Index of maps — 408
Map of London Underground — 415

How to use this guide

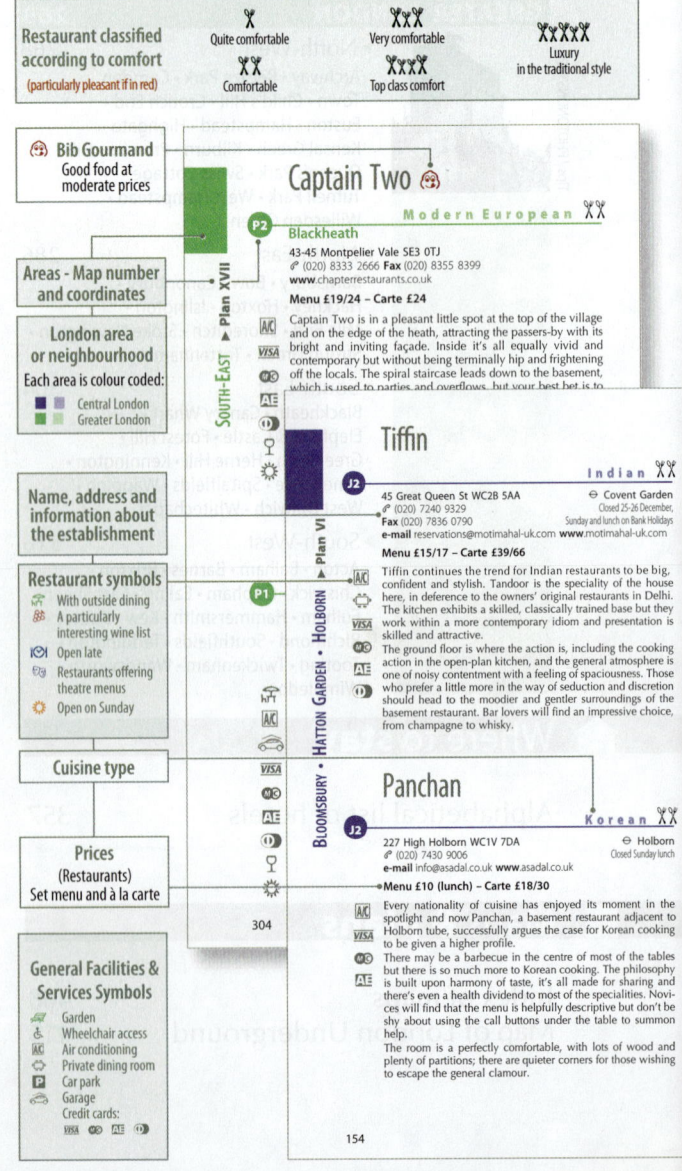

HOW TO USE THIS GUIDE

Hotel classification according to comfort
(particularly pleasant if in red)

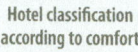 Quite comfortable
 Very comfortable
 Luxury in the traditional style
 Comfortable
 Top class comfort

Hotel symbols

- **39 rm** Number of rooms
- 🍽 Breakfast included (or not)
- ♦/♦♦ Prices for a single/double room
- 🍃 Quiet hotel
- 🍴 With restaurant
- 🏊 Swimming pool
- 💆 Spa
- 🧖 Sauna
- 🎾 Tennis
- 🏋 Exercise room
- 🛗 Lift
- 📶 Broadband connection in bedrooms
- 📡 Wireless access in bedrooms
- 📺 Satellite TV
- 🏢 Equipped conference room

Map coordinates — Underground station

Agatha's

12

15 Charlotte St W1T 1RJ — ⊖ Goodge Street
☎ (020) 7806 2000 Fax (020) 7806 2002
e-mail charlotte@firmdale.com **www**.charlottestreethotel.co.uk

44 rm – ♦£247/282 ♦♦£347, 🍽 £19 – 8 suites
🍴 **Hercule** (See restaurant listing)

...tion, within strolling distance of Soho, or
...own private screening room that attract
...h industry sorts and arty souls who have
...own, but the stimulating way in which it
...and the prevailing vibe.
...warehouse has been deftly transformed
...and proves that comfort and design can
...and that something good has come from
...g a combination of abstract art, sculpture
...rtists of the neighbouring Bloomsbury set,
...be also quite English in tone. The drawing
...ress-free areas, in contrast to the bustle of
...restaurant.
...edrooms are one-off pieces of furniture
...rawer fabrics and fittings, all supported by
...mme of virtually constant refurbishment.
...enthusiastic and confident. The loft and
...l stir emotions of envy and desire or, if

Le Petit François ✿✿

G3

French 🍴XXXX

43 Upper Brook St W1K 7QR — ⊖ Marble Arch
☎ (020) 7408 0881 — Closed Christmas-New Year, Sunday, Saturday
Fax (020) 7491 4387 — lunch and Bank Holidays – booking essential
e-mail bookings@le-gavroche.com **www**.le-gavroche.co.uk

Menu £48 – Carte £60/130

In today's rush for the new and the novel, we sometimes forget about the jewels we already have. Le Petit François is guaranteed its own chapter when the history of British gastronomy is written and today, over forty years after it first opened in Chelsea, it's still maintaining its own high standards and respect for tradition. The service is unerringly professional; this is where any budding restaurateur should come if they want to learn how things are done 'properly' and one can observe the hierarchical structure from one's chair. The room retains a clubby and masculine feel but it also offers a palpable sense of history; those new to the restaurant are guided gently through its customs and politely reminded of its traditions.

The menu represents classic French cuisine and not just an English idea of French cuisine; a style of food which is becoming rarer by the day. A Soufflé Suissesse is rich enough to live on for days and the use of luxury items, from lobster to foie gras, would make Epicurus blanch. Those who prefer a lighter style, however, are not ignored.

MAYFAIR • SOHO • ST JAMES'S ▶ Plan II

WESTMINSTER ▶ Plan V

First Course
- Hot foie gras and crispy duck pancake flavoured with cinnamon.
- Lobster mousse with caviar and champagne butter sauce.

Main Course
- Roast saddle of rabbit with crispy potatoes and parmesan.
- Whole roast John Dory with artichokes, olive oil mashed potato.

Dessert
- Bitter chocolate and praline 'indulgence'.
- Iced amaretto nougat with cherries cooked in red wine syrup.

Area - Map number

Stars for good cooking
✿ to ✿✿✿

✿
Starred restaurant symbol

Sample menu for starred restaurant

A culinary history of London

London, influenced by worldwide produce arriving via the Thames, has always enjoyed a close association with its food, though most of the time the vast majority of its people have looked much closer to home for their sustenance.

Even as far back as the 2nd century AD, meat was on the menu: the profusion of wildlife in the woods and forests around London turned it into a carnivore's paradise, thereby setting the tone and the template. Large stoves were employed to cook everything from pork and beef to goose and deer. The Saxons added the likes of garlic, leeks, radishes and turnips to the pot, while eels became a popular staple in later years.

WHAT A LARK!

By the 13th century, the taste for fish had evolved to the more exotic porpoise, lamprey and sturgeon, with saffron and spices perking up the common-or-garden meat dish. Not that medieval tastes would have been considered mundane to the average 21st century diner: Londoners of the time would think nothing about devouring roasted thrush or lark from the cook's stalls dotted around the city streets. And you'd have been unlikely to hear the cry "Eat your greens!" In the 15th century the vegetable diet, such as it was, seemed to run mainly to herbs such as rosemary, fennel, borage and thyme.

As commercial and maritime success burgeoned in the age of the Tudors, so tables began to groan under the weight of London's penchant for feasting. No excess was spared, as oxen, sheep, boars and pigs were put to the griddle; these would have been accompanied by newly arrived yams and sweet potatoes from America and 'washed down' with rhubarb from Asia. People on the streets could 'feast-lite': by the 17th century hawkers were offering all sorts of goodies on the hoof.

FULL OF BEANS

All of this eating was of course accompanied by a lot of drinking. Though much of it took place in the alehouses and taverns - which ran into the thousands - by the 18th century coffee houses had become extraordinarily popular. These were places to do business as well as being convenient 'for passing evenings socially at a very small charge'.

Perhaps the biggest revolution in eating habits came midway through the 19th century when the first cavernous dining halls and restaurants appeared. These 'freed' diners from the communal benches of the cook-house and gave them, for the first time, the chance for a bit of seclusion at separate tables. This private dining experience was an egalitarian movement: plutocrats may have had their posh hotels, but the less well-off were buttering teacakes and scones served by 'nippies' at the local Lyons Corner House.

Influenced by post-World War II flavours brought in by immigrants from Asia, the Caribbean and Africa, Londoners can now enjoy an unparalleled cuisine alive with global flavours, while the worlds of food and drink have fused remarkably well in recent years with the growing excellence of the gastropub, which had its roots in the creative maelstrom of the capital.

Practical London

Arrival/Departure

Getting to the UK's first city from abroad can try the patience of even the most eager Londonophile, but at least you have plenty of options to choose from.

Planes...

Heathrow, the UK's busiest airport, can suffer from its popularity, but is conveniently located on the Piccadilly Line and so is marvellous for southwest London. Those wishing to be whisked to the centre shouldn't hesitate to board the popular Heathrow Express to Paddington - more expensive than the tube, but you're sped to Zone One four times quicker. Getting a taxi is a much riskier strategy - depending on traffic, the journey can take an hour or more and is correspondingly pricey.

Gatwick to the south is further out in the sticks, but has some convenient rail links from the south terminal. The Gatwick Express runs to Victoria Station taking 30 minutes, although other services get there almost as fast. The Thameslink line, meanwhile, runs through London Bridge and Kings Cross, before going up to burgeoning Luton Airport, the original EasyJet hub.

... or trains?

Stansted was also a cheap flights trailblazer and is known for Norman Foster's modern terminal building. Trains and coaches go to Liverpool Street, convenient for east London. Business travellers, however, should consider flights to London City Airport, with the prospect of amazing views from the plane and a speedy transfer onto the Docklands Light Railway (DLR).

Getting around

You know you're a true Londoner when you've mastered how to use the Tube, but

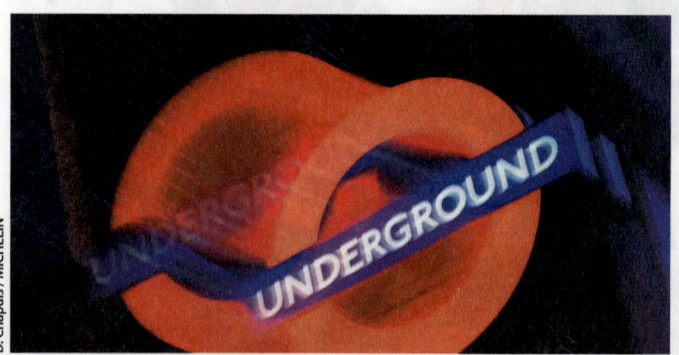

those on a flying visit should not despair - it's easier than it looks.

Tube and oysters

Travelcards go a long way on London's transport system, since unlimited journeys within the zoned areas will work out cheaper than numerous single fares, and the cards can also be used on buses and the DLR. However, those here for a while (or who just want the thrill of swiping their wallet on the little yellow gate pads) would be well-advised to get an Oyster card, which electronically stores travelcard or pre-pay credit. These smartcards have become beloved by Londoners in a very short time - not least because they offer savings on fares and keep the crowds moving quicker.

A bit of nouse can save you a lot of hassle. Remember that tube trains will be packed with commuters during rush hour periods and that platforms can be a long escalator away from ticket barriers. Also be aware that sometimes (especially in central London) a Tube journey isn't necessary at all. Leicester Square, for instance, is but 250m from Covent Garden. Check your AtoZ and if the journey looks relatively straightforward, walk - you'll get a much better view.

Drivetime

Buses provide another alternative and from the top of a double decker you'll get a sight-seeing tour for the price of your fare. The night bus service has improved immeasurably in the past couple of years (a good thing too, since the Tube still stops not long after midnight). But London life would not be complete without the occasional black cab ride home. Look for the illuminated sign on the roof before hailing and make sure you're in the mood for banter.

For those brave enough to drive themselves, the Congestion Charge may have helped to clear your way, but you'll pay a price for it - £8 each day you drive within the charge zone (£10 if you pay the day after). The good news for motorists is that the charge doesn't apply at the weekends, or before 7:00am or after 6.00pm during the week.

LIVING LONDON LIFE

There is something for everyone in London and finding out what's here for you is part of the fun. The trick is to realise that everyone's London is different and it's okay to think outside of the box. For example, the West End may have an international reputation as a theatrical powerhouse, but the most daring work is often found on the fringe, in poky venues above pubs.

Shopping

So by all means head to Oxford Street to revel in London shopping at its most frenetic, but know you'll find similar stores on the (quieter) Kensington High Street and you may prefer to try your luck in the local markets. The West End has an international reputation as a theatrical powerhouse, but the most daring work is often found on the fringe, in poky venues above pubs. Likewise, the superclubs of Clerkenwell and Shoreditch are famous the world over as party palaces, but you may prefer to embrace the Latin rhythms of a salsa evening, and belly dancing classes are also becoming a phenomenon.

Tips and tipping

When it comes to the important bit - eating - there are a few tips to ensure a good old time. Those on a budget need not miss out on fine dining experiences, with many good value lunch menus to be had. Conversely, in the City and with restaurants popular with business folk, dinner is often the cheaper option, while West End pre- and post-theatre menus are ideal for cut-price gourmets. Keeping tabs on water and wine refills should avoid nasty surprises coming with the bill - but note there is no standard procedure for tipping, and although some restaurants leave the amount open, others add a service charge of anything up to 15%. If you're unhappy, speak up.

Finally, it can be pretty frustrating when the perfect restaurant says it can't fit in your cosy table for two until mid-way through 2009. Invite some friends and ask for a table for four and you may have better luck - less romantic, but the food will taste just as good. Bon appétit!

Where to eat

Starred Restaurants

Within this selection, we have highlighted a number of restaurants for their particularly good cooking. When awarding one, two or three Michelin Stars there are a number of factors we consider: the quality and compatibility of the ingredients, the technical skill and flair that goes into their preparation, the clarity and combination of flavours, the value for money and, above all, the taste. Equally important is the ability to produce excellent cooking not once but time and time again. Our inspectors make as many visits as necessary, so that you can be sure of the quality and consistency.

A two or three star restaurant has to offer something very special in its cuisine; a real element of creativity, originality or personality that sets it apart from the rest. Three stars – our highest award – are given to the very best.

Cuisines in any style and of any nationality are eligible for a star. The decoration, service and comfort have no bearing on the award.

We will also point out any restaurants that we feel have the potential to rise further and already have an element of superior quality. These rising stars, along with the existing stars, will continue to be closely watched.

Let us know what you think, not just about the stars but about all the restaurants in this guide.

The awarding of a star is based solely on the quality of the cuisine.

N: highlights those establishments newly promoted to one, two or three stars.

Starred Restaurants

✤✤✤

Exceptional cuisine, worth a special journey.
One always eats here extremely well, sometimes superbly. Distinctive dishes are precisely executed, using superlative ingredients.

Gordon Ramsay	XxXx	216

✤✤

Excellent cooking, worth a detour.
Skilfully and carefully crafted dishes of outstanding quality.

Alain Ducasse at The Dorchester **N**	XxXxX	37	Hibiscus **N**	XxX	45
L'Atelier de Joël Robuchon **N**	X	99	Marcus Wareing at The Berkeley	XxXx	106
The Capital Restaurant	XxX	217	Pied à Terre	XxX	145
Le Gavroche	XxXx	39	The Square	XxXx	41

✤

A very good restaurant in its category.
A place offering cuisine prepared to a consistently high standard.

Amaya	XxX	109	Rasoi	XX	226
Ambassade de L'Ile **N**	XxX	221	Rhodes Twenty Four	XxX	180
Arbutus	X	83	Rhodes W1 (Restaurant)	XxXx	126
Assaggi	X	166	Richard Corrigan at Lindsay House	XxX	54
Aubergine	XxX	220	River Café	XX	339
L'Autre Pied **N**	XX	132	Roussillon	XxX	108
Benares	XxX	49	St John **N**	X	195
Chez Bruce	XX	354	Semplice **N**	XX	64
Club Gascon	XX	184	Sketch (The Lecture Room and Library)	XxXx	42
Foliage	XxX	218	Tom Aikens	XxX	219
The Glasshouse	XX	344	La Trompette	XxX	328
Gordon Ramsay at Claridge's	XxXx	40	Umu	XxX	53
The Greenhouse	XxX	44	Wild Honey	XX	61
Hakkasan	XX	148	Yauatcha	XX	80
Hélène Darroze at The Connaught **N**	XxXx	38	Zafferano	XxX	107

Kai **N**	XxX	55
The Ledbury	XxX	251
Locanda Locatelli	XxX	127
Maze	XxX	46
Murano **N**	XxX	52
Nahm	XX	113
Nobu	XX	60
Nobu Berkeley St	XX	63
Quilon	XxX	110

Rising Stars

For ✤✤✤		
Alain Ducasse at The Dorchester **N**	XxXxX	37
For ✤✤		
The Ledbury	XxX	251
Tom Aikens	XxX	219

Bib Gourmand

Restaurants offering good quality cooking for less than £28 (price of a 3 course meal excluding drinks)

L'Accento	X	167
Al Duca	X	82
The Anchor and Hope	🍴	207
Benja	XX	77
Bradley's **N**	XX	283
The Brown Dog	🍴	324
Brula	X	351
Cafe Spice Namaste	XX	315
Chapters	XX	308
Comptoir Gascon	X	203
Dehesa **N**	X	89
Foxtrot Oscar **N**	X	239
Galvin Bistrot de Luxe	XX	130
Giaconda Dining Room **N**	X	155
Great Queen Street	X	153
The Havelock Tavern	🍴	342
Hereford Road **N**	X	165
Kastoori	X	350
Ma Cuisine (Barnes)	X	324
Ma Cuisine (Kew)	X	345
Ma Cuisine (Twickenham)	X	352
Malabar	X	260
Mango and Silk **N**	X	334
Market **N**	X	274
Medcalf **N**	X	201
Metrogusto	XX	297
The Modern Pantry **N**	X	202
The Narrow	🍴	312
Salt Yard	X	154
Tangawizi	X	353
Upstairs	XX	327
Via Condotti	XX	65

Restaurants by Cuisine Type

American

| Automat | ✗ | 85 |

Asian

Champor-Champor	✗	204
Cicada	✗	200
Cocoon	✗✗	74
Crazy Bear	✗✗	149
E&O	✗✗	256
Eight over Eight	✗✗	237
Great Eastern Dining Room	✗✗	294
Haiku	✗✗	78
Kiasu	✗	168
Singapore Garden	✗✗	284
Taman Gang	✗✗	65
XO	✗✗	272

Beef specialities

Barnes Grill	✗	323
The Grill Room	✗	352
Kew Grill	✗✗	343
Maze Grill	✗✗	70
Notting Grill	✗	261

British

Bedford and Strand	✗	100
Bentley's (Grill)	✗✗✗	56
Bluebird	✗✗	228
Butlers Wharf Chop House	✗	199
Canteen (Southbank)	✗	206
Canteen (Spitalfields)	✗	313
Great Queen Street	✗ ❀	153
Hereford Road	✗ ❀	165
Hix Oyster and Chop House	✗	202
Inn the Park	✗	84
Magdalen	✗	201
Market	✗ ❀	274
Medcalf	✗ ❀	201
Mews of Mayfair	✗✗	73
The National Dining Rooms	✗	88
Paternoster Chop House	✗	198
Quality Chop House	✗	203
Quo Vadis	✗✗✗	51
Rex Whistler	✗✗	115
Rhodes Twenty Four	✗✗✗ ❀	180
Rhodes W1 Brasserie	✗✗	129
Rivington (Greenwich)	✗	311
Rivington (Shoreditch)	✗	300
Roast	✗✗	186
Rules	✗✗	96
St John	✗ ❀	195
St John Bread and Wine	✗	314
Shepherd's	✗✗✗	112

Chinese

Bar Shu	✗	87
China Tang	✗✗✗✗	36
Chinese Experience	✗	86
Dragon Castle	✗✗	310
Good Earth (Chelsea)	✗✗	238
Hakkasan	✗✗ ❀	148
Haozhan	✗✗	79
Kai	✗✗✗ ❀	55
Ken Lo's Memories of China	✗✗	115
Mao Tai	✗✗	337
Maxim	✗✗	333
Memories of China	✗✗	258
Min Jiang	✗✗✗	252
Mr Chow	✗✗	232
Pearl Liang	✗✗	164
Phoenix Palace	✗✗	135
Snazz Sichuan	✗✗	276
Yauatcha	✗✗ ❀	80
Yi-Ban	✗✗	336

Eastern european

| Baltic | ✗✗ | 190 |

French

L'Absinthe	✗	281
Admiralty	✗✗	97
Alain Ducasse at The Dorchester	✗✗✗✗✗ ❀❀	37

Where to **eat** ▶ Cuisine Type

17

Restaurant		Page
Almeida	XX	296
Ambassade de L'Ile	XxX ❀	221
Angelus	XX	162
L'Atelier de Joël Robuchon	X ❀❀	99
Aubaine	X	241
L'Auberge	XX	345
Aubergine	XxX ❀	220
L'Aventure	XX	135
Belvedere	XxX	252
Bibendum	XxX	222
Bistro Aix	X	275
Bleeding Heart	XX	150
Le Boudin Blanc	X	90
Brasserie Roux	XX	68
Brasserie St Jacques	XX	81
Cafe Boheme	X	90
The Capital Restaurant	XxX ❀❀	217
Le Cercle	XX	229
Chez Bruce	XX ❀	354
Chez Kristof	XX	340
The Clerkenwell Dining Room	XX	191
Clos Maggiore	XX	97
Club Gascon	XX ❀	184
Le Colombier	XX	230
Comptoir Gascon	X ⓐ	203
Coq d'Argent	XxX	182
L'Escargot	XxX	48
Galvin at Windows	XxxX	43
Galvin Bistrot de Luxe	XX ⓐ	130
Le Gavroche	XxxX ❀❀	39
Gordon Ramsay	XxxX ❀❀❀	216
Hélène Darroze at The Connaught	XxxX ❀	38
Incognico	XX	146
The Ledbury	XxX ❀	251
Lobster Pot	X	312
Ma Cuisine (Barnes)	X ⓐ	324
Ma Cuisine (Kew)	X ⓐ	345
Ma Cuisine (Twickenham)	X ⓐ	352
Marcus Wareing at The Berkeley	XxxX ❀❀	106
Mon Plaisir	XX	146
Morgan M	XX	290
Notting Hill Brasserie	XX	253
1 Lombard Street	XxX	181
Papillon	XX	233
Pearl	XxX	144
La Petite Maison	XX	67
Poissonnerie de l'Avenue	XX	229
Le Pont de la Tour	XxX	182
La Poule au Pot	X	118
Racine	XX	227
The Restaurant at The Petersham	XxX	348
Rhodes W1 (Restaurant)	XxxX ❀	126
Roussillon	XxX ❀	108
Sauterelle	XX	185
Sketch (The Lecture Room and Library)	XxxX ❀	42
Spread Eagle	XX	311
The Square	XxxX ❀❀	41
Tom's Kitchen	X	240
Les Trois Garcons	XX	313
La Trompette	XxX ❀	328
La Trouvaille	XX	75
Le Vacherin	XX	329
Villandry	XX	136
The Wallace	X	137

Gastropub

The Admiral Codrington	🍺	242
The Anchor and Hope	🍺 ⓐ	207
Anglesea Arms	🍺	341
The Barnsbury	🍺	299
The Bollo	🍺	320
The Brown Dog	🍺 ⓐ	324
Builders Arms	🍺	244
The Bull	🍺	278
Carpenter's Arms	🍺	342
Cat and Mutton	🍺	292
Chelsea Ram	🍺	243
The Coach and Horses	🍺	207
The Cross Keys	🍺	245
The Dartmouth Arms	🍺	310
The Dartmouth Castle	🍺	343
The Devonshire	🍺	331
The Drapers Arms	🍺	298
Duke of Sussex	🍺	320
The Ebury	🍺	120
The Empress of India	🍺	292
The Engineer	🍺	282
The Farm	🍺	338
The Fat Badger	🍺	262
The Fire Stables	🍺	355

The Fox	🍴🍺	301
The Garrison	🍴🍺	209
The Greyhound	🍴🍺	279
The Greyhound at Battersea	🍴🍺	327
The Gun	🍴🍺	309
The Hartley	🍴🍺	208
The Havelock Tavern	🍴🍺 😊	342
The House	🍴🍺	291
Junction Tavern	🍴🍺	284
Lots Road Pub & Dining Room	🍴🍺	246
The Magdala	🍴🍺	277
The Morgan Arms	🍴🍺	291
The Narrow	🍴🍺 😊	312
Norfolk Arms	🍴🍺	157
The Northgate	🍴🍺	298
North London Tavern	🍴🍺	279
L'Oasis	🍴🍺	299
The Old Dairy	🍴🍺	303
The Only Running Footman	🍴🍺	91
The Pantechnicon Rooms	🍴🍺	120
Paradise by way of Kensal Green	🍴🍺	278
The Peasant	🍴🍺	208
The Phoenix (Chelsea)	🍴🍺	245
The Pig's Ear	🍴🍺	244
Prince Albert	🍴🍺	274
Prince Alfred & Formosa Dining Room	🍴🍺	169
Prince Arthur	🍴🍺	293
Prince of Wales	🍴🍺	347
The Princess	🍴🍺	301
Queen's Head & Artichoke	🍴🍺	140
The Queens	🍴🍺	281
The Queens Pub and Dining Room	🍴🍺	276
The Rosendale	🍴🍺	315
St John's	🍴🍺	272
The Salt House	🍴🍺	140
The Salusbury	🍴🍺	282
The Spencer Arms	🍴🍺	347
Swag and Tails	🍴🍺	243
The Thomas Cubitt	🍴🍺	119
The Victoria	🍴🍺	334
The Warrington	🍴🍺	170
The Waterway	🍴🍺	169
The Well	🍴🍺	209
The Wells	🍴🍺	277

Greek

Real Greek Mezedopolio	✗	296

Indian

Amaya	✗✗✗ ❀	109
Benares	✗✗✗ ❀	49
Bengal Clipper	✗✗	185
Bombay Brasserie	✗✗✗	224
Café Lazeez	✗✗	76
Cafe Spice Namaste	✗✗ 😊	315
Chor Bizarre	✗✗	74
Chutney Mary	✗✗✗	223
The Cinnamon Club	✗✗✗	111
Eriki	✗✗	283
Imli	✗	91
Indian Zing	✗✗	338
Jamuna	✗✗	163
Kastoori	✗ 😊	350
Khan's of Kensington	✗✗	234
Malabar	✗ 😊	260
Mango and Silk	✗ 😊	334
Memories of India on the River	✗✗✗	335
Mint Leaf	✗✗	69
Mint Leaf Lounge	✗✗	194
Moti Mahal	✗✗	151
Painted Heron	✗✗	236
La Porte des Indes	✗✗	130
Quilon	✗✗✗ ❀	110
Rasa	✗	302
Rasa Samudra	✗✗	133
Rasa Travancore	✗	302
Rasoi	✗✗ ❀	226
Red Fort	✗✗✗	56
Tamarind	✗✗✗	50
Tangawizi	✗ 😊	353
Urban Turban	✗	168
Vama	✗✗	236
Veeraswamy	✗✗	75
Zaika	✗✗	254

Innovative

Archipelago	✗✗	150
L'Etranger	✗✗	231
Foliage	✗✗✗ ❀	218
The Greenhouse	✗✗✗ ❀	44
Hibiscus	✗✗✗ ❀❀	45
Maze	✗✗✗ ❀	46

Pied à Terre	XxX✪✪	145	Osteria Stecca	XX	136
The Providores	XX	131	Passione	X	152
Texture	XX	128	Pellicano	XX	235
Tom Aikens	XxX✪	219	Quadrato	XxX	308
Trinity	XX	332	Quirinale	XX	112
			Riva	X	323

International

Aquasia	XxX	225
Cantina Vinopolis	X	198
The Ivy	XxX	95
Light House	X	355
Michael Moore	X	137
The Modern Pantry	X🍀	202
Ottolenghi	X	297
Silk	XX	82
Sketch (The Gallery)	XX	66
Union Café	X	138

River Café	XX✪	339
Santini	XxX	111
Sardo	XX	147
Sardo Canale	XX	280
Sartoria	XxX	50
Semplice	XX✪	64
Theo Randall	XxX	47
Timo	XX	257
Toto's	XxX	225
Trenta	XX	163
Vasco and Piero's Pavilion	XX	72
Via Condotti	XX🍀	65
Zafferano	XxX✪	107

Italian

L'Accento	X🍀	167
A Cena	XX	351
Al Duca	X🍀	82
Alloro	XX	62
L'Anima	XxX	300
Arturo	X	167
Assaggi	X✪	166
Avista	XxX	58
Caffé Caldesi	X	138
Caldesi	XX	134
Camerino	XX	152
Cantina Del Ponte	X	197
Caraffini	XX	230
Carpaccio	XX	237
Cecconi's	XxX	51
Cibo	X	260
Il Convivio	XX	114
Daphne's	XX	227
Edera	XX	255
Enoteca Turi	XX	346
Fifteen London	X	295
Franco's	XX	76
Latium	XxX	128
Locanda Locatelli	XxX✪	127
Luciano	XxX	57
Manicomio (Chelsea)	X	240
Manicomio (City of London)	XX	192
Metrogusto	XX🍀	297
Olivo	XX	118
Osteria Emilia	X	273

Italian influences

Acorn House	X	154
Murano	XxX✪	52
Petersham Nurseries Café	X	349
Philpott's Mezzaluna	XX	275
The Phoenix (Putney)	XX	346
Water House	XX	294

Japanese

Aaya	XX	81
Abeno	X	156
Atami	XX	114
Chisou	X	85
Dinings	X	139
Kiku	XX	78
Matsuba	X	348
Matsuri - High Holborn	XX	147
Matsuri - St James's	XX	71
Nobu	XX✪	60
Nobu Berkeley St	XX✪	63
Nozomi	XX	228
Roka	XX	131
Sake No Hana	XxX	58
Sumosan	XX	73
Sushi-Say	X	285
Tatsuso	XX	188
Tsunami	XX	332
Umu	XxX✪	53
Zuma	XX	232

Korean

Asadal	XX	151

Kosher

Bevis Marks	XX	187

Latin american

Floridita	XX	67

Lebanese

Fakhreldine	XX	72
Kenza	XX	192
Levant	XX	134
Noura Brasserie	XX	117
Noura Central	XX	69

Malaysian

Awana	XxX	224

Mediterranean

Aurora	X	87
Le Café du Jardin	X	100
Dehesa	X 🙂	89
11 Abingdon Road	XX	257
Harrison's	X	321
The Lock	XX	303
Moro	X	197
Portal	XX	190
Salt Yard	X 🙂	154
Sam's Brasserie	X	330
Tapas y Vino	X	353

Modern european

Alastair Little	XX	79
Arbutus	X ✿	83
L'Autre Pied	XX ✿	132
The Avenue	XX	71
Axis	XxX	95
Babylon	XX	255
Bank	XX	117
Blueprint Café	X	196
Bonds	XxX	181
The Botanist	XX	238
The Brackenbury	X	340
Bradley's	XX 🙂	283
Brasserie James	X	322
Brula	X 🙂	351
Bumpkin	X	259
Le Café Anglais	XX	162
The Cafe at Sotheby's	X	84
Le Caprice	XX	59
The Chancery	XX	186
Chapters	XX 🙂	308
Charlotte's Place	X	333
Chelsea Brasserie	XX	235
Clarke's	XX	254
Le Deuxième	XX	98
Devonshire Terrace	XX	191
Embassy	XxX	57
Fifth Floor	XxX	223
Fig	X	290
Flâneur	X	155
The Forge	XX	98
Four O Nine	XX	331
Giaconda Dining Room	X 🙂	155
The Glasshouse	XX ✿	344
Gordon Ramsay at Claridge's	XxxX ✿	40
Hoxton Apprentice	X	295
Hush	XX	62
Island	XX	165
Kensington Place	X	259
The Larder	XX	188
Launceston Place	XxX	253
The Mercer	XX	193
Odette's	XX	280
Oscar	XX	129
Oxo Tower	XxX	183
Oxo Tower Brasserie	X	194
Patterson's	XX	59
Plateau	XX	309
Portrait	X	88
Quaglino's	XX	68
Ransome's Dock	X	325
Richard Corrigan at Lindsay House	XxX ✿	54
St Alban	XxX	48
Skylon	XxX	183
Smiths of Smithfield	XX	189
Sonny's	XX	322
Stanza	XX	77
Tate Modern (Restaurant)	X	196
Upstairs	XX 🙂	327
Village East	X	205
Vinoteca	X	199
Wapping Food	X	314

Where to **eat** ▶ Cuisine Type

The Wharf	XX	349
The White Swan	XX	189
Whits	XX	256
Wild Honey	XX ✿	61
The Wolseley	XxX	47
York & Albany	XX	273

Moroccan

Momo	XX	66
Pasha	XX	233

North african

Azou	X	341

Polish

Wódka	X	261

Scottish

Boisdale	XX	116
Boisdale of Bishopsgate	XX	187

Seafood

Bentley's (Oyster Bar)	X	86
Bibendum Oyster Bar	X	242
Deep	XX	336
Fish Hook	X	330
J. Sheekey	XX	96
Olivomare	X	119
One-O-One	XxX	222
Scott's	XxX	43
Wright Brothers	X	205

Spanish

Barrafina	X	89
Cambio de Tercio	XX	234
Cigala	X	153
Fino	XX	149
L Restaurant and Bar	XX	258
Tapas Brindisa	X	204

Thai

Bangkok	X	241
Benja	XX ☺	77
Blue Elephant	XX	337
Chada	XX	325
Chada Chada	X	139
Mango Tree	XX	116
Nahm	XX ✿	113
Nipa	XX	164
Saran Rom	XxX	335
Simply Thai	X	350

Traditional

The Ambassador	X	200
Bellamy's	XX	70
Brew Wharf	X	206
The Butcher and Grill	X	326
Foxtrot Oscar	X ☺	239
High Road Brasserie	XX	329
Konstam at the Prince Albert	X	156
Lamberts	X	321
Langan's Coq d'Or	XX	231
Marco	XX	239
The Ritz Restaurant	XxXxX	36
Tom Ilić	X	326
Walnut	X	285

Turkish

Ozer	XX	133

Vegetarian

Vanilla Black	XX	193

Vietnamese

Au Lac	X	293

Restaurants with outside dining

The Admiral Codrington	🍴	242
Anglesea Arms	🍴	341
Aquasia	✕✕✕	225
Aurora	✕	87
L'Aventure	✕✕	135
Babylon	✕✕	255
BANK	✕✕	117
The Barnsbury	🍴	299
Belvedere	✕✕✕	252
Bevis Marks	✕✕	187
Bleeding Heart	✕✕	150
Boisdale	✕✕	116
The Bollo	🍴	320
Le Boudin Blanc	✕	90
The Brackenbury	✕	340
Brasserie James	✕	322
Brew Wharf	✕	206
The Brown Dog	🍴 ✿	324
The Bull	🍴	278
The Butcher et Grill	✕	326
Butlers Wharf Chop House	✕	199
Canteen	✕	206
Cantina Del Ponte	✕	197
Caraffini	✕✕	230
Carpenter's Arms	🍴	342
Chapter Two	✕✕ ✿	308
Chez Kristof	✕✕	340
Cigala	✕	153
The Coach et Horses	🍴	207
Coq d'Argent	✕✕✕	182
The Dartmouth Arms	🍴	310
The Dartmouth Castle	🍴	343
Deep	✕✕	336
Dehesa	✕ ✿	89
Devonshire Terrace	✕✕	191
The Devonshire House	🍴	331
The Drapers Arms	🍴	298
Duke of Sussex	🍴	320
Embassy	✕✕✕	57
The Empress of India	🍴	292
The Engineer	🍴	282
Fig	✕	290
Great Queen Street	✕ ✿	153
The Greyhound	🍴	279
The Greyhound	🍴	327
The Gun	🍴	309
The Havelock Tavern	🍴 ✿	342
High Road Brasserie	✕✕	329
Hix Oyster and Chop House	✕	202
The House	🍴	291
Hoxton Apprentice	✕	295
Hush	✕✕	62
Indian Zing	✕✕	338
Inn the Park	✕	84
Junction Tavern	🍴	284
Langan's Coq d'Or	✕✕	231
The Ledbury	✕✕✕ ✣	251
Ma Cuisine	✕ ✿	345
The Magdala	🍴	277
Manicomio	✕	240
Medcalf	✕ ✿	201
Memsaab	✕✕✕	335
The Modern Pantry	✕ ✿	202
Momo	✕✕	66
The Morgan Arms	🍴	291
The Narrow	🍴 ✿	312
The Northgate	🍴	298
Notting Grill	✕	261
Odette's	✕✕	280
Olivomare	✕	119
The Only Running Footman	🍴	91
Osteria Stecca	✕✕	136
Oxo Tower	✕✕✕	183
Oxo Tower Brasserie	✕	194
Painted Heron	✕✕	236
Paternoster Chop House	✕	198
Pellicano	✕✕	235
Petersham Nurseries Café	✕	349
The Phoenix	🍴	245
The Phoenix	✕	346
Plateau	✕✕	309
Le Pont de la Tour	✕✕✕	182
La Poule au Pot	✕	118

Where to eat ▶ Outside dining

Outside dining

Prince Albert	🍴	274
Quadrato	XxX	308
The Queens	🍴	281
Queens Pub et Dining Room	🍴	276
Ransome's Dock	X	325
Rex Whistler	XX	115
The Ritz Restaurant	XxXxX	36
River Café	XX ✿	339
The Rockwell		398
The Rosendale	🍴	315
The Salt House	🍴	140
Santini	XxX	111
Saran Rom	XxX	335
Sardo Canale	XX	280
Smiths of Smithfield	XX	189
Asia de Cuba		386
Toto's	XxX	225
La Trompette	XxX ✿	328
The Victoria	🍴	334
Wapping Food	X	314
Water House	XX	294
The Waterway	🍴	169
The Wells	🍴	277
The Wharf	XX	349
York et Albany	XX	273

Open late

Aaya	XX	81	Café Lazeez	XX	76
L'Accento	X ✿	167	Caffé Caldesi	X	138
Alastair Little	XX	79	Caldesi	XX	134
Angelus	XX	162	Cambio de Tercio	XX	234
Arbutus	X ✿	83	Camerino	XX	152
Assaggi	X ✿	166	Cantina Del Ponte	X	197
Aubergine	XxX ✿	220	The Capital Restaurant	XxX ✿✿	217
Automat	X	85	Le Caprice	XX	59
L'Aventure	XX	135	Chada	XX	325
The Avenue	XX	71	Chada Chada	X	139
Axis	XxX	95	Chapters	XX ✿	308
Barnes Grill	X	323	Charlotte's Place	X	333
Barrafina	X	89	China Tang	XxxX	36
Bengal Clipper	XX	185	Chor Bizarre	XX	74
Bentley's (Oyster Bar)	X	86	The Clerkenwell Dining Room	XX	191
Boisdale	XX	116	Clos Maggiore	XX	97
Bombay Brasserie	XxX	224	Cocoon	XX	74
The Botanist	XX	238	Dehesa	X ✿	89
The Butcher and Grill	X	326	Le Deuxième	XX	98
Butlers Wharf Chop House	X	199	L'Escargot	XxX	48
Le Café Anglais	XX	162	Fakhreldine	XX	72
Cafe Boheme	X	90			
Le Café du Jardin	X	100			

Restaurant	Rating	Page
Floridita	XX	67
The Forge	XX	98
Franco's	XX	76
Galvin at Windows	XxxX	43
Galvin Bistrot de Luxe	XX ⓐ	130
Good Earth (Chelsea)	XX	238
Gordon Ramsay	XxxxX ❀❀❀	216
Gordon Ramsay at Claridge's	XxxX ❀	40
The Greenhouse	XxX ❀	44
Hakkasan	XX ❀	148
Haozhan	XX	79
High Road Brasserie	XX	329
Hush	XX	62
Imli	X	91
Incognico	XX	146
The Ivy	XxX	95
Jamuna	XX	163
J. Sheekey	XX	96
Khan's of Kensington	XX	234
Levant	XX	134
Locanda Locatelli	XxX ❀	127
Luciano	XxX	57
Malabar	X ⓐ	260
Mango Tree	XX	116
Marco	XX	239
Marcus Wareing at The Berkeley	XxxX ❀❀	106
Mint Leaf	XX	69
Momo	XX	66
Mr Chow	XX	232
The Narrow	🍺 ⓐ	312
Nobu Berkeley St	XX ❀	63
Notting Hill Brasserie	XX	253
Noura Brasserie	XX	117
Noura Central	XX	69
Olivo	X	118
Oxo Tower	XxX	183
Oxo Tower Brasserie	X	194
Ozer	XX	133
Pasha	XX	233
Patterson's	XX	59
Pearl Liang	XX	164
The Phoenix (Putney)	X	346
Phoenix Palace	XX	135
Pied à Terre	XxX ❀❀	145
Plateau	XX	309
Le Pont de la Tour	XxX	182
La Porte des Indes	XX	130
La Poule au Pot	X	118
Quaglino's	XX	68
Quality Chop House	X	203
Ransome's Dock	X	325
Red Fort	XxX	56
Roka	XX	131
St Alban	XxX	48
Sake No Hana	XxX	58
Santini	XxX	111
Sartoria	XxX	50
Shepherd's	XxX	112
Singapore Garden	XX	284
Sketch (The Gallery)	XX	66
Snazz Sichuan	XX	276
Sumosan	XX	73
Taman Gang	XX	65
Tamarind	XxX	50
Theo Randall	XxX	47
Timo	XX	257
La Trouvaille	XX	75
Via Condotti	XX ⓐ	65
The Wolseley	XxX	47
Yauatcha	XX ❀	80
Zuma	XX	232

Open on Sunday

Name		Page
Aaya	XX	81
Abeno	X	156
L'Absinthe	X	281
Almeida	XX	296
Amaya	XxX ❀	109
Angelus	XX	162
Aquasia	XxX	225
Arbutus	X ❀	83
Arturo	X	167
L'Atelier de Joël Robuchon	X ❀❀	99
Aubaine	X	241
Au Lac	X	293
Automat	X	85
L'Autre Pied	XX ❀	132
Awana	XxX	224
Azou	X	341
Baltic	XX	190
Barnes Grill	X	323
Barrafina	X	89
Bedford and Strand	X	100
Benares	XxX ❀	49
Bengal Clipper	XX	185
Bentley's (Oyster Bar)	X	86
Bibendum	XxX	222
Bibendum Oyster Bar	X	242
Bluebird	XX	228
Bombay Brasserie	XxX	224
The Botanist	XX	238
Le Boudin Blanc	X	90
Brasserie Roux	XX	68
Brew Wharf	X	206
Brula	X 🍴	351
Bumpkin	X	259
Butlers Wharf Chop House	X	199
Le Café Anglais	XX	162
Cafe Boheme	X	90
Le Café du Jardin	X	100
Cambio de Tercio	XX	234
Cantina Del Ponte	X	197
The Capital Restaurant	XxX ❀❀	217
Le Caprice	XX	59
Chapters	XX 🍴	308
Charlotte's Place	X	333
Chelsea Brasserie	XX	235
Chez Bruce	XX ❀	354
Chez Kristof	XX	340
China Tang	XxxX	36
Chutney Mary	XxX	223
Cigala	X	153
Clarke's	XX	254
Daphne's	XX	227
Le Deuxième	XX	98
E&O	XX	256
L'Etranger	XX	231
Fakhreldine	XX	72
Fish Hook	X	330
Foliage	XxX ❀	218
The Forge	XX	98
Foxtrot Oscar	X 🍴	239
Galvin at Windows	XxxX	43
Galvin Bistrot de Luxe	XX 🍴	130
The Glasshouse	XX ❀	344
Good Earth (Chelsea)	XX	238
Gordon Ramsay at Claridge's	XxxX ❀	40
Hakkasan	XX ❀	148
Haozhan	XX	79
Hereford Road	X 🍴	165
High Road Brasserie	XX	329
Hoxton Apprentice	X	295
Imli	X	91
Inn the Park	X	84
Island	XX	165
The Ivy	XxX	95
Jamuna	XX	163
J. Sheekey	XX	96
Kai	XxX ❀	55
Kastoori	X 🍴	350
Kensington Place	X	259
Kew Grill	XX	343
Khan's of Kensington	XX	234
Kiasu	X	168
Launceston Place	XxX	253
The Ledbury	XxX ❀	251
Levant	XX	134
Locanda Locatelli	XxX ❀	127

Restaurant		Page
The Lock	XX	303
L Restaurant and Bar	XX	258
Ma Cuisine (Barnes)	X	324
Ma Cuisine (Kew)	X	345
Malabar	X	260
Mango Tree	XX	116
Mao Tai	XX	337
Matsuri - St James's	XX	71
Memories of India on the River	XxX	335
Mr Chow	XX	232
The Narrow		312
Noura Brasserie	XX	117
Noura Central	XX	69
Nozomi	XX	228
One-O-One	XxX	222
The Only Running Footman		91
Oscar	XX	129
Oxo Tower	XxX	183
Oxo Tower Brasserie	X	194
Ozer	XX	133
Painted Heron	XX	236
Papillon	XX	233
Pasha	XX	233
Pearl Liang	XX	164
Pellicano	XX	235
The Phoenix (Putney)	X	346
Phoenix Palace	XX	135
Le Pont de la Tour	XxX	182
La Porte des Indes	XX	130
Portrait	X	88
La Poule au Pot	X	118
The Providores	XX	131
Quadrato	XxX	308
Quaglino's	XX	68
Quality Chop House	X	203
Quilon	XxX ✾	110
Racine	XX	227
The Restaurant at The Petersham	XxX	348
Rex Whistler	XX	115
Rhodes W1 Brasserie	XX	129
The Ritz Restaurant	XxXxX	36
Rivington (Shoreditch)	X	300
Roka	XX	131
The Rosendale		315
Rules	XX	96
St Alban	XxX	48
St John Bread and Wine	X	314
Sake No Hana	XxX	58
Santini	XxX	111
Saran Rom	XxX	335
Sardo Canale	XX	280
Scott's	XxX	43
Simply Thai	X	350
Singapore Garden	XX	284
Skylon	XxX	183
Smiths of Smithfield	XX	189
Snazz Sichuan	XX	276
Spread Eagle	XX	311
Tamarind	XxX	50
Tom's Kitchen	X	240
Toto's	XxX	225
Trinity	XX	332
La Trompette	XxX ✾	328
Tsunami	X	332
Urban Turban	X	168
Vama	XX	236
Vasco and Piero's Pavilion	XX	72
Veeraswamy	XX	75
Village East	X	205
Walnut	X	285
The Wharf	XX	349
Wild Honey	XX ✾	61
The Wolseley	XxX	47
XO	XX	272
Yauatcha	XX ✾	80
Zafferano	XxX ✾	107
Zuma	XX	232

Where to eat ▶ Open Sunday

Central London

- Mayfair · Soho · St James's **32**
- Strand · Covent Garden **92**
- Belgravia · Victoria **102**
- Regent's Park · Marylebone **122**
- Bloomsbury · Hatton Garden · Holborn **142**
- Bayswater · Maida Vale **158**
- City of London · Clerkenwell · Finsbury · Southwark **172**
- Chelsea · Earl's Court · Hyde Park · Knightsbridge · South Kensington **210**
- Kensington · North Kensington · Notting Hill **248**

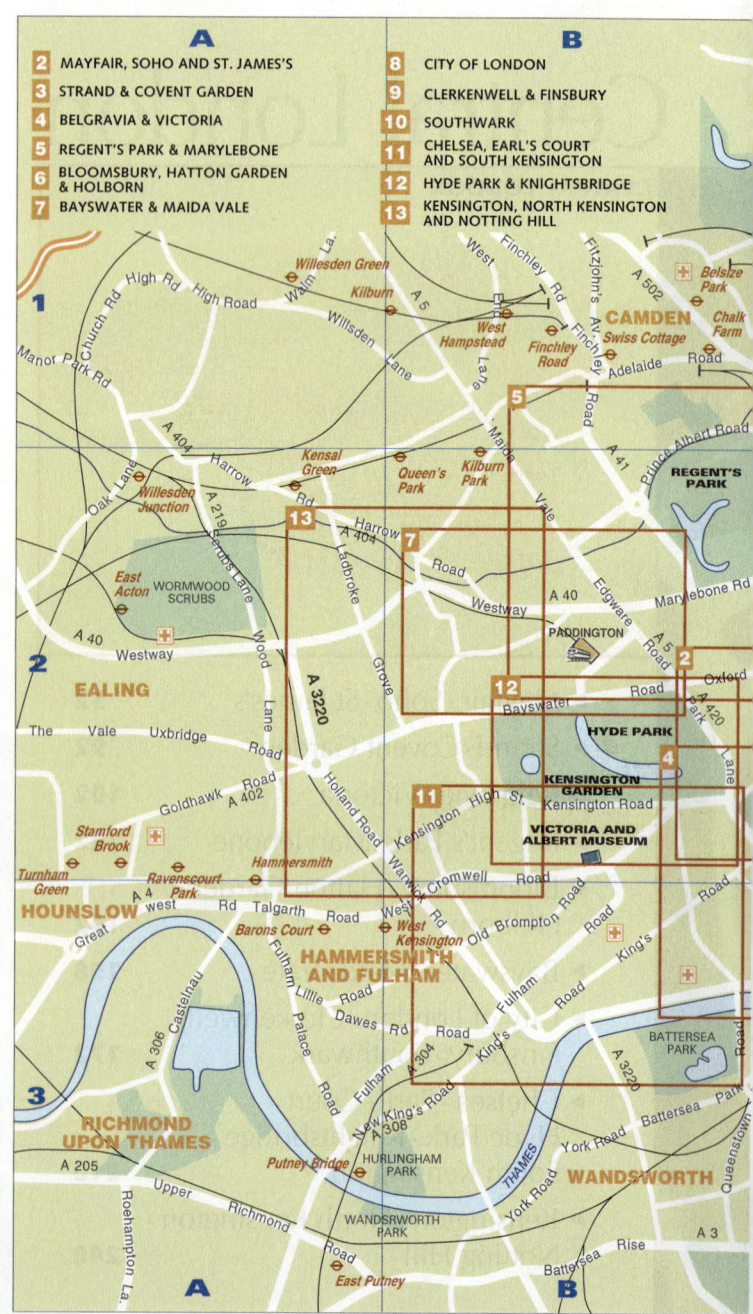

Mayfair · Soho · St James's

There's one elegant dividing line between Mayfair and Soho - the broad and imposing sweep of **Regent Street** - but mindsets and price tags keep them a world apart. It's usual to think of easterly Soho as the wild and sleazy half of these ill-matched twins, with Mayfair to the west the more sedate and sophisticated of the two. Sometimes, though, the natural order of things runs awry: why was rock's legendary wild man Jimi Hendrix, the embodiment of Soho decadence, living in the rarefied air of Mayfair's smart 23 Brook Street? And what induced Vivienne Westwood, punk queen and fashionista to the edgy, to settle her sewing machine in the uber-smart Conduit Street?

Mayfair has been synonymous with elegance for three and a half centuries, ever since the Berkeley and Grosvenor families bought up the local fields and turned them into posh real estate. The area is named after the annual May fair introduced in 1686, but suffice it to say that a raucous street celebration would be frowned upon big time by twenty-first century inhabitants. The grand residential boulevards can seem frosty and imposing, and even induce feelings of inadequacy to the humble passer-by but should he become the proud owner of a glistening gold card, then hey ho, doors will open wide. Claridge's is an art deco wonder, while **New Bond Street** is London's number one thoroughfare for the most chi-chi names in retailing. **Savile Row** may sound a little 'passé' these days, but it's still the place to go for the sharpest cut in town, before sashaying over to compact **Cork Street** to indulge in the purchase of a piece of art at one of its superb galleries. Science and music can also be found here, and at a relatively cheap price: the Faraday Museum in **Albemarle Street** has had a sparkling refurbishment, and the Handel House Museum in Brook Street boasts an impressive two-for-one offer: you can visit the beautifully presented home of the German composer and view his musical scores… before looking at pictures of Hendrix, his 'future' next door neighbour.

Soho challenges the City as London's most famous square mile. It may not have the money of its brash easterly rival, but it sure has the buzz. It's always been fast and loose, since the days when hunters charged through with their cries of 'So-ho!' Its narrow jumbled streets throng with humanity, from the tourist to the tipsy, the libertine to the louche. A lot of the fun is centred round the streets just south of **Soho Square,** where area legends like The Coach & Horses ('Norman's Bar'), Ronnie Scott's and Bar Italia cluster in close proximity. There's 80s favourite, the Groucho Club, too, though some of its lustre may have waned since a corporate takeover. The tightest t-shirts in town are found in **Old Compton Street,** where the pink pound jangles the registers in a swathe of gay-friendly bars and restaurants. To get a feel of the 'real' Soho, where old engraved signs enliven the shop fronts and the market stall cries echo back to the 1700s, a jaunt along **Berwick Street** is always in vogue, taking in a pint at the eternally popular Blue Posts, an unchanging street corner stalwart that still announces 'Watney's Ales' on its stencilled windows.

Not a lot of Watney's ale was ever drunk in **St James's;** not a lot of ale of any kind for that matter. Champagne and port is more the style here, in the hushed and reverential gentlemen's clubs where discretion is the key, and change is measured in centuries rather than years. The sheer class of the area is typified by **Pall Mall's** Reform Club, where Phileas Fogg wagered that he could zip round the world in eighty days, and the adjacent **St James's Square,** which was the most fashionable address in London in the late seventeenth century, when dukes and earls aplenty got their satin shoes under the silver bedecked tables.

The Ritz Restaurant

Traditional

H4

at The Ritz Hotel, ⊖ Green Park
150 Piccadilly ✉ W1J 9BR
✆ (020) 7493 8181 **Fax** (020) 7493 2687
e-mail enquire@theritzlondon.com **www**.theritzlondon.com

Menu £36/45 – Carte £46/88 s

Not only is dinner at The Ritz Restaurant a grand old occasion but it also acts as a history lesson to any students of hospitality on how things were meant to be done. The room is certainly unmatched in the sheer lavishness of its Louis XVI decoration; the table settings positively gleam thanks to all that polishing and there are probably more ranks to the serving team than in a ship's company. Little wonder they insist on jackets and ties. The Ritz Classics could be a saddle of Kentish lamb or a roast sirloin; Ritz Traditions could be smoked salmon carved at your table or Dover Sole filleted in front of you. If you want the full experience, have the Sonata Menu - six courses paired with wine - and go at the weekend for a dinner dance.

China Tang

Chinese

G4

at Dorchester Hotel, ⊖ Hyde Park Corner
Park Lane ✉ W1A 2HJ   Closed 25 December
✆ (020) 7629 9988 **Fax** (020) 7629 9595
e-mail chinatang@dorchesterhotel.com **www**.thedorchester.com

Menu £15 (lunch) – Carte £40/100

Found within The Dorchester Hotel, the Tang of the title is David Tang, entrepreneur and jet-setter extraordinaire, and his restaurant suits him exceptionally well. It's all outrageously glamorous, from the cruise-line style of the stunning bar to the art deco feel of the dining room with its marble, murals, its etched glass and cushions. You really don't know where to look, especially when most of the diners are as decorative as the room. By contrast, the cooking tends to tread a comparatively traditional, if pricey, path through Cantonese cooking, with some modern elements thrown in. How could you not love a place where poetry is recited in the loo and the private dining rooms are called Ping, Pang and Pong?

Alain Ducasse at The Dorchester ✤✤

French

Park Lane ✉ W1K 1QA
☏ (020) 7629 8866 **Fax** (020) 7629 8686
e-mail alainducasse@thedorchester.com
www.alainducasse-dorchester.com
Menu £45/75

⊖ Hyde Park Corner
Closed 3 weeks summer,
5 days early January,
Saturday lunch,
Sunday and Monday

Alain Ducasse

Some restaurants get it right first time; others can take longer to hit their strides, even when they're part of the Alain Ducasse empire. The Fourth Estate may have had their pencils sharpened even before the paint dried but this outpost at The Dorchester steadily improved throughout 2008 in both service and food, although its prices can still daze. The food always reflected Ducasse's lighter, more modern approach to gastronomy but the kitchen now performs to a higher, more consistent and confident level. The cooking is refined and elegant but also satisfying and balanced. No expense was spared on the decoration: Patrick Jouin's design uses plenty of leather and wood, tans and creams but also some 30,000 green silk buttons to reflect the park; 4,500 fibre optics shimmering around the semi-private Table Lumière; portholes to give arrivals a fleeting glimpse of what lies within and tables decorated with a sense of luxury and a little whimsy. Some of the accents may still be a little impenetrable but the service is slick and well organised.

First Course
- Soft-boiled egg, crayfish, wild mushrooms and Nantua sauce.
- Simmered duck foie gras, mango 'dolce forte' sauce.

Main Course
- Fillet of beef and seared foie gras Rossini, 'sacristain potatoes' and Périgueux sauce.
- Baked fillet of sea bass with potato gnocchi.

Dessert
- 'Baba like in Monte-Carlo'.
- Gianduja chocolate.

Hélène Darroze at The Connaught

French

G3

Carlos Place ✉ W1K 2AL
📞 (020) 3147 7200
e-mail info@theconnaught.co.uk **www.**the-connaught.co.uk

Menu £39/75

⊖ Bond St
Booking essential

The Connaught may have had a reputation as a bastion of pin-striped male clubbability but, after 110 years, the hotel now has its second, successive female Head Chef. After the flirtation with Italy, the cooking is now firmly rooted back in La France, with Hélène Darroze at the helm. She comes from a family of chefs going back four generations and divides her time between London and her restaurant in Paris. The main influences on her cooking come from the Landes region and the terroir of South West France, although she is now also acquainted with the best produce from the British Isles. Meals kick off with sliced jambon noir of estimable quality from Bigorre and her cooking is known for its bold and prominent flavours and her creative flourishes; desserts are a particular strength of the kitchen. The restaurant has been redesigned by India Mahdavi, who has created an elegant new look by softening all that original mahogany wall panelling and the tables are possibly the most beautifully laid in London. Service is diligently attentive.

First Course
- Lobster ravioli with spices, citrus and carrot mousseline.
- Le caviar d'Aquitaine.

Main Course
- Irish wild salmon with puy lentils, carrots and spring onions.
- Squab pigeon with confit turnips, lime and ginger sauce.

Dessert
- Peach with pistachio ice cream and sponge.
- Seasonal red fruits set in hibiscus jelly.

Le Gavroche ✿✿

French

43 Upper Brook St ✉ **W1K 7QR** ⊖ Marble Arch
✆ (020) 7408 0881 Closed Christmas-New Year, Sunday, Saturday
Fax (020) 7491 4387 lunch and Bank Holidays – booking essential
e-mail bookings@le-gavroche.com **www**.le-gavroche.co.uk

Menu £48 (lunch) – Carte £58/137

A/C
✿✿
VISA
MC
AE
D

Le Gavroche may now be in its fifth decade as one of London's most fêted and stately restaurants, but 2008 saw two significant events in its history: the retirement of Silvano Giraldin, the longest serving restaurant manager in London; and the recruitment of Rachel Humphrey as Head chef to work alongside Michel Roux, Chef de Cuisine and keeper of the Roux dynasty. The impact of these two events may not be felt for a while but what they prove is that even in traditional places like Le Gavroche, life moves on. Hopefully, though, it won't move on too much because although there are lighter dishes available, the restaurant's greatest appeal is as an antidote to all those low-fat, poly un-this, high-in-that, taste-free foods we're all threatened with. This is classic and extravagant French cooking, where the dishes are rich, the sauces are creamy and the ingredients luxurious. This may not be food you could eat every day but that's what makes it so special. Indulgence is good; it's why exercise bikes were invented.

First Course
- Hot duck foie gras, grapes and crispy pancake flavoured with cinnamon.
- Gratin of langoustines and snails, hollandaise flavoured with Basque pepper and parsley.

Main Course
- Roast saddle of rabbit with crispy potatoes and parmesan.
- Sea bass, lentil and bacon jus, Jerusalem artichoke purée.

Dessert
- Bitter chocolate and praline 'indulgence'.
- Passion fruit soufflé, white chocolate ice cream.

Gordon Ramsay at Claridge's 🌸

Modern European ✕✕✕✕

G3

Brook St ✉ W1K 4HR — ⊖ Bond St
📞 (020) 7499 0099 **Fax** (020) 7499 3099 — Booking essential
e-mail reservations@gordonramsay.com **www**.gordonramsay.com

Menu £30/70

Who'd have thought that such grand art deco surroundings with a long, proud history would attract such a young crowd? Gordon Ramsay at Claridge's is still firmly established on the radar of the fashionable and the famous which inevitably means that getting a table is still a somewhat painstaking process; even guests staying in the hotel get no special queue-jumping privileges. At lunch, where you'll find a particularly good value set menu, the room fills quickly and empties slowly but the atmosphere is never intimidating and the service never rushed. This is largely down to the experienced waiting staff and the impressive number of women in senior roles. Mark Sargeant continues to run things in the kitchen; he may be a loyal lieutenant of Gordon Ramsay but he has his own style and is unafraid of trying new things; his menus focus on seasonality and provenance but also continually develop. Enthusiasts can reserve the Chef's table in the kitchen. Those reluctant to leave can linger in the Lalique bar beside the restaurant.

First Course

- Salad of crab with carrot à la grecque, ginger and carrot dressing.
- Pot-roast wood pigeon, white onion and marjoram velouté.

Main Course

- Roast rib of beef with cep relish and smoked potato purée.
- Black bream, razor clams, samphire, Jersey Royals, mint velouté

Dessert

- Valrhona chocolate and honeycomb fondant with orange yoghurt sorbet.
- Calvados panna cotta, blackberry doughnuts.

The Square ❀❀

French

6-10 Bruton St ✉ W1J 6PU
📞 (020) 7495 7100
Fax (020) 7495 7150
e-mail reception@squarerestaurant.com
www.squarerestaurant.com

Ⓗ Green Park
Closed 25 December, 1 January and
Saturday lunch, Sunday and Bank Holidays

Menu £35/75

The Square is definitive proof that a comfortable, well run and ambitious restaurant does not have to be a painfully ceremonial one. Despite the departure of the long-standing manager, the service continues to impress: every detail is taken care of but it's done with personality and the occasional flicker of flamboyance, while the only starchiness in the place is in the crisp tablecloths. It's unusual to find quite such warmth and conviviality in a room this size but then The Square has never lacked followers and fans; if you come for lunch you'll be likely to witness a few tables eager to spin out the experience well into the grey of the afternoon. But what draws everyone to The Square is the food. Any aspiring chef examining what makes Philip Howard's cooking so accomplished will learn the concept of 'less is more'; there is an innate understanding of flavours and balance so plates are never overburdened with ingredients. This is also cooking which knows how and when to complement a classic repertoire with elements of individuality.

First Course
- Crab lasagne, cappuccino of shellfish, champagne foam.
- Parfait of foie gras, chicken liver, peanut brittle and apple chutney.

Main Course
- Herb crusted saddle of lamb, rosemary and shallot purée.
- Fillet of brill, crab, sea kale, farfalle and chive butter sauce.

Dessert
- Assiette of chocolate.
- Rice pudding soufflé with prunes and armagnac.

Sketch
(The Lecture Room & Library) ✱

French XXXX

First Floor, 9 Conduit St ✉ W1S 2XG ⊖ Oxford Street
✆ (020) 7659 4500 Closed 25-30 December, 2 weeks summer, Saturday
Fax (020) 7629 1683 lunch, Sunday, Monday and Bank Holidays
e-mail info@sketch.uk.com **www**.sketch.uk.com – booking essential

Menu £35/65 – Carte £65/94

The 18C house that is Mourad Mazouz and Pierre Gagnaire's London jewel still bewitches and bedazzles. The 'heavy' and the velvet rope on the door add to that feeling of exclusivity; you're escorted upstairs to the Lecture Room & Library like a visiting luminary and the room's extravagant decoration is as vivid and exhilarating as ever. The menus need to be studied carefully as each course comprises a number of dishes – very much the Pierre Gagnaire signature. The kitchen remains as passionate as ever and is clearly unable to rein in its ambition as this is unrestrained cooking that mixes the best of classical French techniques with more challenging contemporary flavours and combinations. You pay accordingly but then there's no denying you're getting something for your money; the introduction of the 'Gourmet Rapide' lunch menu is a laudable attempt to widen accessibility. The service is rarely less than slick and staff are well informed and confident, offering just the occasional sniff of arrogance.

First Course
- Langoustine 'addressed in five ways'.
- Smoked salmon, tuna and cauliflower.

Main Course
- Fillet of Simmental beef, pancake and truffle.
- Scottish lobster.

Dessert
- Caraïbe chocolate and ground nuts.
- Mini Paris-Brest.

Galvin at Windows

French 𝄞𝄞𝄞𝄞

G4

at London Hilton Hotel,
22 Park Lane ✉ W1K 1BE
✆ (020) 7208 4021 **Fax** (020) 7208 4144
e-mail reservations@galvinatwindows.com
www.galvinatwindows.com

⊖ Hyde Park Corner
Closed Saturday lunch and Bank Holidays

Menu £29/58 – Carte £60/75

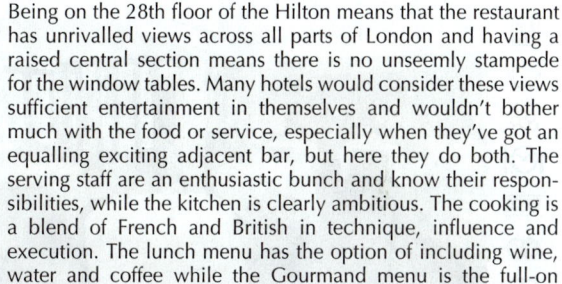

Being on the 28th floor of the Hilton means that the restaurant has unrivalled views across all parts of London and having a raised central section means there is no unseemly stampede for the window tables. Many hotels would consider these views sufficient entertainment in themselves and wouldn't bother much with the food or service, especially when they've got an equalling exciting adjacent bar, but here they do both. The serving staff are an enthusiastic bunch and know their responsibilities, while the kitchen is clearly ambitious. The cooking is a blend of French and British in technique, influence and execution. The lunch menu has the option of including wine, water and coffee while the Gourmand menu is the full-on experience.

Scott's

Seafood 𝄞𝄞𝄞

G3

20 Mount St ✉ W1K 2HE
✆ (020) 7495 7309
Fax (020) 7647 6327
www.scotts-restaurant.com

⊖ Bond St
Closed 25-26 December,
1 January and August Bank Holiday

Carte £38/87

Scott's is a genuine institution. It opened in the 1850s, moved to its current site in the 1960s and is a byword for seafood and oysters. It was revamped and reborn in 2006 by its new owners, Caprice holdings, who have made it once again the epitome of fashion. The menu is a flurry of headings from Crustacea and Mollusc to Smoked Fish and Fish on the Bone. The quality of the seafood and shellfish from across the UK is first rate and the kitchen knows not to interfere too much when it's this fresh. The mark-ups on the wines are kept minimal. They've also managed the clever trick of making something traditional seem new: the oak panelling is juxtaposed with artwork from Young British Artists. The front room, with the oyster bar, is more casual in style than the back.

The Greenhouse ❀

Innovative

G4

27a Hay's Mews ✉ W1J 5NY ⊖ Hyde Park Corner
📞 (020) 7499 3331 Closed 24 December - 6 January,
Fax (020) 7499 5368 Saturday lunch, Sunday and Bank Holidays
e-mail reservations@greenhouserestaurant.co.uk
www.greenhouserestaurant.co.uk

Menu £29/65

Owner Marlon Abela's constant reinvestment into The Greenhouse has ensured that it remains contemporary in design and fresh in feel. The latest refurbishment has used the garden outside as inspiration and the tones are natural and calming. The mostly round tables are generously sized and the experienced manager leads a large team; service is capable and professional, although there is the occasional lapse in polish. The chef is an advocate of the new approach to techniques and cooking and is an acolyte of celebrated French chef, Michel Bras. That means artfully constructed dishes where the main ingredient is subtly enhanced with contrasting textures and creative –and sometimes quite challenging - combinations. France is the main influence but the chef is not afraid of the occasional Moroccan note here or Asian tweak there, although the kitchen can sometimes overreach itself in trying to be original. But the restaurant has clear ambition and this goes a long way in accounting for the number of loyal and supportive guests. The wine list is one of the best around.

First Course
- Foie gras glazed with lemon, honey, apricot and begonia.
- Scallops with cauliflower purée, cobnuts and truffle.

Main Course
- Veal rump with asparagus and tamarind reduction.
- Red mullet, saffron mussels, butternut and kumquat.

Dessert
- 'Snix' - chocolate, salted caramel and peanuts.
- Tonka bean millefeuille, whisky ice cream.

Hibiscus ✿ ✿

H3

Innovative 🍴🍴🍴

29 Maddox St ✉ W1S 2PA ⊖ Oxford Circus
✆ (020) 7629 2999 Closed 2 weeks summer, 2 weeks Christmas,
Fax (020) 7514 9552 Saturday except dinner 1 November
e-mail enquiries@hibiscusrestaurant.co.uk - 20 December and Sunday
www.hibiscusrestaurant.co.uk

Menu £25 (lunch)/60

The clues are in the decoration: the French oak represents the stout figure of Claude Bosi and his nationality, while the Welsh slate acknowledges that it was in Ludlow that he made his name and reputation. That reputation was put on the line by his move from kingpin in a small market town to competing with the big beasts in the battleground of Mayfair. It is testament to his skill that not only has London embraced his restaurant but also that many of his old customers have remained loyal - they just have a longer journey for dinner now. The sign outside is suitably discreet – all the bells and whistles here are on the plate. Bosi's cooking is bold and daring; some combinations are strikingly original but his deft and confident cooking techniques see it through. His time in Ludlow also gave him an appreciation of the UK's finest produce, be that Cornish fish, Welsh lamb or Herefordshire beef. His chocolate tart is a must. Being closed at weekends means that consistency in quality is a given.

First Course
- Sweetbreads with oak smoked goat's cheese, onion fondue.
- Tartare of scallops and mango with sweetcorn.

Main Course
- Chicken stuffed with crayfish, girolles and green mango.
- Roast pigeon with wild chicory, pumpkin and passion fruit purée.

Dessert
- Tart of sweet peas, mint and sheep's whey with coconut ice cream.
- Gratin of banana and coffee, treacle and banana compote.

MAYFAIR • SOHO • ST JAMES'S ▶ Plan II

Maze ✲

Innovative 🍴🍴🍴

G3

10-13 Grosvenor Sq ✉ W1K 6JP ⊖ Bond Street
☎ (020) 7107 0000 **Fax** (020) 7107 0001
e-mail maze@gordonramsay.com **www**.gordonramsay.com

Carte approx. £57 s

Maze continues to blossom and flourish and the addition of the Grill in mid 2008 was a natural result of the restaurant's enduring popularity. The kitchen brigade has now grown to 34 and these young and energetic chefs ensure the kitchen remains as determined and ambitious as ever. Lincolnshire-born Jason Atherton describes his cooking as modern French but he uses a decent amount of produce from the British Isles and also champions ingredients from his own region such as eel, pork and a number of cheeses. His appealingly presented dishes are imaginative deconstructions and are constantly evolving: they are now somewhat larger than before, so ordering four per person should suffice; the clued-up and clued-in staff will offer sound advice to the undecided. The wine list has also developed and the trio of wines in the wine flights are a useful option. The room is a stylish affair, designed by David Rockwell, but don't overlook the bar which is more comfortable than most and well worth a pre or post prandial visit.

First Course
- Crab salad with mooli and apple jelly.
- Roast scallops, cauliflower purée, Muscatel vinegar dressing.

Main Course
- Red mullet and sardine with saffron rice and pimento purée.
- Sussex pork 'head to toe', apple, spiced lentils.

Dessert
- Pineapple carpaccio with seaweed croquette and Malibu lime jelly.
- Peanut butter and cherry jam sandwich, salted nuts, cherry sorbet.

The Wolseley

Modern European 🍴🍴🍴

H4

160 Piccadilly ✉ W1J 9EB
☏ (020) 7499 6996
Fax (020) 7499 6888
www.thewolseley.com

⊖ Green Park
Closed 25 December, 1 January, August Bank
Holiday and dinner 24 and 31 December
– booking essential

Carte £26/53

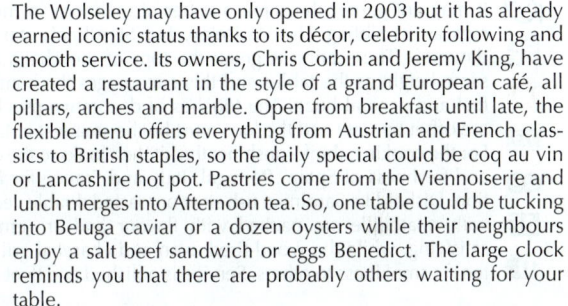

The Wolseley may have only opened in 2003 but it has already earned iconic status thanks to its décor, celebrity following and smooth service. Its owners, Chris Corbin and Jeremy King, have created a restaurant in the style of a grand European café, all pillars, arches and marble. Open from breakfast until late, the flexible menu offers everything from Austrian and French classics to British staples, so the daily special could be coq au vin or Lancashire hot pot. Pastries come from the Viennoiserie and lunch merges into Afternoon tea. So, one table could be tucking into Beluga caviar or a dozen oysters while their neighbours enjoy a salt beef sandwich or eggs Benedict. The large clock reminds you that there are probably others waiting for your table.

Theo Randall

Italian 🍴🍴🍴

G4

at InterContinental Hotel,
1 Hamilton Place, Park Lane
✉ W1J 7QY
☏ (020) 7318 8747
www.theorandall.com

⊖ Hyde Park Corner
Closed 25-26 December,
Saturday lunch, Sunday and Bank Holidays

Menu £25 (weekday lunch) – Carte £43/50

Theo Randall's profile is increasing thanks to greater media exposure and his eponymous restaurant is also bedding in nicely. The philosophy of the River Café, where he was head chef previously, has been drilled into his team: excellent ingredients and clear flavours. The menu is printed before each service depending on what's in season and top condition, although the scallops, veal chop and pasta cappelletti have all become regular features, as has the flourless chocolate cake. The wood oven is a preferred method of cooking. The restaurant may be in a hotel but there's always someone poised to greet you and the atmosphere in the large, contemporary room is refreshingly un-ceremonial; you can even just pop in for some pasta at the bar.

St Alban

Modern European 🍴🍴🍴

4-12 Regent St ✉ SW1Y 4PE — ⊖ Piccadilly Circus
✆ (020) 7499 8558 — Closed 25-26 December and 1 January
Fax (020) 7499 6888
e-mail info@stalban.net www.stalban.net

Menu £20 (lunch weekends) – Carte £22/39

It may not garner the same number of mentions in the shiny rags as its sibling The Wolseley, but St Alban's star is undimmed. The seating is great: the tops of the chairs are the same height as the tables and this encourages the community feel and general buzz. The touches of decorative psychedelia are offset by slate and the loos must be the smartest in London. For the cooking, think sunshine: the kitchen looks to the colours and freshness of Spain, Portugal, Italy and France for inspiration. Dishes like Sardinian fish stew or roasted double veal chop with ratatouille are packed with flavour and are eminently satisfying, while the wood-fired oven and charcoal grill add a terrific smokiness to others. Service is polished and fleet of foot.

L'Escargot

French 🍴🍴🍴

48 Greek St — ⊖ Tottenham Court Road
✉ W1D 4EF
✆ (020) 7437 2679 **Fax** (020) 7437 0790
e-mail sales@whitestarline.org.uk www.lescargotrestaurant.co.uk

Menu £18 (lunch) – Carte £30/33

It has one of the most iconic neon signs in Soho and a long, proud history going back to the 1920s when they used to farm snails in the basement; just walking in can induce feelings of warmth and affection. It's two restaurants in one building: the ground floor is certainly the more fun and comes with a brasserie feel and good value pre/post theatre menus, although more contemporary dishes are encroaching on the more celebrated classics. Ask for a table by the front window. A collection of Picasso lithographs and ceramics, as well as some Chagall pictures, give the upstairs room its name. Here it's all rather formal and hushed, with a kitchen that attempts more ambitious dishes but doesn't always quite pull them off.

Benares

Indian

12a Berkeley Square House
W1J 6BS
(020) 7629 8886 **Fax** (020) 7499 2430
e-mail reservations@benaresrestaurant.com
www.benaresrestaurant.com

Green Park
Closed 25-26 December,
1 January, and Bank Holidays

Menu £30 (lunch) – Carte £39/61

Chef Atul Kochhar may have opened another place in the Hampshire countryside and has clearly become a favourite with Food TV producers but that doesn't mean he's taken his eye off the ball at his smart Mayfair HQ. He has a loyal band of chefs, many of whom have been manning their stations since the opening. Named after the Holy City on the Ganges, the first floor restaurant is a smart but very convivial affair, surrounded by discreet private dining areas; try asking for one of the corner tables, numbers 17 or 24. Alternatively, you can try a 'platter' in the relaxed surroundings of the bar, which has its own identity. Either way, you'll find much to enjoy in the cooking: the influences come from across all parts of India but many of the dishes are given an innovative little twist here or original tweak there. However, flavours remain authentic and that's largely due to the deft spicing. The use of quality ingredients is a given and many of the dishes, especially the vegetables, change regularly.

First Course
- Tandoori roasted quails with red chilli and yoghurt marinade.
- Artichoke fritters, tomato and garlic salsa.

Main Course
- Tiger prawns with curry leaf, onion and tomato sauce.
- Corn-fed chicken, star anise and khorma sauce.

Dessert
- Saffron and mango jelly with coconut.
- Allspice-infused dark chocolate brownie.

Tamarind

G4

Indian 🗙🗙🗙

20 Queen St ✉ W1J 5PR
✆ (020) 7629 3561
Fax (020) 7499 5034
e-mail manager@tamarindrestaurant.com
www.tamarindrestaurant.com

⊖ Green Park
Closed 25-26 December, 1 January and
lunch Saturday and Bank Holidays

Menu £22/52 – Carte £39/61

A/C
🕐
☀
VISA
MC
AE
①

Tamarind may be in a basement but that basement is very well lit, elegant and surprisingly spacious; its subterranean location also adds to the sense of exclusiveness. The restaurant set the standard in Indian cooking for many years, and while many other kitchens may have caught up, it remains a popular destination for aficionados of good quality Indian cuisine, especially with the smarter set who like a bit of comfort with their food. The speciality is the Moghul cooking of the North West and the tandoor oven – the kebabs are their most renowned dishes – and, although there is a subtle European edge to the cooking, it remains loyal to its roots. The restaurant's popularity had lead to the opening of other projects.

Sartoria

H3

Italian 🗙🗙🗙

20 Savile Row ✉ W1S 3PR
✆ (020) 7534 7000
Fax (020) 7534 7070
e-mail sartoriareservations@danddlondon.com
www.danddlondon.com

⊖ Green Park
Closed 25-26 December, 1 January,
Sunday and Bank Holidays

Menu £25 – Carte approx. £35

A/C
🕐
🎭
VISA
MC
AE

Too many restaurants seem to have been just plonked down anywhere but the elegantly dressed and appropriately Italian Sartoria was clearly designed with its locality in mind, in this case Savile Row. The street's proud history and traditions of bespoke tailoring come playfully celebrated in the decoration – and even the bill comes pinned to a cushion. It's also quite a stylish affair, with a warm and inviting glow. Several tables come with sofa-style seating and standard lamps adjacent and all tables offer plenty of elbow room. The menu is extensive, clearly laid out and covers most of the regions of Italy. The kitchen displays a lightness of touch and dishes come attractively presented. The wine list offers a decent selection by the glass.

Quo Vadis

British

I3

26-29 Dean St ⊖ Tottenham Court Road
✉ W1D 3LL Closed Christmas and Sunday
✆ (020) 7437 9585 **Fax** (020) 7734 7593
e-mail info@quovadissoho.co.uk **www**.quovadis.co.uk

Menu £18 (lunch) – Carte £27/54

A/C

VISA

MC

AE

2008 saw the rebirth of this Soho institution, now owned by the Hart Brothers of Fino fame. Once home to Karl Marx, it was first opened in 1926 by Pepino Leonis, the man who introduced lasagne to London. The famous façade has been wisely left as it was while inside, they've lowered the ceiling, renewed the leather seats and parquet floor and generally freshened up the room and the art deco. For the food they revisit the era of classic British Grill restaurants – think steak tartare or smoked salmon, followed by Dover sole or veal sweetbreads, finished off with a treacle tart. The prime ingredients are treated with respect and, even with a couple of side dishes and the cover charge (which includes unlimited water), the prices seem fair.

Cecconi's

Italian

H3

5a Burlington Gdns ✉ W1S 3EP ⊖ Green Park
✆ (020) 7434 1500 Closed 25 December – booking essential
Fax (020) 7434 2020
e-mail giacomo@cecconis.co.uk **www**.cecconis.com

Carte £28/46

A/C

VISA

MC

AE

Clubs have had VIP areas for years so it was inevitable that certain restaurants that pride themselves on their celestial clientele would create a semi-private area for those can't bear the thought of mere mortals watching them eat. That being said, the bar at Cecconi's is an appealing spot and more of a destination than most; their Bellinis are legendary. Those more interested in the food will find that carpaccios and tartares are the house specialities but this type of Italian comfort eating has something for everyone. Lobster spaghetti and veal Milanese are the top sellers and Super Tuscans have a page to themselves on the wine list. Breakfast is as busy as dinner and weekend brunches are languid affairs.

Murano ✿

Italian influences 🗡🗡🗡

20 Queen St ✉ W1J 5PR — ⊖ Green Park
✆ (020) 7592 1222 **Fax** (020) 7592 1213 — Closed Sunday
e-mail murano@gordonramsay.com **www**.angelahartnett.com

Menu £25/55

VISA
MC
AE
D

She may not have her name in the title as she did when running the kitchens at The Connaught, but there is clearly more of Angela Hartnett's personality in Murano, which she opened in partnership with Gordon Ramsay in the late summer of 2008. It comes with fresco panels, pale leather chairs, cream and subtle green colours and, appropriately enough, Murano glassware. This all gives the room a fresh and luminous feel. Service is a tad over anxious but is well organised and not afraid to show a little personality. Angela Hartnett's family background is a mix of Emilia Romagna and Wales and this is reflected in her cooking: it has strong Italian notes but isn't Italian per se, and the Welsh influences are evident in some of the ingredients, such as the lamb. But what this also adds up to is a kitchen that can sing, possibly even literally. Great cured hams, breads and Sicilian olive oil kicks things off and the cooking is delicate yet satisfying. Cheeses are in very good nick and a mix of French and Italian desserts are a real strength.

First Course

- Scallop, watermelon and Joselito ham salad.
- Swiss chard and Sairass ricotta tortelli, sage and butter emulsion.

Main Course

- Duck breast and confit of leg with mustard fruits and potato cakes.
- Roasted turbot, smoked ham stock, pearl barley, summer vegetables.

Dessert

- Apricot soufflé with Amaretto di Saronno ice cream.
- Figs poached in red wine with zabaglione.

Umu ✿

Japanese

14-16 Bruton Pl ✉ W1J 6LX — ⊖ Bond Street
✆ (020) 7499 8881 — Closed 24 December - 7 January,
Fax (020) 7016 5120 — Saturday lunch, Sunday and Bank Holidays
e-mail reception@umurestaurant.com **www**.umurestaurant.com

Menu £21 (lunch) – Carte £34/73

The mere fact that there are over 160 different labels of sake available tells you this is no ordinary Japanese restaurant. The menu is printed on parchment paper held together with bamboo and comes in three parts: the first is the main à la carte offering plenty of choice; the second is sushi – both 'classic' and 'modern' – which comes from the large central sushi counter and the third describes the six seasonally changing, multi-course Kaiseki menus. Sixty percent of diners go for one of these Kaiseki menus and it's easy to understand why: only one decision need be made and the small dishes are delivered from the kitchen in a balanced and harmonious order so that each dish complements the one that went before. The only subsequent involvement of the customer could be with a bit of cooking with the shabu shabu course. The restaurant is well staffed and help with ordering is always at hand, even when it all gets very busy. Natural materials are used throughout and subtle lighting adds to the seductive mood.

First Course
- Sweet shrimp with sake jelly and caviar.
- Tiger prawn tempura.

Main Course
- Grilled skill fish teriyaki, yuzu and citrus flavoured grated radish.
- Grilled lobster, soy velouté, kinome leaf.

Dessert
- Black bean ice cream.
- Kyoto sundae.

Richard Corrigan at Lindsay House ✽

Modern European 🗡🍴🗡

21 Romilly St ✉ **W1D 5AF** ⊖ **Leicester Square**
✆ (020) 7439 0450 Closed 24-27 December and Sunday
Fax (020) 7437 7349
e-mail richardcorrigan@lindsayhouse.co.uk **www**.lindsayhouse.co.uk

Menu £59 (dinner) – Carte lunch £31/52

Regulars are divided on whether the ground or first floor dining room of this 18C house is the better option. The ground floor is the more opulently decorated but the atmosphere upstairs always appears to be more animated, with everyone seemingly having a little more fun. Both rooms boast some interesting pieces of art and dining in a house in Soho lends a little exclusivity to proceedings. Richard Corrigan is the chef with his name above the door but, with his finger inserted into a number of pies these days, his kitchen is entrusted to a long-standing and confident team of loyal deputies, many of whom are also Irish. Their homeland is represented on the menu by the likes of crubeens, soda bread, beef and oysters but the kitchen's priority is sourcing the best ingredients, wherever they may be found; for example, rhubarb comes from Yorkshire and chicken from Lancashire. Dishes are nicely balanced and flavours are pronounced and confident. The Tasting Menu, or Garden menu for vegetarians, is a good introduction. Sadly, the lease is up in May 2009.

First Course
- Carpaccio of octopus with scallop and orange purée.
- Poached duck egg, pea velouté and ham knuckle.

Main Course
- Roast loin of venison, pickled red cabbage, bacon and onion.
- Red wine poached turbot, celeriac, creamed cabbage.

Dessert
- Rhubarb mousse, ginger sablé and horseradish ice cream.
- Milk chocolate and orange pistachio parfait.

Kai ✿

Chinese

65 South Audley St
W1K 2QU
☎ (020) 7493 8988 **Fax** (020) 7493 1456
e-mail kai@kaimayfair.com www.kaimayfair.com

⊖ Hyde Park Corner
Closed 25-26 December and
1 January – booking essential

Menu £24 (lunch) – Carte £34/84

Chef Alex Chow honed his skills at Jade restaurant in Singapore's Fullerton Hotel before joining the well-groomed surroundings of Kai. It's spread over two floors but the lower level is equally as bright and contemporary in style as the ground floor. Service is unobtrusive and very sweet natured; this may be Mayfair but they're not above teasing the occasional regular. The exemplary cooking highlights the rich heritage, depth and variety of Chinese cooking. The chef is under orders to be creative but not for novelty sake and there is a nice balance between the traditional and the more modern. The informative descriptions on the menu support the emphasis that the kitchen places on sourcing the best ingredients. Equal care goes into preparing the 'Imperial Delicacies,' which include the 'Buddha Jumps Over the Wall' soup for which five day's notice is needed for the kitchen, as it does the more recognisable standards whose prices are much more down to earth. There is also a fortnightly changing lunch menu which is even kinder on the pocket.

First Course
- Pan-fried prawns with mustard greens and buttered lettuce.
- Aromatic crispy duck.

Main Course
- Lamb with Sichuan peppercorns, flower mushrooms and bamboo shoot.
- Sea bass with ginger and spring onions.

Dessert
- 'Pumpkin Cream' with purple rice, coconut ice cream.
- Pastry pancake with red bean paste.

Bentley's (Grill)

British ✗✗✗

11-15 Swallow St ✉ W1B 4DG
✆ (020) 7734 4756
e-mail reservations@bentleys.org
www.bentleyoysterbarandgrill.co.uk

⊖ Piccadilly Circus
Closed 25-26 December, 1 January,
Saturday lunch and Sunday

Menu £22 (lunch) – Carte £36/62

The beloved institution called Bentley's continues to enjoy its new lease of life. The green neon sign is still outside but these days the upstairs dining room has a contemporary feel with leather chairs, fabric covered walls and paintings of boats and fish for those who haven't twigged what's on the menu. One thing that will probably never change is the clubby feel and the preponderance of suited male customers. Seafood also remains the draw, with fish on the bone dissected at the table something of a house speciality. Much of the produce comes from St Ives and Looe in Cornwall and the freshness is palpable. Dover and Lemon soles feature strongly, as do oysters and soups whilst the breads and beef remind you that owner Richard Corrigan is Irish.

Red Fort

Indian ✗✗✗

77 Dean St ✉ W1D 3SH
✆ (020) 7437 2525
Fax (020) 7434 0721
e-mail info@redfort.co.uk **www**.redfort.co.uk

⊖ Tottenham Court Road
Closed lunch Saturday,
Sunday and Bank Holidays

Menu £25/35 – Carte £26/46

The Red Fort is now one of the daddies of the Soho scene. Although the delightful doorman is sadly no longer outside and the dimly-lit, throbbing basement bar, Akbar, has become quite a hit, the cooking fortunately continues to hit the spot. It follows the 300 year old traditions of the Moghul Court; there are plenty of dishes which, on closer inspection, reveal themselves to be familiar constructions, but there is also plenty of originality here: try lamb chops with pomegranate or whole quail dishes. The accompanying breads are particularly good. The dining room is well-dressed and divided into two – the far room is best and here they use sandstone, mosaics, Indian art and a water feature in homage to Lal Quila, the Red Fort in Delhi.

Embassy

Modern European XXX

H3

29 Old Burlington St ✉ W1S 3AN
✆ (020) 7851 0956
Fax (020) 7434 3074
e-mail embassy@embassylondon.com **www**.embassylondon.com

⊖ Green Park
Closed Saturday lunch, Sunday,
Monday and Bank Holidays – dinner only

Menu £25 (lunch) – Carte £24/45

A fashionable restaurant in the middle of Old Burlington Street may sound a little unlikely but Embassy sits there rather confidently. The buzzy nightclub downstairs is on the circuit for an assortment of celebrities on lists A to C but the restaurant, found on the ground floor, is no mere addendum to the club and has become a destination in its own right. The large bar, with plenty of brown leather seating, leads up to the dining area which comes decorated in stylish creams with well-spaced tables. Floor to ceiling windows and a pavement terrace give it extra appeal in the summer. The menu is that of a classically trained kitchen and features a fair share of extravagant ingredients, used with flair and understanding.

Luciano

Italian XXX

H4

72-73 St James's St ✉ SW1A 1PH
✆ (020) 7408 1440
Fax (020) 7493 6670
e-mail info@lucianorestaurant.co.uk **www**.lucianorestaurant.co.uk

⊖ Green Park
Closed 25-26 December and Sunday

Menu £22 (lunch) – Carte £30/46

Marco Pierre White goes back to his Italian roots in this restaurant, named after his son. The Man may not, sadly, be cooking any longer but he has put together a good team who deliver satisfyingly wholesome Italian classics, from a balanced and appealing menu. The ubiquitous David Collins designed the space which fits effortlessly into the gracious surroundings of St James's. The art deco bar is a favoured local spot for lunch, but descend a few steps and you'll find yourself in the elegant dining room, where the art comes courtesy of Marco's own collection. Staff are the embodiment of politeness at your table and the kitchen delivers the promise of the menu at the correct pace.

Avista

G3

Italian XXX

at Millennium Mayfair Hotel,
39 Grosvenor Sq ⊠ W1K 2HP
✆ (020) 7596 3444 **Fax** (020) 7596 3443
e-mail reservations@avistarestaurant.com
www.avistarestaurant.com

⊖ Bond Street
Closed 25 December and 1 January

Menu £24 (lunch) – Carte £26/46

Avista occupies the generous space within the Millennium Hotel that was previously farmed out to Brian Turner. Not only have they softened the room but they've also added a separate street entrance which helps in establishing the restaurant's identity, despite the best efforts of the intrusively anodyne music. Veneto born Chef Michele Granziera, a Zafferano alumnus, has created a menu that traverses Italy and marries the rustic with the more refined. There are dishes designed for sharing as well as pre-starter 'snacks' if you really can't wait. The homemade pastas are a particular highlight, while the kitchen's creativity is given full rein on the 'Surprise' seven course menu which is available at dinner.

Sake No Hana

H4

Japanese XXX

23 St James's St ⊠ SW1A 1HA
✆ (020) 7925 8988 **Fax** (020) 7925 8999
e-mail reservations@sakenohana.com **www.**sakenohana.com

⊖ Green Park
Closed 24-25 December

Carte £20/85

This ugly '60s building, built for The Economist, proved too much for a couple of restaurants but is now home to Alan Yau, of Hakkasan and Yauatcha fame, and his first Japanese restaurant. 'Flower of Sake' is reached via escalator, although if you want the sushi bar stay on the ground floor. Designed by Kengo Kuma, it's dominated by a striking cedar wood structure; if you've got your best socks on ask for a tatami table. The 8 page menu groups dishes according to their method of preparation with the traditional rice or noodles to end the meal; influences are a mix of both 'new-style' Japanese and the more traditional kaiseki. Sharing is the thing, although dish sizes do vary. Instead of a wine list, there's a large choice of sake and shochu.

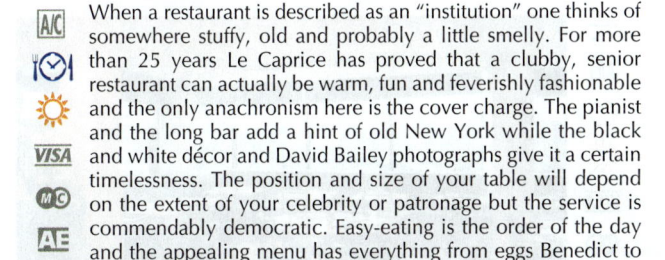

Le Caprice

Modern European

H4

Arlington House, Arlington St
✉ SW1A 1RJ
✆ (020) 7629 2239
Fax (020) 7493 9040
e-mail reservation@le-caprice.co.uk **www**.le-caprice.co.uk

⊖ Green Park
Closed 24-26 December, 1 January and
31 August – Sunday brunch

Carte £37/50

When a restaurant is described as an "institution" one thinks of somewhere stuffy, old and probably a little smelly. For more than 25 years Le Caprice has proved that a clubby, senior restaurant can actually be warm, fun and feverishly fashionable and the only anachronism here is the cover charge. The pianist and the long bar add a hint of old New York while the black and white décor and David Bailey photographs give it a certain timelessness. The position and size of your table will depend on the extent of your celebrity or patronage but the service is commendably democratic. Easy-eating is the order of the day and the appealing menu has everything from eggs Benedict to rump of veal. The Caesar salad and salmon fishcakes are a permanent fixture.

Patterson's

Modern European

H3

4 Mill St ✉ W1S 2AX
✆ (020) 7499 1308 **Fax** (020) 7491 2122
e-mail info@pattersonsrestaurant.co.uk
www.pattersonsrestaurant.com

⊖ Oxford Street
Closed Saturday lunch,
Sunday and Bank Holidays

Menu £25/40 – Carte £20/45

In this age where corporate brands are encroaching on every high street, it is becoming all too rare to come across a genuine family-run restaurant, especially in the salubrious surroundings of Mayfair. But Patterson's is the genuine article: parents, son and daughter are all involved with the day-to-day running of this modern, comfortable eatery on a narrow little street. The décor is stylishly understated and the menu offers up a selection of precisely executed and decoratively presented dishes. Lunchtime sees a well-priced set menu alongside the à la carte, which features a choice of five dishes per course. Service is swift and smooth for those on a time schedule but dinner on the whole is an altogether more relaxed affair.

Nobu

G4

Japanese

at The Metropolitan Hotel,
19 Old Park Lane ✉ W1Y 1LB
✆ (020) 7447 4747 **Fax** (020) 7447 4749
e-mail london@noburestaurants.com
www.noburestaurants.com

⊖ Hyde Park Corner
Closed 25-26 December and
1 January – booking essential

Menu £50/90 – Carte £32/50

London may not have been the first branch of Nobu to open (it was, in fact, the second, after New York) but in the year that saw Number 20 open in Dubai, it remains one of the best and that's largely down to Head Chef Mark Edwards and the levels of consistency he achieves with his brigade of forty chefs. He has also introduced the Osusume menu exclusively for London which is aimed at offering neophytes the opportunity of discovering what makes the food - Japanese with South American influences - quite so interesting: the flavours are unique, the combinations wholly complementary; the ingredients top-notch and desserts have been reinvigorated. It's little wonder its dishes have been plagiarised across the city. The restaurant remains as star-studded as ever but this has always been so much more than a mere celebrity crèche and its paired-down simplicity rightly throws the focus back on the food . If you really can't live without your Nobu, they'll now even come to your home and do your dinner party for you.

First Course
- Tuna sashimi salad, Matsuhisa dressing.
- Tomato rock shrimp ceviche.

Main Course
- Black cod with miso.
- Beef 'Toban' yaki.

Dessert
- Suntory whisky cappuccino.
- Warm chocolate santandagi.

Wild Honey ✽

Modern European

12 St George St ✉ W1S 2FB
☎ (020) 7758 9160
Fax (020) 7493 4549
e-mail info@wildhoneyrestaurant.co.uk
www.wildhoneyrestaurant.co.uk

⊖ Oxford Circus
Closed 25-26 December and 1 January

Menu £17 (lunch) – Carte £23/37

Wild Honey is ticking along nicely, proving that owners Anthony Demetre and Will Smith got things pretty spot-on from day one. This is all about relaxed dining and good food – even the reservation system is not the tortuous ordeal it is elsewhere – and the wood panelling adds to that clubby feel. The menu sees subtle differences as ingredients come in and out of season and, as they are used at their peak, this further helps in keeping costs – and accordingly, menu prices – down. The kitchen is clearly very capable but also respects the customers' own food knowledge: dishes are never showy or overdressed nor ingredients necessarily luxurious but instead every component on the plate plays its part, either in texture or flavour. The set choice menu must be one of the best deals in town. Staples on the à la carte are the bouillabaisse and the wild honey ice cream. The service works equally well: it is unobtrusive yet clued-up and the wine list still offers a great selection by the carafe, which is so much more satisfying that by the glass.

First Course
- Dorset crab, salad of peas and young shoots.
- Dover sole terrine, wild mushrooms and golden sultanas.

Main Course
- Saddle and shoulder of rabbit, gnocchi, olives and tomatoes.
- Cod with spring onions, razor clams and smoked pancetta.

Dessert
- Rum 'Baba', raspberries, Chantilly cream.
- White peach with mascarpone ice cream.

Alloro

Italian

19-20 Dover St ✉ W1S 4LU
✆ (020) 7495 4768
Fax (020) 7629 5348
e-mail alloro@finedininggroup.com
www.londonfinedininggroup.com

⊖ Green Park
Closed Easter, 25 December,
1 January, Saturday lunch and Sunday

Menu £32/35 – Carte £40/60

Alloro represents that new breed of fashionable Italian restaurant where style, good food and slick service blend successfully together. This certainly is not the place for the whisperers who haunt so many places. Thanks to the adjacent bar and the principle of osmosis, the atmosphere here is always pretty exuberant. Lunchtimes are popular with dealers of both the art and wheeler variety while dinner draws a typically metropolitan mix of types, all attracted by both the warm styling of the room and the modernity of the menu. Cooking has a slight Northern Italian attitude and the pasta dishes will no doubt be one of the highlights of your meal. The waiting staff carry out their duties with a confident swagger.

Hush

Modern European

8 Lancashire Court, Brook St
✉ W1S 1EY
✆ (020) 7659 1500 **Fax** (020) 7659 1501
e-mail info@hush.co.uk www.hush.co.uk

⊖ Bond Street
Booking essential

Carte £23/49

The setting is delightful - in the courtyard of a charming mews - and the outside terrace must surely be one of the places to be on a summer's day. You'll easily forget you're in the heart of the city. Hush indeed.

The brasserie on the ground floor is the mainstay of this surprisingly large operation and is quite a perky little number. The vibe is cool with a hint of flirtatiousness in the air. The menu reads like a comprehensive guide to modern European brasserie dining. Those who prefer their dining to be a little more exclusive should head upstairs to The Silver Room: the more formal room where the menu is altogether more your classic French. You'll also find the rather swanky cocktail lounge on this floor.

Nobu Berkeley St ✿

H3

Japanese ××

15 Berkeley St ✉ W1J 8DY
✆ (020) 7290 9222
Fax (020) 7290 9223
e-mail nobuberkeleyst@noburestaurants.com
www.noburestaurants.com

⊖ **Green Park**
Closed 25-26 December, Saturday lunch,
Sunday lunch and Bank Holidays

Menu £28/85 – Carte £33/49

Pop in before service and you'll witness staff using a length of string to create a straight line so that the soy sauce containers on each table are all lined up perfectly. This may be one of the most talked-about celebrity hangouts but they still do things properly here, not least in the kitchen, by demonstrating the Japanese eagerness for perfection. Anyone whose fame does not extend beyond their own home needs to book one month in advance but try pitching up at 7pm and you may get lucky. Alternatively, try lunch and a bento box with some organic juice. There are 45 chefs in the kitchen, 60% of whom are Japanese, and considerable care is evident in the food. Nobu tacos are a great way of getting things started and staff are sincere and well informed if you need help. Greatest hits like yellowtail sashimi, black cod with miso and shrimp tempura remain on the menu but each Nobu has some unique element and here it's the wood oven. The cabbage steak with truffles is a top seller and the crispy pork belly with spicy miso well worth trying.

First Course
- Octopus carpaccio with botargo.
- Seared toro with yuzo miso and jalapeno salsa.

Main Course
- Duck breast with wasabi salsa.
- Wagyu rump tatika, dried white miso.

Dessert
- Chocolate santandagi with pistachios.
- Yuzu tart, Earl Grey ice cream.

Semplice ✼

G3

Italian ✕✕

9-10 Blenheim St ✉ W1S 1LJ
✆ (020) 7495 1509
Fax (020) 7493 7074
e-mail info@ristorantesemplice.com
www.ristorantesemplice.com

⊖ Bond Street
Closed Christmas, Easter, Saturday lunch,
Sunday and Bank Holidays
– booking essential at dinner

Menu £19 (lunch) – Carte £31/47

A/C
⅋
VISA
MC
AE

At a time when a lot of cooking is generic rather than specifically regional, here is one place that knows where it comes from. That place is the north of Italy and the two young but experienced owners, from Brescia and Lake Maggiore, are equally passionate about their native produce. They make frequent trips home for reasons of quality and traceability and, with cooking that keeps to the maxim of the restaurant's name, those ingredients have to shine. Instead of Prosecco, they offer Franciacorta by the glass; they serve Fassone beef, a breed reared in Piedmonte, and their carpaccio is a signature dish, as is the Milanese risotto with saffron and bone marrow. For the fish they only accept the best from the Cornish day boats; make sure you try the cheeses which come with fruit marmalades. The lunch menu provides a great opportunity to experience the clean, fresh flavours of this honest cooking at a very decent price. The room is warm and stylish; and newcomers are greeted with the same degree of effusiveness as regulars. It isn't easy making everything look so simple.

First Course
- Pan-fried goat's cheese with beetroot and balsamic vinegar.
- Ravioli of potato, rosemary and braised oxtail.

Main Course
- Fassone beef with spiced French beans and salad.
- Roast turbot, spinach, Cerignola and Gaeta olives, fresh basil.

Dessert
- Domori chocolate fondant and pistachio ice cream.
- Pineapple and polenta cake, yoghurt sorbet.

THE ARTISTRY OF CHAMPAGNE

www.louis-roederer.com

You've got the right address !

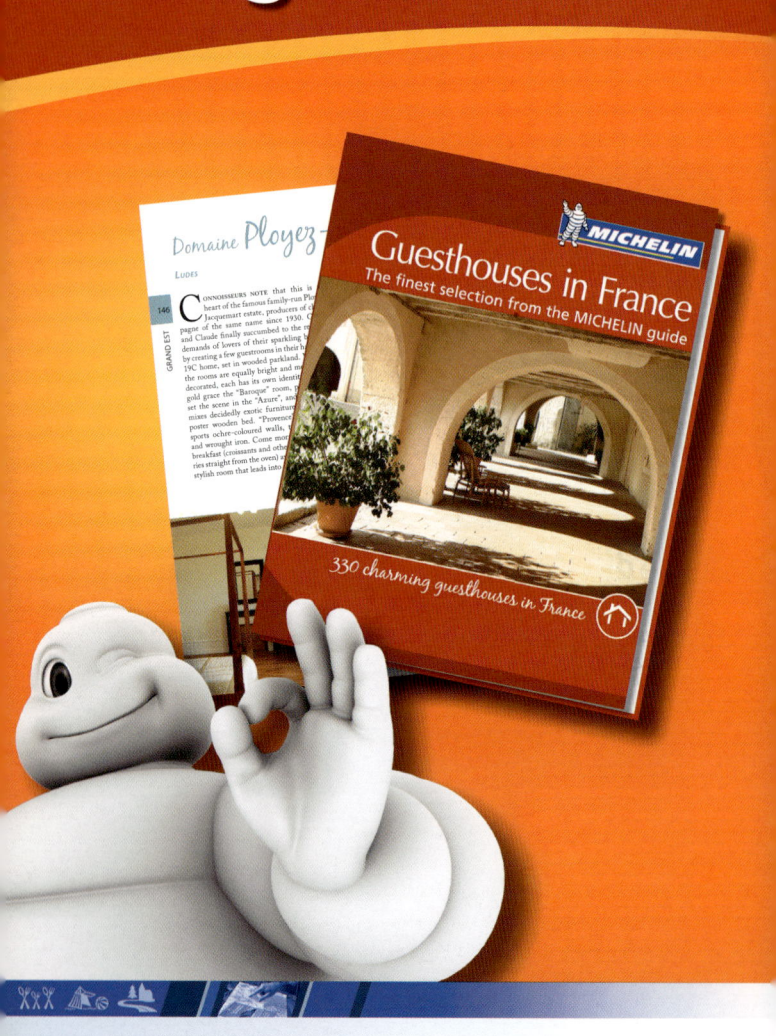

From palaces to bed and breakfasts, from fine restaurants to small bistrot, the MICHELIN guide collection includes 45,000 hotels and restaurants selected by our inspectors in Europe and beyond. Wherever you may be, whatever your budget, you can be sure you have the right address!

www.michelin.co.uk

MICHELIN
A better way forward

Via Condotti

Italian

H3

23 Conduit St ✉ W1S 2XS
✆ (020) 7493 7050
Fax (020) 7409 7985
e-mail info@viacondotti.co.uk **www**.viacondotti.co.uk

⊖ Oxford Circus
Closed Christmas, New Year,
Sunday and Bank Holidays

Menu £19/28

This Italian restaurant is as warm and inviting as its pretty façade suggests. It's busier at lunchtimes but relaxed and unhurried at dinner; it's just a shame the nicer upstairs room is only used as an overflow. The menu also delivers what it promises. The excellent grissini and focaccia get things off to a good start; influences are mostly from the more northerly parts of Italy although many of the ingredients are sourced from within the UK, and there's an appealing earthiness to the cooking. The pasta dishes are particularly good, as are the set prices, even when you add the occasional vegetable side dish. Via Condotti is not only an Italian translation of Conduit Street but is itself an equally glamorous shopper's paradise in Rome.

Taman Gang

Asian

F3

141 Park Lane ✉ W1K 7AA
✆ (020) 7518 3160
Fax (020) 7518 3161
e-mail info@tamangang.com **www**.tamangang.com

⊖ Marble Arch
Closed Sunday and Bank Holidays
– dinner only

Menu £55/75 – Carte £28/73

As they take your coat and lead you downstairs, the number of fresh orchids you pass should alert you to the fact that they're not exactly giving it away here. You'll be led to a table in the central 'horseshoe' shape or on one of the sides; the latter are better for the romantically inclined. 'Pan-Asian' is the catch-all description of the menu. The ubiquitous black cod with miso is there - perhaps it's a legal requirement - as is 'modern' sushi, but the chefs, who are mostly Chinese and Malaysian, know their Asian flavours and ingredients are good. However, that final bill can creep up if you start ordering a number of the tempting sounding 'small plates', especially with the 15% service charge added on top.

Sketch (The Gallery)

International 𝕏𝕏

H3

9 Conduit St ✉ W1S 2XG   ⊖ **Oxford Street**
✆ (020) 7659 4500   Closed 25-26 December Sunday and Bank Holidays
Fax (020) 7629 1683   – booking essential – dinner only
e-mail info@sketch.uk.com   www.sketch.uk.com

Carte £32/52

Art and food have been linked since bison first appeared in Palaeolithic cave drawings; The Gallery at Sketch just connects the two in more of a 21st century sort of way. During the day it's an art gallery, with regularly changing exhibitions featuring mostly video art thanks to the projectors and the huge white space. In the evening it transforms itself into a lively brasserie, with the videos still dancing around the walls. France provides the starting point for the cooking but along the way it picks up influences from Italy to Japan which seems to suit the international crowd. It doesn't come cheap but that's the price for exclusivity. For a less frenzied but more expensive affair, head upstairs to The Lecture Room & Library.

Momo

Moroccan 𝕏𝕏

H3

25 Heddon St ✉ W1B 4BH   ⊖ **Oxford Circus**
✆ (020) 7434 4040 **Fax** (020) 7287 0404   Closed Sunday lunch
e-mail info@momoresto.com   www.momoresto.com

Menu £24/40 – Carte £30/43

Momo is one of those perennially busy places and it's easy to see why. Tucked away on a little side street, it's kitted out like a souk, with window screens and hanging lanterns, but it also comes with a soundtrack. The candlelight and the low slung tables add to the exotic romance of the room, although adoring couples may find intimacy curtailed by the close proximity of the neighbouring table. It's much more fun to come in a group and spend some time in the hip surroundings and the hopping bar, glancing adoringly at all the beautiful people who fill the place on a nightly basis. The food is predominantly Moroccan, with pastilla, couscous and tagines all there, although there are other more contemporary Maghrebian choices available.

La Petite Maison

French ✗✗

G3

54 Brooks Mews ✉ W1K 4EG
☏ (020) 7495 4774
e-mail info@lpmlondon.co.uk **www**.lpmlondon.co.uk

⊖ Bond Street
Closed Sunday dinner

Carte £31/64

Packed from the moment it opened in the summer of 2007, La Petite Maison brings a little piece of Nice to Mayfair. French Mediterranean cooking and its sunny bounty of artichokes, lemons, olives, peppers and tomatoes have clearly caught the prevailing fashion for healthy eating. 'Food is served to help yourself' it proclaims, which translates as 'you may want to share,' but you don't have to, as the dishes are of normal size. However, with over 20 starters including pissaladière, sardines and squid, it may be worth ordering a few. The whole roast black-leg chicken with foie gras has proved a hit, as have the fish main courses. As one would expect, there's plenty of rosé on the wine list. Their slogan is 'Tous célèbres ici', which means lots of all-year tans and good tailoring.

Floridita

Latin American ✗✗

I3

100 Wardour St
✉ W1F 0TN
☏ (020) 7314 4000
Fax (020) 7314 4040
www.floriditalondon.com

⊖ Tottenham Court Road
Closed 24-26 December,
1 January and Sunday – dinner only

Carte £45/62

It's salsa all the way, from the spicy food to the live music and dancing. If you think the ground floor with its Mediterranean tapas is busy, try downstairs for size. Here you'll find yourself in a huge nightclub-style space boasting an impressive cocktail list and a variety of Latin American dishes, from Cuban classics like ropa vieja to a whole-roast suckling pig and a large selection of assorted cuts of Argentinean beef aged for 28 days. It's not cheap but then again everything is done very well and everyone is here for a Big Night Out. The bands are flown in from Cuba, the music starts at 7.30pm and the party atmosphere never lets up. Those whose pace is more Cohiba than Mojito can nip next door to La Casa del Habano.

Brasserie Roux

French

I4

8 Pall Mall ⊠ SW1Y 5NG — ⊖ Piccadilly Circus
℘ (020) 7968 2900 **Fax** (020) 7747 2251
e-mail h3144@accor.com
www.sofitelstjames.com

Menu £20/25 – Carte £32/55

The term 'brasserie' does not really prepare you for the grandeur of a room that once formed part of a banking hall. Those giant lamps are needed to counter such an enormous ceiling and the leather armchairs and large tables up the ante on the comfort front. It is a surprise, therefore, to discover there's a weekly changing set menu that's not only keenly priced but also includes two glasses of wine. The 'brasserie' label certainly makes more sense when talking about the food; expect comforting classics like blanquette de veau or baba au rhum alongside terrines and plenty of grilled meats and fish. Add to this some pasta dishes, a few salads and a children's menu and you'll find that there's something for everyone.

Quaglino's

Modern European

H4

16 Bury St ⊠ SW1Y 6AL — ⊖ Green Park
℘ (020) 7930 6767 — Closed 25-26 December – booking essential
Fax (020) 7930 2732
e-mail quags-res@danddlondon.com **www**.quaglinos.co.uk

Menu £20 (lunch) – Carte £25/46

Quaglino's has been around long enough for us to forget what an impact its opening had, back in the early 1990s. The large bar, the sweeping staircase, the cigarette girls and the bustle of a vast, glamorous restaurant really set London's collective pulse racing. Today, the 'scene' may have moved elsewhere but Quaglino's still offers a good night out. The menu is an appealing mix of brasserie style favourites, with traditional French dishes marked out in red. Grilled meats are done well but the shellfish and seafood are the stars of the show and the kitchen understands the importance of freshness and simplicity. Lunch and early evening set menus are well priced. The bar, with live music, is a great spot for pre or post prandial drinks.

Mint Leaf

Indian

14

Suffolk Pl ✉ SW1Y 4HX ⊖ Piccadilly Circus
✆ (020) 7930 9020 Closed Saturday lunch and Sunday
Fax (020) 7930 6205
e-mail reservations@mintleafrestaurant.com
www.mintleafrestaurant.com

Menu £15 – Carte £27/37

Being surrounded by playhouses has clearly rubbed off because Mint Leaf provides a thoroughly theatrical experience. Just watch your entrance as the stairs down are cloaked in darkness. You'll firstly encounter a long, tenebrous and highly fashionable bar. The dining room beyond splits into five areas, all equal in their moodiness and energised by the constant pulse of lounge music. Don't be alarmed when the staff leave what looks like a catwalk and crouch down at your table – it's their way of offering reassuring service. In such surroundings one would expect decidedly eclectic Indian food but instead they keep things traditional and grounded, except for the very European desserts. Try the specially created Indian salads at lunch.

Noura Central

Lebanese

13

22 Lower Regent St ⊖ Piccadilly Circus
✉ SW1Y 4UJ
✆ (020) 7839 2020 **Fax** (020) 7839 7700
e-mail nouracentral@noura.co.uk **www**.noura.co.uk

Menu £18/40 – Carte £20/39

The nearer one got to Piccadilly Circus, the fewer choices of restaurant one usually had. However, Noura Central changed all that when it opened a few years back. This capacious Lebanese restaurant, together with its equally roomy bar, offers a wide selection of Levantine dishes, in richly colourful surroundings. Assorted mezes, charcoal grilled meats, various fish platters and rich, sweet pastries all feature on the extensive menus and provide sufficiently varied choice for all tastes. The decoration is exuberant and lavish, matched by an atmosphere that's never less than animated, thanks in part to the extensive cocktail list and the decent prices found on the wine list. The occasional DJ also ensures that noise levels never fall below party mode.

Bellamy's

H3   **Traditional**

18 Bruton Pl ✉ W1J 6LY   ⊖ Bond Street
📞 (020) 7491 2727   Closed Saturday lunch, Sunday,
Fax (020) 7491 9990   Christmas, Easter and Bank Holidays
e-mail info@bellamysrestaurant.co.uk
www.bellamysrestaurant.co.uk

Menu £29 – Carte £36/54

First find the little mews of Bruton Place, then snake through the appetising deli out front, glide through the double doors and you'll find yourself in Bellamy's restaurant. This is a decidedly clubby little place with a hint of brasserie about it. It's also perennially full of Mayfair regulars, some of whom are a little more 'Horse and Hounds' and a little less 'Hello'. Prices here are hard to quantify: there is a very reasonable set menu for under £30 but this comes juxtaposed with £340 for Beluga Caviar. The menu covers an equally broad field with everything from whitebait to foie gras, mixing the English with the French. The scrambled eggs with truffles are ideal for the louche late riser. Puds are more your classic French.

Maze Grill

G3   **Beef specialities**

at London Marriott H. Grosvenor   ⊖ Bond Street
Square,
Grosvenor Sq ✉ W1K 6JP
📞 (020) 7107 0000 **Fax** (020) 7514 1528
e-mail maze@gordonramsay.com **www**.gordonramsay.com

Carte £28/31

If Maze is the smooth sophisticate then Maze Grill is its red-blooded American cousin, for this place is all about beef. It also feels more like a part of the Marriott Hotel to which it is attached. The assorted cuts, from Casterbridge grain-fed and Hereford grass-fed through to Creekstone prime USDA corn-fed and Wagyu, are brought to your table and individually described. Your preferred steak is then given a blast in the super-hot broiler before being served on a wooden board. There are plenty of sides and sauces to accompany your meat and these, along with the starters or small plates, can beef up your bill, although the wine prices are kept relatively reasonable. There are other fish and meat choices available for if you don't fancy a steak.

The Avenue

Modern European XX

7-9 St James's St ⊠ SW1A 1EE
℘ (020) 7321 2111
Fax (020) 7321 2500
e-mail avenuereservations@danddlondon.com
www.theavenue-restaurant.co.uk

⊖ Green Park
Closed 25-26 December,
Saturday lunch and Sunday

Menu £23 – Carte £20/43

In contrast to some of the starchier establishments in the street, The Avenue is a loud and confident affair, even though it's been around long enough to be approaching its teenage years. It's easy to spot, thanks to its large billowing flag and it occupies an impressive amount of square footage. White is the predominant colour, although the large artwork which changes three or four times a year tries to compete for your attention. The kitchen keeps things simple and knows not to mess around too much with the ingredients. Expect satisfying European brasserie favourites where the flavours are pronounced and the choice extensive. The pricing of the lunch time set menu is particularly keen when you consider the neighbourhood.

Matsuri - St James's

Japanese XX

15 Bury St ⊠ SW1Y 6AL
℘ (020) 7839 1101 **Fax** (020) 7930 7010
e-mail dine@matsuri-restaurant.com **www.**matsuri-restaurant.com

⊖ Green Park
Closed Christmas and New Year

Menu £35 – Carte £28/60

The façade of this Japanese restaurant may be a little drab but the location - in among the art galleries of Bury Street - explains why lunch is such a busy affair. It is also much nicer all round once you're inside, where you're greeted by a very charming hostess who escorts you downstairs to one of the teppan-yaki tables or, if you're quick, you can grab one of the few seats at the neighbouring sushi bar. The managers have a tendency to stand around looking important while the service is undertaken by very helpful and earnest waitresses, traditionally kitted out. Once you have chosen from one of the many different menus available, watch the chef at your table slice and dice and your appetite will get going immediately.

Vasco and Piero's Pavilion

Italian

H2

15 Poland St
✉ W1F 8QE
✆ (020) 7437 8774
Fax (020) 7437 0467
e-mail eat@vascosfood.com www.vascosfood.com

⊖ Tottenham Court Road
Closed Saturday lunch, Sunday and
Bank Holidays – booking essential at lunch

Menu £30 (dinner) – Carte lunch £29/38

Those who think that Soho is changing too quickly and is beginning to lose its personality can take heart with the continuing presence of Vasco and Piero's Pavilion, which has been in Poland Street since 1989, having first opened in Oxford Street in the 1970s. The menu still changes twice a day and much of the meat, cheese, vegetables and truffles come from small, family producers back in Umbria. Specialities from the region also include guinea fowl and cured pork, while the home-made pastas are an obvious strength. Dishes come with an appetising simplicity that has been perfected over the years and, for this, the restaurant is rewarded with a very loyal clientele, many of whom don't even need to look at a menu.

Fakhreldine

Lebanese

H4

85 Piccadilly ✉ W1J 7NB
✆ (020) 7493 3424 **Fax** (020) 7495 1977
e-mail info@fakhreldine.co.uk www.fakhreldine.co.uk

⊖ Green Park
Closed 24 to 26 December

Menu £19 (lunch) – Carte £28/48

Ascend the marble staircase and you enter into this stylish and urbane Lebanese restaurant which comes with its own smart lounge bar where large sofas provide the perfect spot for pre-dinner cocktails. The restaurant, reinvented by a refurbishment and named after an 18th century Lebanese Prince, benefits from its large picture windows which let in plenty of light, as well as providing great views of Green Park for those with window tables. The stone, oak and muted palate all lend a sensual contemporary edge to the decoration. It's not just the meze which blend the traditional with the modern: the Lebanese home cooking is equally fragrant and no less accomplished, with daily changing specials and tasting plates available.

Sumosan

Japanese ✕✕

H3

26 Albemarle St ✉ W1S 4HY
📞 (020) 7495 5999
Fax (020) 7355 1247
e-mail info@sumosan.co.uk
www.sumosan.com

⊖ Green Park
Closed 25-26 December, New Year,
Saturday lunch, Sunday lunch and
Bank Holidays – dinner only

Menu £23/70 – Carte approx. £70

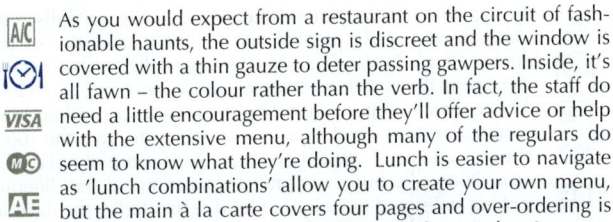

A/C
🍽️⌚
VISA
MC
AE
◐

As you would expect from a restaurant on the circuit of fashionable haunts, the outside sign is discreet and the window is covered with a thin gauze to deter passing gawpers. Inside, it's all fawn – the colour rather than the verb. In fact, the staff do need a little encouragement before they'll offer advice or help with the extensive menu, although many of the regulars do seem to know what they're doing. Lunch is easier to navigate as 'lunch combinations' allow you to create your own menu, but the main à la carte covers four pages and over-ordering is easy. Whilst there are some familiar sounding modern Japanese classics, others exhibit greater originality. Ensure you leave room at the end for some sushi and sashimi, as this is what the kitchen does best.

Mews of Mayfair

British ✕✕

H3

10-11 Lancashire Court, Brook St
(first floor) ✉ W1S 1EY
📞 (020) 7518 9388 **Fax** (020) 7518 9389
e-mail info@mewsofmayfair.com **www**.mewsofmayfair.com

⊖ Bond Street
Closed 25-26 December and Sunday

Menu £23/40 – Carte £36/48

VISA
MC
AE
◐

'Nice' may be a word in need of an image consultant but it applies perfectly to Mews of Mayfair. The room is nice, the service is nice and the food is, well, nice too; it's the sort of place made for daughters taking their mothers out for lunch. In the evening it may all get a bit funkier, with a DJ in the basement and after work packs in the ground floor bar, but the first floor restaurant remains a composed and polished environment. This care extends to the kitchen where they put plenty of effort into their food; there's enough individuality to give it personality but not so much that it becomes gimmicky. There are quite a few set menus to complement an already well-balanced à la carte so choice is bountiful, which is nice.

Chor Bizarre

Indian

16 Albemarle St ✉ W1S 4HW
✆ (020) 7629 9802
Fax (020) 7493 7756
e-mail chorbizarrelondon@oldworldhospitality.com
www.chorbizarre.com

⊖ Green Park
Closed 25-26 December,
1 January and Sunday lunch

Menu £17 (lunch) – Carte £24/38

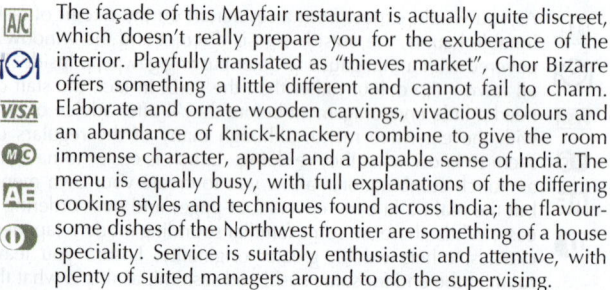

The façade of this Mayfair restaurant is actually quite discreet, which doesn't really prepare you for the exuberance of the interior. Playfully translated as "thieves market", Chor Bizarre offers something a little different and cannot fail to charm. Elaborate and ornate wooden carvings, vivacious colours and an abundance of knick-knackery combine to give the room immense character, appeal and a palpable sense of India. The menu is equally busy, with full explanations of the differing cooking styles and techniques found across India; the flavoursome dishes of the Northwest frontier are something of a house speciality. Service is suitably enthusiastic and attentive, with plenty of suited managers around to do the supervising.

Cocoon

Asian

65 Regent St ✉ W1B 4EA
✆ (020) 7494 7600
Fax (020) 7494 7607
e-mail reservations@cocoon-restaurants.com
www.cocoon-restaurants.com

⊖ Piccadilly Circus
Closed 25-27 December,
Saturday lunch and Sunday

Menu £15 (lunch) – Carte £28/51

A first glance at the menu would suggest a Japanese restaurant: sushi, sashimi, bento boxes and tempura all feature prominently and you may find yourself transfixed by the master craftsman behind one of the counters doing his thing with a very large knife. However, on closer investigation, you'll find dishes whose influences owe more to Korea, China and Thailand, while others are shaped more from the culinary zeitgeist. The common theme, though, is sharing, so ordering should be a group activity, although staff give good advice. The place seats 170 but is cleverly divided and the styling and décor are decidedly space-age. Lunches are relatively calm affairs with shoppers in for salads and bento boxes. It all hots up big-time in the evenings.

Veeraswamy

Indian ✕✕

H3

Victory House, 99 Regent St
(entrance on Swallow St)
✉ W1B 4RS
✆ (020) 7734 1401 **Fax** (020) 7439 8434
e-mail veeraswamy@realindianfood.com www.realindianfood.com

⊖ Piccadilly Circus
Closed dinner 25 December

Menu £20 (lunch) – Carte £36/44

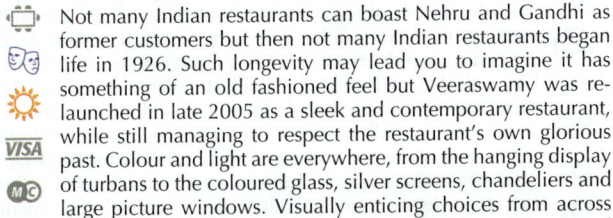

Not many Indian restaurants can boast Nehru and Gandhi as former customers but then not many Indian restaurants began life in 1926. Such longevity may lead you to imagine it has something of an old fashioned feel but Veeraswamy was re-launched in late 2005 as a sleek and contemporary restaurant, while still managing to respect the restaurant's own glorious past. Colour and light are everywhere, from the hanging display of turbans to the coloured glass, silver screens, chandeliers and large picture windows. Visually enticing choices from across India are showcased, from recipes garnered from palaces and royal courts to humble homes, with many designed for sharing. Veeraswamy looks set to be around for another 80 years.

La Trouvaille

French ✕✕

H3

12A Newburgh St ✉ W1F 7RR
✆ (020) 7287 8488
Fax (020) 7434 4170
www.latrouvaille.co.uk

⊖ Oxford Circus
Closed 25 December,
Sunday and Bank Holidays

Menu £20/35

Newburgh Street is a charming cobbled street and La Trouville is the perfect little restaurant to find on it, but don't try the obvious corner door - the entrance is down the alley. The ground floor is a great spot for wine and charcuterie but head upstairs for 'Le Dining Room.' Decoratively it's bright and appealing, if somewhat offbeat: those clear plastic chairs catch your eye but numb your bum. The place is owned and passionately run by a couple of proud Northern Frenchmen and their set menus offer French classics with the occasional modern twist: their frog's legs can come with a curry sauce; their banana bavarois with guava and tamarillo. The wines are mostly organic and all come from the south.

Franco's

H4

Italian ××

61 Jermyn St ✉ SW1Y 6LX ⊖ Green Park
✆ (020) 7499 2211   Closed Christmas- New Year and Sunday
Fax (020) 7495 1375   – booking essential
e-mail reserve@francoslondon.com www.francoslondon.com

Menu £30 (lunch) – Carte £34/49

|A/C|
|⊙|
|☻|
|VISA|
|MC|
|AE|

The first thing you'll notice is wafts of cigar smoke drifting up from the pavement seats but head in and you'll get a friendly greeting, even when this place is busy which appears to be every day from dawn to dusk. It's spread over two floors plus a bar, with slick and attentive service and plenty of regulars. The menu fuses the classic with more modern Italian fare; there are supplementary grills, daily specials and even a seasonal truffle menu. Full of flavour and generous of portion, the cooking is satisfying and enjoyable. If the à la carte prices seem a little rich, then there's a decent value, weekly changing set menu, with a choice of two dishes per course, with a further theatre menu available too.

Café Lazeez

I2

Indian ××

21 Dean St ✉ W1D 3TN ⊖ Tottenham Court Road
✆ (020) 7434 9393 **Fax** (020) 7434 0022 Closed Sunday
e-mail reservations@lazeezsoho.com www.lazeez.sohocom

Carte £27/35

|A/C|
|⊙|
|☻|
|VISA|
|MC|
|AE|
|①|

The ground floor bar, attached to the Soho Theatre, is a lively little number and draws quite a crowd, more for its drinks list, no doubt, than the little Indian delicacies that are on offer. If you prefer to do your eating sitting down, then head downstairs for somewhere a tad quieter. Sketches of former Indian prime ministers adorn the brightly coloured walls, service is conscientious and the best tables are the booths by the staircase. The open-plan kitchen exhibits a certain ambition, encouraged by the restaurant's new owners. Several dishes come appealingly presented in earthenware dishes; there's clarity to the flavours and vigour in their construction. The wine list is also not your normal drab affair.

Stanza

Modern European ✕✕

I3

97-107 Shaftesbury Ave
✉ W1D 5DY
✆ (020) 7494 3020 **Fax** (020) 7494 3050
e-mail reception@stanzalondon.com **www**.stanzalondon.com

⊖ Leicester Square
Closed Saturday lunch and Sunday

Menu £14 (lunch) – Carte £28/64

A/C
🎭
VISA
MC
AE
DC

The name may be a rather tenuous link to neighbouring Theatreland but Stanza does do a decent value pre-show menu and its position on Shaftesbury Avenue means no great rush is needed to make curtain-up. Later on the place all gets pretty busy as it boasts a large and glitzy bar which stays open until 3am. The 80-seater restaurant is more than a mere appendage to that bar and offers a decent menu, which comes complete with a few lines of verse. It also name-checks quite a few suppliers and they clearly take their sourcing, which is chiefly within the British Isles, very seriously. The cooking displays a certain degree of originality but knows what goes with what. Being on the first floor adds a hint of exclusivity.

Benja 😊

Thai ✕✕

H3

17 Beak St ✉ W1F 9RW
✆ (020) 7287 0555
Fax (020) 7287 0056
e-mail info@krua.co.uk **www**.benjarestaurant.com

⊖ Oxford Circus
Closed 24-25 December and Sunday

Carte approx. £34

A/C
VISA
MC
AE

The red façade of a Soho townhouse make this Thai restaurant easy to spot and its seductive style has made it popular with the romantically inclined. Benja means 'five' in Thai: there are five owners and five main colour schemes. The ground floor is used the most but it's probably the least interesting of the three floors. The first floor is the most appealing with its mirrors and carved wooden flowers but requests to be moved upstairs can fall on deaf ears. Unusually, the Thai chef developed his skills at home near Bangkok, rather than in a restaurant, and whilst his cooking may underestimate our ability to enjoy a little spice, he does provide some interesting and unusual specialities alongside the more familiar classics.

Kiku

Japanese ✗✗

H4

17 Half Moon St ✉ W1J 7BE
☏ (020) 7499 4208
Fax (020) 7409 3259
www.kikurestaurant.co.uk

⊖ Green Park
Closed 25 December, 1 January,
lunch Sunday and Bank Holidays

Menu £18/46 – Carte £33/55

A/C
VISA
MC
AE
◐

These days you'll find countless restaurants attempting to 're-interpret' Japanese food but Kiku, a Mayfair stalwart for many years, shows there is a still a demand for tradition. The restaurant feels very bright and fresh, thanks to the minimalist décor of stone and natural wood. There are seats for 50 in the main room but panels break it up and at the back, up a few steps, you'll find the sushi counter. A plethora of menus is on offer so whether it's just soba noodles, a casserole, sushi or the full kaiseki experience you're after then they've got it covered. As expected, the natural flavours of the ingredients are allowed to come through, there's a fierce adherence to seasonality and importance placed on presentation.

Haiku

Asian ✗✗

H3

15 New Burlington Place
✉ W1S 2HX
☏ (020) 7494 4777
www.haikurestaurant.com

⊖ Oxford Circus
Closed Sunday

Menu £22/40 – Carte £40/50

A/C
VISA
MC
AE

It is not just the concept that was imported from South Africa – the original is in Cape Town – but also much of the stone and wood that decorates this moodily lit restaurant spread over three floors. The bar is downstairs but the ground floor is where the action is, although you never quite forget it's all housed within an office block. There are about 18 chefs here, from all over the world, which is a clue as to the food. They've given it the frighteningly unspecific name of 'Asian tapas', but then the menu does feature dishes from Japan, China, India and Thailand. Everything is on offer here, from sashimi and tempura to dim sum, tandoori and curry. Just be prepared to share and to accept that some parts will be greater than the sum.

Alastair Little

13

Modern European ✕✕

49 Frith St ✉ W1D 5SG
☎ (020) 7734 5183
Fax (020) 7734 5206
Menu £23/40

⊖ Tottenham Court Road
Closed Sunday and Bank Holidays
– booking essential

Alistair Little is a reassuring constant in ever-changing Soho. Its shoutier neighbours may display affection for luminous neon lighting but Alistair Little's pared down simplicity and egalitarian interior has always been reflected in its discreet façade. The man himself may no longer be involved but his influence can still be felt in the cooking. The balanced, daily-changing menu uses the freshest of ingredients and inflicts the minimum amount of interference upon them; the plate is never too crowded and flavours - subtly influenced by the Mediterranean - are well defined. But simple food doesn't always mean simple prices and the final bill, after some rather diminutive glasses of wine, can stack up.

Haozhan

13

Chinese ✕✕

8 Gerrard St ✉ W1D 5PJ
☎ (0207) 4343 838 **Fax** (0207) 4349 991
e-mail info@haozhan.co.uk **www**.haozhan.co.uk
Menu £11 (lunch) – Carte £17/33

⊖ Leicester Square

The hardest thing to find in Chinatown has always been a decent Chinese restaurant but in amongst the sea of mediocrity has come Haozhan which translates, appropriately enough, as "good place to eat." The majority of the menu is Cantonese with the odd Sichuan punch and some Taiwanese and Malaysian specialities. Eschew the usual perennials in favour of more modern dishes such as Assam prawns or Sanpei chicken; the homemade tofu is a particular strength. Presentation is strong; ingredients are very fresh; flavours are clear and well judged and it's even worth staying for dessert. Greens and blacks add to the contemporary feel of the place, which is spread over two floors. Service also bucks the local trend, being knowledgeable and helpful.

Yauatcha ✤

Chinese ✗✗

15 Broadwick St
W1F 0DL
☏ (020) 7494 8888 **Fax** (020) 7494 8889
e-mail mail@yauatcha.com

⊖ Tottenham Court Road
Closed 24-25 December

Carte £20/78

Regulars to this swish, modern dim sum restaurant beneath Richard Rogers' Ingeni building are divided as to which floor is best: the brighter, ground floor level, with its pastries and teas and staff in white uniforms or the altogether darker and equally busy downstairs, where the ceiling is covered in twinkly lights and the staff wear black. The only thing most agree on is that the narrow area under the stairs is the least desirable spot. Cantonese dim sum occupies 80% of the menu, where everything is divided by its method of preparation such as steamed, fried, baked or grilled as well as cheung fun and congee dishes. While many of the exquisite and carefully prepared dishes are authentic, the kitchen has developed many creations themselves, such as the prawn and bean curd cheung fun which is already being copied elsewhere. A little charm directed at your waiter/ress is no bad thing as then they'll be more inclined to give some thoughtful and helpful advice. Most dishes contain three pieces so, if your table has an even number, get in quick.

First Course
- Chilean sea bass mooli roll.
- Shiitake and duck roll.

Main Course
- Crispy aromatic duck with Thai spring onion and cucumber.
- XO prawn, scallops and lotus root.

Dessert
- Coconut soufflé with lime sorbet.
- Blue tea blackberry.

Brasserie St Jacques

French

33 St James's Street ✉ SW1A 1HD ⊖ Green Park
☎ (020) 7839 1007 **Fax** (020) 7839 3204 Closed Christmas and New Year
e-mail info@brasseriestjacques.co.uk www.brasseriestjacques.co.uk

Carte £26/38

33 St James's Street has been home to a number of restaurants: most recently Fiore and, most notably, Pétrus. Its newest incumbent is Brasserie St Jacques which represents owner Claudio Pulze's 51st restaurant opening. The layout of the room has never done any of the restaurants any great favours and this time is no exception: the bar may have been moved and some big Gallic posters and smoky mirrors hung but the place does lack that buzz one would expect from a brasserie. But where that name does apply more aptly is in the menu: it offers all the usual favourites from escargots to coq au vin, terrines to entrecôtes; the occasional Gascony accent comes courtesy of Pierre Koffman who's the consultant chef.

Aaya

Japanese

66 Brewer St ✉ W1F 9TR ⊖ Piccadilly Circus
☎ (0207) 3193 888 **Fax** (0207) 3193 889 Closed 25 December
e-mail info@aaya.com

Carte £25/60

Brewer Street hasn't seen this much glitz since Madame Jojo's heyday. Gary Yau (brother of Alan, restaurateur-extraordinaire) opened this supremely and, almost incongruously, stylish Japanese restaurant in 2008 and did so in a discreet, low-key way. There are other contradictions: the door-less doorman; the crisp elegance of the room at odds with the table setting; the trendily-dressed but sometimes indifferent staff. But the mesmerising bar and the extended basement sushi counter are terrific and the food is undeniably good. Much of the produce in imported and the menu combines the classic with the more contemporary. Dishes come artfully presented; the sushi and sashimi follow more traditional lines and are the strengths.

Silk

International 🍴🍴

H3

at Courthouse Kempinksi Hotel,
19-21 Great Marlborough St
✉ W1F 7HL
✆ (020) 7297 5567 **Fax** (020) 7297 5599
e-mail info@courthouse-hotel.com www.courthouse-hotel.com

⊖ Oxford Circus
Closed 22 December-1 January,
Sunday and Monday – dinner only

Menu £25 – Carte £23/38

A/C VISA MC AE

Those who find themselves in Soho but regard the local atmosphere as a little too strident and lawless can seek sanctuary in the hushed surroundings of Silk which was once a magistrate's court, appropriately enough. Unburdened by fashion, or indeed popularity, it is, nonetheless, a well run place with a novel culinary style that works a lot better in practice than on paper. The menu takes as its influence that part of the 'silk route' which passed through India and Asia. In reality, this means largely Indian dishes with some Thai added on, while the desserts are more European in design. The presentation can sometimes be a tad fiddly but the actual cooking is undertaken with good ingredients and a certain care.

Al Duca 😊

Italian 🍴

H4

4-5 Duke of York St
✉ SW1Y 6LA
✆ (020) 7839 3090 **Fax** (020) 7839 4050
e-mail info@alduca-restaurants.co.uk www.alduca-restaurant.co.uk

⊖ Piccadilly Circus
Closed Christmas, New Year,
Sunday and Bank Holidays

Menu £27/28

A/C 🎭 VISA MC AE ⓓ

Fresh and invigorating Italian cooking is the draw at Al Duca, nestling among the galleries, outfitters and old pubs of St James's. The set menus offer an appealing mix of dishes, many of which come in a modern, understated way with a nicely balanced simplicity. There's a daily changing pasta and risotto and the kitchen demonstrates a light and confident touch, as well as an obvious appreciation of the ingredients. Furthermore, it represents very good value, especially when you consider the location. Service makes up in efficiency what it lacks in personality. The crisp terracotta interior of tiles and stone means that noise has a tendency to bounce around the place a little when busy, which it nearly always is - and deservedly so.

Arbutus ❀

Modern European

63-64 Frith St
W1D 3JW
☏ (020) 7734 4545 **Fax** (020) 7287 8624
e-mail info@arbutusrestaurant.co.uk **www**.arbutusrestaurant.co.uk

⊖ Tottenham Court Road
Closed 25-26 December and 1 January

Menu £16 (lunch) – Carte £31/36

It may now have a sibling, Wild Honey, but no eyes have been taken off the ball at Arbutus. Neither is there any sign of the credit crunch here and when you look at the formula, it's easy to understand why: it serves classic dishes that are packed with flavour but priced fairly. There is the occasional 'turned on its head' dish, like the egg, duck and rillettes starter but generally this is about good 'cheffing' – using less expensive cuts of meat, like bavette of beef or less popular fish such as Silver mullet, in technically accomplished and carefully executed dishes that brings out the best from those ingredients. The menu can change twice in a day as dishes prove popular or certain ingredients become available. The lunch and pre-theatre menus are a positive steal and the obvious consideration towards their customers is further reflected in the wine list where wines are available by bottle or carafe. The place has an appealing lack of formality and an energetic atmosphere. Those without reservations can try their luck at the counter by the entrance.

First Course
- Smoked eel, beetroot and horseradish cream.
- Soft boiled egg, duck breast and rillettes.

Main Course
- Saddle of rabbit, cottage pie and peas.
- Silver mullet, crushed new potatoes, Cornish cockles.

Dessert
- Doughnuts, pistachio, honey and lemon thyme ice cream.
- Warm chocolate soup, caramelised milk ice cream.

Inn the Park

British

St James's Park ✉ SW1A 2BJ
✆ (020) 7451 9999
Fax (020) 7451 9998
e-mail info@innthepark.com **www**.innthepark.com

⊖ Charing Cross
Closed 25 December and dinner
January-February and October-November

Carte £28/32

Oliver Peyton's eco-friendly pavilion sits in St James's Park, the oldest Royal Park, and blends into its environment wonderfully well - even the roof is covered with grass. The terrace is a hard place to beat on a warm day and the views over the lake are terrific. It's also open all day and gains plaudits as much for its Britishness as its concern about sustainability and environmental damage. The kitchen may not always quite deliver the promise of the menu but all the ingredients, from crab to rabbit and duck to mutton, remind us what great produce we have in good old Blighty. There is also a children's menu of wholesome 'real' food, while the puddings are of the properly filling variety and may include treacle tart or apple pie.

The Cafe at Sotheby's

Modern European

34-35 New Bond St ✉ W1A 2AA
✆ (020) 7293 5077
Fax (020) 7293 6993
www.sothebys.com

⊖ Bond Street
Closed 24 December-4 January,
Saturday and Sunday
– booking essential – lunch only

Carte £25/33 s

'Café' is something of a misnomer as this is a thoroughly civilised, comfortable and urbane little spot for morning coffee, lunch or afternoon tea, located within the world famous auction house. It spills into the lobby but the best tables are those against the wall, with the banquette seating. Mirrors and Cecil Beaton photographs lighten the space and the waitresses are a charming and efficient group. The lunch menu is a short but well balanced affair, mixing the light with the more substantial and dishes are fresh and invigorating, including the popular lobster sandwich, a permanent feature. The wine list is also diminutive but the dozen or so wines are varied and well chosen. Bookings are essential, especially on sale days.

Chisou

Japanese

H2

4 Princes St ✉ W1B 2LE
☏ (020) 7629 3931 **Fax** (020) 7629 5255
e-mail chisou@xln.co.uk www.chisou.co.uk

⊖ Oxford Circus
Closed Sunday

Menu £17 (lunch) – Carte £24/43

Chisou proves that size should be no obstacle to providing good service and you'll find plenty of staff are on hand to guide you through the Japanese food. While it may be intimate, they are generous with the table size and spacing. The kitchen is headed up by a Japanese speaking Sri Lankan; he's often seen manning the sushi counter and has the owner's permission to source ingredients entirely on quality rather than cost restrictions. Specialities, from a menu that covers all points, include Tuna yukke, Gyu tataki (seared beef) and Hourensou (spinach) salad. There are some good value lunch set menus and next door is the useful 'Go Chisou,' where the growing local Japanese community go to get their Bento boxes.

Automat

American

H3

33 Dover St ✉ W1S 4NF
☏ (020) 7499 3033
Fax (020) 7499 2682
e-mail info@automat-london.com www.automat-london.com

⊖ Green Park
Closed 25 December and 1 January

Carte £39/52

Automat, an American-style brasserie, comes divided into three: the first section by the entrance is the least enticing as those waiting for tables will stand around near yours; the midsection comes decked out in the style of a railway carriage and the third is undoubtedly where the action is. The open kitchen and noise bouncing of the white tiles creates quite a buzzy vibe. The menu could have come direct from NYC. You'll find chowder, cakes of the crab and cheese variety, burgers and steaks, although in portions more European than Stateside. Brunch here is the genuine article. Where the authenticity falls down is in the service which lacks that energetic confidence and relentless efficiency one usually finds across the pond.

Chinese Experience

Chinese ✕

118 Shaftesbury Ave ✉ W1D 5EP
☏ (020) 7437 0377
e-mail info@chineseexperience.com **www.**chineseexperience.com

⊖ Leicester Square
Closed 25 December

Menu £15 – Carte approx. £19

A/C ☼ VISA MC

The location and that blaze of neon light may make you think this is nothing more than another touristy Chinese restaurant that couldn't find room in Chinatown, but Chinese Experience is, in fact, a thoroughly authentic and enthusiastically run restaurant. You'll notice this as soon as you step into its bright and airy interior and are greeted by friendly and obliging staff. It's divided into two rooms: the first with bench tables for those communally inclined and the larger second, with individual tables and a simple, crisp décor of white or red walls. The dim sum is served both for lunch and dinner and is worthy of note; the main menu is also extensive, mixing the familiar with those dishes of a more individual nature.

Bentley's (Oyster Bar)

Seafood ✕

11-15 Swallow St ✉ W1B 4DG
☏ (020) 7734 4756
Fax (020) 7758 4140
e-mail reservations@bentleys.org
www.bentleysoysterbarand grill.co.uk

⊖ Piccadilly Circus
Closed 24-26 December and 1 January

Carte £28/64

A/C 🍽 ☼ VISA MC AE

Once the place where sons took their ageing fathers or bewildered tourists took themselves, but now, following its full makeover a couple of years back, it's attracting an altogether sprightlier group of pescatarians. The elements remain largely the same: white jacketed staff open native or rock oysters by the bucket load, while others serve smoked salmon, fish pie, Dover sole and assorted seafood dishes. The difference is that the cooking is undertaken with a little more care these days. The panelled walls, marble topped tables and leather banquettes are also a great improvement and provide highly civilised surroundings in which to indulge. Reservations are not taken for the rather smart place settings up at the bar, so get in early if you want one of these.

Aurora

H3

Mediterranean

49 Lexington St ✉ W1F 9AP
📞 (020) 7494 0514
Carte approx. £25

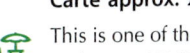

⊖ Piccadilly Circus
Closed Christmas and Sunday
– booking essential

This is one of those no-nonsense restaurants where most of the customers are regulars who just get on with it. It all happens in a cramped 18th century house, with a rough and ready feel enlivened with more than a hint of gothic. Tables are tightly packed and the ground floor is a buzzy place; go downstairs if you're after some intimacy. The menu changes every month and the cooking is satisfying, rustic and relatively straightforward; the best dishes are those that have roots closer to home. Those regulars ensure the steak is never removed and there's always a pasta and a salad dish. The jewel is the delightful walled garden – unique in Soho. It all works at Aurora, which is why it is now virtually an institution.

Bar Shu

I3

Chinese

28 Frith St ✉ W1D 5LF
📞 (020) 7287 8822
Fax (020) 7287 8858

⊖ Leicester Square
Closed 25-26 December – booking advisable

Carte £20/25

The fiery flavours of China's Sichuan Province are featured at the perennially busy Bar Shu and those who like their food hot will not be disappointed. Liberal amounts of peppers and chillies are used by the Sichuanese to combat the effects of a humid, wet climate while the region's reputation as a land of plenty are reflected in the variety of ingredients and the large number of specialities. The waiting team may appear reluctant to engage with their customers but the menu helpfully has pictures of the various dishes to help the novice. Sichuan cooking is also well-known for the strange names it gives its more famous dishes and most are featured, so look out for 'pock marked old woman's bean curd' or 'husband and wife meat slices.'

The National Dining Rooms

13

British

Sainsbury Wing, The National
Gallery, Trafalgar Sq
✉ WC2N 5DN
☏ (020) 7747 2525
e-mail enquiries@thenationaldiningrooms.co.uk
www.thenationaldiningrooms.co.uk

⊖ Charing Cross
Closed Christmas – lunch only and dinner Wednesday

Menu £30 – Carte £28/45

The UK's dismal culinary reputation abroad may be hopelessly outdated but will remain so until overseas visitors see evidence to the contrary. Credit then to Oliver Peyton for opening a restaurant in one of our great popular landmarks - The National Gallery. This Peyton place is on the first floor of the Sainsbury Wing, looking down over Trafalgar Square. The menu is a decidedly British affair, with carefully sourced ingredients from across our sceptred isle. So, Dorset crab can be followed by Scottish beef and the cheese selection shows off our great repertoire. Adjacent to the David Collins designed restaurant is a 'bakery', serving up evocative treats like jammy dodgers and fig rolls for those who haven't been to a gallery since that school trip.

Portrait

13

Modern European

3rd Floor, National Portrait Gallery, St Martin's Pl ✉ WC2H 0HE
☏ (020) 7312 2490
Fax (020) 7925 0244
e-mail portrait.restaurant@searcys.co.uk **www**.searcys.co.uk

⊖ Charing Cross
Closed 25-26 December
– booking essential – lunch only

Carte £23/32

Portrait is on the third floor of the Ondaatje wing of the National Portrait Gallery and is run by the Searcy's catering company. You needn't ask for a window seat because the views, of recognisable rooftops and Nelson standing proudly in Trafalgar Square, are just as good from any of the tables. Although open for breakfast and tea, this is principally a lunchtime operation, with dinner limited to Thursdays and Fridays - the nights of the gallery's extended opening hours. The à la carte menu keeps things relatively light and the influences mostly from Europe; there is a good value set menu at weekends. This is a useful spot, not only for gallery visitors but for those attending matinee performances at the numerous theatres nearby.

Barrafina

Spanish

54 Frith St ⊠ W1D 3SL
✆ (020) 7813 8016
Fax (020) 7734 7593
e-mail info@barrafina.co.uk www.barrafina.co.uk

⊖ Tottenham Court Rd
Closed Christmas, Easter and Bank Holidays
– bookings not accepted

Carte £18/37

London has been a bit iffy about restaurants that don't take reservations but Barrafina is the likely candidate to buck that trend. This is the newest sibling to the Hart brothers' Fino restaurant and its success is down to its mix of satisfyingly unfussy and authentic tapas and a buzzy atmosphere. Seafood is a speciality and the fish displays an exhilarating freshness; the Jabugo ham is also well worth trying. Four dishes per person is about par and the choice varies from razor clams a la plancha and tuna tartar to grilled chorizo and lamb sweetbreads with capers. It all centres around a counter, with seating for 20, so be prepared to talk to your neighbour. That's another thing that's never caught on in the capital. Be sure to try one of the sherries.

Dehesa

Mediterranean

25 Ganton St ⊠ W1F 9BP
✆ (020) 7494 4170
Fax (020) 7494 4175
e-mail info@dehesa.co.uk www.dehesa.co.uk

⊖ Oxford Circus
Closed 1 week Christmas and Sunday dinner

Carte £20/40

Dehesa is a few streets away from its sister restaurant, Salt Yard, and repeats the format of offering delicious Spanish and Italian tapas. The menu is not an exact copy but the bestsellers all feature: the pork belly with cannellini beans; courgette flowers with Monte Enebro and honey and the soft chocolate cake with Frangelico ice cream. They recommend 2-3 plates per person. Between 3pm and 5pm the kitchen takes a breather so the choice becomes ham on or off the bone, charcuterie and cheese. The drinks list is worthy of a visit in itself. The corner location is an inviting spot; they don't take bookings at dinner but neither do they rush their customers. Dehesa is a wooden area and home to Ibérico pigs who produce such great ham.

Le Boudin Blanc

French

G4

5 Trebeck St ✉ W1J 7LT
& (020) 7499 3292 **Fax** (020) 7495 6973
e-mail reservations@boudinblanc.co.uk
www.boudinblanc.co.uk

⊖ Green Park
Closed 25 December

Menu £15 (lunch) – Carte £28/48

Shepherd Market is the true heart of Mayfair, as it was here that the original May fair was held before the area was developed in the 18C into the village-like quarter it is now. The atmosphere may be a little less licentious these days but there's still a certain breeziness in the air and Le Boudin Blanc brings along some Gallic joie de vivre. The place is always busy and there's seating for about 150 but the first floor is marginally less frantic. The crowds are attracted by authentic and satisfying French classics, from snails and fish soup to confit of duck or beef tartare. Side orders can push up the final bill but there's a good value lunch and early evening menu. If you want more responsive service, try practising your French.

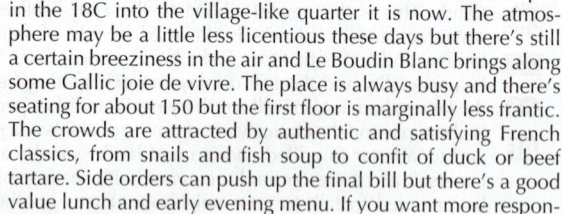

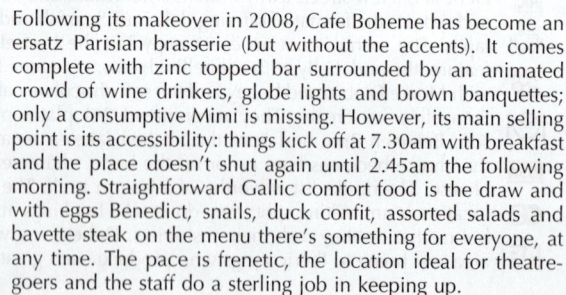

Cafe Boheme

French

I3

13 Old Compton St
✉ W1D 5GQ
& (020) 7734 0623 **Fax** (020) 7434 3775
e-mail info@cafeboheme.co.uk
www.cafeboheme.co.uk

⊖ Leicester Square
Closed 25 December

Carte £24/36

Following its makeover in 2008, Cafe Boheme has become an ersatz Parisian brasserie (but without the accents). It comes complete with zinc topped bar surrounded by an animated crowd of wine drinkers, globe lights and brown banquettes; only a consumptive Mimi is missing. However, its main selling point is its accessibility: things kick off at 7.30am with breakfast and the place doesn't shut again until 2.45am the following morning. Straightforward Gallic comfort food is the draw and with eggs Benedict, snails, duck confit, assorted salads and bavette steak on the menu there's something for everyone, at any time. The pace is frenetic, the location ideal for theatre-goers and the staff do a sterling job in keeping up.

Imli

Indian

I3

167-169 Wardour St
✉ W1F 8WR
✆ (020) 7287 4243
Fax (020) 7287 4245
e-mail info@imli.co.uk www.imli.co.uk

⊖ Tottenham Court Road
Closed 25-28 December,
1 January and lunch Bank Holidays

Menu £18 (lunch) – Carte £15/23

'Relatively timely food' may not sound quite as snappy as 'fast food' but Imli proves that, if you don't want to linger long over a meal, there are alternatives to multinationals. It may be an Indian restaurant but 'tapas' is the shorthand for dishes that are diminutive and involve sharing. The menu is short, well priced and to the point; three dishes per person should suffice, although the hungry should go for the 'Taste of Imli'. The cooking is a combination of street food and some regional, particularly Northern Indian, influences; vegetarians will find themselves with plenty of choice. Where Imli has borrowed from the 'experts' is in its use of bright lighting and vivid colours to encourage a rapid turnover.

The Only Running Footman

Gastropub

H3

5 Charles St. ✉ W1J 5DF
✆ (020) 7499 2988 **Fax** (020) 7491 8162
e-mail info@therunningfootman.biz
www.therunningfootman.biz

⊖ Green Park

Carte £29/39

Anyone who despairs about pubs serving Thai curry should head to this charming, historic pub which re-opened in 2007. That Union flag flying outside tells you everything about their attitude, for here our own culinary heritage is celebrated. The ground floor is small, atmospheric and always packed – it's first-come-first-served. The menu hits the bullseye: who can resist an Omelette Arnold Bennett for breakfast, potted shrimps for lunch or some haddock for dinner? You can even order a sausage sarnie to take away. Upstairs you can book, it's all rather plush and the menu is more ambitious. You do get to order the rib of beef for two; otherwise you may just wish you were downstairs with a pork pie and piccalilli.

Strand · Covent Garden

It's fitting that Manet's world famous painting 'Bar at the Folies Bergère' should hang in the **Strand** within a champagne cork's throw of theatreland and Covent Garden. This is the area perhaps more than any other which draws in the ticket-buying tourist, eager to grab a good deal on one of the many shows on offer, or eat and drink at fabled shrines like J.Sheekey or Rules. It's here the names already up in lights shine down on their potential usurpers: celeb wannabes heading for The Ivy, West Street's perennially fashionable restaurant. It's here, too, that Nell Gwyn set up home under the patronage of Charles II, while Oscar Wilde revelled in his success by taking rooms at the Savoy.

The hub of the whole area is the piazza at **Covent Garden,** created by Inigo Jones four hundred years ago. It was given a brash new lease of life in the 1980s after its famed fruit and veg market was pulled up by the roots and re-sown in Battersea. Council bigwigs realised then that 'what we have we hold', and any further redevelopment of the area is banned. Where everyone heads is the impressive covered market, within which a colourful jumble of arts and crafts shops gels with al fresco cafés and classical performers proffering Paganini with your cappuccino. Outside, under the portico of St Paul's church, every type of street performer does a turn for the tourist trade. The best shops in Covent Garden, though, are a few streets north of the market melee, emanating out like bicycle spokes from Seven Dials.

For those after a more highbrow experience, one of London's best attractions is a hop, skip and *grand jeté* from the market. Around the corner in **Bow Street** is the city's famed home for opera and ballet, where fire – as well as show-stopping performances – has been known to bring the house down. The **Royal Opera House** is now in its third incarnation, and it gets more impressive with each rebuild. The handsome, glass-roofed Floral Hall is a must-see, while an interval drink at the Amphitheatre Café Bar, overlooking the piazza, is de rigeur for show goers. At the other end of the Strand the **London Coliseum** offers more opera, this time all performed in English. Down by Waterloo Bridge, art lovers are strongly advised to stop at **Somerset House** and take in one of London's most sublime collections of art at the Courtauld Gallery. This is where you can get up close and personal to Manet's barmaid, as well as an astonishing array of Impressionist masters and twentieth century greats. The icing on the cake is the compact and accessible eighteenth century building that houses the collection: real icing on a real cake can be found in a super little hidden-away café downstairs.

Of a different order altogether is the huge **National Gallery** at

Trafalgar Square which houses more than two thousand Western European pieces (it started off with 38). A visit to the modern Sainsbury Wing is rewarded with some unmissable works from the Renaissance. It can get just as crowded in the capital's largest Gallery as in the square outside, so a good idea is to wander down **Villiers Street** next to Charing Cross station and breathe the Thames air along the Victoria Embankment. Behind you is the grand Savoy Hotel, which reopens in 2009 after major refurbishment; for a better view of it, you can head even further away from the crowds on a boat trip from the **Embankment,** complete with on-board entertainment. And if the glory of travel in the capital, albeit on the water, has whetted your appetite for more, then pop into the impressively renovated Transport Museum in Covent Garden piazza, where gloriously preserved tubes, buses and trains from the past put you in a positive frame of mind for the real live working version you'll very probably be tackling later in the day.

Strand & Covent Garden
(Plan III)

BLOOMSBURY, HATTON GARDEN & HOLBORN (Plan VI)

STRAND AND COVENT GARDEN

Key locations

- BRITISH MUSEUM
- GRAY'S INN FIELD
- GRAY'S INN
- BLOOMSBURY SQ.
- Holborn
- SIR JOHN SOANE'S MUSEUM
- LINCOLN'S INN FIELDS
- LINCOLN'S INN
- New Sq.
- Chancery Lane
- ST CLEMENT DANES
- TEMPLE
- Le Deuxième
- L'Atelier de Joël Robuchon
- Covent Garden
- The Ivy
- The Forge
- ROYAL OPERA HOUSE
- Le Café du Jardin
- Clos Maggiore
- COVENT GARDEN
- LONDON TRANSPORT MUSEUM
- One Aldwych
- Axis
- SOMERSET HOUSE
- Temple
- ST PAUL'S
- Rules
- J. Sheekey
- St Martins Lane
- Bedford & Strand
- ST MARTIN-IN-THE-FIELDS
- Admiralty
- VICTORIA EMBANKMENT GARDENS
- NATIONAL PORTRAIT GALLERY
- TRAFALGAR SQUARE
- CHARING CROSS
- OLD ADMIRALTY
- HORSE GUARDS
- BANQUETING HOUSE
- SOUTHBANK CENTRE
- Canteen
- Skylon
- LAMBETH
- JUBILEE GARDENS
- WATERLOO
- COUNTY HALL
- Westminster

Edge references

- MAYFAIR, SOHO AND ST JAMES'S (Plan II)
- BLOOMSBURY, HATTON GARDEN & HOLBORN (Plan VI)
- CITY OF LONDON (Plan VIII)
- SOUTHWARK (Plan X)
- BELGRAVIA & VICTORIA (Plan IV)

Legend

- ● Hotel
- ● Restaurant

0 200 m
0 200 yards

Axis

Modern European XXX

1 Aldwych ✉ WC2B 4RH
✆ (020) 7300 0300
Fax (020) 7300 0301
e-mail axis@onealdwych.com **www**.onealdwych.com

⊖ Temple
Closed Saturday lunch,
Sunday and Bank Holidays

Menu £18 (lunch) – Carte £28/37

Axis has had a little makeover: they have added some soft green fabrics on the walls and a bamboo-effect façade to the enormous futuristic mural. But they have also reduced the number of tables and spread things out a little more which means that the parties of larger tables don't dominate the room as they once did. Anticipation is still heightened by the spiral marble staircase leading down to the restaurant, which must have one of the highest ceilings in London. The menu is more British than before and greater emphasis is placed on provenance: you may find Lincolnshire rabbit, Herdwick lamb or Loch Duart salmon on the menu. The Grill section remains and there are also dishes for two, such as Rump of veal or Tarte Tatin.

The Ivy

International XXX

1-5 West St ✉ WC2H 9NQ
✆ (020) 7836 4751 **Fax** (020) 7240 9333
www.the-ivy.co.uk

⊖ Leicester Square
Closed 24-26 December,
1 January and August Bank Holiday

Carte £26/50

Despite being given a run for its money by the likes of The Wolseley, The Ivy remains the restaurant of choice for those 'celebrities' who appreciate their public as long as they don't have to see them when they're eating. And they get to have their photo taken on the way out. The format is much-copied but rarely so successful: if the restaurant knows you, you'll get in, if they don't then book well ahead and if you still haven't got it, then re-watch Ricky Gervais' 'Extras'. The menu is a hard one to pin down as it has something for everyone, whether you're a late riser and want eggs Benedict, need comfort food like shepherd's pie or something more exotic like Thai sea bass. The place does runs like clockwork.

J. Sheekey

I3

Seafood ××

28-32 St Martin's Court
✉ WC2 4AL
✆ (020) 7240 2565
Fax (020) 7497 0891
e-mail reservations@j-sheekey.co.uk www.j-sheekey.co.uk

⊖ Leicester Square
Closed 25-26 December, 1 January and August Bank Holiday – booking essential

Carte £31/51

When one thinks of fashionable restaurants one usually thinks of the glossy and the new but J. Sheekey has been doing its thing since 1896 and its sense of Englishness and links to the theatre still draw a crowd. It helps that they also do fish and seafood rather well, by keeping it all simple. The reassuring sight of potted shrimps, fruits de mer, fishcakes, fish pies and Dover Sole all feature and can be followed by uncomplicated fruit tarts or chocolate puddings so you leave feeling immeasurably satisfied, although a little lighter in the wallet. There are five sections and if you're a regular or your name's been up in lights, the more choice of table you'll have. Those tables are compact but that just adds to the bonhomie.

Rules

J3

British ××

35 Maiden Lane ✉ WC2E 7LB
✆ (020) 7836 5314 **Fax** (020) 7497 1081
e-mail info@rules.co.uk www.rules.co.uk

⊖ Leicester Square
Closed 4 days Christmas – booking essential

Carte £33/47

Such is the transient nature of restaurants that anywhere over 15 years old is referred to as 'well-established'. Rules opened its doors in 1798 and, as London's oldest restaurant, is fully entitled to look down on all those johnny-come-latelys. It's bursting with character and history and its quintessential Englishness is something to behold. Every inch of wall is covered with paintings, cartoons and drawings and its customers, from Charles Dickens to Charlie Chaplin, have always been drawn from the literary and theatrical worlds. The cooking also celebrates the best of British by specialising in game, often from its own estate on the Pennines, so this is the place for grouse, partridge and pheasant or a great steak and kidney pie.

146 YEARS OF EXPERIENCE, 27 HERBS AND SPICES, 1 PERFECT BLEND

BÉNÉDICTINE
Liqueur

DOM BÉNÉDICTINE. A TRADITION OF TASTE.

INTERNATIONAL WINE & SPIRIT COMPETITION BEST IN CLASS: 2005, 2007, 2008

MICHELIN ATLASES
Let your imagination take you away.

Get the most from your traveling with Michelin atlases
- Detailed road network coverage, updated annually
- Unique atlas format designed for the way you drive
- Route-planning made easy for business and leisure

www.michelin.co.uk

MICHELIN
A better way forward

Clos Maggiore

French ✕✕

I3

33 King St ✉ WC2E 8JD
☎ (020) 7379 9696
Fax (020) 7379 6767
e-mail enquiries@closmaggiore.com **www**.closmaggiore.com

⊖ Leicester Square
Closed lunch Saturday and Sunday

Menu £20 (lunch) – Carte £35/47

Exceptional value lunch and pre-theatre (up to 6.30pm) menus ensure that Clos Maggiore is never anything other than very busy. But despite its touristy location, this is not a restaurant merely pandering to a transient trade but one with a surprisingly neighbourly feel and plenty of regulars. The cooking shows flair and ambition, with its roots firmly within France; those set menus show off the kitchen's shrewd purchasing and imagination. Meanwhile, the extensive à la carte allows the chef full reign and his dishes are creative, neat and balanced; the wine list is a serious volume. The best seats are at the back in the conservatory; the roof opens in summer. Service is structured, quite formal but also comes with personality.

Admiralty

French ✕✕

J3

Somerset House, The Strand
✉ WC2R 1LA
☎ (020) 7845 4646 **Fax** (020) 7845 4658
e-mail info@theadmiraltyrestaurant.com
www.theadmiraltyrestaurant.com

⊖ Temple
Closed 25-26 December and Sunday

Menu £22/25 – Carte £27/38

There are many number of reasons to visit the magnificent 18C Somerset House, one of them being the restaurant in the south building. The Admiralty acknowledges the palace's link with the Royal Navy in its name and in the ship shaped chandeliers hanging in the two rooms into which the restaurant is divided. The high ceiling and arched windows ensure plenty of light; although it's the shame the riverside outside terrace is a separate operation. The menu offers an appealing selection that covers plenty of bases, from the earthiness of regional French cuisine to the more international influences of contemporary cooking. It can be a little on the corporate side at lunch but has a much more romantic atmosphere at dinner.

Le Deuxième

J3   **Modern European** XX

65a Long Acre ✉ WC2E 9JH   ⊖ Covent Garden
☏ (020) 7379 0033 **Fax** (020) 7379 0066   Closed 24-25 December
e-mail info@ledeuxieme.com **www**.ledeuxieme.com

Menu £17 (lunch) – Carte £28/33

Depending on which direction you've come from, this is either the first, or the last, restaurant in Covent Garden. Either way, it's a world away from the plethora of tourist joints which cover the surrounding streets. For a start, the service is enthusiastic, while the room has a warmth and an unthreatening neutrality. The cooking is also above this neighbourhood's norm. Lunch and pre-theatre menus are a steal and come with sufficient choice. The à la carte, meanwhile, offers a balanced and comprehensive choice and whilst there may be the occasional Asian note, the thrust remains within Europe, with a Franco-Italian emphasis. Expect risotto, gnocchi, foie gras and lemon tart. It shares the same owners as Le Café du Jardin.

The Forge

I3   **Modern European** XX

14 Garrick Street ✉ WC2E 9BJ   ⊖ Leicester Square
☏ (020) 7379 1432 **Fax** (020) 7379 1530   Closed 24 and 25 December
e-mail info@theforgerestaurant.co.uk
www.theforgerestaurant.co.uk

Menu £17 (lunch) – Carte £31/35

The owners appear to have Covent Garden sewn up as this is their third venture in the neighbourhood, after Le Café du Jardin and Le Deuxième. However, restaurant genealogists will recognise the place as Inigo Jones, whose star sparkled in the late '70s. The Forge has clearly looked more towards local stalwarts like The Ivy for inspiration: the menu is a long A3 affair, offering everything from eggs Benedict and plates of pasta to foie gras or Dover sole. The lunch and pre/post theatre menus are competitively priced. Apart from the odd Asian note, most influences are kept within the Med but there's also a willingness to use seasonal British produce. It's a large, open room with a downstairs bar and last orders are taken at midnight.

L'Atelier de Joël Robuchon ✿✿

French

13-15 West St ✉ WC2H 9NE — Leicester Square
✆ (020) 7010 8600 **Fax** (020) 7010 8601
e-mail info@joelrobuchon.co.uk **www**.joel-robuchon.com

Menu £25 (lunch) – Carte £33/85

Being a 'branch' or 'chain' restaurant usually suggests diminishing returns or bland homogeny – but every L'Atelier that appears around the world is testament to the vision of Joël Robuchon and his commitment to top quality cooking. Here in London there are two restaurants within one building: La Cuisine is more your structured affair, with moody black the predominant shade. The idea is for it to have something of a kitchen feel, although most people's kitchens do not have an army of French waiters with impenetrable accents. Downstairs on the ground floor is where you sit at the counter to watch the chefs at work and this is the more fun and relaxed choice. Both floors, however, share the same standards of cuisine as you would expect from somewhere employing over forty chefs. The food is predominantly French but there are Spanish and Italian influences too. Dishes are small, precise and exquisitely flavoured so ordering a number of them is usually the popular route; the problem lies in knowing when to stop for the sake of your wallet.

First Course
- Pig's trotter on parmesan toast with black truffle.
- Scottish lobster salad.

Main Course
- Langoustine with mango and basil relish.
- Quail stuffed with foie gras and truffled mashed potato.

Dessert
- La Boule surprise.
- Strawberry iced lollipop, mulled wine cherries.

Le Café du Jardin

Mediterranean

J3

28 Wellington St ✉ WC2E 7BD
☏ (020) 7836 8769 **Fax** (020) 7836 4123
e-mail info@lecafedujardin.com **www**.lecafedujardin.com

⊖ Covent Garden
Closed 24-25 December

Menu £17 (lunch) – Carte £25/32

The advantage of a theatre-land restaurant is that you'll be offered a good value set price menu and be guaranteed to be in your seat in time for curtain-up. Le Café du Jardin fulfils these duties admirably, with a weekly changing set menu with plenty of choice and staff whose commitment cannot be faulted, especially considering last orders are taken up to midnight. The downside is that the service can take time to change gear and those in for a more leisurely meal later in the evening could find themselves nursing their coffees sooner than they expect. Cooking is sunny and Mediterranean in influence, with plenty of pastas and grilled meats and fish. The ground floor is where the bustle is; downstairs is calmer but cooler in summer.

Bedford & Strand

British

J3

1a Bedford St ✉ WC2E 9HH
☏ (020) 7836 3033
e-mail hello@bedford-strand.com
www.bedford-strand.com

⊖ Charing Cross
Closed 25-26 and 31 December,
1 January, Saturday lunch,
Sunday and Bank Holidays – booking essential

Menu £16 – Carte £22/35

They call themselves a 'wine room and bistro' which neatly sums up both the philosophy and the style of the place - interesting wines, reassuringly familiar food and relaxed surroundings. It's named, American-style, after the cross streets so it's easy to find and the basement location shouldn't be off-putting. The after-work crowd have largely dispersed by 8ish in the evening but it all remains fairly energetic, helped along by a bright and sprightly team. British and Mediterranean comfort food is the feature of the menu, with a choice ranging from fish soup and risotto to cottage pie, with classic deli food served at the bar. The wine list has been thoughtfully put together and comes accompanied by some sensible pricing.

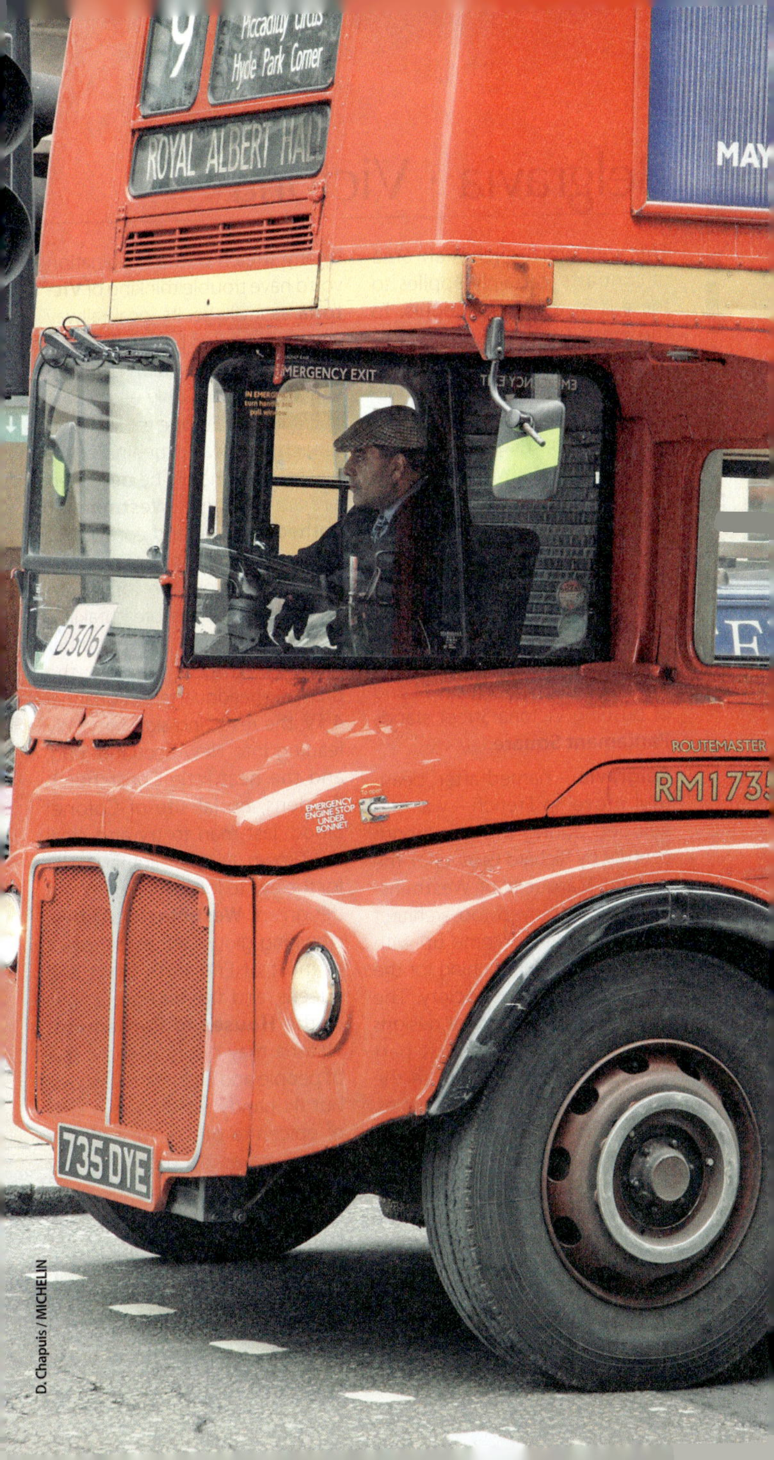

D. Chapuis / MICHELIN

Belgravia · Victoria

The well-worn cliché 'an area of contrasts' certainly applies to these ill-matched neighbours. To the west, Belgravia equates to fashionable status and elegant, residential calm; to the east, Victoria is a chaotic jumble of backpackers, milling commuters and cheap-and-not-always-so-cheerful hotels. At first sight, you might think there's little to no common ground, but the umbilical cord that unites them is, strange to say, diplomacy and politics. Belgravia's embassies are dotted all around the environs of **Belgrave Square,** while at the furthest end of bustling Victoria Street stands **Parliament Square.**

Belgravia – named after 'beautiful grove' in French - was developed during the nineteenth century by Richard Grosvenor, the second Marquess of Westminster, who employed top architect Thomas Cubitt to come up with something rather fetching for the upper echelons of society. The grandeur of the classical designs has survived for the best part of two centuries, evident in the broad streets and elegant squares, where the rich rub shoulders with the uber-rich beneath the stylish balconies of a consulate or outside a high-end antiques emporium. You can still sample an atmosphere of the village it once was, as long as your idea of a village includes exclusive designer boutiques and even more exclusive mews cottages.

By any stretch of the imagination you'd have trouble thinking of **Victoria** as a village. Its local railway station is one of London's major hubs and its bus station brings in visitors from not only all corners of Britain, but Europe too. Its main 'church', concealed behind office blocks, could hardly be described as humble, either: **Westminster Cathedral** is a grand concoction based on Istanbul's Hagia Sophia, with a view from the top of the bell tower which is breathtaking. From there you can pick out other hidden charms of the area: the dramatic headquarters of Channel 4 TV, the revolving sign famously leading into New Scotland Yard, and the neat little Christchurch Gardens, burial site of Colonel Blood, last man to try and steal the Crown Jewels. Slightly easier for the eye to locate are the grand designs of **Westminster Abbey,** crowning glory and resting place of most of England's kings and queens, and the neo-gothic pile of the **Houses of Parliament.** Victoria may be an eclectic mix of people and architectural styles, but its handy position as a kind of epicentre of the Westminster Village makes it a great place for political chit-chat. And the place to go for that is The Speaker, a pub in Great Peter Street, named after the Commons' centuries-old peacekeeper and 'referee'. It's a backstreet gem, where it's not unknown for a big cheese from the House to be filmed over a pint.

Winston Churchill is someone who would have been quite at home holding forth at The Speaker, and half a mile away in King Charles Street, based within the **Cabinet War Rooms** – the secret underground HQ of the war effort – is the Churchill Museum, stuffed full of all things Churchillian. However, if your passion is more the easel and the brush, then head down to the river where another great institution of the area, **Tate Britain,** gazes out over the Thames. Standing where the grizzly Millbank Penitentiary once festered, it offers, after the National Gallery, the best collection of historical art in London. There's loads of space for the likes of Turner and Constable, while Hogarth, Gainsborough and Blake are well represented, too. Artists from the modern era are also here, with Freud and Hockney on show, and there are regular installations showcasing upwardly mobile British talent. All of which may give you the taste for a trip east along the river to Tate Modern. This can be done every twenty minutes courtesy of the Tate-to-Tate boat service, which handily stops en-route at the London Eye, and even more handily sports eye-catching Damien Hirst décor and a cool, shiny bar.

Belgravia & Victoria
(Plan IV)
MAYFAIR, SOHO AND ST JAMES'S (Plan II)
CHELSEA, EARL'S COURT AND SOUTH KENSINGTON (Plan XI)
F
G
H
4
5
7
Hotel
Restaurant
HYDE PARK
Serpentine Road
South Carriage Drive
APSLEY HOUSE WELLINGTON MUSEUM
Park Lane
Curzon St.
Half Moon St.
Green Park
Piccadilly
Old Park Lane
SPENCER HOUSE
GREEN PARK
The Lanesborough
Brompton Rd
Hyde Park Corner
Constitution Hill
The Berkeley
Marcus Wareing at The Berkeley
Knightsbridge
Grosvenor Crescent
The Halkin
BUCKINGHAM PALACE GARDENS
Nahm
Grosvenor Place
BUCKINGHAM PALACE
Basil St.
Sloane St.
Wilton Crescent
Chapel St.
The Pantechnicon Rooms
Amaya
BELGRAVE SQ.
Chester St.
ROYAL MEWS
Buckingham Gate
Zafferano
Lowndes St.
BELGRAVIA
Mango Tree
Palace St.
HANS PL.
Cadogan Pl.
Noura Brasserie
Lower Grosvenor Pl.
Eaton Pl.
Beeston Pl.
Bressenden Pl.
Pont St.
Chesham Pl.
Eccleston St.
The Goring
Sloane Street
Chesham Street
Lyall St.
Eaton Sq.
Eaton Pl.
EATON SQ.
Olivomare
Victoria Street
Rd
CADOGAN SQ.
Santini
Victoria
Vauxhall
Carlisle Place
Ken Lo's Memories of China
Palace St.
VICTORIA
Wilton
B+B Belgravia
Street
Olivo
St.
King's Road
The Thomas Cubitt
Boisdale
Bridge
South Eaton Pl.
Gillingham St.
Road
Draycott Pl.
Il Convivio
Elizabeth St.
Belgrave
SLOANE SQ.
Bourne St.
Row
Chester St.
Semley Pl.
Buckingham
Saint
ECCLESTON SQ.
Warwick
King's Road
Lower Sloane St.
Ebury
Way
Road
La Poule au Pot
The Ebury
George's
WARWICK SQ.
Pimlico Road
Warwick
St.
Cheltenham Terrace
Franklin's Row
Roussillon
Alderney
Cumberland
Road
Sutherland
Chelsea Bridge Road
Street
Gloucester
Drive
BURTON'S COURT
Road
Ebury Bridge
St.
St.
Street
Hospital
THE ROYAL HOSPITAL
Lupus
Churchill Gardens
NATIONAL ARMY MUSEUM
Embankment
Grosvenor Road
Chelsea
THAMES
Chelsea Bridge

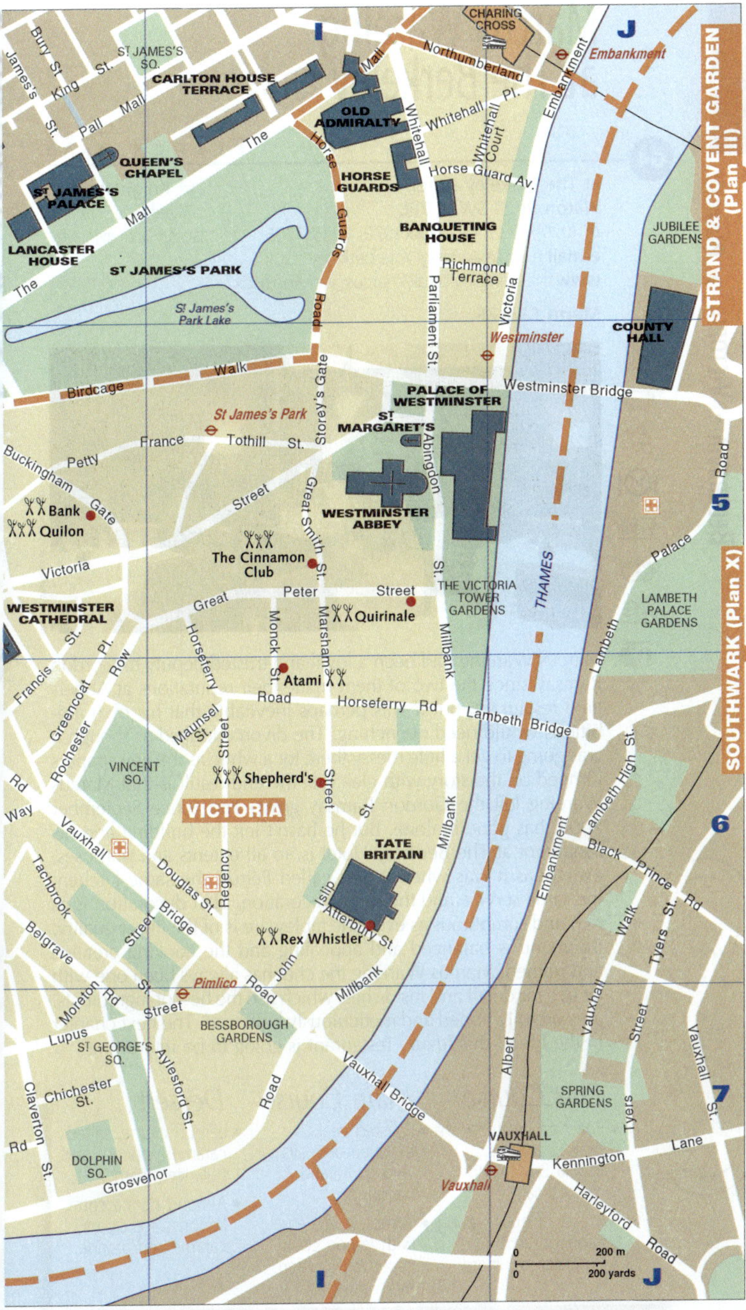

CHARING CROSS
Embankment
STRAND & COVENT GARDEN (Plan III)
Northumberland
ST JAMES'S SQ.
CARLTON HOUSE TERRACE
OLD ADMIRALTY
Whitehall
Whitehall Court
Horse Guard Av.
QUEEN'S CHAPEL
ST JAMES'S PALACE
HORSE GUARDS
BANQUETING HOUSE
JUBILEE GARDENS
LANCASTER HOUSE
ST JAMES'S PARK
St James's Park Lake
Richmond Terrace
Parliament St.
Victoria
Westminster
COUNTY HALL
Birdcage Walk
PALACE OF WESTMINSTER
Westminster Bridge
St James's Park
ST MARGARET'S
Tothill St.
Storey's Gate
Buckingham Gate
Petty France
WESTMINSTER ABBEY
Bank
Quilon
The Cinnamon Club
Victoria Street
Great Smith St.
THE VICTORIA TOWER GARDENS
THAMES
Lambeth Palace Road
LAMBETH PALACE GARDENS
WESTMINSTER CATHEDRAL
Great Peter Street
Quirinale
Atami
Horseferry Road
Monck St.
Marsham St.
Millbank
Lambeth Bridge
SOUTHWARK (Plan X)
Maunsel St.
VINCENT SQ.
Shepherd's
VICTORIA
TATE BRITAIN
Lambeth High St.
Black Prince Rd
Vauxhall Bridge Road
Douglas St.
Regency Street
Atterbury St.
Rex Whistler
John Islip St.
Tachbrook Street
Belgrave Rd
Pimlico
Moreton St.
BESSBOROUGH GARDENS
Lupus Street
ST GEORGE'S SQ.
Aylesford St.
Chichester St.
Claverton St.
DOLPHIN SQ.
Grosvenor Rd
Vauxhall Bridge
Albert Embankment
Vauxhall Walk
Tyers Street
SPRING GARDENS
VAUXHALL
Vauxhall
Kennington Lane
Harleyford Road
Vauxhall St.
200 m
200 yards

Marcus Wareing at The Berkeley ✿✿

French

G4

at The Berkeley Hotel,
Wilton Pl ✉ SW1X 7RL
☎ (020) 7235 1200 **Fax** (020) 7235 1266
e-mail marcuswareing@the-berkeley.co.uk
www.the-berkeley.co.uk/marcus_wareing.aspx

⊖ Knightsbridge
Closed 25-26 December,
Saturday lunch and Sunday

Menu £35/75

Marcus Wareing had been a loyal and trusted deputy to Gordon Ramsay since the two of them made their reputations at Aubergine restaurant, but it was perhaps inevitable that his own ambitions would need quenching. The divorce looked as though it was going to get a little messy there for a while as the newspapers jumped on the story with glee, but the end result is that Marcus Wareing left the Gordon Ramsay group and, since September 2008, has gone it alone. But he hasn't left the building and his restaurant at The Berkeley Hotel is, to all extents and purposes, exactly as it was when it was called Pétrus: the same kitchen, the same service and the same decoration. That decoration is as rich and sumptuous as ever; the tableware is of the finest quality; the menu is balanced and appealing and the cooking creative and refined. Marcus Wareing the chef has always been one with an eye for detail and his dishes, which use the best of ingredients, are carefully honed and meticulously balanced. The next chapter in the life of this luxury restaurant is going to be interesting.

First Course

- Poached lobster with braised trotters, vanilla butter and roasted salsify.
- Breast of quail, spring cabbage and Pommery mustard.

Main Course

- Roasted veal, fricassee of snails, wild garlic and bacon.
- Turbot, frogs legs with lemon confit, caper and golden raisin purée.

Dessert

- Lemon crème, salted caramel popcorn and milk ice cream.
- Almond panna cotta, liquorice ice cream, caramelised orange.

Zafferano

Italian

15 Lowndes St ⊠ SW1X 9EY ⊖ Knightsbridge
𝒞 (020) 7235 5800 Closed 2 weeks Christmas-New Year
Fax (020) 7235 1971 – booking essential
e-mail info@zafferanorestaurant.com
www.zafferanorestaurant.com

Menu £35/45

Zafferano is well-known for its loyal clientele and there has certainly been no decline in its popularity: there's always an early evening rush and no let up from there, although the full menu can always be taken at the bar. What is less known is that the man who has been running the kitchen for years, and was also the restaurant's first employee, is a Yorkshireman, Andy Needham; although he could pass as an Italian such is his passion for all that Italy has to offer. Having such a following means that the menu never stays too far from its core dishes, although there are always daily specials. If they ever took the linguine with lobster or the tiramisu off the menu the police would find themselves dealing with some very well-dressed rioters in the Belgravia area. The pasta really is special here and the food is fresh, seasonal and unfussy. The wine list continues to evolve; some top-end French names have moved in and there is more champagne. If you want to take some of the experience home then try their deli, which has really taken off.

First Course
- Sliced cured beef, rocket and goat's cheese.
- Burrata with artichokes and peas.

Main Course
- Grilled monkfish with courgettes and sweet chilli.
- Roast corn-fed chicken with lemon and capers.

Dessert
- Chocolate fondant with Gianduia ice cream.
- Vanilla panna cotta with strawberry and basil sugar.

BELGRAVIA · VICTORIA ▶ Plan IV

Roussillon ✽

French

G6

16 St Barnabas St ✉ SW1W 8PE
✆ (020) 7730 5550
Fax (020) 7824 8617
e-mail alexis@roussillon.co.uk
www.roussillon.co.uk

⊖ **Sloane Square**
Closed 25-26 December, Easter,
Saturday lunch and Sunday

Menu £35/55

These days we are lead to believe that anyone under the age of 18 finds the idea of eating vegetables an abhorrent proposition. Perhaps they could all be brought along to Roussillon to find out how vegetables can taste when they are cooked at the peak of their seasonal freshness, for this is the great strength of Alexis Gauthier's kitchen; he even offers an 8 course Menu Légume. Carnivores are still made just as welcome and will find themselves faced with plenty of choice. The cooking is classical French in its influences and techniques, but ingredients are largely British; and flavours subtle and nuanced. The sommelier and his wine list are the other attractions: his list contains plenty of gems from Roussillon, the Languedoc and the South West of France. Of all the starred restaurants in London, Roussillon, with its pretty bay window façade, is probably the least known and that is probably its great strength: it knows what it's doing and has a loyal, grown-up clientele. Who all eat their vegetables.

First Course
- Sesame seed crusted langoustines with basil and tomato broth.
- Potato gnocchi with parmesan, girolle and courgette flower tempura.

Main Course
- Red deer with celeriac and truffle purée, poached pear.
- Wild sea bass with tomato, chard and ratatouille jus.

Dessert
- Louis XV crunchy praline and chocolate.
- Blackcurrant soufflé with caramel ice cream and shortbread.

Amaya ✽

Indian 🍴🍴🍴

F5

Halkin Arcade, 19 Motcomb St
✉ SW1X 8JT
☎ (020) 7823 1166 **Fax** (020) 7259 6464
e-mail amaya@realindianfood.com
www.realindianfood.com

Menu £22/40 – Carte approx. £34

⊖ Knightsbridge
Closed 25 December

'Delicate' and 'restrained' are words rarely used when discussing Indian cooking but here at Amaya they sum up the approach perfectly. The tandoor, the tawa griddle and the sigri charcoal grill are used expertly to create small, tantalising plates, where the spicing enhances rather than masks the natural flavours. Kebabs are the most popular items on the menu and finishing with a curry is recommended but not imperative. Particular attention is paid to the quality of the seasonal vegetables, and the Vegetarian tasting menu, along with the Gourmand selection, are big hits. Desserts, too, shouldn't be overlooked as they are taken seriously and are subtly original. Most dishes are finished off in the show kitchen with its coloured lighting, so tables with clear views are the most sought after. As with all types of multi-plate dining, timing is everything and the kitchen keeps things moving at just the right pace. The multi-national staff know their menu well and offer sensible advice and the Keralan artwork adds warmth to the chic décor.

First Course
- Tandoori ocean prawns, tomato and ginger.
- Punjab chicken wing lollipops with chilli and lime.

Main Course
- Grilled lamb chops with lime and coriander.
- Griddled fillet of Dover sole with a coconut, coriander and mint crust.

Dessert
- Whipped chocolate and yoghurt.
- 'Three refreshers' - coconut; blackcurrant; melon and ginger.

BELGRAVIA • VICTORIA ▶ Plan IV

Quilon ✿

Indian

H5

at Crowne Plaza London
- St James Hotel,
41 Buckingham Gate ✉ SW1 6AF
✆ (020) 7821 1899 **Fax** (020) 7233 9597
e-mail info@quilonrestaurant.co.uk **www**.quilon.co.uk

Menu £20/35 – Carte £35/46

⊖ St James's Park
Closed Saturday lunch

A/C
☀
VISA
MC
AE

The vibrant and colourful decoration goes some way towards creating a general feeling of wellbeing and also offsets the slight hotel feel. Indian scenes painted on a canvas and made to look like murals add a hint of exoticism and, thanks to subtle lighting and the shape of the room, it feels quite intimate for a restaurant with seating for ninety. As with all good kitchens, the starting point is using exemplary ingredients and Quilon is no exception: for example, only corn-fed chicken is used and the chef is committed to sustainability. The kitchen also displays a healthy respect for the traditions of Indian cooking and this is particularly evident in the spicing of dishes; but Sriram Aylur and his brigade are also not afraid of pushing boundaries. Vegetarians are very well looked after and, appropriately for a restaurant that specialises in Southern Indian cuisine (the restaurant name refers to the port on the south west coast), Keralan fish dishes are of particular note. The service is well organised and endearingly professional.

First Course
- Marinated scallops grilled and served with spiced coconut cream.
- Batter-fried shrimps, oyster and fish in fiery masala.

Main Course
- Lobster with mango, ginger, kokum and curry leaves.
- Guinea fowl, onion, green chilli, cardamom and coconut milk.

Dessert
- Almond delight with praline, yoghurt and almond ice cream.
- Jackfruit milk pudding with strawberry purée.

BELGRAVIA · VICTORIA ▶ Plan IV

Santini

G5

Italian 🗙🗙🗙

29 Ebury St ✉ SW1W 0NZ
✆ (020) 7730 4094
Fax (020) 7730 0544
e-mail info@santini-restaurant.com **www**.santini-restaurant.com

⊖ Victoria
Closed 24-27 December and Easter

Carte £31/51

Whether it is the relatively discreet location, the long-standing family ownership or the classic Italian cooking, what is certain is that over the years Santini has attracted its fair share of the high profile celebrity market, from Presidents to actors and all points in between. The décor is sleek and understated and the service formal and deliberate. A pretty foliage-fringed terrace provides a pleasant spot for alfresco dining for those unafraid or unlikely to be troubled by passing admirers. The menu keeps it classic with a subtle Venetian accent and the focus rightly falls on the quality of the ingredients. Those whose ambition outweighs their wallet should try the more reasonably priced pre-theatre menu.

The Cinnamon Club

I5

Indian 🗙🗙🗙

30-32 Great Smith St
✉ SW1P 3BU
✆ (020) 7222 2555
Fax (020) 7222 1333
e-mail info@cinnamonclub.com **www**.cinnamonclub.com

⊖ St James's Park
Closed 26 December, 1 January,
Sunday and Bank Holiday Mondays

Menu £22 (lunch) – Carte £34/54

The Grade II listed former Westminster library may seem an unlikely setting for an Indian restaurant but it works surprisingly well. The shelves of books are still there on the mezzanine level of the large main room where the action is, although the smaller front room has better air-conditioning. There are two bars: the one downstairs is the livelier. A variety of menus are on offer and prices can get quite steep but the cooking clearly displays ambition and innovation. Many of the ingredients may be more European, like Herdwick lamb or Anjou pigeon, but the cooking techniques, colours and spices are resolutely Indian. Staff are on the ball, as you'd expect from somewhere serving over 200 people twice a day.

Shepherd's

British ✗✗✗

Marsham Court, Marsham St
✉ SW1P 4LA
☎ (020) 7834 9552 **Fax** (020) 7233 6047
e-mail admin@langansrestaurants.co.uk
www.langansrestaurants.co.uk

⊖ Pimlico
Closed Saturday,
Sunday and Bank Holidays
– booking essential

Menu £34

Looking at the number of shiny pates and pin-striped suits that pile into Shepherd's for lunch you'd be forgiven for thinking that 'Blair's Babes' never left much of a legacy. This is a classic, old-school blokey institution that could show some of those new restaurants a thing or two; for starters, it runs on wheels and gives the punters what they want. The atmosphere is animated throughout, but the booths are the best places to sit. The menu is a combination of classic dishes and brasserie favourites but your best bet is to head for those bits of the menu that read like a UKIP manifesto – the fiercely British specialities, like the daily roast or the Dover Sole, followed by an indulgent dessert like a sponge pudding.

Quirinale

Italian ✗✗

North Court, 1 Great Peter St
✉ SW1P 3LL
☎ (020) 7222 7080
Fax (020) 7233 3080
e-mail info@quirinale.co.uk www.quirinale.co.uk

⊖ Westminster
Closed August, 1 week Christmas - New Year,
Saturday, Sunday and Bank Holidays

Carte £34/40

Named after one of the Seven Hills of Rome where the Italian head of state resides, Quirinale lies in the shadow of Parliament. It's easy to miss as the discreet entrance is tucked inside a mansion block entrance. Descend the wide tiled staircase and you'll find yourself in a surprisingly bright and contemporary styled restaurant, where the service is scrupulously slick and the atmosphere discreet. The chef hails from Brescia but his seasonally-changing menu is all-encompassing, with a few more Sicilian and Neapolitan touches. Pastas are home-made, cooking shows a light touch and the wine list covers all parts. There's a large selection of cheeses that are worth exploring, all sourced from small, artisan suppliers.

Nahm ✽

Thai

at The Halkin Hotel,
5 Halkin St ✉ SW1X 7DJ
✆ (020) 7333 1234
Fax (020) 7333 1100
e-mail res@nahm.como.bz **www**.halkin.como.bz

⊖ Hyde Park Corner
Closed Christmas, Easter,
lunch Saturday-Sunday, and Bank Holidays
– booking advisable

Menu £26/55 – Carte £40/46

Nahm is still one of London's most original restaurants. The soothing surroundings are a subtle blend of copper tones, wood and candlelight; the understated hint of Asian design sits well within the boutique surroundings of the The Halkin Hotel. The staff appear to have raised their game in their knowledge and enthusiasm for David Thompson's superlative dishes which are based on Royal Thai traditions and are prepared with a sure hand and an innate understanding by his head chef, Matthew Albert. The fresh and fragrant salads are a great way to start and provide balance to the rich curries which have real intensity, depth but also balance. You can opt for the 'nahm arharn' set menu but that does mean the table all get the same dishes and there is such variety on the à la carte. The kitchen will offer to provide starters separately but prefer to serve the meal in true Thai style which means all together. The only slight niggle is that the super-efficient air-conditioning can cool the dishes rather too quickly.

First Course
- Salted chicken wafers, longans, Thai basil.
- Pumpkin curry puffs.

Main Course
- Pork belly, braised with peanuts.
- Red curry of duck with lychee.

Dessert
- Coconut cake with rambutans and perfumed syrup.
- Fresh Thai fruits.

BELGRAVIA • VICTORIA ▶ Plan IV

Atami

Japanese ✕✕

I6

37 Monck St ⊖ Pimlico
(entrance on Great Peter St) Closed Saturday lunch
✉ SW1P 2BL
✆ (020) 7222 2218 **Fax** (020) 7222 2788
e-mail mail@atami-restaurant.com **www**.atami-restaurant.com

Menu £23/45 – Carte approx. £35

A/C
VISA
MC
AE

Named after one of Japan's best known hot spring resorts, Atami is the latest in a line of stylishly decorated Japanese restaurants that have proved very popular over the last few years by mixing the traditional with the decidedly contemporary. The difference is that here prices are a little more down to earth. The serving team will offer the novice expert guidance around the menu; alongside the sushi and sashimi, expect to find ingredients of a more European provenance, paired in some unexpected yet delicate combinations. Bamboo, leather, mirrors, glass and natural woods combine to create a sensual and striking space, illuminated by four large ceiling orbs. The bar is tucked away discreetly but is equally appealing and strangely calming.

Il Convivio

Italian ✕✕

G6

143 Ebury St ✉ SW1W 9QN ⊖ Sloane Square
✆ (020) 7730 4099 Closed 25-26 December,
Fax (020) 7730 4103 Sunday and Bank Holidays
e-mail comments@etruscarestaurants.com
www.etruscarestaurants.com

Menu £22 (lunch) – Carte approx. £34

A/C
⊟
VISA
MC
AE

You know you're in a serious Italian restaurant when the autumnal truffle season produces specialities on the menu featuring the white truffle - tartufo bianco, the king of truffles. Indeed, there's no denying the quality of the produce here, whether it's the milk-fed lamb, Angus beef or wild sea bass. Pasta is also something of a house speciality and any of the half-dozen choices can be taken as a starter, middle or main course. Found within an attractive Georgian house, the poet Dante is celebrated in the name and the decoration of the restaurant and lines of his poetry are embossed on the wall. The best place to sit is either at the front, overlooking the street, or right at the back under the retractable roof.

Rex Whistler

British ✕✕

I6

Tate Britain, Millbank ✉ SW1P 4RG
☎ (020) 7887 8825
Fax (020) 7887 4969
e-mail britain.restaurant@tate.org.uk **www**.tate.org.uk

⊖ Pimlico
Closed 24-26 December
– booking essential – lunch only

Carte £28/37

Galleries everywhere are finally seeing the value of having a decent restaurant but the one here at Tate Britain has been going since 1972. It's a spacious, masculine room, offering the added appeal of being surrounded by the striking Rex Whistler mural 'In Pursuit of Rare Meats', painted in 1927. Just as the gallery celebrates British art, so the menu does its bit for Blighty: there's a daily catch from the Newlyn day boats and the chips are even cooked in dripping. Meanwhile, the fruity puddings illustrate why this part of the meal is our culinary crowning glory. The wine list is truly excellent: it is intelligently laid out, has over 80 half bottles, many of which are from wines rarely seen in halves, and it is full of gems.

Ken Lo's Memories of China

Chinese ✕✕

G6

65-69 Ebury St ✉ SW1W 0NZ
☎ (020) 7730 7734 **Fax** (020) 7730 2992
www.memories-of-china.co.uk

⊖ Victoria
Closed 25-26 December,
Sunday lunch and Bank Holidays

Menu £20/32 – Carte £31/51

The restaurant may have changed hands over the years but the late Ken Lo was responsible for putting the place on the map all those years ago and so it's appropriate to find his name still in the title. The restaurant belies its age in its looks. It is bright, modern and quite minimalist in its design but also manages to be warm and welcoming. Chinese script, lattice panels and well dressed tables ensure a sense of comfort and style. The length of the menu can appear a little bewildering, as can the seemingly eccentric numbering system, but the dishes come carefully prepared. The set menus are often the easier option and take you on a gastronomic tour of China. Service is positive, well marshalled and clued-up.

Boisdale

G6

Scottish ××

15 Eccleston St ⊠ SW1W 9LX — ⊖ Victoria
☏ (020) 7730 6922 — Closed Christmas,
Fax (020) 7730 0548 — Saturday lunch and Sunday
e-mail info@boisdale.co.uk www.boisdale.co.uk

Carte £29/91

Those waiting for the day when a Scottish Embassy opens in London can more than make do with Boisdale, for they will be unlikely to find anywhere, outside of Scotland, more Scottish than this. The owner is a proud Macdonald and the Macdonald tartan is everywhere, along with a plethora of prints and paintings. The menu showcases the best of Scotland's fine produce from salmon to game and matured beef. There is a choice of dining room within this charming Regency town house, from the clubby atmosphere of the Macdonald Bar to the more formal and demure surroundings of the Auld restaurant. In summer the retractable roof makes the Courtyard Garden a popular choice. The one element to break from all things Scottish is the nightly jazz band.

Mango Tree

G5

Thai ××

46 Grosvenor Pl ⊠ SW1X 7EQ — ⊖ Victoria
☏ (020) 7823 1888 — Closed 24-25 December and 1 January
Fax (020) 7838 9275
e-mail info@mangotree.org.uk www.mangotree.org.uk

Menu £18/40 – Carte approx. £25

There are other Mango Trees in Bangkok and Dubai which tells you that this branch is not going to be some humble little local – we're talking loud, polished and none too cheap. That being said, it still equates to a good night out, thanks to the large bar and the clued-up team, who all have the latest ordering gizmos at their disposal. The menu covers all bases and is logically laid out; there are plenty of milder stir-fries, hotter curries and appealing starters and dishes are prepared with almost unexpected care and respect. With some judicious ordering and sharing, that final bill can be kept to moderate levels. Anyone not sated can order the Dessert Selection: a taster of all the desserts. The loos are virtually a taxi ride away.

Bank

H5

Modern European ✕✕

45 Buckingham Gate
✉ SW1E 6BS
☏ (020) 7630 6644
Fax (020) 7630 5665
e-mail reservations.westminster@bankrestaurants.com
www.bankrestaurants.com

⊖ St James's Park
Closed Saturday lunch, Sunday and
Bank Holidays – booking essential at lunch

Carte £29/45

Adjoined to the Crowne Plaza Hotel but with its own street entrance, this branch of Bank is a little less frenzied than the one that used to exist in Aldwych but can, nonetheless, still provide a fun night out. You do first have to get past the Zander Bar, which purports to be the longest bar in the country, and those who find themselves unable to ever pass a bar will find it also has a food menu. The restaurant itself is a large conservatory affair and looks out onto an attractive Victorian courtyard. The lunchtime clientele can be a little more business orientated but is less so in the evenings. You'll find classic, familiar choices alongside more contemporary influences on the extensive à la carte, which is supplemented by a fixed priced option.

Noura Brasserie

G5

Lebanese ✕✕

16 Hobart Pl ✉ SW1W 0HH
☏ (020) 7235 9444 **Fax** (020) 7235 9244
e-mail noura@noura.co.uk **www**.noura.co.uk

⊖ Victoria

Menu £18/40 – Carte £24/39

Having made their name in Paris, the owners set their sights across the Channel and opened their first London restaurant here in Belgravia in 2000. It undoubtedly challenged any preconceptions by being a big, bold and brash room which was both decidedly contemporary and reflective of the zeitgeist. Today, it's as busy as ever, especially with larger tables and parties for whom the surroundings are ideal. Nonetheless, the staff remain stoically immune to the enthusiasm of their customers. A slightly less formal approach is adopted at lunch, with a keenly priced lunch menu on offer. The main menu is a dazzlingly long affair, with authentic Lebanese delicacies designed for sharing. Those new to it all should try the set menus or selected platters.

Olivo

G6   Italian 🍴

21 Eccleston St ✉ SW1W 9LX   ⊖ Victoria
✆ (020) 7730 2505   Closed Bank Holidays,
Fax (020) 7823 5377   lunch Saturday and Sunday
e-mail maurosanna@oliveto.fsnet.co.uk **www**.olivorestaurant.com

Menu £23 (lunch) – Carte £25/33

All restaurants work best when the owner is present. At Olivo, Mauro not only keeps a steady hand on the tiller but he also ensures that the atmosphere remains bright and welcoming - that's what makes Olivo such an attraction. It still feels like a local restaurant, although some diners are prepared to travel quite some distance to get here, and its twenty year anniversary bears testament to its continued popularity. The rustic décor and the closely set tables within this relatively small space further ensure a highly convivial feel, helped along by a keen team of servers. The menu and the wine list are both Italian, with subtle hints of Sardinia. The chargrill is a house speciality, dishes are colourful and satisfying and the produce used is top notch.

La Poule au Pot

G6   French 🍴

231 Ebury St ✉ SW1W 8UT   ⊖ Sloane Square
✆ (020) 7730 7763   Closed 25-26 December and 1 January
Fax (020) 7259 9651

Menu £18 (lunch) – Carte £29/42

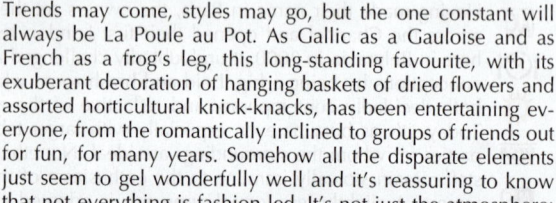

Trends may come, styles may go, but the one constant will always be La Poule au Pot. As Gallic as a Gauloise and as French as a frog's leg, this long-standing favourite, with its exuberant decoration of hanging baskets of dried flowers and assorted horticultural knick-knacks, has been entertaining everyone, from the romantically inclined to groups of friends out for fun, for many years. Somehow all the disparate elements just seem to gel wonderfully well and it's reassuring to know that not everything is fashion led. It's not just the atmosphere: the classic country cooking is also responsible for drawing the crowds. Expect a selection of rustic favourites from coq au vin to crème brûlée, supplemented by daily specials.

Olivomare

G5

Seafood 🍴

10 Lower Belgrave St ✉ SW1W 0LJ   ⊖ Victoria
✆ (020) 7730 9022 **Fax** (020) 7823 5377   Closed Sunday and Bank Holidays
e-mail maurosanna@oliveto.fsnet.co.uk **www**.olivorestaurants.com

Carte £28/33

A new cog in the local Olivo chain was added in May 2007 with the opening of Olivomare. Seafood is the theme here, with a subtle Sardinian subtext, which means you'll find bottarga, intensely flavoured grey mullet roe, grated on spaghetti; fregola, Sardinia's own version of couscous, with the classic accompaniment of clams and some chilli heat; cassola di pesce, a version of fish soup, and lorighittas - earring-shaped pasta. The pasta dishes are available as a starter or main course, although the individually priced veg and breads can nudge the bill northward. The decor is minimalistic chic, with snow-blind white and a mural of intertwined fish – stare at this for long enough and apparently you'll see a boat.

The Thomas Cubitt

G6

Gastropub 🍺

44 Elizabeth Street   ⊖ Sloane Square.
✉ SW1W 9PA   Closed 25 December, Good Friday
✆ (020) 7730 6060 **Fax** (020) 7730 6055   – booking essential
e-mail reservations@thethomascubitt.co.uk
www.thethomascubitt.co.uk

Menu £25 – Carte £30/60

Welcome the world of the pub, Belgravia style. Thomas Cubitt was the master builder responsible for landmark local squares, Eaton and Belgrave, and he would surely have approved of this decidedly handsome establishment. Regency and Georgian styles have been put to good effect, with oak flooring, panelling and fireplaces, to create a warm and welcoming feel, from the delightful ground floor bar in which to enjoy more casual dining to the charming and more formal upstairs room where the period feel really comes into its own. Here the menu is more structured and features seasonal produce, carefully sourced from across the British Isles, in unfussy and flavoursome dishes. Service also hits the right note in its unobtrusiveness and warmth.

The Ebury

Gastropub

G6

11 Pimlico Rd ✉ SW1W 8NA — ⊖ Sloane Square
✆ (020) 7730 6784 **Fax** (020) 7730 6149 — Closed 25 December
e-mail info@theebury.co.uk **www**.theebury.co.uk

Menu £20 (lunch) – Carte £30/45

A/C
VISA
MC
AE

On the ground floor one finds the busy and lively brasserie/pub with floor to ceiling windows and a thrusting young crowd with a bar that is equally adept at satisfying their demands. Ascend the oak staircase and you come upon altogether more tranquil and restful surroundings, where the added formality and pretty decorative touches help create a very soothing ambience. There's a crustacean bar, ideal for those who wish to share their food, while the main menu reads like a manifesto for modern European cooking: there's everything from foie gras, pork belly and rump of lamb to other less artery-bothering offerings like roast cod with Puy lentils and guinea fowl with root vegetables. Desserts will be hard to resist.

The Pantechnicon Rooms

Gastropub

G5

10 Motcomb St ✉ SW1X 8LA — ⊖ Knightsbridge
✆ (020) 7730 6074 — Closed 25 December and Good Friday
Fax (020) 7730 6055
e-mail reservations@thepantechnicon.com
www.thepantechnicon.com

Menu £25 (lunch) – Carte £25/50

VISA
MC
AE
(1)

It took the owners over a year to transform the distinctly unprepossessing Turks Head and turn it into this smart new pub that matches their other place nearby, The Thomas Cubitt. It's named after the art and antique repository that once graced Motcomb Street until it was destroyed by fire in 1874; a painting of which graces the smart upstairs restaurant. The menu is a sophisticated number, with oysters, caviar and shellfish having their own sections, along with cocktails and champagne. Downstairs the menu gets tweaked slightly so that the starters become 'small plates' but otherwise there is little difference; influences are kept within Europe, the seafood is well worth exploring and dishes come daintily presented.

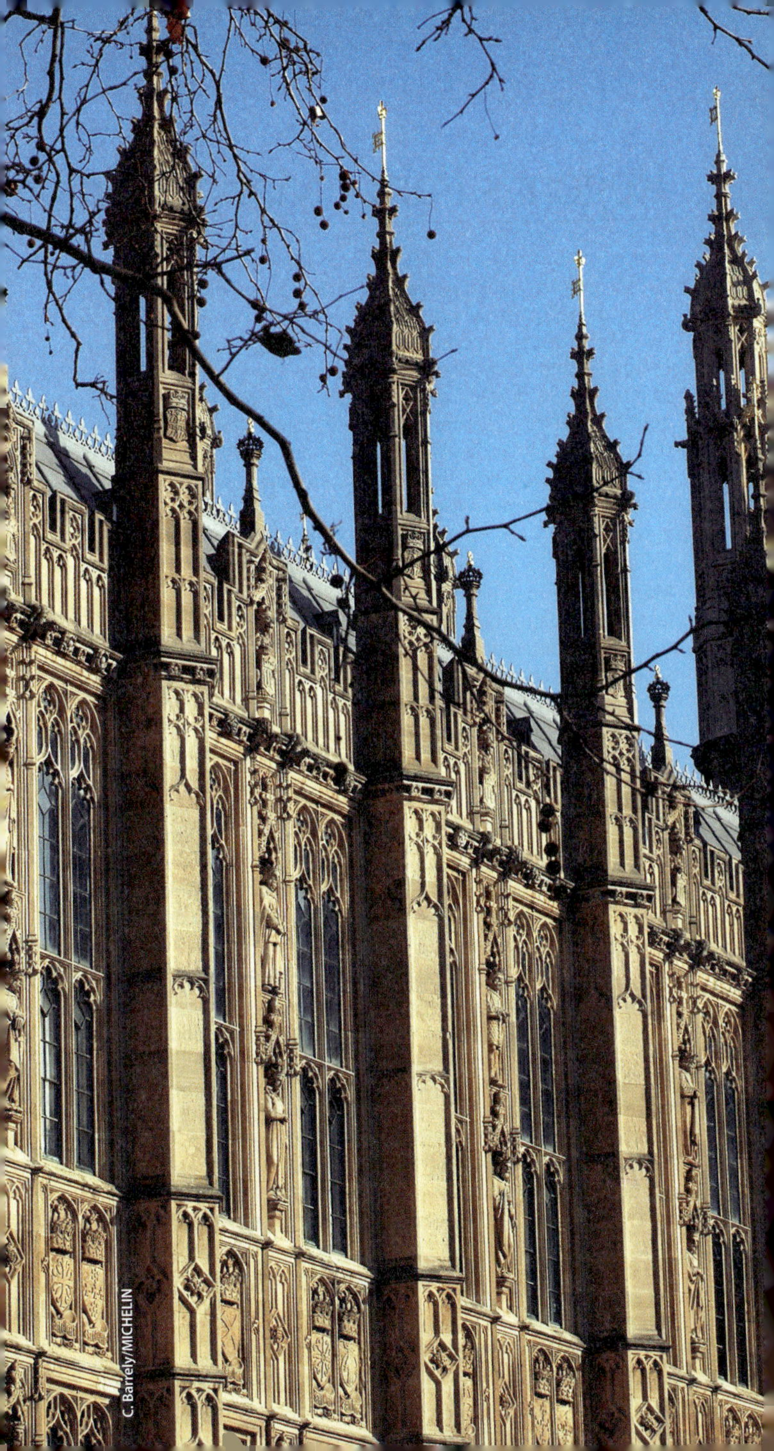
C. Barrely/MICHELIN

Regent's Park · Marylebone

The neighbourhood north of chaotic Oxford Street is actually a rather refined place where shoppers like to venture for the smart boutiques, and where idlers like to saunter for the graceful parkland acres full of rose gardens and quiet corners. In fact, Marylebone and Regent's Park go rather well together, a moneyed village with a wonderful park for its back garden.

Marylebone may now exude a fashionable status, but its history tells a very different tale. Thousands used to come here to watch executions at Tyburn gallows, a six hundred year spectacle that stopped in the late eighteenth century. Tyburn stream was covered over, and the area's modern name came into being as a contraction of St Mary by the Bourne, the parish church. Nowadays the people who flock here come to gaze at less ghoulish sights, though some of the inhabitants of the eternally popular Madame Tussauds deserved no better fate than the gallows. South across the busy Marylebone Road, the preponderance of swish restaurants and snazzy specialist shops announces your arrival at **Marylebone High Street.** There are patisseries, chocolatiers, cheese shops and butchers at every turn, nestling alongside smart places to eat and drink. At St Marylebone Church, each Saturday heralds a posh market called Cabbages & Frocks, where artisan food meets designer clothing in a charming garden. Further down, the century old Daunt Books has been described as London's most beautiful bookshop: it has long oak galleries beneath graceful conservatory skylights. Close by, the quaintly winding Marylebone Lane boasts some truly unique shops like tiny emporium The Button Queen, which sells original Art Deco, Victorian and Edwardian buttons. In complete contrast, just down the road from here is the mighty **Wigmore Hall,** an art nouveau gem with great acoustics and an unerringly top-notch classical agenda that can be appreciated at rock-bottom prices. Meanwhile, art lovers can indulge an eclectic fix at the **Wallace Collection in Manchester Square,** where paintings by the likes of Titian and Velazquez rub shoulders with Sevres porcelain and grand Louis XIV furniture.

Regent's Park – an idyllic Georgian oasis stretching off into London's northern suburbs - celebrates its two hundredth birthday in a couple of years. Before architect John Nash and his sponsor The Prince Regent gave it its much-loved geometric makeover, it had been farming land, and prior to that, one of Henry VIII's hunting grounds. His spirit lives on, in the sense that various activities are catered for, from tennis courts to a running track. And there are animals too, albeit not roaming free, at **London Zoo,** in the park's northerly section. Most people, though, come here to while away an hour or two around the boating lake or amble the Inner Circle which contains **Queen Mary's Gardens** and their enchanting bowers of fragrant roses. Others come for a summer sojourn to the Open Air Theatre where taking in a performance of 'A Midsummer Night's Dream' is very much *de rigueur*. The Regent's Canal provides another fascinating element to the park. You can follow its peaceful waters along a splendid walk from the **Little Venice** houseboats in the west, past the golden dome of the **London Central Mosque,** and on into the north-west confines of Regent's Park as it snakes through London Zoo, before it heads off towards Camden Lock. On the other side of Prince Albert Road, across from the zoo, the scenic glory takes on another dimension with a climb up Primrose Hill. Named after the grassy promontory that sets it apart from its surrounds, to visitors this is a hill with one of the best panoramas in the whole of London; to locals (ie, actors, pop stars, media darlings and the city set) it's an ultra fashionable place to live with pretty Victorian terraces and accordingly sky-high prices. Either way you look at it (or from it), it's a great place to be on a sunny day with the breeze in your hair.

BAYSWATER & MAIDA VALE (Plan VII)
HYDE PARK & KNIGHTSBRIDGE (Plan XII)
D
E
F
0.1
0
1
2
3
The Salt House
L'Aventure
Osteria Stecca
Dinings
St John's Wood
Maida Vale
Warwick Avenue
Edgware Rd
Paddington
Bayswater
Lancaster Gate
PADDINGTON
MARYLEBONE
PRIMROSE
HYDE PARK
NORFOLK CRESCENT
Dorset Square
Grand Union Canal
Abbey Road
Belsize Road
Boundary Road
Boundary Rd
Greville Pl.
Greville Road
Clifton Hill
Carlton Hill
Loudoun Road
Marlborough Hill
Finchley Road
St John's Wood Park
Queen's Grove
Ordnance Hill
Elsworthy Road
Avenue Road
Townshend Road
St Edmund's Terrace
Acacia Road
Wellington Road
St John's Wood Terrace
Allitsen Road
Prince Albert Road
Outer Circle
Grove End Road
Circus Road
Hamilton Terrace
Marlborough Place
Abercorn Pl.
Randolph Avenue
Elgin Avenue
Lauderdale Road
Sutherland Avenue
Warrington Crescent
Clifton Gardens
Warwick Avenue
Blomfield Rd
Blomfield Road
Maida Avenue
Hall Road
St John's Wood Road
Lodge Road
Lisson Grove
Orchardson St.
Penfold Street
Church Street
Broadley St.
Bell Street
Rossmore Road
Harewood Ave
Park Road
Edgware Road
Harrow Road
Westway
A 40
Marylebone Road
Old Marylebone Rd
Chapel St.
Seymour Place
Crawford Street
Gloucester Terrace
Westbourne Terrace
Bishop's Bridge Road
Eastbourne Terrace
South Wharf Rd
Praed Street
Cleveland Terrace
Gloucester Terrace
Spring St.
Sussex Gardens
Sussex Pl.
Radnor Pl.
Harrowby St.
George Street
Kendal St.
Connaught St.
Hyde Park St.
Inverness Terrace
Leinster Gardens
Queen's Gardens
Craven Hill
Craven Road
Craven Terrace
Stanhope Terrace
Bayswater Road
North Carriage Drive
0
400 m
0
400 yards

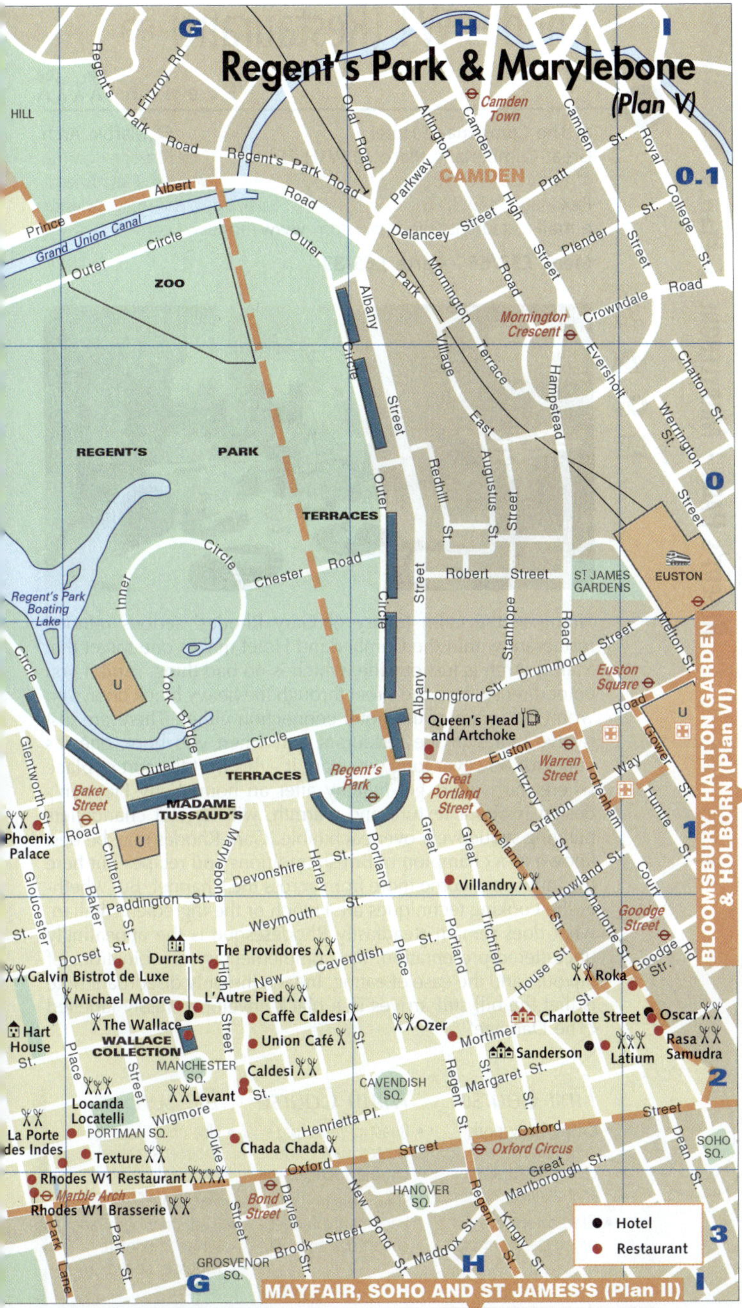

ated above
Rhodes W1 (Restaurant) ❀

French ✖✖✖✖

F3

at The Cumberland Hotel,
Great Cumberland Place ✉ W1H 7DL
☏ (020) 7616 5930
Fax (020) 7479 3888
e-mail restaurant@rhodesw1.com **www**.rhodesw1.com

⊖ Marble Arch
Closed Christmas - New Year,
1 week August, Saturday lunch,
Sunday and Monday – booking advisable

Menu £32/65 – Carte £65/83

VISA · MC · AE

Sitting in the calm luxury of Gary Rhodes' serious minded restaurant within the Cumberland Hotel makes one forget that Marble Arch is just outside, which is no bad thing. And if you enter directly from the street through the heavy black door, you won't be aware of the hotel connection either. There are just twelve tables in the restaurant and when you book one it's yours for however long you want it – this isn't the sort of place where the waiters get twitchy after an hour. Kelly Hoppen's design is about texture and warmth, with crystal chandeliers hanging seductively over each table. Gary Rhodes may be best known as a champion of British traditions and recipes but here the influences come more from across the Channel. But whether the cooking techniques are French or the ingredients Italian, what does remain steadfastly Rhodesesque is the appealingly uncluttered presentation, the complementary combinations of flavours and the ease of eating. In fact, the only discordant note is that the bill still arrives in a black envelope crassly labelled "The Damage".

First Course
- Crispy belly pork, langoustine, caramelised apple and vanilla.
- Glazed lobster omelette thermidor.

Main Course
- Roast pigeon, pig's trotter, navet and chutney sauce.
- Slow poached sea bass, confit fennel, cucumber and dill.

Dessert
- Hot chocolate moelleux, salted chocolate mousse, crème fraîche sorbet.
- Iced strawberry and white chocolate mousse, strawberry salad.

Locanda Locatelli

Italian

8 Seymour St ✉ W1H 7JZ — Marble Arch
℘ (020) 7935 9088 **Fax** (020) 7935 1149 Closed 25 December
e-mail info@locandalocatelli.com
www.locandalocatelli.com

Carte £41/58

Locanda Locatelli

The creamy leather seating has been given a good buffing, the cherry wood has been polished, the porthole mirrors still gleam and now they've even gone and got some Damien Hirst. In a few short years, Locanda Locatelli has become a London landmark and the David Collins' designed interior has been kept fresh and invigorated. The kitchen too has lost none of its sparkle. It still insists on using the best possible produce; the fact that many more of their ingredients now come from the British Isles speaks volumes for how we, as a nation, are producing some pretty high quality foods. It all kicks off with a terrific basket of bread, served with wonderfully fruity olive oil. Great antipasti awake the senses, the pasta dishes are undoubtedly the kitchen's greatest strength, while the fish and meat dishes are a lesson in balance and honesty. Not having four courses would be like watching AC Milan and leaving at half time and there would be riots in Portman Square if they ever took their tiramisu off the menu. The choice of pre and post dinner drinks has been expanded.

First Course
- Deep fried calf's foot salad and mustard fruit.
- Pan-fried scallops, saffron vinaigrette

Main Course
- Veal with Parma ham, sage and aubergine.
- Char-grilled sardines, bread and tomato salad

Dessert
- Tasting of Amedei chocolate.
- Cheese crème caramel, tomato and raspberry jam.

Latium

Italian

21 Berners St, Fitzrovia
✉ W1T 3LP
☏ (020) 7323 9123
Fax (020) 7323 3205
e-mail info@latiumrestaurant.com **www**.latiumrestaurant.com

⊖ Oxford Circus
Closed Christmas, New Year,
Saturday lunch, Sunday and Bank Holidays

Menu £20/30

In contrast to the über trendy Sanderson Hotel opposite, Latium has steadily built up a loyal following by providing surroundings which are less challenging and altogether more down to earth. That is not to say the restaurant is without personality for it has a certain well-groomed, understated chic, but comfort and relaxation are clearly the priorities. The strength also lies in the service which is executed with a confidence which comes from having pride and belief in your establishment - names and faces of returning customers are remembered. The chef-owner hails from Lazio and his set-price menu offers a balanced selection of specialities which all come with a certain degree of elaboration and top-notch ingredients.

Texture

Innovative

34 Portman Square ✉ W1H 7BY
☏ (020) 7224 0028
e-mail info@texture-restaurant.co.uk
www.texture-restaurant.co.uk

⊖ Marble Arch
Closed 2 weeks Christmas - New Year,
2 weeks August, Sunday and Monday

Menu £22/45 – Carte £48/59

The two young and ambitious owners, one from Iceland the other from France, met when working at Raymond Blanc's Le Manoir aux Quat'Saisons as head chef and head sommelier respectively. This is their first venture and the name hints at the style of cooking: expect innovative construction and contrasting textures. There is no doubt about the quality of the ingredients, especially the Icelandic produce like cod or lamb; heights are sometimes hit and the cooking is largely free of butter or cream. However, over elaboration means that dishes don't always add up to the sum of their parts. The high-ceilinged space is relaxed and unassuming in its style: it's worth spending time in the front Champagne bar and examining the excellent wine list.

Rhodes W1 Brasserie

F3

British XX

at The Cumberland Hotel, ⊖ Marble Arch
Great Cumberland Pl ✉ W1A 4RF
✆ (020) 7616 5930 **Fax** (020) 7479 3888
e-mail brasserie@rhodesw1.com www.garyrhodes.com

Carte £25/42

[A/C] [☼] [VISA] [MC] [AE]

From the street entrance look out for the candelabras and keep heading through the bustling bar. The main dining room is a pretty big affair, but panels and glass break it up a little and the staff appear to be able to cope. The cooking takes the brasserie theme and mixes European dishes with a little British twist here and an emphasis there, so, alongside risotto and fish soup, you'll find terrines of ham hock with piccalilli, sausage and mash and an assortment of grilled meats and fish. For dessert, the choice can range from cheesecake and tarts to rice pudding and tiramisu. The kitchen is confident, times things well and offers something to suit everyone. For a less frenetic experience, head to the eponymous chef's more formal restaurant adjacent.

Oscar

I2

Modern European XX

at Charlotte Street Hotel, ⊖ Goodge Street
15 Charlotte St ✉ W1T 1RJ Closed Sunday lunch
✆ (020) 7907 4005 **Fax** (020) 7806 2002 – booking essential
e-mail charlotte@firmdale.com www.charlottestreethotel.co.uk

Carte £31/46

[A/C] [☼] [VISA] [MC] [AE] [D]

Charlotte Street always appears to be full of life and the sheer range of restaurants, snack bars and cafés may be the cause or the effect. The unimaginatively, but undeniably accurately, named Charlotte Street Hotel offers up another popular option with their Oscar restaurant. It's located at street level in this fashionable hotel, while its bar fills the front and often spills out onto the pavement. The place is a wonderfully colourful affair, with murals, stained glass lanterns and striped seating. The pace can be quite frenetic and reminds us all that restaurants are there as places of enjoyment, not worship. Cooking is decidedly modern and dishes come neatly presented. They offer a commendable number of wines by the glass.

Galvin Bistrot de Luxe 😊

French ✕✕

G2

66 Baker St ✉ W1U 7DJ — Baker Street
✆ (020) 7935 4007 Closed 25-26 December and 1 January
Fax (020) 7486 1735
e-mail info@galvinuk.com **www**.galvinuk.com

Menu £16 (lunch) – Carte £24/35

Some said a restaurant would never succeed on this site, the 'wrong end' of Baker Street. Well, Galvin opened in September 2005 and there has hardly been a spare table since. The Galvin brothers proved the doomsayers wrong by pooling their considerable culinary experience and expertise in creating what they describe as a bistrot de luxe. They took as their model the new wave of bistrots modernes and their cooking is a refreshingly uncomplicated celebration of French cuisine and one executed with care and understanding. The L shaped room also has the character of a Parisian bistro, with wood panelling, slate flooring and large globe lights hanging from the ceiling. You feel that everyone is dining in their favourite restaurant.

La Porte des Indes

Indian ✕✕

F2

32 Bryanston St ✉ W1H 7EG — Marble Arch
✆ (020) 7224 0055 Closed 25-26 December,
Fax (020) 7224 1144 1 January and Saturday
e-mail london.reservation@laportedesindes.com
www.laportedesindes.com

Menu £15/28 – Carte £27/42

The façade gives little away but step in and you'll be instantly transported to what looks like the set from the latest Bollywood movie. Spread over two floors, La Porte des Indes really is vast and it's decorated in a spectacularly unrestrained display of palms trees, murals and waterfalls. The equally exuberant Jungle Bar is a popular place to kick off the evening. The menu offers something for everyone, including specialities from Pondicherry and others influenced by French India. Vegetarians are particularly well catered for and cookery demonstrations are held regularly for those wishing to learn more about Indian food. For those after a memento of their meal here, there is a little shop in the entrance lobby.

The Providores

Innovative 🍴🍴

G2

109 Marylebone High St ⊖ Bond Street
✉ W1U 4RX Closed 25-26 December and 1-2 January
✆ (020) 7935 6175 **Fax** (020) 7935 6877
e-mail anyone@theprovidores.co.uk **www**.theprovidores.co.uk

Menu £44 (dinner) – Carte £19/61

A/C
☀
VISA
MC
AE

New Zealander Peter Gordon showcases his unique style of fusion cooking upstairs at The Providores. It uses flavours, spices and ingredients from around the world, including many from Australasia, in complex but texturally estimable dishes. The most recent development is that all dishes for dinner now come in starter-size. This more labour-intensive menu means a greater choice – three dishes plus a dessert should suffice for most – although it doesn't come cheap. It's still a bunfight in the ground floor Tapa Room, with its global tapas, but fight your way through it and up the stairs and you'll be greeted by charming and helpful staff, a simply furnished room and a lively atmosphere. The wines are almost exclusively from New Zealand.

Roka

Japanese 🍴🍴

I2

37 Charlotte St ⊖ Tottenham Court Road
✉ W1T 1RR Closed 25 December and 1 January
✆ (020) 7580 6464 **Fax** (020) 7580 0220
e-mail info@rokarestaurant.com **www**.rokarestaurant.com

Carte approx. £29

A/C
🕐
☀
VISA
MC
AE
①

When a restaurant has been designed by a company called 'Super Potato' you can be pretty sure it's going to be all shiny and modern, and Roka doesn't disappoint. The walls are made of glass so expect passers-by to gaze covetously at your lunch and they open up fully in summer (the walls, not the passers-by). There's also a lot of wood, from the tables to the large counter wrapped around the robata grill where the chefs all do their thing in full view. The menus can appear a little bewildering at first so don't be afraid to ask for help. The grill is the main event but it's certainly worth ordering from a variety of sections and the dishes have a robustness that belies their delicate presentation. There's a great bar downstairs.

L'Autre Pied ❀

Modern European ✕✕

G2

5-7 Blandford Street ✉ W1U 3DB
✆ (020) 7486 9696 **Fax** (020) 7486 5067
e-mail info@lautrepied.co.uk
www.lautrepied.co.uk

⊖ Bond Street
Closed 23-29 December

Menu £20 (lunch) – Carte £35/46

The Other Foot is Charlotte Street's Pied à Terre which is one of London's senior restaurants. In late 2007 owners David Moore and Shane Osborn opened this restaurant in what local estate agents call Marylebone Village, with their former sous chef, Marcus Eaves, as partner and chef. The interior has changed relatively little from its previous incarnation as Blandford Street: red leather seating, back-lit screens and closely set tables, creating a largely stress-free environment. As it's all designed just as much for the locals, the staff ensure that everything stays fairly informal but they also keep their eye on the ball. Don't, however, equate these more relaxed surroundings with simpler food: this is not some sort of diffusion line or even Pied à Terre Lite – there is some serious ambition in the kitchen here. For starters, that kitchen can't disguise the influence exerted by its alma mater, for this is creative cooking with a healthy dollop of originality. The chef is not afraid of using unfamiliar cuts; he likes his game and combinations are well thought out.

First Course
- Seared foie gras, artichokes and pineapple sorbet.
- Crab, avocado, tzatziki mousse, parmesan tuille.

Main Course
- Saddle of rabbit, courgette, polenta with chorizo and black olive jus.
- Line-caught pollock, sauté Jerusalem artichoke and thyme.

Dessert
- Black Forest millefeuille.
- Warm financier, almond milk, coffee sorbet.

Ozer

Turkish ✕✕

H2

4-5 Langham Pl, Regent St
✉ W1B 3DG
✆ (020) 7323 0505 **Fax** (020) 7323 0111
e-mail info@sofra.co.uk **www**.sofra.co.uk

⊖ Oxford Circus

Menu £21 – Carte £17/25

The front section, for cocktails, can take a good pounding in the evenings, especially in the summer when the large windows at the front are thrown open onto Regent Street, and the place is seemingly packed with BBC staff from across the road. If you fight your way through, you'll find yourself in a spacious yet equally frenetic restaurant. It's decorated in very bold colours of red and gold and framed by an ornately modern chandelier. Noise levels remain high, especially when the music is pumped up. Service makes up in efficiency what it may lack in personality, while the menu offers a full range of fresh and revitalising Turkish food. Fish lovers and vegetarians are particularly well catered for.

Rasa Samudra

Indian ✕✕

I2

5 Charlotte St ✉ W1T 1RE
✆ (020) 7637 0222
Fax (020) 7637 0224
www.rasarestaurants.com

⊖ Goodge Street
Closed 24 December-1 January and lunch Sunday and Bank Holidays

Menu £23/30 – Carte £13/24

So how best to draw attention to yourself when you're competing for business in a street filled with an abundance of restaurants and cafés? Full marks go to Rasa Samudra for painting their façade a shocking shade of pink, which certainly makes them stand out, although intriguingly they have also decided to paint the interior in the same hue. The front room fills up first but go through to the rooms at the back which are far more inviting. The restaurant is also decorated with silks, carvings and assorted Indian ornaments but the food's the main attraction here with the menu divided into two main parts: rich and creamy seafood specialities from Kerala and fragrant vegetarian dishes. Begin your meal by trying typical Keralan tea shop snacks.

Levant

G2 — **Lebanese** XX

Jason Court, 76 Wigmore St ⊖ Bond Street
✉ W1U 2SJ
✆ (020) 7224 1111 **Fax** (020) 7486 1216
e-mail reservations@levant.co.uk **www**.levant.co.uk

Menu £37 (dinner) – Carte £35/40

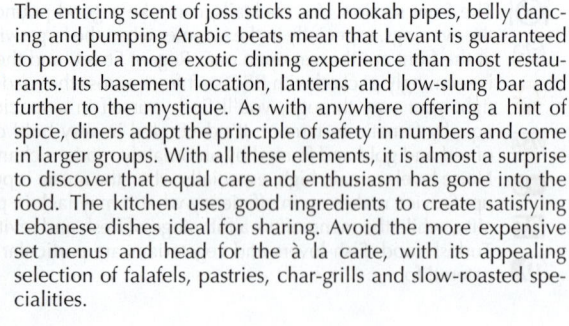

The enticing scent of joss sticks and hookah pipes, belly dancing and pumping Arabic beats mean that Levant is guaranteed to provide a more exotic dining experience than most restaurants. Its basement location, lanterns and low-slung bar add further to the mystique. As with anywhere offering a hint of spice, diners adopt the principle of safety in numbers and come in larger groups. With all these elements, it is almost a surprise to discover that equal care and enthusiasm has gone into the food. The kitchen uses good ingredients to create satisfying Lebanese dishes ideal for sharing. Avoid the more expensive set menus and head for the à la carte, with its appealing selection of falafels, pastries, char-grills and slow-roasted specialities.

Caldesi

G2 — **Italian** XX

15-17 Marylebone Lane ⊖ Bond Street
✉ W1U 2NE Closed Saturday lunch,
✆ (020) 7935 9226 **Fax** (020) 7935 9228 Sunday and Bank Holidays
e-mail tuscan@caldesi.com **www**.caldesi.com

Carte approx. £53

There's something reassuring about a restaurant bearing the owner's name, in this case Giancarlo's, who has been here since 1994. The abundance of mirrored panelling makes the room feel larger than it actually is, while the candlelight adds to the general atmosphere of intimacy and warmth. Chairs can be a little uncomfortable for those who have insufficient padding of their own. Signor Caldesi hails from Tuscany and it is to this region of Italy that the kitchen seeks inspiration, with the appropriately muscular wines to match. The waiters come dressed in black, know what they're doing and deliver chosen dishes promptly. The striking upstairs room used for private parties comes colourfully painted and has its own bar.

L'Aventure

D0.1

French 🍴🍴

3 Blenheim Terrace ⊖ St John's Wood
✉ NW8 0EH Closed 2 weeks August, 1 week January,
✆ (020) 7624 6232 Saturday lunch, Sunday and Bank Holidays
Fax (020) 7625 5548

Menu £19/35

Tailor-made for anyone with a sound grasp of French wishing to impress a date: the menu is written entirely in French so politely decline the waiter's offer of a quick translation and wait for the admiring looks. What's more, if it's a warm day, you'll be sitting in the enchanting front terrace, where the shrubs are covered in twinkly lights. This is a charming neighbourhood restaurant, with a cosy and warm interior, owned and run by the delightful Catherine who'll make you feel you're being unfaithful if you don't return. The set menu is good value at lunch but pricier at dinner when the well-heeled locals come out. Expect the French bourgeois classics, from artichoke salad to rack of lamb and an ile flottante to finish.

Phoenix Palace

F1

Chinese 🍴🍴

3-5 Glentworth St ✉ NW1 5PG ⊖ Baker Street
✆ (020) 7486 3515 **Fax** (020) 7486 3401
e-mail info@phoenixpalace.uk.com **www**.phoenixpalace.uk.com

Menu £25 (dinner) – Carte approx. £20

The habit of displaying photos of visiting celebs is usually limited to places once patronised by Telly Savalas or a finalist from Opportunity Knocks but at Phoenix Palace there's a genuinely impressive wall of fame. They come for the carefully prepared food and infectious atmosphere. The menu is an undeniably lengthy tome but it's sensibly divided; the sections to look out for are the fish dishes, like steamed sea bass which is ideal for sharing, and the chef's specials at the back, with the dim sum the best lunch option. The twenty chefs, who are mostly from Hong Kong, exhibit a lightness of touch which is evident in the dishes. The room is vast but the service is capable and well-organized; orders are taken up to 11.30pm.

Villandry

French ✕✕

H1

170 Great Portland St
✉ W1W 5QB
✆ (020) 7631 3131
Fax (020) 7631 3030
e-mail contactus@villandry.com **www**.villandry.com

⊖ Regent's Park
Closed 25-26 and 31 December,
1 January and Sunday dinner

Menu £30/35 – Carte £27/43

Villandry goes from strength to strength. The shop at the front features fantastic breads and pastries; you can sit in the Charcuterie Bar in amongst the cookbooks and jars; have something from the stir-fry station where you can try your own recipe or grab a smoothie at Villandry Rapide. All this before you even get to the restaurant. Here you'll find a bright, high-ceilinged room with doors opening onto the pavement. It serves appealing French-biased food like mussels, cassoulet and steak tartare; the plat du jour attracts quite a following. There's a separate Oysters and Shellfish section on the menu and a decently priced wine list divided by style. Parents on Saturday can have lunch while the kiddies get a "cookie class".

Osteria Stecca

Italian ✕✕

D0

1 Blenheim Terrace
✉ NW8 0EH
✆ (020) 7328 5014
e-mail info@osteriastecca.com **www**.osteriastecca.com

⊖ St John's Wood
Closed Monday lunch

Menu £16 (lunch) – Carte dinner approx. £40

The eponymous Stecca is Stefano, who was once the chef here during the restaurant's previous incarnation as Rosmarino and now he's back as the owner too. He's the sort of stout, effusive, full-on Italian that even Central Casting would consider a cliché; when he's out of the kitchen you'll certainly know it. The terrace, white walls and a front conservatory mean that bright light bounces around indiscriminately, hence perhaps the startled expressions of some of the neatly coiffed St. John's Wood locals. The menu covers all points of the country and has a large pasta section; dishes are fairly undemanding and, refreshingly, they come fully garnished so there are no side dishes to bump up the final bill. Lunch represents particularly good value.

The Wallace

G2

French

Hertford House, Manchester Sq
✉ W1U 3BN
✆ (020) 7563 9505
e-mail reservations@thewallacerestaurant.com
www.thewallacerestaurant.com

⊖ Bond St
Closed 25 December – lunch only

Menu £25 – Carte £30/41

Along with the Old Masters, The Wallace Collection is famed for its galleries of 18C French paintings, furniture and porcelain. It's appropriate then that Oliver Peyton's restaurant has an equally Gallic tone. Housed in a delightful glass-roofed courtyard at the rear, with an all-day café to one side, the restaurant offers a comprehensive selection of classic French fare. Terrines are a speciality and come with a large jar of cornichons, cheeses are in good condition and main courses could include everything from escargots to bouillabaisse. For dessert it has to be Tarte Tatin or Baba au rhum. The wine list is also exclusively French and comes with realistic prices. It gets busy, so book - especially on a summer's day.

Michael Moore

G2

International

19 Blandford St ✉ W1U 3DH
✆ (020) 7224 1898
Fax (020) 7224 0970
e-mail info@michaelmoorerestaurant.com
www.michaelmoorerestaurant.com

⊖ Baker Street
Closed Christmas-New Year, Saturday lunch, Sunday and Bank Holidays

Menu £19 (lunch) – Carte £33/49

Michael Moore is a classically trained chef who has created a welcoming little restaurant. He describes his cooking as 'global cuisine' but that really just means the occasional Asian note to what are fairly conventional combinations and constructions. There may be a slight tendency towards over-elaboration but there's no doubting the quality of the produce and the attractive presentation. The menu changes every six weeks, although the regulars insist that certain favourite dishes remain. The room is cosy and compact, with small tables and seating for just thirty-two. By contrast, the service is surprisingly formal and somewhat ceremonial which occasionally leads to a bottleneck in the middle of the room.

Union Café

International

G2

96 Marylebone Lane ✉ W1U 2QA
℘ (020) 7486 4860
Fax (020) 7935 1537
e-mail unioncafe@brinkleys.com **www.**brinkleys.com

⊖ Bond Street
Closed Sunday dinner and Bank Holidays

Carte £31/38

The egalitarianism suggested by the name is entirely matched by its quasi-industrial looks; the exposed ducts, open kitchen and bustling atmosphere tell you straight away that this is no place for standing on ceremony. Mind you, the chairs now have cushions so lingering over lunch is no longer quite so numbing an experience. Service is pretty laid back but does get the job done, with just the occasional prompt required, while the menu exhibits a veritable hotchpotch of influences; expect to find everything from dim sum to risotto, burgers to pork belly and crab cakes to calves liver. The cooking is undertaken with more care than you expect and with these satisfying crowd-pleasers it's easy to see why the place is perennially busy.

Caffé Caldesi

Italian

G2

1st Floor, 118 Marylebone Lane ✉ W1U 2QF
℘ (020) 7935 1144 **Fax** (020) 7935 8832
e-mail caffe@caldesi.com **www.**caldesi.com

⊖ Bond Street
Closed Sunday dinner

Carte £21/42

Simpler is often better but that doesn't always mean cheaper. Caffé Caldesi is the informal relation to Caldesi further down the road and offers a more relaxed environment. The ground floor of this converted corner pub is the all-day café-bar part of the operation with the main restaurant upstairs. Here you'll find a bright and colourful room with a very genial atmosphere. The cheeses may be Tuscan but otherwise there's no single dominant Italian region on the menu. Instead it offers a selection of satisfying and earthy dishes, with the home-made pastas particularly good. Plates arrive with appetisingly simple presentation and flavours are bold and balanced, but you may find that the final bill is a little more than you were expecting.

Chada Chada

G2

Thai

16-17 Picton Pl ✉ W1U 1BP
✆ (020) 7935 8212
Fax (020) 7924 2791
e-mail enquiry@chadathai.com **www**.chadathai.com

⊖ Bond Street
Closed Sunday and Bank Holidays

Menu £14 (lunch) – Carte approx. £37

A/C
🕐
VISA
MC
AE
①

In Picton Place, just slightly removed from the melee of populist eateries in James Street, sits Chada Chada, a Thai restaurant and offspring of the Battersea original. Its comforts may be modest but it has an appealingly sweet atmosphere, thanks largely to the staff who always appear to have just been told a good joke. The first half of the restaurant allows you views of the open kitchen and there is a nicely decorated downstairs room which is used more as an overflow. The seats are not overly upholstered but fortunately delivery from the kitchen is fairly swift. The dishes on the menu are numbered and go all the way up to 112 but are clearly divided. They come authentically prepared, generously proportioned and appropriately priced.

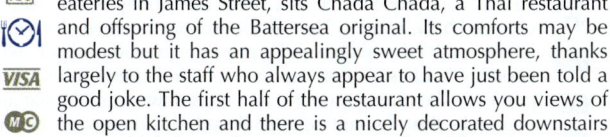

Dinings

F2

Japanese

22 Harcourt St. ✉ W1H 4HH
✆ (020) 7723 0666
Fax (020) 7723 3222

⊖ Marylebone
Closed Sunday and Bank Holidays
– booking essential

Carte £24/62

VISA
MC
AE
①

The smiling chefs greet you from behind the sushi counter which acts as a prompt to the girls in the basement to rush upstairs and escort you back down below. The idea behind Dinings is to resemble an after-work Japanese izakaya, or pub, and this they achieve. Staff outnumber guests and their service is endearingly sweet, while comfort levels are modest – chairs are built for purpose rather than comfort. The atmosphere is chummy and music loud. The young owner has come from Nobu-land and the food calls itself 'Japanese tapas'; shorthand for small plates of diligently prepared dishes, similar in style to his alma mater in its mix of traditional and modern, but without the lofty price tag. Puddings are more your classic French.

The Salt House

Gastropub

D0.1

63 Abbey Road, St John's Wood ✉ NW8 0AE
⊖ St John's Wood.
Closed 25 December
✆ (020) 7328 6626
e-mail salthousemail@majol.co.uk
www.thesalthouse.co.uk

Carte £20/36

First it was The Salt House, then The Abbey Road, then it changed back again to The Salt House. But whatever the name, it has remained a reliable and inviting neighbourhood pub, with cooking that has a sunny, country feel and comes in man-size portions. The dining room's a few steps down from the bar and overlooks the pleasant semi-enclosed outside terrace and its style is of the relaxed, higgledy-piggledy school. The bill can tot up without you noticing but there's plenty of interest on the menu, whether that's the sea bass cartoccio, the rack of lamb with sweet potatoes or the top-notch quality Scottish beef. There are always assorted pasta dishes available as well as more unusual offerings like rabbit casserole or honey-glazed poussin.

Queen's Head & Artichoke

Gastropub

H1

30-32 Albany St ✉ NW1 4EA
⊖ Great Portland Street.
✆ (020) 7916 6206
e-mail info@theartichoke.net **www.theartichoke.net**

Carte £19/25

The location may be just about spot-on: bordering the park to catch the strollers and close enough to the Euston Road to get the office bods. The formula also hits the spot: modern European influenced food mixed with a large selection of 'tapas' in its loosest form. The place is certainly always jumping. The licence can be traced back to good Queen Bess and apparently she loved a bit of artichoke. Today's customers can all enjoy completely differing culinary experiences. One might be having pâté followed by roast lamb while their partner has chicken satay followed by red duck curry. Tapas is the nebulous term for a huge and appealing mix of small dishes where the influences take in North Africa, the Middle East as well as Europe and is offered all day.

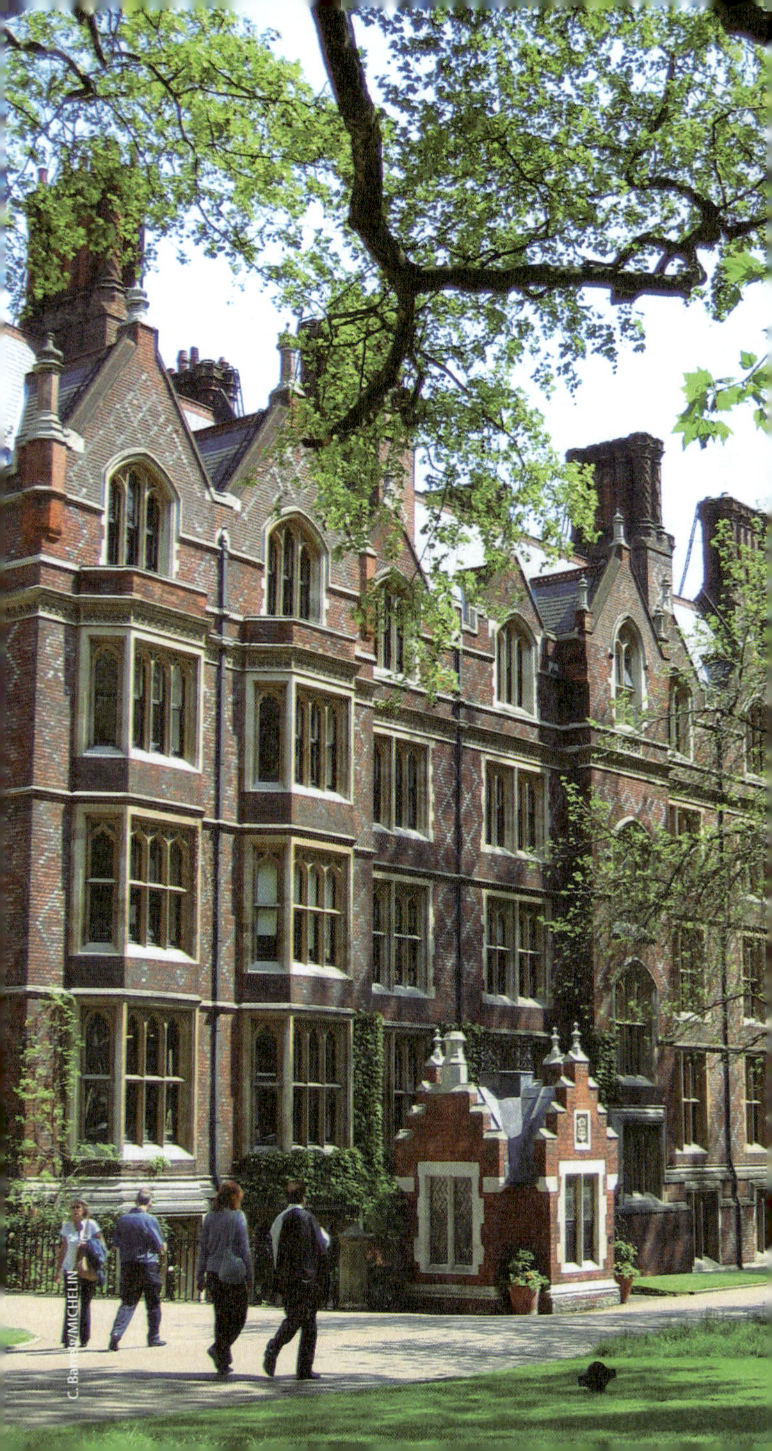
MICHELIN

Bloomsbury · Hatton Garden · Holborn

A real sense of history pervades this central chunk of London. From the great collection of antiquities in the British Museum to the barristers who swarm around the Royal Courts of Justice and Lincoln's Inn; from the haunts of Charles Dickens to the oldest Catholic church in Britain, the streets here are dotted with rich reminders of the past. Hatton Garden's fame as the city's diamond and jewellery centre goes back to Elizabethan times while, of a more recent vintage, Bloomsbury was home to the notorious Group (or Set) who, championed by Virginia Woolf, took on the world of art and literature in the 1920s.

A full-on encounter with **Holborn** is, initially, a shock to the system. Coming up from the tube, you'll find this is where main traffic arteries collide and a rugby scrum regularly ensues. Fear not, though; the relative calm of London's largest square, part-flanked by two quirky and intriguing museums, is just round the corner. The square is **Lincoln's Inn Fields,** which boasts a canopy of characterful oak trees and a set of tennis courts. On its north side is **Sir John Soane's Museum,** a gloriously eccentric place with twenty thousand exhibits where the walls open out like cabinets to reveal paintings by Turner and Canaletto. On its south side, the Hunterian Museum, refitted four years ago, is a fascinating repository of medical bits and pieces. Visitors with a Damien Hirst take on life will revel in the likes of animal digestive systems in formaldehyde, or perhaps the sight of half of mathematician Charles Babbage's brain. Others not so fascinated by the gory might flee to the haunting silence of **St Etheldreda's church** in Ely Place, the only surviving example of thirteenth-century Gothic architecture in London. It survived the Great Fire of 1666, and Latin is still the language of choice.

Contemplation of a different kind takes centre stage in the adjacent **Hatton Garden.** This involves eager-eyed couples gazing at the glittering displays of rings and jewellery that have been lighting up the shop fronts here for many generations, ever since the leafy lane and its smart garden environs took the fancy of Sir Christopher Hatton, a favourite of Elizabeth I. After gawping at the baubles, there's liquid refreshment on hand at one of London's most atmospheric old pubs, the tiny Ye Old Mitre hidden down a narrow passageway. The preserved trunk of a cherry tree stands in the front bar, and, by all accounts, Elizabeth I danced the maypole round it (a legend that always seems more believable after the second pint).

Bloomsbury has intellectual connotations, and not just because of the writers and artists who frequented its townhouses in the twenties. This is where the University of London has its headquarters, and it's also home to the **British Museum,** the vast treasure trove of international artefacts that attracts visitors in even vaster numbers. As if the exhibits themselves weren't lure enough, there's also the fantastic glass-roofed Great Court, opened to much fanfare at the start of the Millennium, which lays claim to being the largest covered public square in Europe. To the north of here by the Euston Road is the **British Library,** a rather stark red brick building that holds over 150 million items and is one of the greatest centres of knowledge in the world. Meanwhile, Dickens fans should make for the north east corner of Bloomsbury for the great man's museum in **Doughty Street:** this is one of many London houses in which he lived, but it's the only one still standing. He lived here for three years, and it proved a fruitful base, resulting in Nicholas Nickleby and Oliver Twist. The museum holds manuscripts, letters and Dickens' writing desk. If your appetite for the written word has been truly whetted, then a good tip is to head back west half a mile to immerse yourself in the bookshops of Great Russell Street.

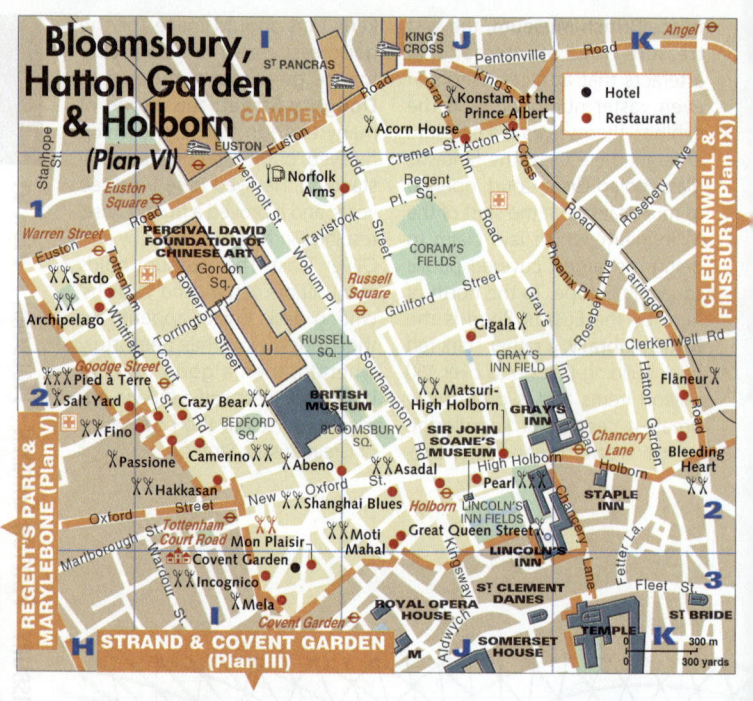

Pearl

J2 — French

at Renaissance Chancery Court Hotel,
252 High Holborn ✉ WC1V 7EN
✆ (020) 7829 7000
Fax (020) 7829 9889
e-mail info@pearl-restaurant.com www.pearl-restaurant.com

⊖ Holborn
Closed last 2 weeks August,
25-26 December,
Saturday lunch and Sunday

Menu £29/54 – Carte approx. £50

Pearl's a zinger. A room as grand and ornate as this could only have been a banking hall; its name refers to its former life as the Pearl Assurance Building. There is a hotel attached but you're not aware of it. The long catwalk of a bar gets a pasting in the evenings but is being pushed as a lunch spot with small tasting plates, while the pillars, hanging beads and pearls break up what is a very large restaurant. Service copes well and is on the ball. Jun Tanaka's cooking is French at its core but the influences stretch far and wide and he's not afraid of strong flavours. Dishes come artfully assembled and are made up of several components. The appropriately vast wine list includes 55 choices by the glass.

Pied à Terre ✿✿

12

Innovative XXX

34 Charlotte St ✉ W1T 2NH ⊖ **Goodge Street**
📞 (020) 7636 1178 Closed first week January,
Fax (020) 7916 1171 Saturday lunch and Sunday
e-mail reservations@pied-a-terre.co.uk
www.pied-a-terre.co.uk

Menu £32/69

Despite opening a more informal offshoot, L'Autre Pied, in late 2007, owners David Moore and Shane Osborn haven't taken any of their feet off the pedals at Pied à Terre. This remains a steadfastly ambitious and firmly established restaurant, supported by a loyal and appreciative clientele. The restaurant certainly makes the best of the fairly limited space available: there is an underused bar upstairs and the main room at the rear is warm and comfortable. Most reassuringly, this is a restaurant that's miles away from those whispering temples of gastronomy. Granted, one does get somewhat assailed by staff at the beginning of the meal but then it all calms down once you've answered all the questions and made all the decisions. The kitchen, meanwhile, is forever moving things forward. The dishes may come artfully presented but this is all about flavours; there is also plenty of originality to the cooking but without recourse to unusual or jarring combinations. This is highly accomplished and intuitive cooking.

First Course
- Crayfish and garlic gnocchi, broccoli, Lardo di Colonnata and grapefruit.
- Saddle of rabbit, boudin blanc, smoked eel.

Main Course
- Suckling pig, beetroot, girolles and apple cider sauce.
- Roast sea bream with fennel, artichoke and shallot dressing.

Dessert
- Bitter sweet chocolate tart, stout ice cream and macadamia nut cream.
- Mango and coconut rice pudding, coconut and chilli panna cotta.

BLOOMSBURY • HATTON GARDEN • HOLBORN ▶ Plan VI

Mon Plaisir

French XX

13

21 Monmouth St ⊠ WC2H 9DD   ⊖ Covent Garden
℘ (020) 7836 7243   Closed 25 December-2 January,
Fax (020) 7240 4774   Saturday lunch, Sunday and Bank Holidays
e-mail monplaisirrestaurant@googlemail.com
www.monplaisir.co.uk

Menu £17 (lunch) – Carte £28/41

London's oldest French restaurant is also one of its most gloriously unpretentious and individual. If you think the Eurostar transports you to France in an instant, try walking into Mon Plaisir, family run for over fifty years, where cries of 'Bonjour!' greet every arrival. The walls are decorated with a plethora of posters, pictures and paraphernalia and the bar is from a Lyonnais brothel. Regulars all have their favourite of the numerous interconnecting rooms, all of which ooze unmistakeable Gallic charm. But this is no themed restaurant. This is as real as the coq au vin or cassolette d'escargots. The fixed price lunch and pre-theatre menus represent excellent value and periodically held evenings featuring a particular region of France are popular events.

Incognico

French XX

13

117 Shaftesbury Ave   ⊖ Tottenham Court Road
⊠ WC2H 8AD   Closed 1 week Christmas,
℘ (020) 7836 8866 **Fax** (020) 7240 9525   Sunday and Bank Holidays
e-mail incognicorestaurant@gmail.com **www.**incognico.com

Menu £33 (lunch) – Carte £30/35

The smart brasserie look remains largely the same, thanks to its worn-in leather, art deco styling, panelling and neatly laid tables. Table 25, enveloped in an alcove, is still the table of choice for the romantically inclined and the service continues to be well organised. But the main change is the elusiveness of those good value set menus; there is one available but you sometimes have to tease it out of them. The cooking has a French base but with prominent Italian influences and the menu is heavily supported by daily specials. It's frill-free and confidently executed but side dishes are needed and can push up the final bill. It still beats hands down all those tourist joints that this part of town attracts.

Sardo

H1

Italian

45 Grafton Way ✉ W1T 5DQ
☏ (020) 7387 2521
Fax (020) 7387 2559
e-mail info@sardo-restaurant.com **www**.sardo-restaurant.com

⊖ Warren Street
Closed 24-29 December, 1 January,
Saturday lunch and Sunday

Carte £23/32

A/C
VISA
MC
AE
⦿

It's worth booking as Sardo is nearly always full - entirely understandably, as this is the sort of restaurant regulars turn up to on an almost daily basis. The owner, chef and most of the kitchen hail from Sardinia and the island provides most of the influences. The ravioli and speciality pastas are made in-house and the kitchen uses particularly hard wheat imported from small suppliers in Sardinia. The cooking is fresh, unpretentious and uses a lot of char-grilling; the menu is helped out by the daily changing blackboard specials. The wine list also remains faithful as Sardinian wines make up half the list. The room is neat and tables are simply laid; those at the back are slightly lighter, thanks to the ceiling window.

Matsuri - High Holborn

J2

Japanese

Mid City Pl, 71 High Holborn
✉ WC1V 6EA
☏ (020) 7430 1970 **Fax** (020) 7430 1971
e-mail eat@matsuri-restaurant.com **www**.matsuri-restaurant.com

⊖ Holborn
Closed 25 December, 1 January,
Sunday and Bank Holidays

Menu £27/47 – Carte £19/75

VISA
MC
AE
⦿

This more modern branch of the Japanese Matsuri restaurants contrasts with the rather traditional feel of the Bury Street original. The shiniest part of the large room is the very long sushi bar to the right as you enter, while the main dining room is the darker area at the back; those who come for teppan-yaki – the third part of the operation – should head downstairs. The best plan for those in the dining room is to order one of the set menus, which includes a kaiseki option for those wanting the full Japanese experience. Otherwise, the soft shell crabs and the sashimi are highlights for anyone going down the à la carte route. Lunch is certainly the busiest part of the day, when staff are less inclined to stand around.

Hakkasan ✿

Chinese ✕✕

8 Hanway Place ⊖ Tottenham Court Road
✉ W1T 1HD Closed 24-25 December
✆ (020) 7927 7000 **Fax** (020) 7907 1889
e-mail reservations@hakkasan.com **www.**hakkasan.com

Menu £40/55 – Carte £37/110

Despite ambitions for world domination - with openings of Hakkasans happening in culinary hotspots around the globe - the original appears to be in no danger of dilution. The dreary, dimly-lit alley and the dark basement location both somehow add to the mystique and sense of exclusivity. Inside it's sexy, sultry and sophisticated and, even with the music and the bustle, can still feel intimate, thanks to the tactical lighting and clever design. The surly doorman has been replaced by a far friendlier welcome and all the staff appear genuinely eager to please; they will tell you when you've over-ordered and the sommelier has been known to direct his customers towards a less expensive alternative from his helpfully laid-out list. The risk of over-ordering is high, as the extensive menu has huge appeal, with dim sum the lunchtime attraction. Go for dishes that offer contrasts in textures, such as the crispy duck salad and the delicately sweet silver cod. With some judicious ordering, it is possible to keep that final bill to a more reasonable level.

First Course
- Roasted mango duck with lemon sauce.
- Soft shell crab with red chilli and curry leaf.

Main Course
- Stir-fried ostrich in yellow bean sauce.
- Steamed Dover sole with spinach, soya and crispy ginger.

Dessert
- Rum and caramel banana cookie crumble.
- Coconut cheesecake with cherry sorbet.

Fino

Spanish ✗✗

33 Charlotte St (entrance on Rathbone St) ✉ W1T 1RR
✆ (020) 7813 8010 **Fax** (020) 7813 8011
e-mail reception@finorestaurant.com
www.finorestaurant.com

⊖ Goodge Street
Closed 25 December, Saturday lunch, Sunday and Bank Holidays

Carte approx. £30

They don't make it easy on themselves by giving their address as Charlotte Street when, in fact, the discreet entrance to this basement restaurant is actually on Rathbone Street. Perhaps that's the reason why, once you've descended the staircase, you'll find that it has something of a secretive and local vibe. Tapas is the order of the day, although it's all structured slightly more formally than you'd find in Spain and the room itself is decidedly more stylish than you'd expect. Five or six dishes per couple to share should suffice, although set menus are available for the undecided. Try a sherry or something from the exclusively Spanish wine list. Helpful waitresses are more than willing to offer advice as well as a translation of unfamiliar words.

Crazy Bear

Asian ✗✗

26-28 Whitfield St ✉ W1T 2RG
✆ (020) 7631 0088
Fax (020) 7631 1188
e-mail enquiries@crazybear-london.co.uk
www.crazybeargroup.co.uk

⊖ Goodge Street
Closed Saturday lunch, Sunday and Bank Holidays

Carte £29/41

The sign is still concealed but that probably adds to the sense of exclusivity and furtiveness. Crazy Bear's clientele are a young bunch, attracted by the chance to dress up for the busy basement bar and the ground floor restaurant. The lighting is moody and the tables are small, so some juggling is required if you want to share plates - and sharing is certainly the best option. The menu is a lengthy issue, covering a number of cuisines, from China to Thailand and from mild and comforting to larynx-laceratingly hot. Dim sum is served all day, and the menu is divided into starters, soups, salads, meat, seafood and curries, as well as eleven or twelve plate tasting menus. Ingredients are good and the choice sufficient to suit all tastes.

Archipelago

Innovative ××

H1

110 Whitfield St ✉ W1T 5ED
✆ (020) 7383 3346
Fax (020) 7383 7181
e-mail info@archipelago-restaurant.co.uk
www.archipelago-restaurant.co.uk

⊖ Goodge Street
Closed Christmas -New Year,
Saturday lunch and Sunday

Menu £39 – Carte £27/37

On a rainy night it takes on the atmosphere of a steamy colonial outpost and you half expect a hunter in a pith helmet to walk past your table. This restaurant is certainly not for the squeamish while those of an overly serious disposition may not get it either. 'Eclectic' is an oft-bandied word to describe hybrid cooking but here it's truly merited. Where else can you eat crocodile, zebra, kangaroo or wildebeest? Peacock has also recently appeared and scorpion has made the odd appearance in the past. The cooking itself often takes on an Asian element and the staff are all faultlessly well informed. Every surface is covered in feathers, trinkets and carvings, all for sale, and your local will seem very dull after this.

Bleeding Heart

French ××

K2

Bleeding Heart Yard (off Greville St)
✉ EC1N 8SJ
✆ (020) 7242 8238
Fax (020) 7831 1402
e-mail bookings@bleedingheart.co.uk **www**.bleedingheart.co.uk

⊖ Farringdon
Closed Christmas-New Year,
Sunday and Bank Holidays
– booking essential

Carte £25/39

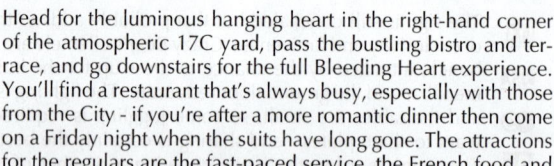

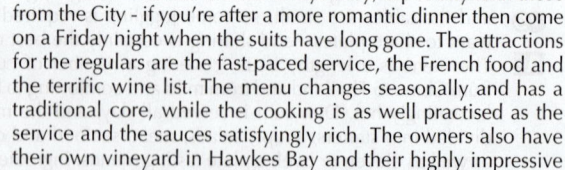

Head for the luminous hanging heart in the right-hand corner of the atmospheric 17C yard, pass the bustling bistro and terrace, and go downstairs for the full Bleeding Heart experience. You'll find a restaurant that's always busy, especially with those from the City - if you're after a more romantic dinner then come on a Friday night when the suits have long gone. The attractions for the regulars are the fast-paced service, the French food and the terrific wine list. The menu changes seasonally and has a traditional core, while the cooking is as well practised as the service and the sauces satisfyingly rich. The owners also have their own vineyard in Hawkes Bay and their highly impressive wine list has a bias towards New Zealand and France.

Moti Mahal

J2

Indian ✗✗

45 Great Queen St ✉ WC2B 5AA
✆ (020) 7240 9329
Fax (020) 7836 0790
e-mail reservations@motimahal-uk.com **www**.motimahal-uk.com

↔ Holborn
Closed 24-29 December and Sunday

Menu £15/20 – Carte £35/51

From the outside Moti Mahal looks more like a cocktail bar than an Indian restaurant, while inside they've clearly let the barman choose the music. It's divided between two floors: the lower level has great semi-circular booths but unfortunately this room is used more for private parties or as an overflow for the bright ground floor. The chefs perform their kitchen duties behind a large window which allows diners the chance to see the action and the star of the show is undoubtedly the tandoor oven. The innovative menu is ambitious in its reach and far removed from the usual standards; the ingredients are top notch, which means that prices are also higher than average. Service is keen and sincere.

Asadal

J2

Korean ✗✗

227 High Holborn ✉ WC1V 7DA
✆ (020) 7430 9006
e-mail info@asadal.co.uk **www**.asadal.co.uk

↔ Holborn
Closed 25-26 December,
1 January and Sunday lunch

Menu £10 (lunch) – Carte £10/18

Every nationality of cuisine has enjoyed its moment in the spotlight and now Asadal, a basement restaurant adjacent to Holborn tube, successfully argues the case for Korean cooking to be given a higher profile. There may be a barbecue in the centre of most of the tables but there is so much more to Korean cooking. The philosophy is built upon harmony of taste, it's all made for sharing and there's even a health dividend to most of the specialities. Novices will find that the menu is helpfully descriptive but don't be shy about using the call buttons under the table to summon help. The room is perfectly comfortable, with lots of wood and plenty of partitions; there are quieter corners for those wishing to escape the general clamour.

Camerino

Italian ✗✗

16 Percy St ✉ **W1T 1DT** ⊖ **Tottenham Court Road**
✆ (020) 7637 9900 Closed 24-26 December, Saturday lunch,
Fax (020) 7637 9696 Sunday and Bank Holidays
e-mail info@camerinorestaurant.com
www.camerinorestaurant.com

Menu £17 – Carte £20/28

Thanks to the twin appeal of decent food and wallet-friendly prices, Camerino is always one of the busiest restaurants around these parts, especially before curtain up. It's a colourful place, from the pink neon sign outside to the large red curtains inside that explain the name – Camerino is Italian for 'theatre dressing room'. The personable owner is a constant presence and he ensures that the service remains on the ball. The à la carte menu offers a comprehensive synopsis of familiar Italian dishes, with a good value set menu running alongside. Homemade pasta is something of a speciality and portions are generous in size, healthy in composition and stout in flavour. Desserts are prepared with particular dexterity.

Passione

Italian ✗

10 Charlotte St ⊖ **Tottenham Court Road**
✉ **W1T 2LT** Closed Christmas-New Year, Bank Holidays,
✆ (020) 7636 2833 Saturday lunch and Sunday – booking essential
Fax (020) 7636 2889
e-mail liz@passione.co.uk **www.**passione.co.uk

Carte £40/47

Chef owner Gennaro Contaldo, Jamie Oliver's great mentor, hails originally from Amalfi and it is from the sun-drenched Southern Italian coast that he seeks inspiration for his cooking. The menu offers a wide selection of dishes using the very best fresh and seasonal produce and dishes such as rabbit with rosemary and wild sorrel risotto remain perennial favourites. The restaurant, like the cooking, comes refreshingly free of unnecessary adornment. It is warm, simply decorated and brightly coloured. In a street offering a plethora of dining options, Passione stands out not just for the quality of the cooking but also for its intimate and relaxed atmosphere. Many clearly agree as it is always busy, so reservations are essential.

Cigala

Spanish

J1

54 Lamb's Conduit St
WC1N 3LW
(020) 7405 1717
Fax (020) 7242 9949
e-mail tasty@cigala.co.uk **www**.cigala.co.uk

⊖ **Russell Square**
Closed 24-26 December, 1 January and Easter
– booking essential

Menu £18 (lunch) – Carte £24/35

Lamb's Conduit hustles and bustles these days and Cigala fits right in. It's quite stark and a bit echoey but once all the regulars pile in they create their own infectious vibe. They come for the authentic and appealingly priced Spanish cooking. The menu changes daily, the highlight being the long list of tapas/starters: two of these plus a main course should more than suffice. There are dishes for two, such as paella and arroz caldoso, that are worth waiting the 30 minutes and the Spanish drinks list is equally tempting. Owner Jake Hodges now spends a lot of his time in Spain and the kitchen can sometimes be lacking in a little lustre, but this is still a good place to spend a winter's evening when summer seems a long way off.

Great Queen Street 😊

British

J2

32 Great Queen St WC2B 5AA
(020) 7242 0622
Fax (020) 7404 9582

⊖ **Holborn**
Closed Christmas-New Year, Monday lunch,
Sunday dinner and Bank Holiday weekends
– booking essential

Carte £24/38

You can be sure that a team garnered from the Anchor & Hope and St John will know what they're doing and, sure enough, Great Queen Street is doing all the right things. Just about the only sign outside that this is a restaurant is the daily menu posted in the window; the inside is all about pared-down simplicity. The menu is also a model of understatement; written simply as 'charcuterie and figs', 'potted shrimps' or 'venison pie', the cooking is full-bodied, confident and satisfying and at prices that are laudably low. Dishes such as rib of Hereford beef and seven hour shoulder of lamb are made for sharing and puds like caramel custard continue the British theme. It's always packed, gets very noisy and the amiable service can sometimes struggle to keep up.

Salt Yard

Mediterranean

H2

54 Goodge St ✉ W1T 4NA
✆ (020) 7637 0657
Fax (020) 7580 7435
e-mail info@saltyard.co.uk **www**.saltyard.co.uk

⊖ Goodge Street
Closed 24 December -3 January, Sunday,
Saturday lunch and Bank Holidays

Carte £20/37

The first thing you get is a smiley welcome and then it's a straight choice between the bar-like ground floor or the more traditionally laid out dining room downstairs; the former is usually more fun. You'll then have a few snacks with something from the mostly Italian wine list, work up to ordering some charcuterie and go from there. It's this kind of flexibility, as well as the competitive pricing, that makes this place so appealing. Spanish is obviously the main influence but the kitchen also adds some Italian specialities and these vibrant Mediterranean aromas fill the air in an enticing way. Flavours are punchy, varied and effective while puddings, such as soft chocolate cake with frangelico ice cream, are prepared with care.

Acorn House

Italian influences

J0

69 Swinton St ✉ WC1X 9NT
✆ (020) 7812 1842
e-mail info@acornhouserestaurant.com
www.acornhouserestaurant.com

⊖ King's Cross
Closed 24-28 December,
Sunday and Bank Holidays

Carte £27/44

This restaurant is a joint venture between the Terence Higgins and Shoreditch Trusts and is London's first eco-friendly training restaurant. They buy local and organic, use renewable 'green' electricity, purify their water, compost waste and recycle. They also hope to develop their training of chefs. Not only do they do all that, but the food happens to be rather good too. It's modern European with largely Italian influences and the mentoring chefs have instilled the importance of keeping it simple; portions are generous and the flavours fresh and natural. Pastas are something of a house speciality. How nice also to see staff smiling and seemingly enjoying their work. Any chef using Peruvian asparagus should be sent to Acorn House.

Giaconda Dining Room

Modern European

I2

9 Denmark Street
✉ WC2H 8LS
✆ (020) 7240 3334
e-mail paulmerrony@gmail.com
www.giacondadining.com

⊖ Tottenham Court Road
Closed Saturday, Sunday, August and
1 week between Christmas and
New Year – booking essential

Carte £22/27

A/C
VISA
MC
AE

In the shadow of Centrepoint lies a frayed little area that's 'not quite Soho'. Here you'll find Denmark Street - London's own historic Tin Pan Alley - now home to the Giaconda Dining Room. Aussies Paul and Tracey Merrony have opened a small but perfectly formed little place: spartanly decorated, busy from day one and great fun. Paul describes his cooking as "Frenchy, with day trips to Italy," which translates on the plate as confident, gutsy, no-nonsense and immeasurably satisfying. Tripe; steak tartare; pork sausage stew; risotto; a deconstructed pig's trotter and a daily changing fish or grilled dish special: there's something for everyone and, with most wine bottles in the £20s, it's all done at a credit-crunch busting price.

Flâneur

Modern European

K2

41 Farringdon Rd ✉ EC1M 3JB
✆ (020) 7404 4422
Fax (020) 7831 4532
e-mail mail@flaneur.com **www**.flaneur.com

⊖ Farringdon
Closed 24 December-2 January and Sunday
– Saturday brunch

Menu £26 – Carte approx. £27

VISA
MC
AE
D

This veritable kingdom of foodie heaven shines ever brightly on the otherwise rather non-descript Farringdon Road. Part food-hall, packed to the gunnels with produce ranging from charcuterie and pasta to oils and sauces, and part-restaurant with outsized chairs lending a certain Alice in Wonderland quality, the aroma alone is enough to stimulate the most jaded of taste buds. Lunch can be a little 'on the hoof' but dinner is usually a slightly more relaxed affair as the store quietens. The menu is tweaked daily to reflect the freshness of the produce and the style is modern European, refreshingly free from unnecessary frills. The wine list, slanted more towards France, reflects what's on the shelves.

Konstam at the Prince Albert

Traditional

J0

2 Acton St
✉ WC1X 9NA
✆ (020) 7833 5040
Fax (020) 7833 5045
e-mail princealbert@konstam.co.uk **www**.konstam.co.uk

⊖ King's Cross St Pancras
Closed 25 December-3 January, Saturday lunch,
Sunday and Bank Holidays

Carte £25/36

Gentrification may remain elusive but at least King's Cross now offers a few dining options. Oliver Rowe has taken a shabby Victorian pub, named it after his great grandfather and has kept the décor functional, save for a striking ornamental lighting feature. However, what makes this restaurant so unusual is that the produce is nearly all sourced from within the boundaries of the London transport network. Using local supplies is easy when you're in Devon but Central London throws up its own challenges and you'll spend most of the time wondering where exactly some of the ingredients on your plate came from. The open kitchen means that if curiosity gets the better of you, then the chefs are within questioning range.

Abeno

Japanese

I2

47 Museum St
✉ WC1A 1LY
✆ (020) 7405 3211 **Fax** (020) 7405 3212
e-mail okonomi@abeno.co.uk **www**.abeno.co.uk

⊖ Tottenham Court Road
Closed 24-26 and 31 December and 1 January

Menu £11 (lunch) – Carte £16/39

Okonomi-yaki is the speciality of this modest but very charming little Japanese place. That's a pancake-like dish, prepared at your table, where you decide on which toppings you want. They are surprisingly rich so a side order of salad or pickle is worth considering but don't ignore the rest of the menu, nor the desserts – the green tea ice cream is particularly good. With only eight tables it can get busy, especially with the British Museum being just yards away but they are open all day and do take reservations. It's best to come with friends as it's a fun experience and the staff, in their natty red T-shirts, are sweet tempered and dextrous on that hotplate. The sake cocktails will get any party off to a flying start.

Norfolk Arms

Gastropub

IJ1

28 Leigh Street ✉ WC1H 9EP
✆ (020) 7388 3937
e-mail info@norfolkarms.co.uk
www.norfolkarms.co.uk

⊖ Russell Square
Closed 25-26 December, 1 January

Carte £19/22

VISA
MC
AE

A onetime drinkers' paradise, the transformation of The Norfolk Arms to gastropub was as welcome as it was absolute. The bench-strewn exterior is beautifully tiled and the inside is just as charming, with ornate ceiling squares, raw plaster walls and tables neatly laid with teacloth napkins. Dried peppers, chillies and strings of onions hang from the walls and light fittings, and cured hams and salami decorate the bar. On the menu you will find some British dishes, but it's heavily influenced by the Mediterranean and particularly Spain, and dominated by appealingly colourful tapas. Food comes served in ceramic dishes and suits the surroundings perfectly hence the occasional queue. Wines are also chosen carefully.

BLOOMSBURY • HATTON GARDEN • HOLBORN ▶ Plan VI

Couverts (X...XXXXX) indicate the level of comfort found at a restaurant. The more Xs, the more formal a restaurant will be.

Bayswater · Maida Vale

There may not appear to be an obvious link between Maida Vale and Italy, but the name of this smart area to the west of central London is derived from a battle fought over two hundred years ago in Southern Italy, and the most appealing visitor attraction in the neighbourhood is the charming canalside **Little Venice.** To stroll around here on a summer's day brings to mind promenading in a more distant European clime; it's hard to believe that the ear-shattering roar of the Westway is just a short walk away. South of this iconic elevated roadway – a snaking route out from Marylebone to the western suburbs – is Bayswater, a busy area of imposing nineteenth century buildings that's the epicentre of London's Middle Eastern community.

During its Victorian heyday, **Bayswater** was a grand and glamorous address for affluent and elegant types who wanted a giant green space (Hyde Park) on their doorstep. The whole area had been laid out in the mid 1800s, when grand squares and cream stuccoed terraces started to fill the acres between Brunel's curvy Paddington station and the park. But during the twentieth century Bayswater's cachet nose-dived, stigmatised as 'the wrong side of the park' by the arrivistes of Knightsbridge and Kensington. Today it's still a backpacker's paradise: home to a bewildering number of shabby tourist hotels, bedsits and b&bs, converted from the grand houses. But this tells only a fraction of the modern story, because the area is undergoing a massive facelift that will transform it forever. The hub of this makeover is the **Paddington Basin,** a gigantic reclamation of the old Grand Union Canal basin in the shadow of the rail terminus. From a ramshackle wasteground, it's now a shimmering zone of metal, steel and glass, a phantasmagoria of blue chip HQs, homes, shops and leisure facilities. Even the barges have been turned into permanently moored 'retail opportunities'. Tree-lined towpaths along the perimeter complete the picture of a totally modern waterscape.

Lovers of the old Bayswater can still relish what made it famous in the first place: radiating out from **Lancaster Gate,** away from Hyde Park, is a web of streets with handsome squares and tucked-away mews, and it still retains pockets of close-knit communities, such as Porchester Square, west of Paddington station. Meanwhile, the 'cathedral' of the area, Whiteleys shopping centre in **Queensway**, remains a pivotal landmark, as it has been for more than a century. Just beyond Whiteleys heading away from central London, **Westbourne Grove** is still reassuringly expensive, or at least the bit that heads determinedly towards Notting Hill. But the wind of change has rustled other parts of the neighbourhood: Connaught Street has evolved into a villagey quarter of boutiques, galleries and restaurants, while, further west, Craven Hill Gardens is the height of chic, courtesy of The Hempel, a boutique hotel.

Little Venice pretty much acts as a dividing line between Bayswater and Maida Vale. Technically, it's the point where the Paddington arm of the Grand Union Canal meets the **Regent's Canal,** but the name, coined by poet Robert Browning who lived close by, has come to encompass the whole area just to the north of the soaring Westway. Narrow boat moorings vie for attention alongside the cafés and pubs that mercifully lack the frantic high street buzz so typical of their kind away from the water's edge. The permanently moored boats were here a long time before those upstarts at Paddington Basin. This is where you can find old-time favourites including a floating art gallery and a puppet theatre barge, and all overseen by the Warwick Castle pub, a stalwart of the area that's a minute's walk from the canal. Suitably refreshed, a wander round the residential streets of Maida Vale is very pleasant, dominated by the impressive Edwardian blocks of flats that conjure up a distinctive well-to-do scene.

KENSINGTON, NORTH KENSINGTON AND NOTTING HILL (Plan XIII)
Prince Alfred & Formosa Dining Room
The Waterway
Westbourne Park
Royal Oak
Urban Turban
Miller's
L'Accento
Assaggi
Hereford Road
Le Cafe Anglais
Bayswater
Kiasu
The Hempel
Queensway
Harrow Road
Westway
Westbourne Grove
Westbourne Park Road
Westbourne Park Villas
Chepstow Road
Porchester Road
Queensway
Bayswater Road
WESTBOURNE GARDENS
PORCHESTER SQ.
QUEEN ANNE'S GATE
LEINSTER SQ.
KENSINGTON GDNS SQ.
PRINCES SQ.
PEMBRIDGE SQ.
CLEVELAND SQ.
0 200 m
0 200 yards

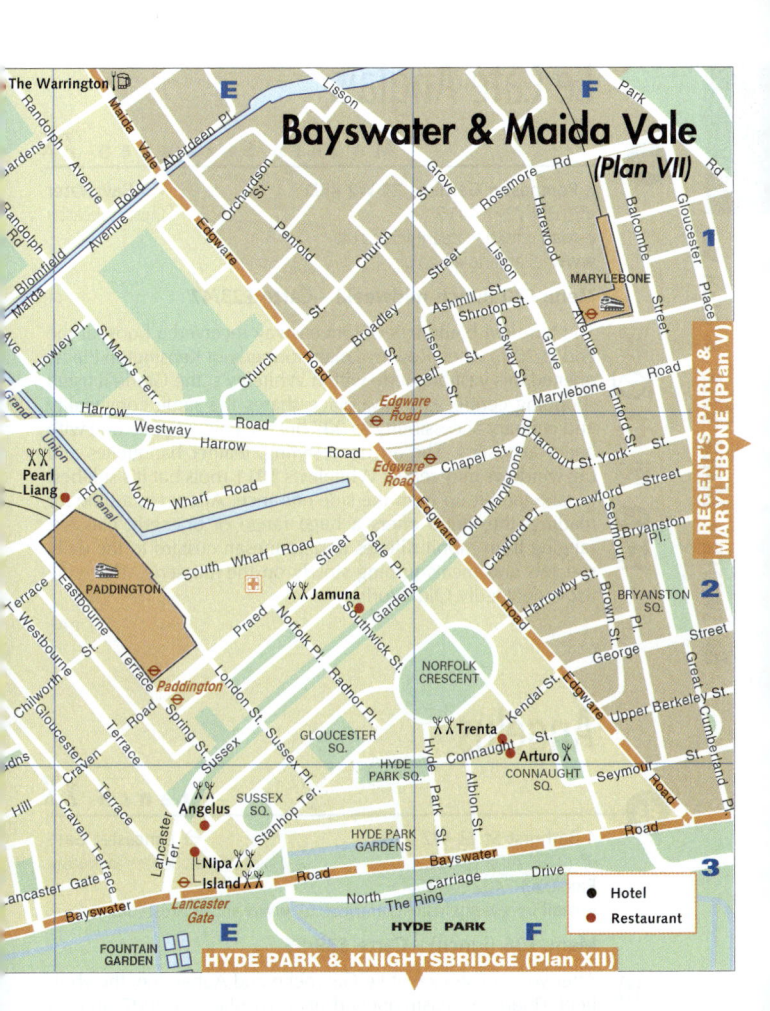

Bayswater & Maida Vale
(Plan VII)

Le Café Anglais

Modern European ✗✗

D2

8 Porchester Gardens ✉ W2 4BD   ⊖ Bayswater
✆ (020) 7221 1415   Closed 26 December
e-mail info@lecafeanglais.co.uk
www.lecafeanglais.co.uk

Menu £20 (lunch midweek) – Carte £23/47

The terminal blandness of Queensway received a boost at the end of 2007 when Rowley Leigh, formerly of Kensington Place, opened this vast brasserie within Whiteley's, the Grade II listed shopping centre. His new place shares the same conviviality and culinary accessibility as 'KP' but on a bigger scale and with better acoustics. The art deco styling, leather banquettes and big windows may reflect Whiteley's 1911 roots but it's still best to take the lift up from the side entrance. Allow extra time for reading: the menu offers a huge range of brasserie classics, ranging from rabbit rillettes and parmesan custard to the daily specials and meats turning slowly on the rotisserie. The wine list is decidedly Old World.

Angelus

French ✗✗

E3

4 Bathurst St ✉ W2 2SD   ⊖ Lancaster Gate
✆ (020) 7402 0083   Closed Christmas-New Year and Monday
Fax (020) 7402 5383
e-mail info@angelusrestaurant.co.uk **www**.angelusrestaurant.co.uk

Menu £36 (lunch) – Carte £39/55

After years of service at Le Gavroche and Aubergine, the ebullient Thierry Tomasin opened his own place in 2007 and his pride was plainly evident. He found a pub that, despite being listed, had lain idle for 18 months and, within it, he created a plausibly French brasserie, thanks to the studded leather banquettes and specially commissioned pieces like the huge art nouveau mirror and Murano chandeliers. There's a lounge bar at the back and private dining in the cellar. The cooking is French, with the occasional foray across the Med, and simplicity is the key: there are rarely more than three or four flavours per plate. The foie gras crème brûlée has swiftly become a house favourite and the buttery pommes purée is wonderfully artery-troubling.

Trenta

F2

Italian XX

30 Connaught St ⊠ W2 2AF — ⊖ Marble Arch
☏ (020) 7262 9623
Fax (020) 7262 9636
Closed Christmas-New Year,
Sunday and Bank Holidays
– dinner only and lunch Thursday and Friday

Carte £23/31

A/C
VISA
MC
AE

The locals are doing their bit for the surrounding area by attempting to rechristen it 'Connaught Village.' That may be stretching things somewhat but, then again, places like the diminutive but engagingly run Trenta do offer a palpable sense of neighbourhood. The chef hails from Emilia Romagna and the richer cooking of this region informs his style. The set menu offers bags of choice; dishes come fully attired and generously proportioned and there's an honesty to the cooking. Desserts are steeped in the flavours of Italy and there's also a good affogati section. The wine list offers a concise but adequate tour across Italy. The restaurant is compact but bright, although try to avoid the less animated downstairs.

Jamuna

E2

Indian XX

38A Southwick St ⊠ W2 1JQ — ⊖ Edgware Road
☏ (020) 7723 5056
Fax (020) 7706 1870
Closed 25-26 December – dinner only
e-mail info@jamuna.co.uk **www**.jamuna.co.uk

Menu £30 (lunch) – Carte £37/60

A/C
🕔
☼
VISA
MC
AE

Its largely transient population means that Bayswater has never been an area particularly noted for the quality of its restaurants. Jamuna is the latest to try its luck and its distinctly smart looking façade tells you that this is no ordinary Indian restaurant. It's similarly well turned-out inside, with neatly laid tables and modern artwork for sale on the walls, although, curiously, there are no clues in the décor with regard to the nationality of the cooking. The cooking is more than sound. It has a broad regional base but with few predictable offerings. Dishes, particularly those involving seafood, are vibrant and fresh, display a certain refinement and are full of flavour. The wine list is extensive and thoughtfully put together.

Pearl Liang

Chinese ××

8 Sheldon Sq., Paddington Central
✉ W2 6EZ
✆ (020) 7289 7000
www.pearlliang.co.uk

⊖ Paddington
Closed 25-26 December

Menu £15 (lunch) – Carte £25/65 s

Paddington Central, to those who don't work in the area, is a relatively recent office and residential development, best reached via Platform 8 from Paddington Station. One of the first restaurants to open was Pearl Liang, a Chinese restaurant. It's big but comfy, with an eye-catching, specially commissioned painting on one wall. When the 'neighbourhood' takes off then the generously proportioned dim sum will surely be the local lunch of choice. After 5pm check out the specialities on the à la carte, such as fresh abalone, shark's fin soup or even the pot of 'Buddha jump over the wall'; there are three balanced set menus as well. From Shanghai dumplings to Szechuan chicken, the choice is extensive. All that's missing is a tad more enthusiasm from the staff.

Nipa

Thai ××

at Royal Lancaster Hotel,
Lancaster Terrace ✉ W2 2TY
✆ (020) 7551 6039
Fax (020) 7724 3191
www.niparestaurant.co.uk

⊖ Lancaster Gate
Closed 24-30 December, 1-4 January,
Saturday lunch, Sunday and Bank Holidays

Menu £27 – Carte £23/32

You'll find Nipa to be a little oasis of calm and hospitality, once you've made it up to the first floor of the Royal Lancaster and sidestepped the businessmen on their laptops in the adjacent lounge. Its teak panelling and ornaments are all imported from Thailand and they've done a convincing job of replicating the original Nipa in Bangkok's Landmark Hotel – if anything, it's even a little smarter. The menu is comprehensive, with a mix of the recognisable blended with more regional specialities. Dishes are marked 1-3 in chillies for their respective heat, come in decent sizes and the harmonious blend of flavours and textures successfully delivers what the aromas promise. Set menus are at the back and provide a convenient all-round experience.

Island

Modern European ✕✕

E3

at Royal Lancaster Hotel, ⊖ Lancaster Gate
Lancaster Terrace ✉ W2 2TY
✆ (020) 7551 6070 **Fax** (020) 7551 6071
e-mail eat@islandrestaurant.co.uk **www**.islandrestaurant.co.uk

Menu £21 – Carte £28/43

The Island in question may be more 'traffic' than 'tropical' but there's no denying they've made the best of an unpromising location. It's actually part of the huge Royal Lancaster Hotel but you wouldn't know it if you approach this large glass structure from the park. Inside it's all very crisp and bright; there's a bar to one side with views of the park (and that traffic) but the atmosphere is relaxed and the staff demonstrate commendable enthusiasm. The menu tries to appeal to everyone by offering an easy mix of grilled steaks, European brasserie favourites, a bit of Asia here and some American there. So expect everything from crab cakes and burgers to sea bass and risotto, all prepared on view through the hatch into the kitchen.

Hereford Road 🙂

British ✕

C2

3 Hereford Road ✉ W2 4AB ⊖ Bayswater
✆ (020) 7727 1144 Closed 25-30 December – booking essential
e-mail info@herefordroad.org
www.herefordroad.org

Carte £24/32

The clues are all there: the adoption of the street name, unassuming décor, enthusiastic service and splendidly British cooking. Yes, Tom Pemberton was ordained by St John in Clerkenwell, and the locals should be delighted he's pitched up here. The first sight is the narrow open kitchen (this was once a butcher's) and the six tables for two with side-by-side seating. The main body is down a few steps, with the four booths being the prize seats. Dishes are as uncomplicated as their menu descriptions suggest and at prices commendably lower than at his alma mater. You might find duck hearts, calf's brains, braised rabbits, pork with fennel or brill with courgettes. Don't miss the dishes for two, such as a whole oxtail or roe shoulder.

Assaggi ✤

Italian

39 Chepstow Pl, (above Chepstow pub) ✉ W2 4TS
✆ (020) 7792 5501
e-mail nipi@assaggi.demon.co.uk
www.assaggi.com

⊖ Bayswater
Closed 2 weeks Christmas and Sunday
– booking essential

Carte £31/46

The clue is in the name: this is all about Taste, with a capital T. The cherubic chef-proprietor Nino Sassu specialises in producing Italian food that just zings with flavour and this is down to the wonderful produce he uses and his knowing when to leave alone. That produce is delivered every morning of every day of the week he's open and at the end of each dinner service he has run out of everything. The menu is written exclusively in Italian and any one of the delightful girls will be happy to elucidate when your Italian culinary vocabulary lets you down. Salads are prepared with just as much care and respect as pasta; the veal cutlet is a real speciality; it's all very seasonal and the flourless chocolate cake is a perennial favourite. Maybe because it's just a room above a pub between rows of terraced houses or because that room is modestly but brightly furnished but eating at Assaggi – for which you must plan ahead as it's forever busy – always engenders a feeling of belonging to some sort of exclusive club; of being 'in the know.'

First Course
- Pecorino con San Daniele e Rucola.
- Crab tagliolini.

Main Course
- Pan-fried calf's liver with balsamic vinegar.
- Grilled tuna, Sicilian caponata.

Dessert
- Panna cotta, orange sauce, toasted almonds.
- Tiramisu with strawberries and chocolate.

Arturo

F2

Italian

23 Connaught St ⌧ W2 2AY
☎ (020) 7706 3388
Fax (020) 7402 9195
e-mail enquiries@arturorestaurant.co.uk
www.arturorestaurant.co.uk

⊖ Marble Arch
Closed 25-26 December, 1 January,
Good Friday and Easter Sunday

Menu £17 (lunch) – Carte £22/30

Ubiquitous beige is the prevailing shade of this slickly designed neighbourhood restaurant, surrounded by antique and art emporia and the growing signs of gentrification. It's all clean and crisp inside, with the clear lines only interrupted by the unevenly shaped customers. Service is confident but phlegmatic. The menu offers up an unchallenging selection of fresh and colourfully presented Italian dishes. Seasoning can occasionally be a little hit and miss but pasta dishes are sensibly proportioned and desserts are nicely balanced. Those who don't mind eating early are rewarded with an inexpensive set menu with adequate choice, as are those coming for lunch. The exclusively Italian wine list keeps things affordable.

L'Accento 😊

C2

Italian

16 Garway Rd ⌧ W2 4NH
☎ (020) 7243 2201
Fax (020) 7243 2201
e-mail laccentorest@aol.com   **www**.laccentorestaurant.co.uk

⊖ Bayswater
Closed Sunday and Bank Holidays

Menu £24 – Carte £27/33

L'Accento has been a feature in Garway Road now for eighteen years; it knows exactly what it does and it does it very well. That means earthy, flavoursome and satisfying Italian cooking, served in casual surroundings at a very decent price. The à la carte offers a rounded trip throughout Italy but it's hard to ignore the right hand side of the menu where the set menu is printed – this also offers some choice and comes at an exceptionally good price. The more familiar your face, the better the service you'll get, but whoever you are, you'll find the atmosphere's always convivial. Avoid the duller back room, though, and don't bother asking for the corner table – that's where the owner sits.

Kiasu

Asian

D3

48 Queensway ✉ W2 3RY — ⊖ Bayswater
✆ (020) 7727 8810 **Fax** (020) 7727 7220
e-mail info@kiasu.co.uk **www**.kiasu.co.uk

Carte £12/26

A/C
☀
VISA
MC

Queensway is awash with similar looking restaurants, but when there's one named after the Hokkien Chinese word for 'afraid to be second best' then it must be worth exploring. The owner of Kiasu is Malaysian and the Strait of Malacca, a passageway between the Indian and Pacific oceans, is the inspiration behind his food. That means exotically sounding specialities like nasi lemak or otak-otak but also dishes from neighbouring countries like Indonesia and Singapore. Some are hot and spicy, others light and fragrant and this is food designed for sharing; as your dishes arrive in no particular order and the tables are a little small, you may have to do some juggling. The place is always packed out; it's simply but brightly decorated and good fun.

Urban Turban

Indian

C2

98 Westbourne Grove ✉ W2 5RU — ⊖ Bayswater
✆ (020) 7243 4200 **Fax** (020) 7243 4080
e-mail info@urbanturban.uk.com **www**.urbanturban.uk.com

Carte £24/26

A/C
🚇
☀
VISA
MC
AE

Mumbai street food is the inspiration behind this latest venture from Vineet Bhatia. The idea is to order a number of not-so-small dishes, which arrive is no particular order, and share them with friends. These range from tangy scallops and lamb kebabs to chicken tossed in spring onion and soya sauce, reflecting the influence of the Chinese on some of those street stalls. For the particularly gregarious there are whole platters to share while those who would no sooner share a fork than a dish should head straight for the 'classic helpings'. The ground floor is where the bustle is, along with the bar and the lounge music; the relatively calmer downstairs section is the far nicer spot for eating in. The name is at least easy to remember.

The Waterway

Gastropub

54 Formosa St ✉ W9 2JU ⊖ Warwick Avenue
✆ (020) 7266 3557 **Fax** (020) 7266 3547
e-mail info@thewaterway.co.uk **www**.thewaterway.co.uk

Carte £30/40

A glimpse of sun and we're all outside so praise be for places like The Waterway. Not only does it have a large terrace but its pleasing vista takes in the canal, barges and the church spire beyond, although you'll have to be quick off the mark to get a spot. Spit and sawdust this is not. Instead you'll find quite a swanky affair - all wood and leather, with the staff dressed in black. The kitchen successfully balances the traditional with the contemporary. So, the 'classics' section on the menu may include moules or burgers and there are barbecues and Sunday roasts, but you'll also find more restaurant food involving sea bass or pork belly. Puds are quite delicate little things, and it's nice to see cheese being taken seriously.

Prince Alfred & Formosa Dining Room

Gastropub

5A Formosa St ✉ W9 1EE ⊖ Warwick Avenue
✆ (020) 7286 3287
e-mail princealfred@youngs.co.uk **www**.princealfred.co.uk

Menu £10 – Carte £23/33

It is possible, if you're approaching from Warrington Crescent, to find yourself seated in the Formosa Dining Room and be virtually unaware of the pub to which it is attached. This would be a crying shame as the Prince Alfred is a magnificent Grade II listed pub which dates back to 1863. Its most striking feature, along with the etched glass, is the partitions creating individual private booths. Heritage enthusiasts may shudder at the more contemporary, almost semi-industrial, dining room which has been attached but local diners seemingly have little regard for such sensibilities and just enjoy the space. The very open open-kitchen produces robust gastropub staples with global influences, while the wine lists features over thirty choices by the glass.

The Warrington

Gastropub

93 Warrington Crescent ✉ W9 1EH   ⊖ Maida Vale.
✆ (020) 7592 7960 **Fax** (020) 7592 1603
e-mail thewarrington@gordonramsay.com
www.gordonramsay.com

Carte £25/35

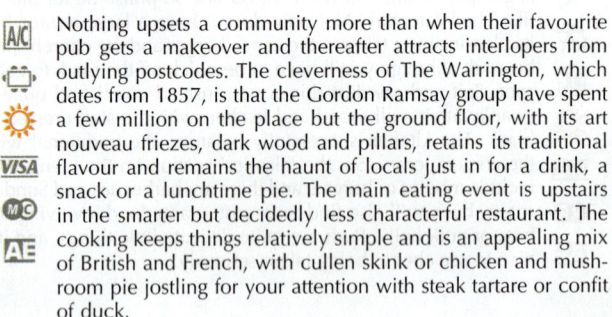

Nothing upsets a community more than when their favourite pub gets a makeover and thereafter attracts interlopers from outlying postcodes. The cleverness of The Warrington, which dates from 1857, is that the Gordon Ramsay group have spent a few million on the place but the ground floor, with its art nouveau friezes, dark wood and pillars, retains its traditional flavour and remains the haunt of locals just in for a drink, a snack or a lunchtime pie. The main eating event is upstairs in the smarter but decidedly less characterful restaurant. The cooking keeps things relatively simple and is an appealing mix of British and French, with cullen skink or chicken and mushroom pie jostling for your attention with steak tartare or confit of duck.

The sun is out – let's eat alfresco! Look for a terrace 🍽.

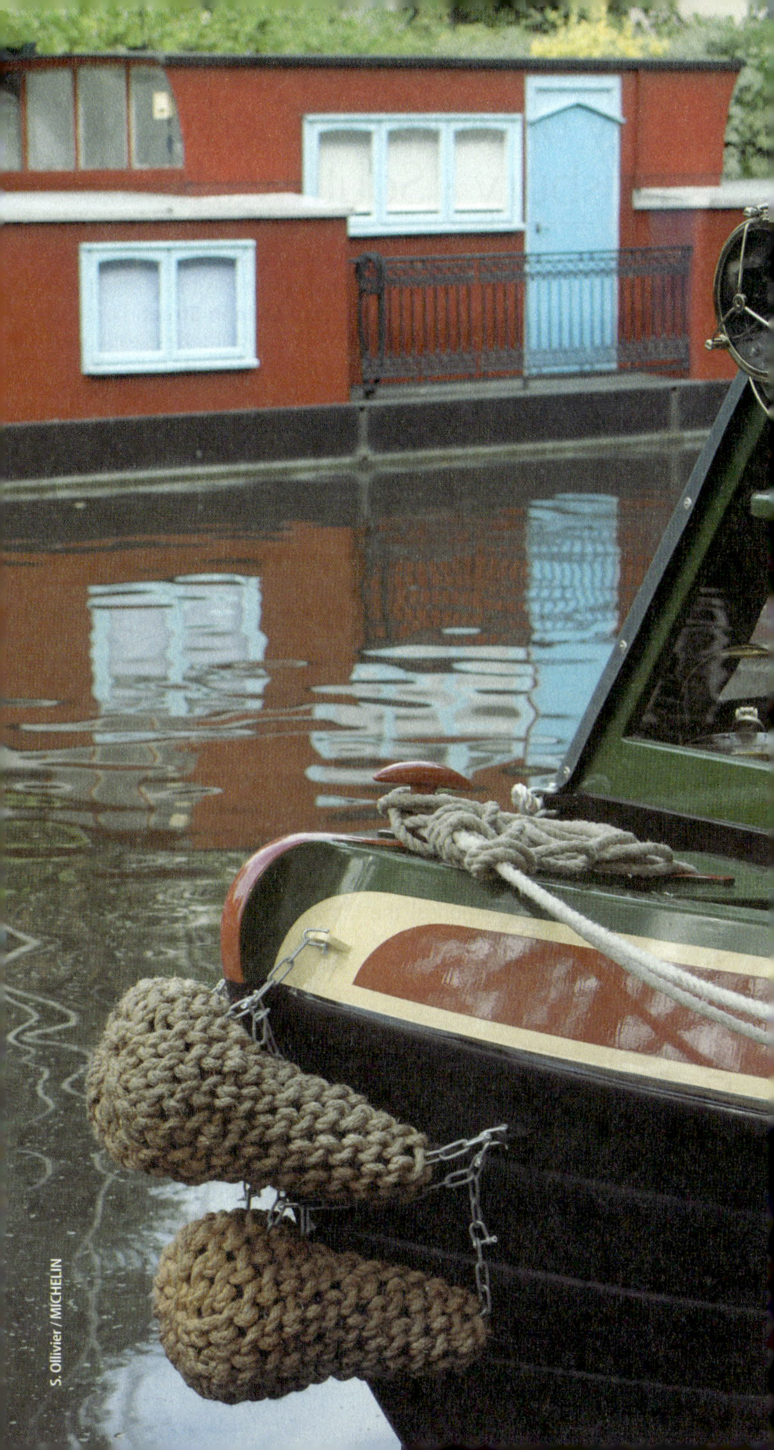

S. Ollivier / MICHELIN

City of London · Clerkenwell Finsbury · Southwark

Say what you like about London, **The City** is the place where it all started. The Romans developed this small area – this square mile – nearly two thousand years ago, and today it stands as the economic heartbeat of not only the capital, but the country as a whole. Each morning it's besieged with an army of bankers, lawyers and traders, and each evening it's abandoned to an eerie ghost-like fate. Of course, this mass exodus is offset by the two perennial crowd-pullers, **St Paul's** and the **Tower of London**, but these are both on the periphery of the area, away from the frenetic commercial zone within. The casual visitor tends to steer clear of the City, but for those willing to mix it with the daytime swarm of office workers, there are many historical nuggets hidden away, waiting to be mined. You can find here, amongst the skyscrapers, a tempting array of Roman ruins, medieval landmarks and brooding churches designed by Wren and Hawksmoor. One of the best ways of encapsulating everything that's happened here down the centuries is to visit the Museum of London, on London Wall, which tells the story of the city from the very start, and the very start means 300,000 BC.

For those seeking the hip corners of this part of London, the best advice is to head slightly northwest, using the brutalist space of the **Barbican Arts Centre** as your marker. You're now entering **Clerkenwell**. Sliding north/south through here is the bustling and buzzy **St John Street,** home to some of the funkiest eating establishments and gastropubs in London, their proximity to **Smithfield** meat market giving a clue as to much of the provenance. Clerkenwell's revivalist vibe has seen the steady reclamation of old factory space: during the Industrial Revolution, the area boomed with the introduction of breweries, print works and the manufacture of clocks and watches. After World War II decline set in, but these days city professionals and loft-dwellers are drawn to the area's zeitgeist-leading galleries and clubs, not to mention the wonderful floor-to-ceiling delicatessens. Clerkenwell is home to The Eagle, one of the city's pioneering gastropubs and still a local favourite, brimming over with newspaper journalists (it's near The Guardian offices). It even has its own art gallery upstairs. Meanwhile, the nearby **Exmouth Market** teems with trendy bars and restaurants, popular with those on their way to the perennially excellent dance concerts at Sadler's Wells Theatre.

The area was once a religious centre, frequented by monks and nuns; its name derives from the parish clerks who performed Biblical mystery plays around the Clerk's Well set in a nunnery wall. This can be found in **Farringdon Lane** complete with an exhibition explaining all. Close by in St John's

Lane is the 16C gatehouse which is home to the Museum of the Order of St John (famous today for its ambulance services), and chock full of fascinating objects related to the Order's medieval history.

Not too long ago, a trip over London Bridge to **Southwark** was for locals only, its trademark grimness ensuring it was well off the tourist map. These days, visitors treat it as a place of pilgrimage as three of London's modern success stories reside here. **Tate Modern** has become the city's most visited attraction, a huge former power station that generates a blistering show of modern art from 1900 to the present day, its massive turbine hall a must-see feature in itself. Practically next door but a million miles away architecturally is Shakespeare's **Globe,** a wonderful evocation of medieval showtime. Half a mile east is the best food market in London: **Borough Market.** Foodies can't resist the organic feel-good nature of the place, with its mind-boggling number of stalls selling produce ranging from every kind of fruit and veg to rare-breed meats, oils, preserves, chocolates and breads. And that's just for hors d'œuvres…

City of London
(Plan VIII)

CLERKENWELL & FINSBURY (Plan IX)

BLOOMSBURY, HATTON GARDEN & HOLBORN (Plan VI)

STRAND & COVENT GARDEN (Plan III)

- Hotel
- Restaurant

174

M
N
1
2
3
4
5
SHOREDITCH
SPITALFIELDS
Street
Banner Street
Whitecross St.
Dufferin St.
Bunhill Row
Leonard Street
City Road
Tabernacle Street
Paul Street
St. Luke St.
Scrutton Street
Curtain Road
Great Eastern St
Shoreditch High Street
Redchurch St
Club Row
Bethnal Green Rd
Whater St.
Worship Street
Quaker Street
Calvin St.
Commercial St.
Folgate St
Spital Square
Hanbury St.
Chiswell Street
Sun Street
Earl St.
Wilson St.
Appold Street
Silk Street
Lane
ST GILES CRIPPLEGATE
Moor Lane
Fore St.
Wall
Tatsuso
LIVERPOOL STREET
Sun Street Passage
Bishopsgate
Brushfield Street
Artillery Lane
Fashion St.
Moorgate
Eldon St.
FINSBURY CIRCUS
Liverpool Street
Middlesex Street
Boisdale of Bishopsgate
Andaz Liverpool Street
London Wall
Devonshire Terrace
Bell Lane
Wentworth Street
Commercial Street
Basinghall St.
GUILDHALL
Rhodes Twenty Four
Kenza
Harrow Place
Goulston St.
ST MARGARET LOTHBURY
Mint Leaf Lounge
Houndsditch
Street
King St.
ST HELEN BISHOPSGATE
Bevis Marks
St Mary Axe
1 Lombard Street
Bonds
Aldgate
Aldgate East
Aldgate High St.
Braham St.
Coq d'Argent
Princes St.
Sauterelle
ROYAL EXCHANGE
The Mercer
ST ANDREW UNDERSHAFT
MANSION HOUSE
Bank
ST PETER UPON CORNHILL
Leadenhall Street
LLOYD'S BUILDING
Mansell St.
ST STEPHEN WALBROOK
King William
ST EDMUND THE KING AND MARTYR
Queen St.
Cannon St.
Fenchurch Street
Lane
Mark Lane
Friars
Minories
FENCHURCH STREET
ST MARY ABCHURCH
ST CLEMENT EAST CHEAP
ST MARGARET PATTENS
Crutched
ST MICHAEL PATERNOSTER ROYAL
Monument
Eastcheap
ST OLAVE'S
CANNON STREET
MONUMENT
Gt Tower St.
ST MARY AT HILL
Tower Hill
Shorter St.
Lower Thames Street
Byward St.
Tower Hill
ST MAGNUS THE MARTYR
ALL HALLOWS BY THE TOWER
TOWER OF LONDON
Tower Bridge Approach
LONDON BRIDGE
ST KATHARINE DOCK
THAMES
SOUTHWARK CATHEDRAL
TOWER BRIDGE
CITY HALL
Tooley Street
Street
London Bridge
St Thomas Street
Pond
Maze
LONDON BRIDGE
Bermondsey St.
GEORGE INN
High
Borough
Great
St Thomas St.
Street
Tower Bridge Rd
Shad Thames
0
200 m
200 yards
SOUTHWARK (Plan X)

BLOOMSBURY, HATTON GARDEN & HOLBÖRN (Plan VI)

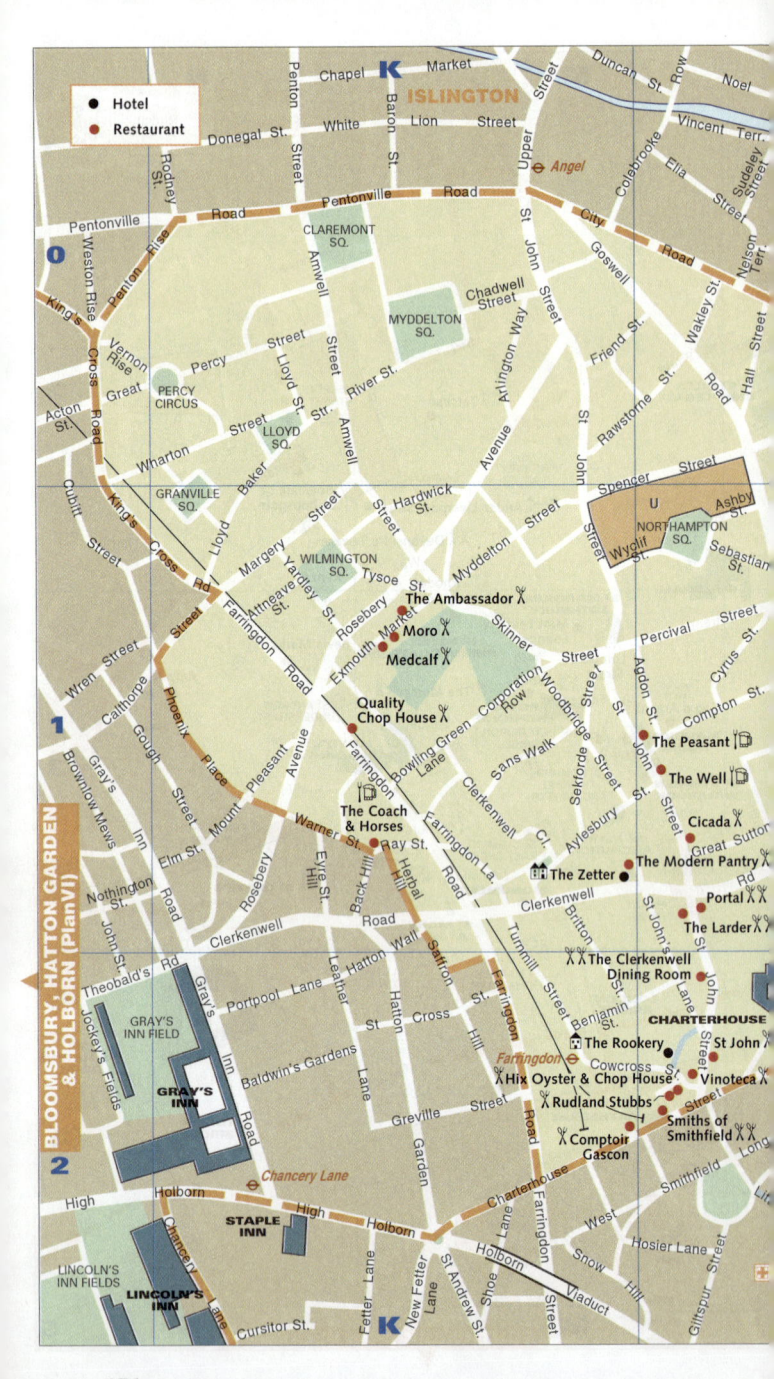

Legend:
- ● Hotel
- ● Restaurant

Areas/Districts labelled:
- ISLINGTON
- CLAREMONT SQ.
- MYDDELTON SQ.
- PERCY CIRCUS
- LLOYD SQ.
- GRANVILLE SQ.
- WILMINGTON SQ.
- NORTHAMPTON SQ.
- CHARTERHOUSE
- GRAY'S INN FIELD
- GRAY'S INN
- STAPLE INN
- LINCOLN'S INN FIELDS
- LINCOLN'S INN

Restaurants / Hotels marked:
- Angel
- The Ambassador
- Moro
- Medcalf
- Quality Chop House
- The Coach & Horses
- The Peasant
- The Well
- Cicada
- The Modern Pantry
- The Zetter
- Portal
- The Larder
- The Clerkenwell Dining Room
- The Rookery
- St John
- Hix Oyster & Chop House
- Vinoteca
- Rudland Stubbs
- Smiths of Smithfield
- Comptoir Gascon

Clerkenwell & Finsbury
(Plan IX)

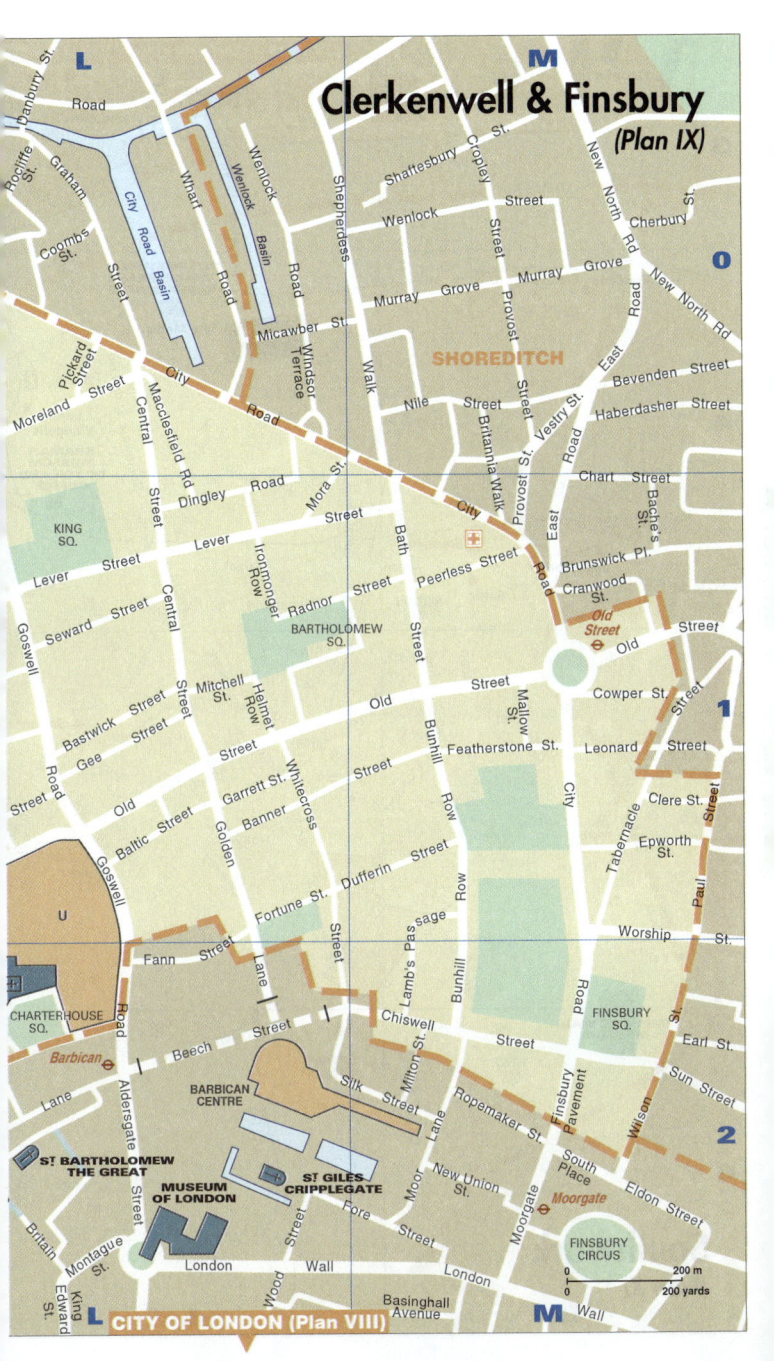

Southwark (Plan X)

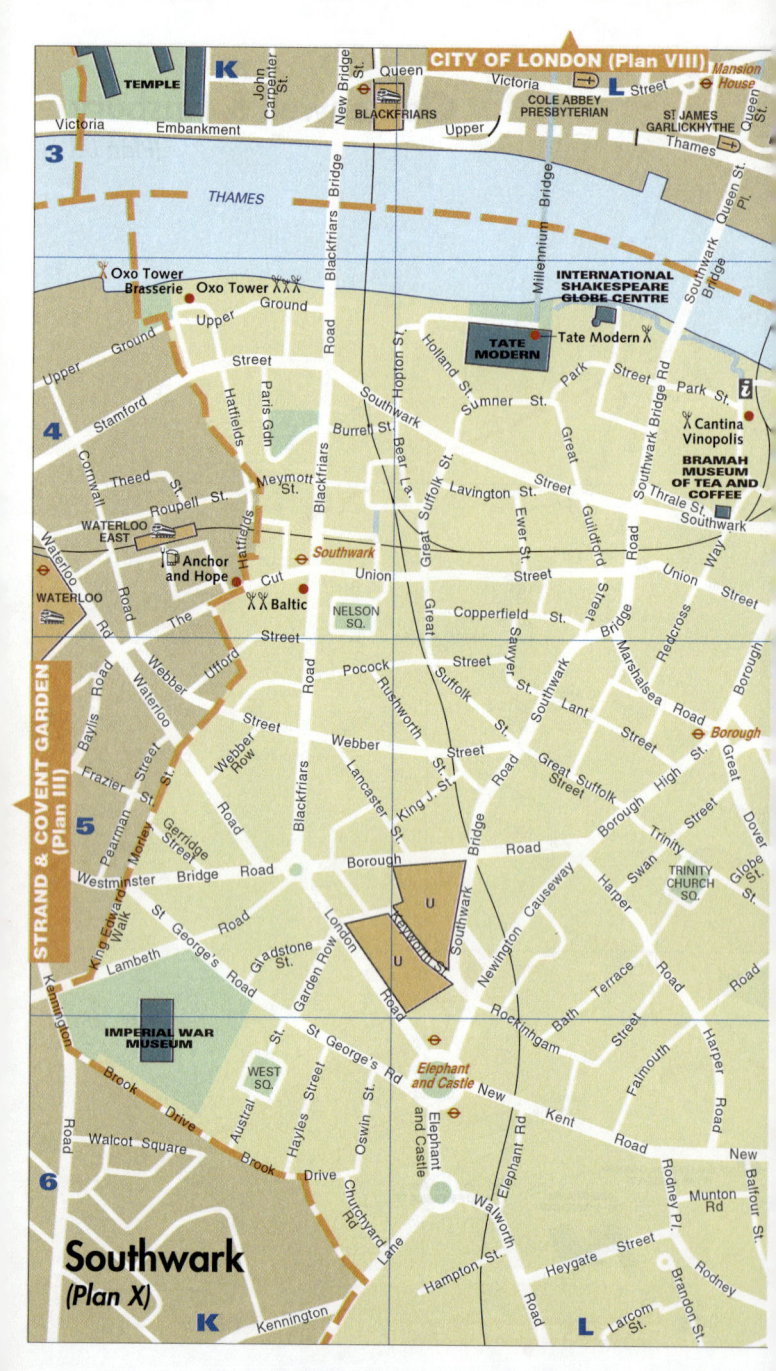

Map: Southwark / Tower Bridge area

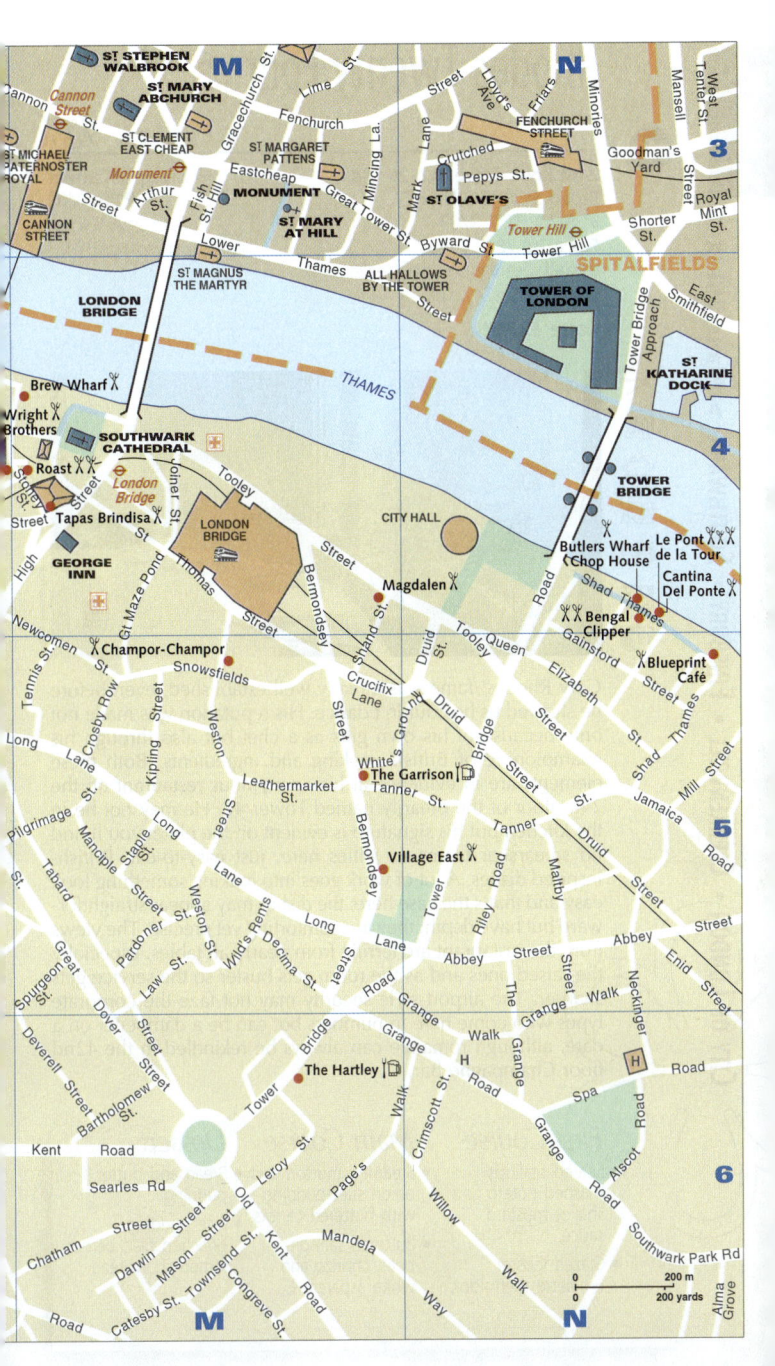

Landmarks and streets (north to south, west to east):

- ST STEPHEN WALBROOK
- ST MARY ABCHURCH
- ST MICHAEL PATERNOSTER ROYAL
- ST CLEMENT EAST CHEAP
- ST MARGARET PATTENS
- Monument
- MONUMENT
- ST MARY AT HILL
- ST OLAVE'S
- FENCHURCH STREET
- Cannon Street
- CANNON STREET
- ST MAGNUS THE MARTYR
- ALL HALLOWS BY THE TOWER
- Tower Hill
- SPITALFIELDS
- TOWER OF LONDON
- ST KATHARINE DOCK
- LONDON BRIDGE
- THAMES
- Brew Wharf
- Wright Brothers
- Roast
- Tapas Brindisa
- SOUTHWARK CATHEDRAL
- London Bridge
- LONDON BRIDGE (station)
- GEORGE INN
- CITY HALL
- TOWER BRIDGE
- Butlers Wharf Chop House
- Le Pont de la Tour
- Cantina Del Ponte
- Magdalen
- Bengal Clipper
- Blueprint Café
- Champor-Champor
- Snowsfields
- The Garrison
- Village East
- The Hartley

Streets:
Cannon Street, Gracechurch St, Lime St, Fenchurch St, Lloyd's Ave, Friars, Minories, West Tenter St, Mansell St, Crutched Friars, Pepys St, Great Tower St, Eastcheap, Mincing La, Mark Lane, Byward St, Tower Hill, Goodman's Yard, Shorter St, Royal Mint St, East Smithfield, Tower Bridge Approach, Lower Thames Street, Arthur St, Fish St Hill, Tooley Street, Joiner St, Thomas St, Bermondsey St, Druid St, Gainsford St, Shad Thames, Queen Elizabeth St, Mill Street, Jamaica Road, Abbey Street, Enid Street, Neckinger, Grange Walk, Spa Road, Southwark Park Rd, Alscot Road, Grange Road, Tower Bridge Road, Crucifix Lane, Leathermarket St, White's Grounds, Tanner St, Maltby St, Riley Rd, Decima St, Wild's Rents, Long Lane, Weston St, Kipling St, Crosby Row, Snowsfields, Newcomen St, Tennis St, Pilgrimage St, Tabard St, Manciple St, Staple St, Pardoner St, Law St, Great Dover St, Spurgeon St, Deverell St, Bartholomew St, Kent Road, Searles Rd, Chatham St, Darwin St, Mason St, Old Kent Road, Townsend St, Congreve St, Catesby St, Leroy St, Page's Walk, Mandela Way, Crimscott St, Willow Walk, Alma Grove

Scale: 200 m / 200 yards

179

Rhodes Twenty Four

British

M3

24th floor, Tower 42, 25 Old Broad St ✉ EC2N 1HQ
✆ (020) 7877 7703
Fax (020) 7877 7788
e-mail reservations@rhodes24.co.uk
www.rhodes24.co.uk

Carte £37/55

⊖ Liverpool Street
▶ **Plan VIII**
Closed Christmas-New Year, Saturday, Sunday and Bank Holidays

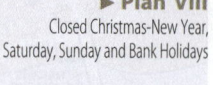

Gary Rhodes' fame was already well established, even before he showed us he couldn't dance. His reputation was made not only because of his own gifts as a chef but also through his championing of British cooking and ingredients. Both these elements are in evidence at his eponymous restaurant on the 24th floor of the drearily named Tower 42. He may not be in the kitchen but his signature is evident on the plate: you'll find no smears or foams or jellies here, just easy-to-eat, British-inspired dishes. A lot of work goes into making something look easy and that's the case here: the dishes may appear straightforward but have depth; they are comforting yet precise. The views from the restaurant are terrific from nearly all tables, especially the raised ones and as the room gets busier so the service gets sharper. The airport-style security may not faze the corporate types who come here in numbers but can be a dampener on a date, although romance can always be rekindled in the 42nd floor Champagne Bar.

First Course
- Seared scallops, mashed potato and shallot mustard sauce.
- Glazed lobster omelette thermidor.

Main Course
- Steamed mutton and onion suet pudding with buttered carrots.
- Buttered salmon, peas, chorizo and white asparagus.

Dessert
- Bread and butter pudding.
- Rice pudding, poached blackberries, lemon shortbread.

Bonds

M3

Modern European 🗡🗡🗡

at Threadneedles Hotel,
5 Threadneedle St ✉ EC2R 8AY
📞 (020) 7657 8088 **Fax** (020) 7657 8089
e-mail bonds@theetongroup.com
www.theetoncollection.com

⊖ Bank
▶ **Plan VIII**
Closed Saturday,
Sunday and Bank Holidays

Menu £18 (lunch) – Carte £28/46

One wonders if they considered the more culinary apt 'Stocks' or the more hospitable 'Shares' before settling on 'Bonds' as the name for this City restaurant, part of the Threadneedles Hotel, converted from an 1856 banking hall. The suited executives, unmoved by the irony of another financial institution enjoying life as a restaurant, come here to enjoy its striking surroundings and good cooking. Enter through the hotel and check out the stained glass cupola in reception, as well as the cocktails available in the bar, which also serves tapas. The grand restaurant, with its pillars, marble and panelling provides the backdrop for sophisticated food that's more elaborate in style than the descriptively understated menu lets on.

1 Lombard Street

M3

French 🗡🗡🗡

1 Lombard St ✉ EC3V 9AA
📞 (020) 7929 6611
Fax (020) 7929 6622
e-mail hb@1lombardstreet.com
www.1lombardstreet.com

⊖ Bank
▶ **Plan VIII**
Closed 25 December- 6 January, Saturday,
Sunday and Bank Holidays
– booking essential at lunch

Menu £44/45 – Carte £52/62

There's a choice of restaurant within the same converted Grade II listed banking hall: you have the bustling front brasserie with its impressive domed skylight and large central bar or, if you're after a more discreet atmosphere, then head for the restaurant at the rear which has a comfortable if somewhat sober appearance. Here you will find quite elaborately presented, tried and tested dishes. The cooking displays mostly classical leanings but is not afraid of adding the occasional Asian note; there's plenty of choice, including some dishes designed for two, such as sea bass, rib of beef or suckling pig and an assortment of tasting menus for the whole table, which can represent better value than the à la carte.

Coq d'Argent

French 𝕏𝕏𝕏

M3

No.1 Poultry ✉ EC2R 8EJ ⊖ Bank
𝒞 (020) 7395 5000 ▶ **Plan VIII**
Fax (020) 7395 5050 Closed Christmas, Easter,
e-mail coqd-argent@danddlondon.com Saturday lunch, Sunday dinner and
www.danddlondon.com Bank Holidays – booking essential

Menu £29 – Carte £34/50

There are only a few London restaurants that offer great views and fewer still that look like a bow of a ship when you gaze up at them. Not only does Coq d'Argent look down over the Square Mile but it also has a great terrace and fantastic roof garden. The bar may get a regular pounding but the noise levels are contained. Service in the restaurant is slick and well-organised but they are so used to busy lunches that dinner can sometimes be served at too quick a pace. The cooking is regional French and dishes come with a certain refinement. There's a good balance between the traditional and more contemporary, with shellfish a popular option. The à la carte can also be a little lofty too, especially as the main courses require side dishes.

Le Pont de la Tour

French 𝕏𝕏𝕏

N4

36d Shad Thames, Butlers Wharf ⊖ London Bridge
✉ SE1 2YE ▶ **Plan X**
𝒞 (020) 7403 8403 **Fax** (020) 7940 1835
e-mail lepontdelatour@danddlondon.com
www.danddlondon.com

Menu £25 (lunch) – Carte £37/52

The regeneration of the River and Butlers Wharf were there for all to see in 1991 when Le Pont de la Tour opened and its glamorous reputation was done no harm when Tony Blair entertained Bill Clinton here in 1997. The elegant room provides diners with terrific views of Tower Bridge and the activity on the river, especially from the delightful terrace, while the menu offers a comprehensive selection of dishes that borrow heavily from France, all served by a well-drilled team. For those after less formal surroundings then head for the Bar & Grill which specialises in crustaceans and fruits de mer while those wanting something to take home are catered for by an impressive array of produce in the adjacent food store.

Oxo Tower

Modern European XXX

K4

(8th floor), Oxo Tower Wharf, Barge House St ✉ SE1 9PH
✆ (020) 7803 3888 **Fax** (020) 7803 3838
e-mail oxo.reservations@harveynichols.com
www.harveynichols.com

⊖ Southwark
▶ **Plan X**
Closed 24-26 December

Menu £33 – Carte £45/61

The Oxo Tower Restaurant is the smarter, more serious and ambitious sibling to the next door brasserie but both share terrific views and wonderful terraces from their location on the 8th floor of the iconic former Oxo riverside factory. The restaurant appears to be permanently busy and this means staff are sometimes a little too eager to tell you what time you have to vacate your table rather than making you feel welcome. The place is roomy, bright and open, with plenty of bustle; the cooking is contemporary and mostly European in influence while the kitchen uses plenty of top-end ingredients. Those views really are great but, on a clear day, you can see plenty of more reasonably priced restaurants.

Skylon

Modern European XXX

J4

1 Southbank Centre, Belvedere Rd ✉ SE1 8XX
✆ (020) 7654 7800 **Fax** (020) 7654 7801
e-mail skylon@danddlondon.com **www.**skylonrestaurant.co.uk

⊖ Waterloo
▶ **Plan III**

Menu £27 (lunch)/30 – Carte £29/40

The dining flagship in the revamped Royal Festival Hall offers a choice: a Grill to one side, with a raised cocktail bar making the most of the river views, and a Restaurant to the other, where things are a little more sedate and a tad more comfortable. This was the first project from D&D London, following their management buy-out of Conran Restaurants, but the 1950s styling and imaginative design makes it a natural addition to the existing portfolio. The Grill offers an easy-to-eat menu, from eggs Benedict to bowls of pasta, as well as pre and post performance menus and something for the kids. The restaurant offers up more ambitious dishes that display a greater degree of complication, finer ingredients and higher prices.

Club Gascon

French

L2

57 West Smithfield ✉ EC1A 9DS — Barbican
☎ (020) 7796 0600 ▶ **Plan VIII**
Fax (020) 7796 0601 Closed January, Saturday lunch, Sunday and
e-mail info@clubgascon.com Bank Holidays – booking essential
www.clubgascon.com

Menu £28/42 – Carte £34/48

The diet of your average Gascon involves prodigious amounts of duck, goose, liver and fat but levels of heart disease in this South West region of France are found to be well below average. This is known as The Gascony Paradox and must surely keep your average dietician awake at night. Being armed with this information makes eating at Club Gascon a guilt-free, blissfully indulgent pleasure as it is this region that the restaurant celebrates. Pascal Aussignac's menu is divided up into five sections: starters; potages; foie gras; fish and meat, with around five dishes per section. The idea is to choose at least three dishes, followed by a dessert; each one is perfectly formed and bursting with flavour. There is also a seasonal set menu available, with wine pairings, for the whole table. Animated conversations ensure that the atmosphere is never less than buzzing. The service from the mainly French staff all dressed in black is polite and knowledgeable, although they can sometimes struggle to keep up when the room is full.

First Course
- Abalone and razor clams à la plancha, parsnip and seaweed tartare.
- Grilled duck foie gras and grapes.

Main Course
- Cappuccino of black pudding and lobster.
- Wild turbot, garden peas, verbena purée, crispy pork.

Dessert
- Rhubarb and champagne sorbet, rose Chantilly.
- White chocolate boule, lime jelly and pineapple.

Sauterelle

French ✕✕

M3

The Royal Exchange ✉ EC3V 3LR
☏ (020) 7618 2483
www.restaurantsauterelle.com

⊖ Bank
▶ **Plan VIII**
Closed Saturday and Sunday

Menu £21 (dinner) – Carte £33/56

A/C
🛆
VISA
MC
AE
①

Opened originally in 1565, The Royal Exchange may have been rebuilt twice, most recently in 1842, but today it is one of the great rousing landmarks in the City. Within the Exchange and to complement the Grand Bar and Café, one finds, on its mezzanine level, Sauterelle. It opened in late 2005 and is another in the D&D collection of restaurants. From its lofty position, Sauterelle (meaning 'grasshopper' in French) provides slick and comfortable surroundings and the well-drilled staff make light of the busy lunchtimes. The menu concentrates on classic bourgeois French cooking, with rillettes, marmites and saucissons to the fore. Expect scallops with Jerusalem artichoke, magret of duck and, to finish, a crème brûlée.

Bengal Clipper

Indian ✕✕

N4

Cardamom Building, Shad
Thames, Butlers Wharf
✉ SE1 2YR
☏ (020) 7357 9001 **Fax** (020) 7357 9002
e-mail mail@bengalclipper.co.uk www.bengalclipper.co.uk

⊖ London Bridge
▶ **Plan X**

Carte £14/20

A/C
🕓
☀
VISA
MC
AE

Set among the converted wharves and warehouses by the part of the Thames where cargoes of Indian teas and spices were once traded, you'll find, fittingly enough, Bengal Clipper, a firmly established Indian restaurant whose reputation has been based on reliable cooking and big, bustling surroundings. The size means that the restaurant is often the chosen venue of larger parties and tables so the atmosphere, particularly in the evenings, is usually fairly hectic, although the smartly kitted out staff are an unflappable lot. Specialities from all parts of India are showcased, along with several originally conceived dishes which includes, in honour of the building in which the restaurant sits, a chicken curry flavoured with cardamom.

The Chancery

Modern European 𝖃𝖃

K2

9 Cursitor St ✉ EC4A 1LL ⊖ Chancery Lane
✆ (020) 7831 4000 ▶ **Plan VIII**
Fax (020) 7831 4002 Closed 25 December, Saturday and Sunday
e-mail reservations@thechancery.co.uk **www**.thechancery.co.uk

Menu £34

Surrounded by the law courts, The Chancery, open only during the week, provides the perfect spot for that last meal of freedom or the post-trial celebratory acquittal. It is the sister restaurant to The Clerkenwell Dining Room and the bright main room benefits from the large picture windows and understated decoration. This is room in which to reserve your table, rather than the basement which can lack something in atmosphere. Service is sufficiently fleet of foot and efficient to reassure those with an eye on the adjournment. The cooking also comes suitably well-judged and is modern in style but underpinned by a solid understanding of the ingredients. The wine list has some well-chosen bottles under £25.

Roast

British 𝖃𝖃

M4

The Floral Hall, Borough Market ⊖ London Bridge
✉ SE1 1TL ▶ **Plan X**
✆ (020) 7940 1300 Closed 25 December and Sunday dinner
Fax (020) 7655 2079 – booking essential
e-mail info@roast-restaurant.com **www**.roast-restaurant.com

Carte £33/48

It's in the one place where you don't look when you find yourself in the deliciously enticing surroundings of Borough Market – up. Jump into the lift and upstairs you'll be greeted and led into a vast room; the best seats are in the raised section beyond the bar. The place is always busy and the young team are a friendly bunch, although they can sometimes appear to be a man down. The food is all about being British and proud of it, reflecting the values of the market below and the importance of provenance. Start with the cocktail of the week, move on to Cornish herring or Arbroath smokie followed by roast lamb or steak and onion pudding and finish with a Bakewell tart or rhubarb crumble. You'll leave whistling 'Land of Hope and Glory'.

Boisdale of Bishopsgate

Scottish ✕✕

N2

Swedeland Court, 202 Bishopsgate ✉ EC2M 4NR
☏ (020) 7283 1763
Fax (020) 7283 1664
e-mail info@boisdale-city.co.uk **www.**boisdale.co.uk

⊖ Liverpool Street
▶ **Plan VIII**
Closed 25 December - 3 January,
Saturday, Sunday and Bank Holidays

Carte £25/59

It's easy to miss and the ground floor is a popular spot for those who like some champagne and oysters on their way home; but follow the tartan carpet down to the relative calm of the cosy and characterful restaurant, complete with live music. That carpet was a clue as this is all about Scotland. Admittedly some of the accents are as unconvincing as Mel Gibson's but there is no denying that the food is the real thing. The large menu is made up of plenty of Scottish specialities and reminds us just how spectacular the produce is north of the border. Salmon, shellfish, beef and, of course, haggis are the perennial favourites but so are the daily specials of game, fish and assorted pies. You'll leave with an urge to hike somewhere.

Bevis Marks

Kosher ✕✕

N3

Bevis Marks ✉ EC3A 5DQ
☏ (020) 7283 2220
Fax (020) 7283 2221
e-mail enquiries@bevismarkstherestaurant.com
www.bevismarkstherestaurant.com

⊖ Aldgate
▶ **Plan VIII**
Closed Saturday,
Sunday and Jewish Holidays

Carte £32/39

The restaurant is, in essence, an extension to the Bevis Marks synagogue which opened in 1701 and is the oldest Jewish place of worship in the UK. The glass enclosed space - with a retractable roof - was originally constructed for a festival, after which it was decided to turn it into a restaurant. Look out for the billboard and menu otherwise you'll never find it. 'Innovative kosher' describes the cooking and the choice is fairly extensive. The kitchen not only updates such classics as chicken soup with matzo balls but adds an Asian influence to some dishes like Sichuan duck and Cantonese chicken. Others have more of a European accent such as cassoulet and fettuccine. Wines are well chosen and several are Mevushal.

Tatsuso

M2

Japanese ✗✗

32 Broadgate Circle
✉ EC2M 2QS
✆ (020) 7638 5863
Fax (020) 7638 5864
e-mail info.tatsuso@btinternet.com

⊖ Liverpool Street
▶ **Plan VIII**
Closed Christmas, New Year, Saturday,
Sunday and Bank Holidays – booking essential

Carte £35/80

Tatsuso was among that pioneering wave of Japanese restaurants responsible for introducing Japanese food to inquisitive Londoners. Today it's one of The City's more mature restaurants and remains a favourite, although one that's beginning to slightly show its age. There is a choice of dining room and, with them, two different dining experiences. On the ground floor it's teppan-yaki, where you sit round the counters and the chefs do their thing in front of you. Prices can rise to fairly lofty heights with some of the set menus, especially if you opt for the Kobe beef. Downstairs is where you'll find more your traditional Japanese restaurant and prices here are a little more down-to-earth. Service is exceptionally polite and well meaning.

The Larder

L1

Modern European ✗✗

91-93 St John St ✉ EC1M 4NU
✆ (020) 7608 1558
Fax (120) 7253 9285
e-mail info@thelarderrestaurant.com
www.thelarderrestaurant.com

⊖ Farringdon
▶ **Plan IX**
Closed 23 December - 5 January, Saturday
lunch, Sunday and Bank Holidays

Carte £24/35

An appropriate name as there is bounty galore. On one side is the bakery with plenty of artisanal breads and cakes. The restaurant, meanwhile, is one of those large, semi-industrial places with exposed brick and pipes and an open kitchen at the back. This kind of hard-edged space can push up the decibels but that's part of its appeal. Think modern European comfort food, from moules marinière to roast salmon with pumpkin ravioli, but alongside the halloumi you might find Lancashire cheese and next to the chicken breast with Puy lentils could be a Barnsley chop, so the Union flag is raised occasionally (the owners are from Leeds). A side dish to accompany the main course is recommended and some thought has gone into them.

The White Swan

Modern European 🍴🍴

K2

108 Fetter Lane ✉ EC4A 1ES
📞 (020) 7242 9696
Fax (020) 7404 2250
e-mail info@thewhiteswanlondon.com
www.thewhiteswanlondon.com

⊖ Temple
▶ **Plan VIII**
Closed Christmas, Saturday, Sunday,
Monday dinner and Bank Holidays

Menu £28 (lunch) – Carte £26/30

You'll find something akin to an assault course at the White Swan because to get to the first floor restaurant you have to fight your way through the drinkers in the ground floor bar and, at lunch time, this is more challenging than you think. Once upstairs, you'll find a small but neat room and service that is polite and friendly but also well paced and professional. The mirrored ceiling and large windows add plenty of light, although the closeness of the tables can make private conversation tricky. However, the cooking is good enough to induce the odd contented silence. It is classical in its base but with the occasional contemporary tweak and dishes display a certain refinement. Pricing is also fair when one considers the location.

Smiths of Smithfield

Modern European 🍴🍴

L2

Top Floor, 67-77 Charterhouse St
✉ EC1M 6HJ
📞 (020) 7251 7950
Fax (020) 7236 5666
e-mail reservations@smithsofsmithfield.co.uk
www.smithsofsmithfield.co.uk

⊖ Barbican
▶ **Plan IX**
Closed 24 December
- 2 January and Saturday lunch

Carte £34/47

If you ever arrange a get-together with a friend here just remember to be a little precise in your meeting spot. Smiths is housed in a vast building where all four of its floors are given over to eating, drinking and general merry making. As a rule of thumb, prices and levels of formality go up the higher up you go yourself. The ground floor is a relaxed bar with an exposed brick warehouse feel and easy, snacky menu. Then it's the cocktail bar, followed by the large and lively 'dining room' which is actually more a brasserie and finally the 'top floor' which has a more corporate, groomed feel and boasts terrific views of the surrounding rooftops. Cooking is decidedly modern with well sourced meats something of a speciality.

Portal

Mediterranean 🍴🍴

L1

88 St John St ✉ EC1M 4EH
📞 (020) 7253 6950 **Fax** (020) 7490 5836
e-mail reservations@portalrestaurant.com
www.portalrestaurant.com

⊖ Farringdon
▶ **Plan IX**
Closed Saturday lunch,
Sunday and Bank Holidays

Carte £34/56

You may be tempted to stay in the front bar, where they serve an appealing array of petiscos or Portuguese tapas, but once through the throng you'll find yourself in pleasant, semi-industrial surroundings, with neatly dressed tables. The service is enthusiastic and helpful, as one would expect from somewhere family owned and run. It is to Southern Europe and particularly Portugal where the kitchen seeks inspiration, so head for the fish, shellfish and pork specialities, like bacalhau or bisaro; if you're in a big group think of pre-ordering the suckling pig. The kitchen commendably concentrates more on flavours rather than presentation. Portugal also features heavily on the wine list and there's an impressive selection of port by the glass.

Baltic

Eastern European 🍴🍴

K4

74 Blackfriars Rd ✉ SE1 8HA
📞 (020) 7928 1111 **Fax** (020) 7928 8487
e-mail info@balticrestaurant.co.uk
www.balticrestaurant.co.uk

⊖ Southwark
▶ **Plan X**
Closed 24-26 December and 1 January

Menu £18 (lunch) – Carte £25/30

The façade may be a little unprepossessing but persevere and you'll find yourself in a slick bar. If you can resist the tempting array of vodkas, including some appealingly original home-made flavours, then proceed further and you'll end up in the arresting space of the restaurant. Alcoves around the edge and, above, a wooden trussed ceiling with vaulted glass combine with bright white walls to give this former industrial space a vividly modernist feel. At this point you'll probably expect some sort of pan-Asian fusion thing but fortunately Baltic enjoys the same ownership as Wódka, so the cooking here covers the altogether more muscular cuisines of Eastern Europe and the Baltic states. It is robust, full of flavour and requires an appetite.

The Clerkenwell Dining Room

French ✗✗

L2

69-73 St John St ✉ EC1M 4AN
✆ (020) 7253 9000
Fax (020) 7253 3322
e-mail reservations@theclerkenwell.com **www**.theclerkenwell.com

⊖ Farringdon
▶ **Plan IX**
Closed Saturday lunch and Sunday

Menu £20 – Carte £30/40

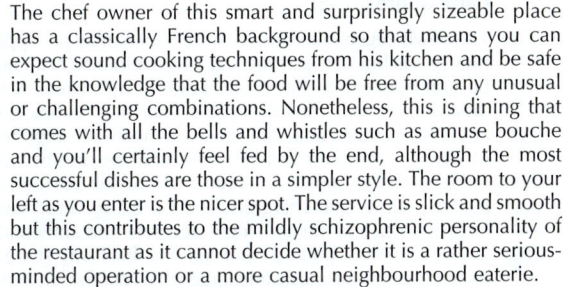

The chef owner of this smart and surprisingly sizeable place has a classically French background so that means you can expect sound cooking techniques from his kitchen and be safe in the knowledge that the food will be free from any unusual or challenging combinations. Nonetheless, this is dining that comes with all the bells and whistles such as amuse bouche and you'll certainly feel fed by the end, although the most successful dishes are those in a simpler style. The room to your left as you enter is the nicer spot. The service is slick and smooth but this contributes to the mildly schizophrenic personality of the restaurant as it cannot decide whether it is a rather serious-minded operation or a more casual neighbourhood eaterie.

Devonshire Terrace

Modern European ✗✗

N2

Devonshire Sq ✉ EC2M 4YY
✆ (020) 7256 3233 **Fax** (020) 7256 3244
e-mail info@devonshireterrace.co.uk
www.devonshireterrace.co.uk

⊖ Liverpool Street
▶ **Plan VIII**
Closed Christmas-New Year,
Saturday and Sunday

Carte £22/34

Devonshire Terrace is all about flexibility. Not only is it open from 7am until midnight, but the idea is to create your own main course by choosing the sauce and the side dishes to accompany your tiger prawns, veal chop, fishcakes or other brasserie-style offering. Those who would no sooner create their own main course than offer to help wash-up should choose salad or pastas dishes which come fully dressed. Apart from the two terraces, one of which is an all-year affair within the atrium, try to snare one of the booths in the bright restaurant with its high ceiling and open kitchen. The elephant motif? This was once an ivory store for the East India Company and the restaurant sponsors an elephant in South Africa.

Kenza

Lebanese ✕✕

N2

10 Devonshire Square
✉ EC2M 4YP
✆ (020) 7929 5533
Fax (020) 7929 0303
e-mail info@kenza-restaurant.com **www.**kenza-restaurant.com

⊖ Liverpool Street
▶ **Plan VIII**
Closed Saturday lunch and Sunday

Carte approx. £35

A/C · ⌨ · VISA · MC · AE · ①

The newly regenerated Devonshire Square may not appear that mysterious but descend the stairs down into Kenza and you'll be transported into the exotic Levant. The name, Arabic for 'treasure,' is well chosen and the floor tiles, lamps, carvings, colourful candles and satin cushions were all imported from Morocco. Moroccan and Lebanese cooking are the two main influences; the choices include samboussek pastries, kibbeh parcels, pureés and chargrills. There are also 'feast' menus for larger parties and the cooking is accurate and authentic; finish with theatrically poured mint tea and baklava. There's belly dancing, pumping music and large tables but the kitchen proves that a party atmosphere and good food are not mutually exclusive.

Manicomio

Italian ✕✕

L3

6 Gutter Lane ✉ EC2V 7AD
✆ (020) 7265 010 **Fax** (020) 7265 011
e-mail gutterlane@manicomio.co.uk
www.manicomio.co.uk

⊖ St Paul's
▶ **Plan VIII**
Closed Christmas-New Year,
Saturday and Sunday

Carte £22/35

A/C · VISA · MC · AE

This sibling to the King's Road branch opened in the summer of 2008 and is on the first floor of a Norman Foster-designed building. On the ground floor is the deli/café while the bar is kept separately on the top floor, away from the restaurant which makes a nice change in this part of town. The owners' other business is importing Italian produce so they know their cipollas. There's also plenty of British meat, game and fish but prepared in an Italian way, with top-notch Italian accompaniments. The cooking covers many regions, with daily specials; one or two side dishes are needed for the main course and these, together with the bread, may bump the bill up. The room has a bright, fresh feel; all the furniture is imported from Italy.

Domaines Ott ★

L'infini pluriel

Route du Fort-de-Brégançon - 83250 La Londe-les-Maures - Tél. 33 (0)4 94 01 53 53
Fax 33 (0)4 94 01 53 54 - domaines-ott.com - ott.particuliers@domaines-ott.com

You've got the right address!

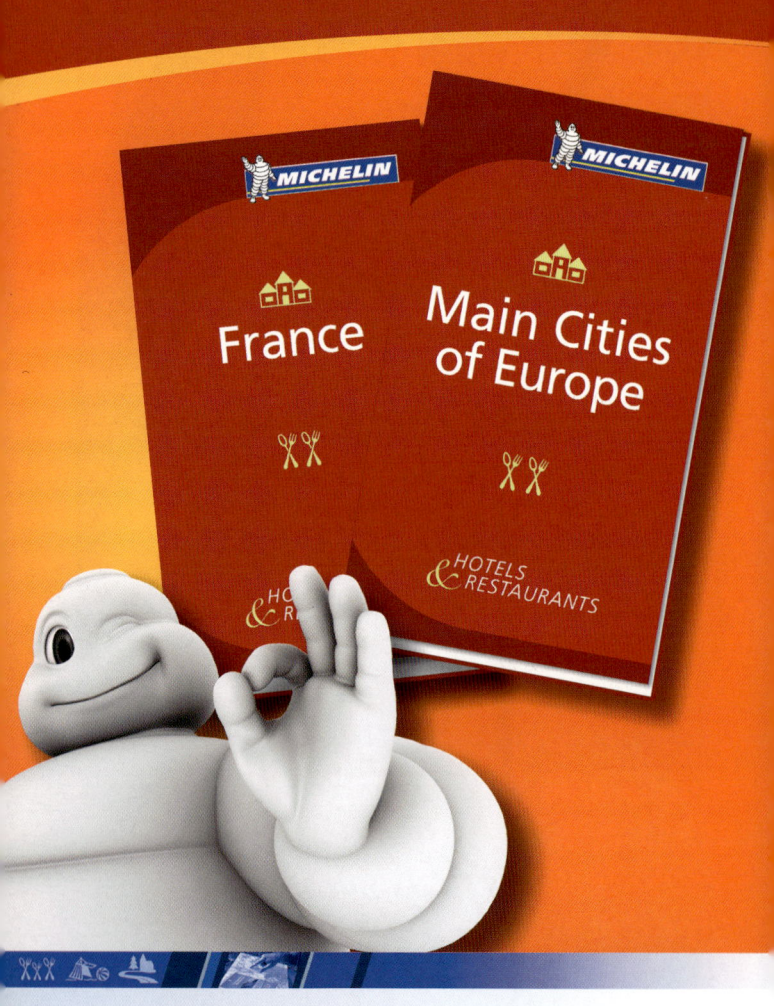

From palaces to bed and breakfast, from fine restaurants to small bistrots, the MICHELIN guide collection includes 45,000 hotels and restaurants selected by our inspectors in Europe and beyond. Wherever you may be, whatever your budget, you are sure you have the right address!

www.michelin.co.uk

MICHELIN
A better way forward

The Mercer

M3

Modern European XX

34 Threadneedle St ✉ EC2R 8AY ⊖ Bank
𝒞 (020) 7628 0001 **Fax** (020) 7588 2822 ▶ **Plan VIII**
e-mail info@themercer.co.uk Closed 25 December - 1 January,
www.themercer.co.uk Saturday, Sunday and Bank Holidays

Carte £29/50

A/C
⊗
VISA
MC
AE

The credit crunch means it's even less likely that a restaurant will ever be converted into a bank so, at the moment, the trend remains from bank to restaurant; here at The Mercer you can even see where the tellers used to sit. The high ceilings and windows let in plenty of light and the place has a pleasingly animated brasserie feel, with service that is slick and well paced. Open from breakfast, the kitchen concentrates on familiar flavours and comforting classics. While the cooking may not always live up to the promise of the menu, it is nonetheless satisfying. Scottish beef features in the Grill section and there are daily specials which could be corned beef hash or a fish pie. There's a huge choice of wines by the glass or carafe.

Vanilla Black

K2

Vegetarian XX

17-18 Tooks Court ✉ EC4A 1LB ⊖ Chancery Lane
𝒞 (020) 7242 2622 ▶ **Plan VIII**
www.vanillablack.co.uk Closed Saturday, Sunday and 2 weeks Christmas

Menu £23/30

A/C
VISA
MC
AE

Those who think vegetarian food is all nut cutlets and knitted muesli should get along to Vanilla Black. Run by a Teesside couple who had a restaurant of the same name in York, they prove that vegetarian food can be varied, flavoursome and filling. The room is neat but quite stark and crisp in its decoration; sufficient warmth comes from the owner and her team of waiting staff. The set priced menu represents fair value and the cooking displays sufficient originality and imagination. Certainly no one leaves hungry as the flavoursome dishes use liberal amounts of cheese and potato. This is a proper restaurant that could heal the wounds of any carnivore scarred in their youth by an unpleasant vegetarian experience.

Mint Leaf Lounge

M3

Indian

12 Angel Court, Lothbury ✉ EC2R 7HB
℘ (020) 7600 0992 **Fax** (020) 7600 6628
e-mail reservations@mintleaflounge.com
www.mintleaflounge.com

⊖ Bank
▶ **Plan VIII**
Closed 22 December-3 January,
Saturday lunch and Sunday

Menu £23 (lunch) – Carte £28/44

This was formerly NatWest's HQ and has been turned into a stylish and slick Indian restaurant. The bar is bigger and the dining area smaller than the original branch in St James's, but with the stock market the way it's been, you can't blame them for that. The menu cleverly allows for flexibility in that many of the dishes are available in both starter and main course size and the presentation on the plate is quite contemporary. The majority of influences come from the more southerly parts of India and dishes demonstrate genuine care in preparation. Fish, meat or vegetarian platters are available and there's a good value set lunch menu. Knowledgeable staff in ubiquitous black provide nicely paced service.

Oxo Tower Brasserie

K4

Modern European

(8th floor), Oxo Tower Wharf, Barge House St ✉ SE1 9PH
℘ (020) 7803 3888 **Fax** (020) 7803 3838
e-mail oxo.reservations@harveynichols.com
www.harveynichols.com

⊖ Southwark
▶ **Plan X**
Closed 24-26 December

Menu £25 (lunch) – Carte £39/50

If you find the prices in the Oxo Tower Restaurant rather vertiginous but still fancy eating somewhere with great views, then you have the Oxo Tower Brasserie: it's on the same floor and is markedly more fun. It's all enclosed in glass and its bustling atmosphere is enlivened with live music. It's a great place to entertain those new to the city and timing your arrival to coincide with the changing light at dusk is well worth it, especially if it's warm enough to sit out on the terrace. 'Brasserie' may describe the room but the dishes on offer are far from what traditionalists would call brasserie classics: the extensive menu is made up of dishes that range from classic Mediterranean to those influenced more by Thailand and Asia.

St John ✿

British

L2

26 St John St ⌂ EC1M 4AY
✆ (020) 7251 0848
Fax (020) 7251 4090
e-mail reservations@stjohnrestaurant.com
www.stjohnrestaurant.com

⊖ Barbican
▶ **Plan IX**

Closed Christmas, Easter, Saturday lunch,
Sunday and Bank Holidays
– booking essential

Carte £26/39

There has never been any doubt about the uniqueness and importance of St John: not only has it influenced countless numbers of chefs but it has always made us all feel good about our own culinary heritage. It now comes with the one thing that was always a little lacking – greater consistency. This was once a 19th century smokehouse and the bakery they have at the front adds a wonderfully welcoming aroma. The restaurant is bright and perennially packed – this is probably not the place for that romantic dinner à deux. Waiters wear chef jackets, which is appropriate as they know everything about the food they serve. That food is correctly summed up by their slogan 'nose to tail eating:' it's as seasonal as they come (the menu changes twice daily) and strong on offal, but also champions unusual cuts and unfamiliar, regional specialities. Flavours are intense and unsullied, thanks to the right union of ingredients and where else can a dozen people on one table share a whole suckling pig? St John reminds us what a physical pleasure eating can be.

First Course
- Brown shrimps and white cabbage.
- Lamb's tongues, green beans and shallots.

Main Course
- Venison liver and lentils.
- Smoked eel, bacon and mash.

Dessert
- Eccles cake and Lancashire cheese.
- Bread pudding and butterscotch sauce.

City of London • Clerkenwell • Finsbury • Southwark ▶ Plans VIII-IX-X

Blueprint Café

Modern European

N5

Design Museum, Shad Thames,
Butlers Wharf ✉ SE1 2YD
☏ (020) 7378 7031
Fax (020) 7357 8810
e-mail blueprintcafe@danddlondon.com www.danddlondon.com

⊖ London Bridge
▶ **Plan X**
Closed 24-27 December and Sunday dinner

Menu £20 – Carte £29/43

VISA MC AE ○

The first thing one notices is the great views of Tower Bridge and The Thames, which, thanks to the restaurant's raised position, are terrific - and on sunny days, the windows fully retract. The Blueprint Café forms an integral part of the Design Museum, which opened in 1989, and it enjoys its own shiny and sleek simplicity; the atmosphere is never less than breezy. The cooking is very much of the no-nonsense, what-you-read-is-what-you-get school and the long-standing chef uses flavours that are pronounced, sunny and seasonal. Dishes from his daily-changing menu, such as smoked eel with horseradish, veal with girolles and lemon posset, come with confident simplicity and, as a result, are easy to eat.

Tate Modern (Restaurant)

Modern European

L4

7th Floor, Tate Modern, Bankside
✉ SE1 9LS
☏ (020) 7401 5020
e-mail tate.modernrestaurant@tztc.org
www.tate.org.uk/modern/information/eating.htm

⊖ Southwark
▶ **Plan X**
Closed 25 December – lunch only and
dinner Friday-Saturday

Carte £24/35

VISA MC

Floor to ceiling windows on two sides and a large mural on a third allow light and colour to fill this large restaurant on the 7th floor of the Tate Modern and balance all that black. Even if you don't get a window table you'll still get a great view of St Paul's. There's seating for 145 but they stop taking reservations when they get to 100 to allow for the impulse diner. Lunch starts at 11.30 and ends at 3pm; there's every possibility of getting in but waiting at the bar is no hardship. The menu is an appealing mix of light, seasonal, fresh and zesty dishes, with a daily fish from Newlyn. The influences are mostly British, with the occasional Italian note. There's a good choice of wines by the glass and carafe as well as assorted soft drinks.

Cantina Del Ponte

N4

Italian

36c Shad Thames, Butlers Wharf ⊖ London Bridge
✉ SE1 2YE ▶ **Plan X**
✆ (020) 7403 5403 **Fax** (020) 7940 1845 Closed 24-26 December
e-mail cantina@danddlondon.com www.danddlondon.com

Menu £18 (lunch)/15 – Carte approx. £25

A refurbishment late in 2007 made this Italian stalwart a little darker and more atmospheric, although they've kept the mural; the best tables on a summer's day remain those on the riverside terrace under the bright orange awning. The menu has also been tweaked: it's out with the pizzas and in with a greater degree of authenticity. The focus is on appealing and flavoursome dishes and the set menu, which is available until 7pm, represents very good value. The à la carte offers an appealing selection, from recognisable standards to others displaying greater originality. Those flavours are well defined and portions are bigger than expected. The wine list covers all of Italy and there's a good choice by the glass.

Moro

K1

Mediterranean

34-36 Exmouth Market ✉ EC1R 4QE ⊖ Farringdon
✆ (020) 7833 8336 **Fax** (020) 7833 9338 ▶ **Plan IX**
e-mail info@moro.co.uk Closed Easter, Christmas,
www.moro.co.uk Sunday and Bank Holidays – booking essential

Carte £29/35

Despite being a feature of Exmouth market for over a decade, Moro remains one of the busiest restaurants around, but anyone left frustrated by not getting a table should consider just pitching up and sitting at the zinc-topped bar: it's a great spot for tapas and some wonderful sherries, you'll get the full benefit of the wondrous aromas from the open kitchen and be able to watch the chefs in action. Moorish cooking is the draw which means Spain and the Muslim Mediterranean. The wood-burning oven and charcoal grill provide the smokiness and charring to improve and enhance the poultry, meat and sourdough bread. The cooking is colourful and invigorating and the menu changes fully every two weeks.

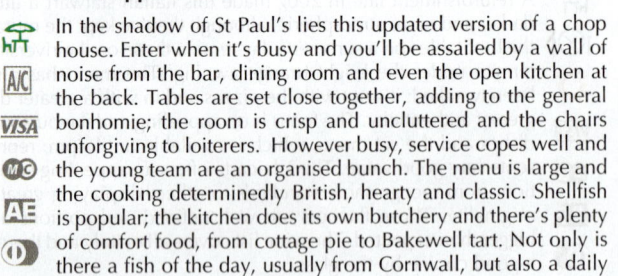

Paternoster Chop House

British

L3

Warwick Court, Paternoster Square ⊖ St Paul's
✉ EC4N 7DX ▶ **Plan VIII**
☏ (020) 7029 9400 Closed 10 days Christmas,
Fax (020) 7029 9409 dinner Sunday, Saturday and Bank Holidays
e-mail paternosterr@danddlondon.com **www**.danddlondon.com

Carte approx. £30

In the shadow of St Paul's lies this updated version of a chop house. Enter when it's busy and you'll be assailed by a wall of noise from the bar, dining room and even the open kitchen at the back. Tables are set close together, adding to the general bonhomie; the room is crisp and uncluttered and the chairs unforgiving to loiterers. However busy, service copes well and the young team are an organised bunch. The menu is large and the cooking determinedly British, hearty and classic. Shellfish is popular; the kitchen does its own butchery and there's plenty of comfort food, from cottage pie to Bakewell tart. Not only is there a fish of the day, usually from Cornwall, but also a daily beast, such as Galloway beef.

Cantina Vinopolis

International

L4

No.1 Bank End ✉ SE1 9BU ⊖ London Bridge
☏ (020) 7940 8333 **Fax** (020) 7089 9339 ▶ **Plan X**
e-mail cantina@vinopolis.co.uk Closed Sunday dinner and Bank Holidays
www.cantinavinopolis.com

Menu £30 – Carte £23/34

Southwark is becoming something of a Utopia for today's gastronauts. Food supplies can be garnered at the wonderful Borough Market and oenologists will find relief and fulfilment at Vinopolis, the wine merchant and museum. Cantina Vinopolis is the wine attraction's public restaurant and is housed under vast, magnificent Victorian arches that lend a palpable sense of history and atmospherics to the whole place. The exposed kitchen offers a menu that flits between continents and, as one would expect, the wine list offers an interesting and correspondingly diverse selection with many well priced bottles. The styling and comforts are simple and uncomplicated and the service is smoothly effective.

Butlers Wharf Chop House

British

N4

36e Shad Thames, Butlers Wharf
✉ SE1 2YE
✆ (020) 7403 3403 **Fax** (020) 7940 1855
e-mail bwchophouse@danddlondon.com
www.danddlondon.com

⊖ London Bridge
▶ **Plan X**
Closed 1-2 January

Menu £26 – Carte £26/38

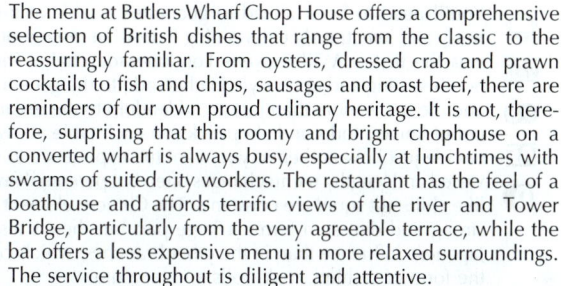

The menu at Butlers Wharf Chop House offers a comprehensive selection of British dishes that range from the classic to the reassuringly familiar. From oysters, dressed crab and prawn cocktails to fish and chips, sausages and roast beef, there are reminders of our own proud culinary heritage. It is not, therefore, surprising that this roomy and bright chophouse on a converted wharf is always busy, especially at lunchtimes with swarms of suited city workers. The restaurant has the feel of a boathouse and affords terrific views of the river and Tower Bridge, particularly from the very agreeable terrace, while the bar offers a less expensive menu in more relaxed surroundings. The service throughout is diligent and attentive.

Vinoteca

Modern European

L2

7 St John St ✉ EC1M 4AA
✆ (020) 7253 8786 **Fax** (020) 7490 4282
e-mail enquiries@vinoteca.co.uk
www.vinoteca.co.uk

⊖ Farringdon
▶ **Plan IX**
Closed Christmas-New Year,
Sunday and Bank Holidays
– booking essential at lunch

Carte £25/30

'Think of a number, double it and add ten' seems to be how most wines are marked up these days. This makes it even more refreshing to find a place like Vinoteca, where the wine comes at realistic and reasonable prices and the choice is both varied and innovative. Vinoteca calls itself a 'Bar, Wine Shop and Kitchen' and it does all three things well. At dinner you order at the bar from a subtly southern European influenced menu where each dish is paired with a recommended wine; table service is provided at lunch which is a far busier time. But the wine is the king here and those who haven't set foot in anything remotely resembling a 'wine bar' since its apotheosis or nadir (depending on your viewpoint) in the 1980s should think again.

Cicada

Asian

L1

132-136 St John St ✉ EC1V 4JT ⊖ Farringdon
℘ (020) 7608 1550 ▶ **Plan IX**
Fax (020) 8608 1551 Closed 23 December-3 January, Saturday lunch,
e-mail cicada@rickerrestaurants.com Sunday and Bank Holidays
www.rickerrestaurants.com

Menu £15 (lunch)/50 – Carte £15/30

You'll need to book ahead to guarantee a table at this busy, noisy and infectiously entertaining Pan Asian restaurant, which was the first in Will Ricker's London-wide chain. The semi-booth seating and open style kitchen add to the general drama and the bar is more than just an addendum to the restaurant. A pot of knives, forks and chopsticks on each table allow you to decide just how authentic you want the experience to be. The varied and lengthy menu changes often but perennial favourites like chilli salt squid are constants. The Chinese element is quite strong and dim sum forms a large part but there's also more Japanese influence than in the other branches, which comes in the form of sashimi, maki rolls and tempura.

The Ambassador

Traditional

K1

55 Exmouth Market ✉ EC1R 4QL ⊖ Farringdon
℘ (020) 7837 0009 ▶ **Plan IX**
e-mail clive@theambassadorcafe.co.uk Closed 24 December-2 January,
www.theambassadorcafe.co.uk Sunday dinner and Bank Holidays

Menu £16 (lunch) – Carte £19/31

Despite some serious competition in the immediate area of Exmouth Market, The Ambassador is holding its own by being true to its principles. These include using carefully sourced and seasonally pertinent ingredients and offering a daily changing menu to reflect what's available. This honesty is reflected in the cooking which is gutsy and satisfying with flavours lasting and true, whether that's slow-cooked mutton or roasted halibut. The place also gives the customers what they want, which is a relaxed, all-day operation where they can meet up over waffles or drop by for bacon sandwiches first thing. The understated and knowingly retro décor – less spit 'n' sawdust, more languor 'n' lino – provides fitting surroundings.

Medcalf

British

K1

40 Exmouth Market ✉ EC1R 4QE
✆ (020) 7833 3533 **Fax** (020) 7833 1321
e-mail mail@medcalfbar.co.uk
www.medcalfbar.co.uk

⊖ Farringdon
▶ **Plan IX**
Closed 24 December-2 January,
Sunday dinner and Bank Holidays
– booking essential

Carte £26/35

There is something very 'proper' about Medcalf: maybe that's the no-frills décor that celebrates the original butcher's shop that was here from 1912 (the lights are held up by meat hooks); maybe it's the loud and buzzy pub-like atmosphere, with the good range of draught beers, wines by the glass and assorted snacks or maybe it's the fresh, appealing and very seasonal British cooking, with dishes like Barnsley chop or Calves liver, which has a satisfyingly robust, masculine feel to it. Whatever it is, it works, as the restaurant gets very busy, very quickly. Those who think jellies and foams should only be found at children's playtime rather than on a dinner plate will find much to celebrate here at Medcalf.

Magdalen

British

M4

152 Tooley St ✉ SE1 2TU
✆ (020) 7403 1342
Fax (020) 7403 9950
e-mail info@magdalenrestaurant.co.uk
www.magdalenrestaurant.co.uk

⊖ London Bridge
▶ **Plan X**
Closed last 2 weeks August,
1 week Christmas,
Saturday lunch and Sunday

Menu £19 (lunch) – Carte £28/45

How you pronounce it may depend on your education, but what is certain is that Magdalen is an appealing addition to this part of town. Owned by a triumvirate of chefs, the place is divided between two floors (no bookings are taken on the ground floor) and has the look of a French brasserie about it. The cooking, however, looks closer to home for influence; what you read is, laudably, what you get, and you'll find hugely appealing words like 'roast', 'potted' and 'dripping' appearing regularly. This is all about being fancy-free and full of flavour; there's still the odd Gallic flavour but even the snails come with a nettle soup. There are also dishes made for two, like whole calves kidney or custard tart. Service is pitched just right.

Hix Oyster and Chop House

British

L2

36-37 Greenhill Rents ⊠ EC1M 6BN — Farringdon
📞 (0207) 017 1930 ▶ **Plan IX**
Fax (0207) 017 1931 Closed Saturday lunch and Sunday dinner
e-mail chophouse@restaurantsetcltd.co.uk
www.restaurantsetcltd.com

Carte £24/62

Utilitarian surroundings, seasonal British ingredients, plenty of offal and prissy-free cooking: this may sound like a description of St John but is in fact the solo venture of Mark Hix, the chef who made The Ivy more than just a celebrity love-in. Smithfield Market seems an appropriate location for a restaurant that not only celebrates Britain's culinary heritage with old classics like rabbit brawn, nettle soup and beef and oyster pie but also reminds us of our own natural bounty, from sand eels and asparagus, whiting to laver bread. It's also called an Oyster & Chop House for a reason, with four types of oyster on offer as well as plenty of meat, including Aberdeen beef aged for 28 days and served on the bone.

The Modern Pantry 😊

International

L2

47-48 St John's Sq ⊠ EC1V 4JJ — Farringdon
📞 (020) 7250 0833 ▶ **Plan IX**
e-mail enquiries@themodernpantry.co.uk Closed Christmas-New Year and
www.themodernpantry.co.uk Bank Holidays – booking advisable

Carte £25/32

Summer 2008 saw Anna Hansen, formerly of The Providores, open her first restaurant in a Georgian building that's been everything from a foundry to a carpentry workshop. Bold and zingy flavours full of vitality are the hallmarks of her cooking; its roots are fusion but tempered with an understanding of when to leave alone. The small plates, such as chorizo and feta fritters, are perfectly formed nibbles and full-bodied main courses like the rabbit stew can pack an unexpected chilli punch. Earl Grey or rosewater provide original flavours to desserts. The communal feel and café style of the ground floor is the best place to be; the atmosphere upstairs is a little more restrained and there are plans for it to have a separate menu.

Comptoir Gascon

French

K2

61-63 Charterhouse St ⊠ EC1M 6HJ
℘ (020) 7608 0851 **Fax** (020) 7608 0871
e-mail info@comptoirgascon.com
www.comptoirgascon.com

⊖ Barbican
▶ **Plan IX**
Closed Christmas-New Year,
Sunday and Monday

Carte £20/32

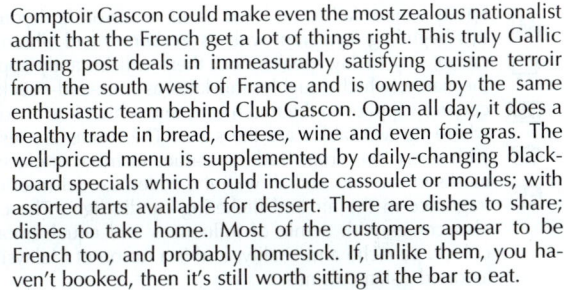

A/C
VISA
MC
AE

Comptoir Gascon could make even the most zealous nationalist admit that the French get a lot of things right. This truly Gallic trading post deals in immeasurably satisfying cuisine terroir from the south west of France and is owned by the same enthusiastic team behind Club Gascon. Open all day, it does a healthy trade in bread, cheese, wine and even foie gras. The well-priced menu is supplemented by daily-changing blackboard specials which could include cassoulet or moules; with assorted tarts available for dessert. There are dishes to share; dishes to take home. Most of the customers appear to be French too, and probably homesick. If, unlike them, you haven't booked, then it's still worth sitting at the bar to eat.

Quality Chop House

British

K1

94 Farringdon Rd ⊠ EC1R 3EA
℘ (020) 7837 5093 **Fax** (020) 7833 8748
e-mail enquiries@qualitychophouse.co.uk
www.qualitychophouse.co.uk

⊖ Farringdon
▶ **Plan IX**
Closed 25-26 December,
1 January and Saturday lunch

Carte £21/38

A/C
🕑
☼
VISA
MC
AE

This late 19C chop house, with the words 'Progressive working class caterer' etched into the window, goes some way to dispelling this idea that serving classic British food in simple surroundings is some sort of ground-breaking new development. The straightforward decoration of benches, booths and tiling fits perfectly with the menu of some of Britain's greatest culinary hits. Granted, there may be the occasional Frenchie gatecrasher but how can snails or fish soup compare to jellied eels or potted shrimps? Just stick to the liver and bacon, the Cumberland sausage or the steak and kidney pie, feel proud of the sauce bottles on the table and you'll leave with thoughts of buying a bulldog and a cigar on the way home.

Champor-Champor

Asian ✕

M5

62-64 Weston St ✉ SE1 3QJ
✆ (020) 7403 4600
e-mail mail@champor-champor.com
www.champor-champor.com

⊖ London Bridge
▶ **Plan X**
Closed Easter, 1 week Christmas and Sunday – booking essential – dinner only

Menu £24/30 – Carte £28/36

A/C
🍽
VISA
MC
AE

Spirits cannot fail to be lifted as soon as you find yourself in this beguiling restaurant with its exuberant and vibrant decoration; any Malay speakers out there will instantly appreciate the name, which roughly translates as 'mix-and-match'. That certainly applies to the two rooms into which it is divided and where no two tables are the same. The rooms are festooned with everything from Buddha statues to tribal artefacts, from masks to carvings and all with the added exoticism of incense fragrance in the air and flickering candle light. The cooking also comes with a mix of influences and equal amounts of colour, panache and vitality, and is a fusion of Malaysian and assorted Asian cuisines.

Tapas Brindisa

Spanish ✕

M4

18-20 Southwark St, Borough Market ✉ SE1 1TJ
✆ (020) 7357 8880
e-mail office@tapasbrindisa.com
www.brindisa.com

⊖ London Bridge
▶ **Plan X**
Closed 25-26 December, 1 January, Sunday and Bank Holidays – bookings not accepted

Carte £12/37

VISA
MC
AE

As in Spain, you have the option of standing or sitting for your tapas. The bar is a great place for a glass of Fino while you watch the acorn-fed Iberian charcuterie being sliced, and the list of hot and cold tapas is extensive, from cured fish and speciality cheeses to grilled chorizo and sautéed chicken livers. It all happens on the edge of Borough Market in what was once a potato warehouse; the owners spent years importing Spanish produce so they know what they're talking about. With its tightly packed tables and convivial atmosphere, it does get very busy and as they don't take reservations, be prepared to wait; if they are full then ask nicely and you can put your name down and then wander around the market.

Wright Brothers

Seafood

L4

11 Stoney St, Borough Market
✉ SE1 9AD
☏ (020) 7403 9554
Fax (020) 7403 9558
e-mail reservations@wrightbros.eu.com **www**.wrightbros.eu.com

⊖ London Bridge
▶ **Plan X**
Closed Sunday, Christmas and Bank Holidays

Carte £22/35

This started life as an oyster wholesaler and then developed around the theme of an oyster and porter house – porter, or dark ale, being the traditional accompaniment to oysters. The range of oysters is huge; they come from all over the world and are served either in their natural state or cooked in a variety of classic ways. Accompanying them is a range of prime shellfish, from winkles and crab to whelks and razor clams, as well as a handful of prepared dishes like fish pie. There's a shellfish barbecue on Saturdays. Don't expect chips or any type of potato – the oyster is the main event and full marks for that. And there's no dessert, except for cheese and truffles. Decoratively, it's equally no-nonsense and the atmosphere is all the better for it.

Village East

Modern European

M5

171 Bermondsey St ✉ SE1 3UW
☏ (020) 7357 6082 **Fax** (020) 7403 3360
e-mail info@villageeast.co.uk
www.villageeast.co.uk

⊖ London Bridge
▶ **Plan X**
Closed 25-26 December

Menu £15 (lunch) – Carte £23/34

Clever name - sounds a bit downtown Manhattan. But while Bermondsey may not be London's East Village, what Village East does is give this part of town a bit more 'neighbour' and a little less 'hood'. It's tricky to find so look for the glass façade and you'll find yourself in one of the bars, still wondering if you've come to the right place. Once, though, you've seen the open kitchen you know the dining area's not far away. Wood, brick, vents and large circular lamps give it that warehouse aesthetic. The menu is laid out a little confusingly but what you get is ample portions of familiar bistro style food, as well as some interesting combinations. The separately priced side dishes are not really needed and can push the bill up.

Brew Wharf

Traditional

Brew Wharf Yard, Stoney St
✉ SE1 9AD
✆ (020) 7378 6601
Fax (020) 7940 5997
e-mail brewwharf@vinopolis.co.uk www.brewwharf.com

⊖ London Bridge
▶ **Plan X**
Closed Christmas-New Year and Sunday dinner

Menu £26 – Carte £19/29

If you've been fighting the crowds at Borough Market and don't fancy eating on the hoof or queuing for a table then head over to Brew Wharf; it's conveniently located just around the corner under the railway arches. It's a bar, restaurant and micro brewery combined, so there should be something that appeals. These beers, along with an extensive range of imported bottles, prove to be the main draw for many, especially the weekday after-work crowd, and the menu, which doubles as a place mat, provides just the right sort of no-nonsense food you'll fancy when you've got a beer in your hand. These include rotisserie dishes such as marinated whole or half chickens, rib-eye steak sandwiches, Caesar salads and pints of prawns.

Canteen

British

Southbank Centre, Belvedere Rd
✉ SE1 8XX
✆ (0845) 686 1122
e-mail rth@canteen.co.uk www.canteen.co.uk

⊖ Waterloo
▶ **Plan III**
Closed 25 December and 1 January

Carte £35/40

The area around the Royal Festival Hall is rapidly becoming a new cultural and social hub, although it looks like all the chain restaurants have got in quickly. Fortunately, in amongst the plethora of brands sits The Canteen, which adopts the same principles as the first Canteen in Spitalfields: it offers classic British food, from daily roasts to assorted pies, potted shrimps to fish and chips; and that great British institution of breakfast is served all day. Desserts may include treacle tart, Eton mess or jelly and prices are kept reasonable. There are booths and shared refectory tables, as well as a large terrace but it's sadly not on the river side. At busy times, service can sometimes struggle to keep up.

The Anchor & Hope 🐶

Gastropub

K4

36 The Cut
✉ SE1 8LP
☏ (020) 7928 9898
Fax (020) 7928 4595
e-mail anchorandhope@btconnect.com

⊖ Southwark.
▶ **Plan X**
Closed 2 weeks at Christmas, Easter,
May Bank Holidays, last 2 weeks in August
– bookings not accepted

Menu £30 – Carte £20/35

The Anchor & Hope is always understandably busy, due to some degree to its proximity to both Vic theatres, but mostly because of its culinary reputation. The fact that they don't take reservations means that it's worth getting here early - in fact very early - to secure a table, although if you're willing to share, you'll be seated sooner. From the tiny kitchen comes forth immensely satisfying dishes, in a rustic and earthy style, drawing on influences from St John in Islington, but at prices which make the queuing worth it. Menu descriptions are understated but infinitely appealing: crab on toast, grilled razor clams, rare roast venison with duck fat potato cake, beef on dripping toast and seven hour lamb shoulder.

The Coach & Horses

Gastropub

K1

26-28 Ray St ✉ EC1R 3DJ
☏ (020) 7278 8990 **Fax** (020) 7278 1478
e-mail info@thecoachandhorses.com
www.thecoachandhorses.com

⊖ Farringdon
▶ **Plan IX**
Closed Christmas to New Year,
Easter weekend, Bank Holidays

Carte £22/28

The Coach and Horses may have a palpable sense of its own Victorian heritage but it's still moving with the times. A recent refreshment of the dining room has turned it into a very pleasant environment. Here, the menu is a reflection of the self-taught chef's enthusiasm for all things European, especially its sunnier Mediterranean parts. There are Spanish and Italian influences aplenty, with everything from osso bucco to polenta, chorizo to chilled soups. But our own British contribution to cuisine is not forgotten, especially in the bar where the appealing list of snacks includes Scotch eggs with mustard - surely a near perfect accompaniment to a pint. Any summer warmth provokes a stampede for the enclosed decked yard.

The Hartley

Gastropub

M6

64 Tower Bridge Road ✉ SE1 4TR
☎ (020) 7394 7023
e-mail enquiries@thehartley.com
www.thehartley.com

⊖ Borough.
▶ **Plan X**
Closed 25-26 December and Bank Holidays

Carte £20/27

A/C ☼ VISA MC AE ①

There may not be too much local competition to fight off but The Hartley still makes an effort in flying the local gastro-pub flag. This red-bricked Victorian pub is also doing its bit to remember the diminishing local heritage by honouring, in name and decoration, the Hartley Jam Factory which once stood opposite and is now, predictably, a residential development. There are original posters, black and white photos and even jars of jam scattered around the place. The open plan kitchen produces robust and appetite-satisfying food from the commendably concise menu, supplemented by daily-changing blackboard specials. Service is relaxed and cool headed. The locals of this parish are clearly taken with The Hartley.

The Peasant

Gastropub

L1

240 St John St ✉ EC1V 4PH
☎ (020) 7336 7726 **Fax** (020) 7490 1089
e-mail gapsbairs@aol.com
www.thepeasant.co.uk

⊖ Farringdon
▶ **Plan IX**
Closed 25 December to 3 January
– booking essential

Menu £14/18 – Carte £25/40

☼ VISA MC AE

Originally called the George & Dragon, it changed to The Peasant to celebrate Wat Tyler's revolting ones of 1381 who gathered near this spot. However, what really made the name of this classic Victorian pub was its being in the vanguard of the original gastro-pub movement. The busy ground floor bar, with its tiles, arched windows, high ceiling and mosaics is a great place for some heartening fare, from sausage and mash to plates of charcuterie or meze, to go with your beer. Upstairs, it's more your proper restaurant experience with decoration courtesy of a fairground/circus theme and a more formal feel. Here, you'll find a degree of originality in the cooking, but the kitchen is at its best when it keeps things relatively simple.

The Well

L1

Gastropub

180 St John St ⊠ EC1V 4JY
✆ (020) 7251 9363 **Fax** (020) 7253 9683
e-mail drink@downthewell.co.uk
www.downthewell.co.uk

⊖ Farringdon
▶ **Plan IX**
Closed 25-26 December

Carte £23/30

A fairly frenetic atmosphere is guaranteed at The Well as it's quite small inside and the locals clearly rather like the place. It has built its reputation on giving the menu just the right balance and level of sophistication, so that you can order a pint of prawns or something a little more ambitious like saffron risotto or one of the daily specials. The sliding screen windows let in the light and the wooden floorboards and exposed brick walls add to the atmosphere of a committed metropolitan pub. The benches outside are popular, particularly with those who don't mind a side order of CO_2 with their beer. Downstairs you'll find an altogether sexier bar, complete with fish tank, which is available for private hire - the bar, not the tank.

The Garrison

M5

Gastropub

99-101 Bermondsey St
⊠ SE1 3XB
✆ (020) 7089 9355
e-mail info@thegarrison.co.uk
www.thegarrison.co.uk

⊖ London Bridge
▶ **Plan X**
Closed 25-26 December, 1 January
– booking essential at dinner

Carte £28/45

Close to the owners' other place, Village East, sits The Garrison, part shabby-chic gastropub, part boho brasserie. The pub's full of bustle and life and the ideal venue for meeting up with friends, especially if you can snare one of the booths. If you're an even bigger party then consider hiring the downstairs room which doubles as a mini cinema. There's a refreshing wholesomeness to the cooking; there are blackboard specials, everything's homemade except for the quince paste which comes with the cheese and the menu changes every eight weeks. Dishes display this no-nonsense approach by being full in flavour and decent in size, whether that's a meatloaf with purple sprouting broccoli or a smoked haddock with bubble and squeak.

Chelsea · Earl's Court · Hyde Park · Knightsbridge · South Kensington

Though its days of unbridled hedonism are long gone - and its 'alternative' tag is more closely aligned to property prices than counter-culture - there's still a hip feel to **Chelsea.** The place that put the Swinging into London has grown grey, distinguished and rather placid over the years, but tourists still throng to the **King's Road,** albeit to shop at the chain stores which have steadily muscled out SW3's chi-chi boutiques. It's not so easy now to imagine the heady mix of clans that used to sashay along here, from Sixties mods and models to Seventies punks, but for practically a quarter of a century, from the moment in 1955 when Mary Quant opened her trend-setting Bazaar, this was the pavement to parade down.

Chelsea's most cutting-edge destination these days is probably the gallery of modern art that bears the name of Margaret Thatcher's former favourite, Charles Saatchi. Which isn't the only irony, as Saatchi's outlandishly modish exhibits are housed in a one-time military barracks, the Duke of York's headquarters. Nearby, the traffic careers round **Sloane Square,** but it's almost possible to distance yourself from the fumes by sitting amongst the shady bowers in the centre of the square, or watching the world go by from a prime position in one of many cafés. Having said that, *the* place to get away from it all, and yet still be within striking distance of the King's Road, is the delightful **Physic Garden,** down by the river. Famous for its healing herbs for over 300 years, it's England's second oldest botanic garden.

Mind you, if the size of a green space is more important to you than its medicinal qualities, then you need to head up to **Hyde Park,** the city's biggest. Expansive enough to accommodate trotting horses on Rotten Row, swimmers and rowers in the Serpentine, up-to-the-minute art exhibitions at the Serpentine Gallery, and ranting individualists at Speakers' Corner, the park has also held within its borders thousands of rock fans for concerts by the likes of the Rolling Stones, Simon and Garfunkel and Pink Floyd.

Just across from its southern border stands one of London's most imperious sights, The **Royal Albert Hall,** gateway to the cultural hotspot that is South Kensington. Given its wings after the 1851 Great Exhibition, the area round **Cromwell Road** invested heavily in culture and learning, in the shape of three world famous museums and three heavyweight colleges. But one of its most intriguing museums is little known to visitors, even though it's only a few metres east of the Albert Hall: the Sikorski is, by turns, a moving and spectacular showpiece for all things Polish.

No one would claim to be moved by the exhibits on show in nearby **Knightsbridge,** but there are certainly spectacular credit card transactions made here. The twin retail shrines of Harvey Nichols and Harrods are the proverbial honey-pots to the tourist bee, where a 'credit crunch' means you've accidentally trodden on your visa. Between them, in **Sloane Street,** the world's most famous retail names line up like an A-lister's who's who. At the western end of Knightsbridge is the rich person's Catholic church of choice, the Brompton Oratory, an unerringly lavish concoction in a baroque Italianate style. Behind it is the enchanting Ennismore Gardens Mews, a lovely thoroughfare that dovetails rather well with the Oratory.

Further west along Old Brompton Road is **Earl's Court,** an area of grand old houses turned into bedsits and spartan hotels. An oddly bewitching contrast sits side by side here, the old resting alongside the new. The old in this case is Brompton Cemetery, an enchanting wilderness of monuments wherein lie the likes of Samuel Cunard and Emmeline Pankhurst. At its southwest corner, incongruously, sits the new, insomuch as it's the home of a regular influx of newcomers from abroad, who are young, gifted and possessed of vast incomes: the players of Chelsea FC.

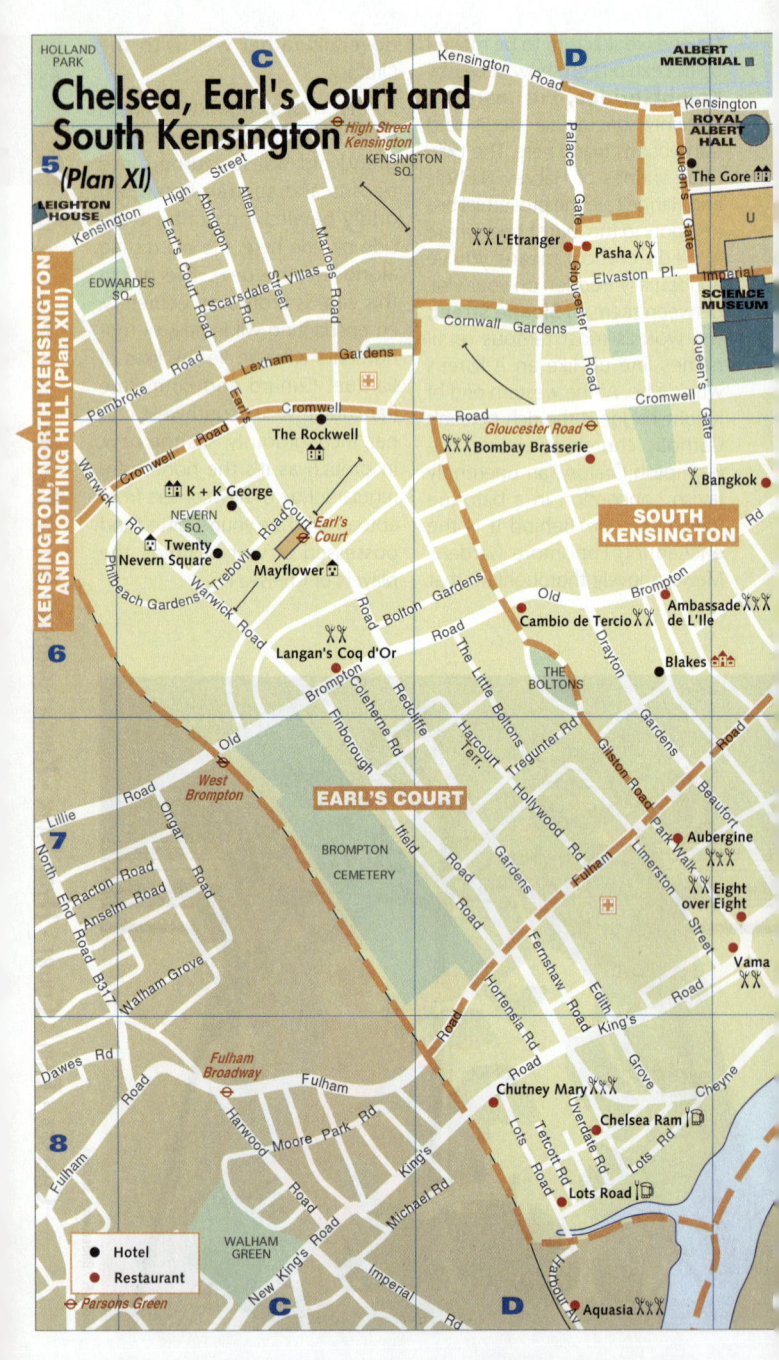

Chelsea, Earl's Court and South Kensington
(Plan XI)

KENSINGTON, NORTH KENSINGTON AND NOTTING HILL (Plan XIII)

HOLLAND PARK
LEIGHTON HOUSE
EDWARDES SQ.
KENSINGTON SQ.
High Street Kensington
Kensington Road
ALBERT MEMORIAL
ROYAL ALBERT HALL
The Gore
L'Etranger
Pasha
SCIENCE MUSEUM
Cornwall Gardens
Lexham Gardens
Cromwell Road
Gloucester Road
The Rockwell
Bombay Brasserie
K + K George
NEVERN SQ.
Twenty Nevern Square
Mayflower
Earl's Court
Bangkok
SOUTH KENSINGTON
Cambio de Tercio
Ambassade de L'Ile
Langan's Coq d'Or
THE BOLTONS
Blakes
West Brompton
EARL'S COURT
BROMPTON CEMETERY
Aubergine
Eight over Eight
Vama
Fulham Broadway
Chutney Mary
Chelsea Ram
Lots Road
WALHAM GREEN
Parsons Green
Aquasia

- ● Hotel
- ● Restaurant

212

Chelsea Map

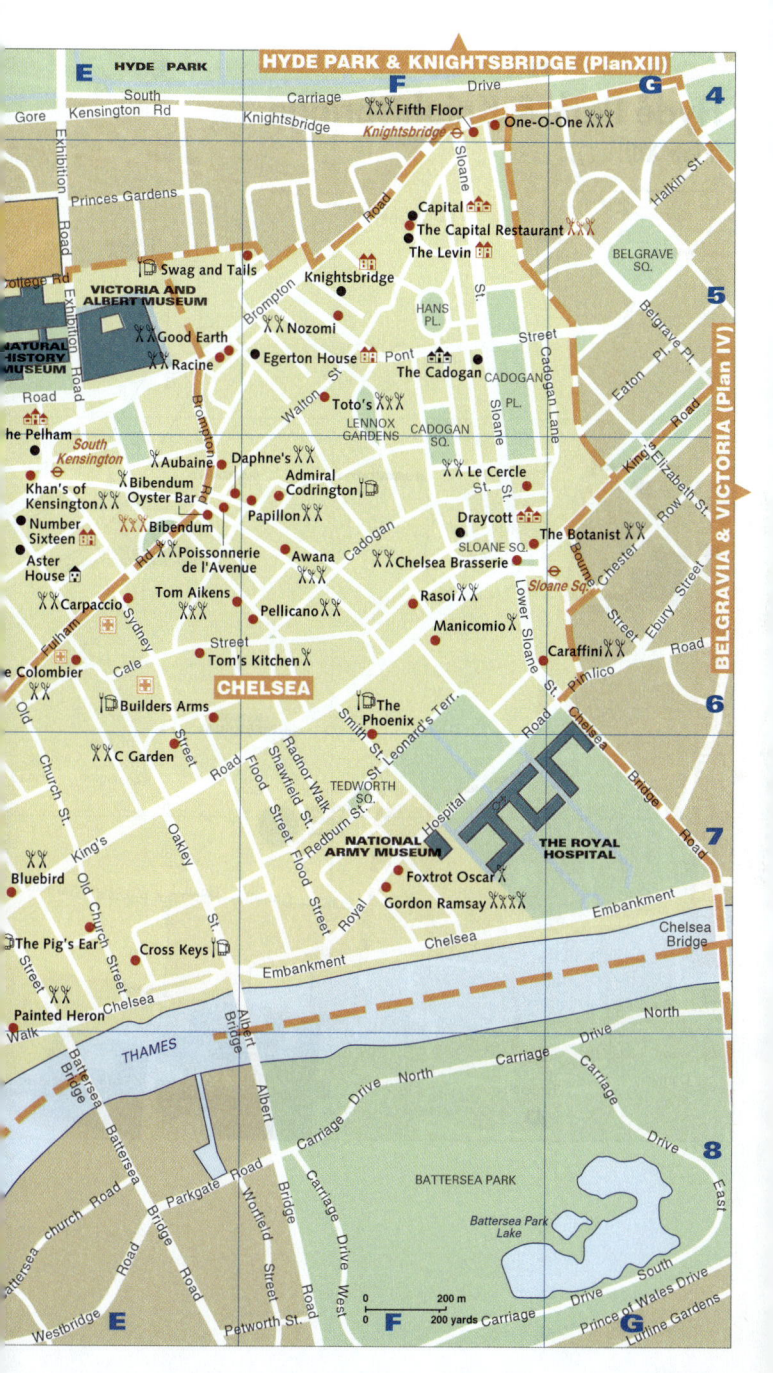

Grid E4–G4 (North, Hyde Park & Knightsbridge area):
- HYDE PARK
- HYDE PARK & KNIGHTSBRIDGE (Plan XII)
- South Carriage Drive
- Gore / Kensington Rd / Knightsbridge / Sloane St
- Fifth Floor
- Knightsbridge (station)
- One-O-One

Grid E5–G5:
- Exhibition Road
- Princes Gardens
- College Rd
- VICTORIA AND ALBERT MUSEUM
- NATURAL HISTORY MUSEUM
- Swag and Tails
- Capital
- The Capital Restaurant
- The Levin
- BELGRAVE SQ.
- Halkin St.
- Belgrave
- Knightsbridge
- Brompton Road
- Good Earth
- Racine
- Nozomi
- HANS PL.
- Egerton House
- Pont
- The Cadogan
- CADOGAN
- Eaton Pl.
- Elizabeth St.
- King's Road
- Walton St.
- Toto's
- LENNOX GARDENS
- CADOGAN PL.
- Sloane St.
- Cadogan Lane

Grid E6–G6:
- he Pelham
- South Kensington
- Aubaine
- Daphne's
- Admiral Codrington
- Le Cercle
- Khan's of Kensington
- Bibendum Oyster Bar
- Papillon
- Draycott
- The Botanist
- Number Sixteen
- Bibendum
- Awana
- SLOANE SQ.
- Chester
- Aster House
- Poissonnerie de l'Avenue
- Cadogan
- Chelsea Brasserie
- Sloane Sq. (station)
- Row St.
- Ebury St.
- Carpaccio
- Tom Aikens
- Pellicano
- Rasoi
- Fulham Road
- Sydney St.
- Manicomio
- Lower Sloane St.
- Caraffini
- e Colombier
- Cale Street
- Tom's Kitchen
- Pimlico Road
- Old Church St.
- Builders Arms
- CHELSEA
- The Phoenix
- Smith St.
- St. Leonard's Terr.

Grid E7–G7:
- C Garden
- King's Road
- Radnor Walk
- Shawfield St.
- Redburn St.
- Flood St.
- Royal Hospital Road
- TEDWORTH SQ.
- NATIONAL ARMY MUSEUM
- THE ROYAL HOSPITAL
- Chelsea Bridge Road
- Bluebird
- Oakley St.
- Foxtrot Oscar
- Gordon Ramsay
- Chelsea Bridge
- The Pig's Ear
- Cross Keys
- Chelsea Embankment
- Painted Heron
- Cheyne Walk

Grid E8–G8:
- THAMES
- Battersea Bridge
- Albert Bridge
- Carriage Drive North
- Chelsea Bridge
- North Carriage Drive
- Battersea church Road
- Parkgate Road
- Bridge Road
- Worfield St.
- Carriage Drive West
- Westbridge Road
- Petworth St.
- BATTERSEA PARK
- Battersea Park Lake
- South Carriage Drive
- East Carriage Drive
- Prince of Wales Drive
- Lurline Gardens

0 200 m / 0 200 yards

BELGRAVIA & VICTORIA (Plan IV)

213

Hyde Park & Knightsbridge
(Plan XII)

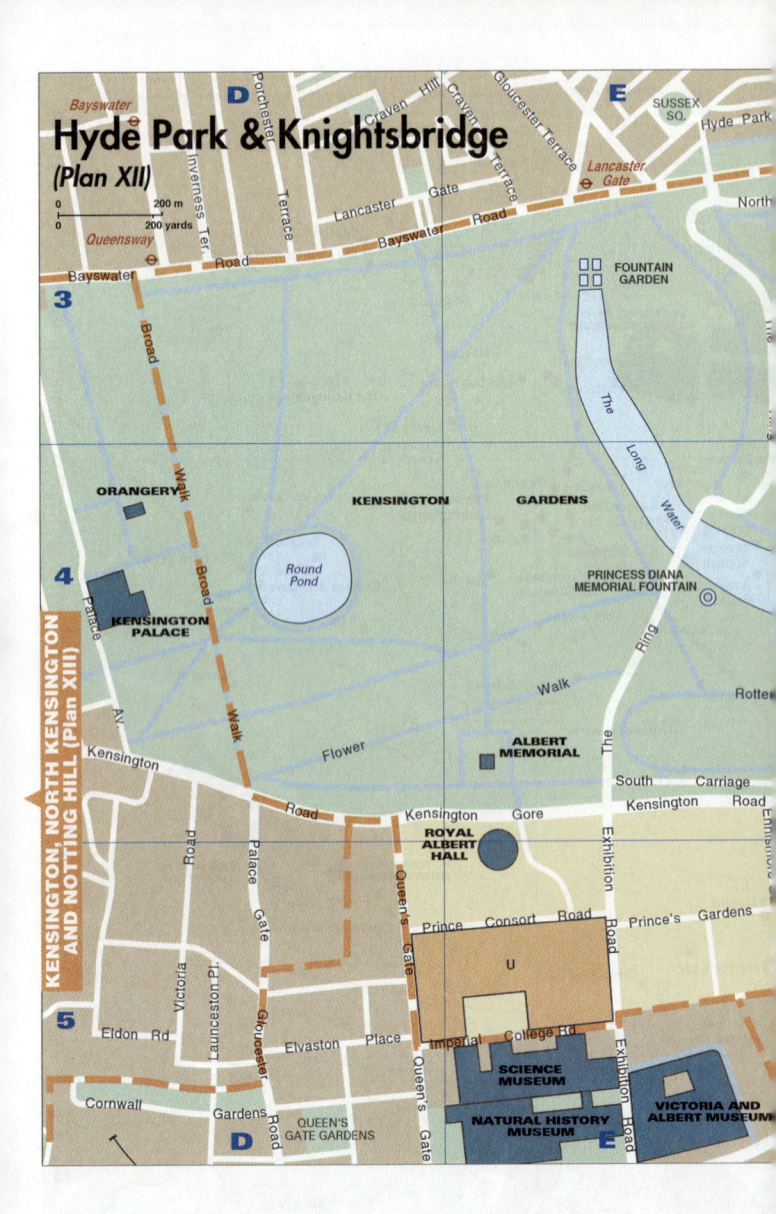

BAYSWATER & MAIDA VALE (Plan VII)

- Hotel
- Restaurant

MAYFAIR, SOHO AND ST JAMES'S (Plan II)

HYDE PARK

The Serpentine

APSLEY HOUSE
WELLINGTON MUSEUM

Mandarin Oriental Hyde Park
Foliage
Mr Chow
Knightsbridge Green
Zuma

Hyde Park Corner

BELGRAVE SQ.

HANS PL.

BELGRAVIA & VICTORIA (Plan IV)

CHELSEA, EARL'S COURT AND SOUTH KENSINGTON (Plan XI)

215

Gordon Ramsay ✿✿✿

French 𝕏𝕏𝕏𝕏

68-69 Royal Hospital Rd
✉ SW3 4HP
✆ (020) 7352 4441
Fax (020) 7352 3334
www.gordonramsay.com

⊖ Sloane Square
▶ **Plan XI**
Closed 1 week Christmas - New Year,
Saturday and Sunday – booking essential

Menu £45/90

'Celebrity chef' may be the nebulous moniker now seemingly lent to anyone with a frying-pan and a personality disorder, but there are chefs out there in TV-land with the talent to match the fame and Gordon Ramsay is foremost amongst them. This is the mother lode of his global empire and it is not difficult to understand why it has remained at the top of the tree. Firstly, the restaurant has never stood still nor rested on its reputation and, secondly, it is staffed by an equally committed crew. The most recent David Collins design is sleek and crisp while the service is as polished as ever and proves that this sort of detailed care doesn't have to be at the expense of personality. Most importantly, the cooking continues to develop. The newest name in the kitchen, Clare Smyth, has added sparkle and an extra eye for detail, while the menu is a clever mix of the classic Ramsay dishes with newer additions. The Menu Prestige has proved so popular that it is now available at lunch, alongside the excellent value Menu of the Day.

First Course

- Roasted Scottish lobster tail, bouillabaisse sauce, cabbage and ratatouille.
- Pressed foie gras, smoked and confit duck, liver, bone marrow crouton.

Main Course

- Best end of lamb and confit of shoulder, spinach and thyme jus.
- Pan-fried sea bass, oyster beignet and caviar velouté.

Dessert

- Prune and armagnac soufflé with chocolate sorbet.
- Granny Smith parfait, honeycomb, bitter chocolate, champagne foam.

The Capital Restaurant ✿✿

French

F5

at Capital Hotel,
22-24 Basil St ✉ SW3 1AT
📞 (020) 7589 5171 **Fax** (020) 7225 0011
e-mail reservations@capitalhotel.co.uk
www.capitalhotel.co.uk

⊖ Knightsbridge
▶ **Plan XI**
Booking essential

Menu £38/58

The Capital

Good service is not something one should necessarily be aware of: it should just happen around you. The unobtrusive staff at The Capital are a case in point: they are all so well organised and choreographed that you barely notice anything happening around you at all. The dining room itself is comfortable and elegant without being too stuffy or serious. To fully indulge those feelings of superiority and sophistication one usually gets when spending time in a luxury hotel, be sure to begin with an aperitif in the discreet bar beforehand. The enthusiastic and committed Frenchman Eric Chavot leads the kitchen brigade and the cooking is very much a reflection of him: he doesn't follow fads and knows exactly what he is trying to achieve on the plate. While the same ingredients may be found in any number of London restaurants, few prepare them with such dexterity and understanding. The preparation is intricate and involved but the end result is dishes that are innovative, creative and even occasionally playful.

First Course
- Crab lasagne with langoustine cappuccino.
- Fricassée of frogs legs, veal sweetbread and cèp purée.

Main Course
- Saddle of rabbit provençale with seared calamari.
- Roast monkfish, caramelised endive and ginger.

Dessert
- Iced coffee parfait with chocolate fondant.
- Vanilla pearls, roasted banana, rum panna cotta and mango sorbet.

Foliage ✽

Innovative 🍴🍴🍴

F4

at Mandarin Oriental Hyde Park Hotel,
66 Knightsbridge ✉ SW1X 7LA
✆ (020) 7201 3723 **Fax** (020) 7235 4552
e-mail molon-dine@mohg.com
www.mandarinoriental.com/london

⊖ Knightsbridge
▶ **Plan XII**
Closed 26 December and 1 January

Menu £35/40

The building work outside means that the view into the park is not quite what it was, and it's still a bit of a fight to get through the bar, but Foliage remains something of an oasis within the splendour of the Mandarin Oriental Hotel. Try to ask for a table on the roomier lower level near the window. As a laudable repost to florid menu descriptions everywhere, the dishes are merely a list of their three or four components, such as Pigeon/Red cabbage/Endive tart Tatin/Ceps. Where it also breaks with tradition is in offering four courses as a standard: a starter, followed by an intermediate course of which most are fish, the main courses where meat prevails and dessert. They assure diners that, in terms of volume of food, this equates to a standard meal but they must have had some pretty big three course meals. There is also a tasting menu for those who wish to eat at a more leisurely pace. The cooking is still detailed and precise but has forsaken the precious tendency towards over elaboration and unnecessary experimentation.

First Course
- Sweetbreads, glazed leeks and morels.
- Beetroot, feta cheese and walnuts.

Main Course
- Pigeon, red cabbage, endive tart Tatin.
- Scallops, squid ink, orzo and almonds.

Dessert
- Calvados soufflé, iced apple parfait, sea salt caramel.
- Banana tart, amaretto and caramel.

Tom Aikens

E6

Innovative

43 Elystan St ✉ SW3 3NT
📞 (020) 7584 2003
Fax (020) 7584 2001
e-mail info@tomaikens.co.uk
www.tomaikens.co.uk

Menu £29/65

South Kensington
▶ **Plan XI**
Closed last two weeks August,
10 days Christmas-New Year,
Saturday, Sunday and Bank Holidays

His chippie failed to enthuse the locals but his eponymous restaurant in Elystan Street still draws in plenty of customers from the surrounding postcodes and he remains on the radar of those fashionistas who know their food. Tom Aikens' attention may have been pulled this way and that in 2008, but he is well aware that it is his name above the door and that it is his reputation at stake. That reputation comes from having worked with an impressive list of names but it also has meant that perhaps it took him a while to develop his own true cooking style. He still may favour grandiose presentation but now appreciates balance and subtlety, in construction and flavour combination. He is becoming a veritable champion of sustainability and adapting the principles to the luxury end of the eating-out market. From a diners point of view the only thing that matters is the feeling one has at the end of the meal: this usually involves feeling extremely well fed, nicely looked after and generally impressed.

First Course
- Lobster and rabbit roasted in vanilla butter with cannelloni.
- Poached pigeon with foie gras mousse and watercress.

Main Course
- Cutlet and belly of pork with squid.
- Dover sole with snails and salsify.

Dessert
- Truffle and vanilla panna cotta with truffle mousse.
- Meringue with vanilla parfait and toffee popcorn.

Aubergine ✽

French 🍴🍴🍴

D7

11 Park Walk ✉ SW10 0AJ
📞 (020) 7352 3449
Fax (020) 7351 1770
e-mail info@auberginerestaurant.co.uk
www.auberginerestaurant.co.uk

⊖ South Kensington
▶ **Plan XI**

Closed 2 weeks Christmas, Easter, Saturday lunch, Sunday and Bank Holidays – booking essential

Menu £34/64

A/C · 🕐 · VISA · MC · AE · ◐

"Food is food" says William Drabble, the chef who has really made Aubergine his own, and by that he means it should be free of gimmicks and the vicissitudes of fashion. But that doesn't mean he's not passionate about it because he most decidedly is, especially when it comes to the sourcing of ingredients - he's even been known to point out to staff the location of a particular farm through the wonders of Google Earth. His cooking remains faithful to the roots of classical cooking and his dishes are confident in flavour and bold in their presentation and they all showcase those superlative ingredients. Equally importantly, he displays an inherent understanding of what goes with what. The relatively new service team also show an understandable respect for the reputation the restaurant has built over the years. This may not be the most fashionable restaurant in London but the loyal clientele know a good thing when they see it. One excellent thing is the very good value lunch, which includes a ½ bottle of wine.

First Course
- Assiette of foie gras.
- Carpaccio of scallops, truffle vinaigrette.

Main Course
- Baked fillets of sole, apple, mussels and chives.
- Pot-roast pigeon, Madeira jus, celeriac fondant.

Dessert
- Iced clementine mousse with rhubarb.
- Honey parfait, citrus fruit salad.

Ambassade de L'Ile ✿

French

D6

117-119 Old Brompton Rd
✉ SW7 3RN
✆ (020) 7373 7774 **Fax** (020) 7373 4472
e-mail direction@ambassadedelile.com
www.ambassadedelile.com

Menu £65 – Carte £63/88

⊖ Gloucester Road
▶ **Plan XI**
Closed Sunday

Ambassade de L'Ile

The latest French chef to try his luck in London is the multi-syllabled Jean-Christophe Ansanay-Alex. He runs a successful restaurant in Lyon and for his London outpost he has chosen the former Edwardian library that was previously home to Lundum's Danish restaurant and, for those with longer memories, Chanterelle. However, few previous diners will recognise the interior. Perhaps the French have a greater sense of irony but no one has seen this much shag-pile carpet and white leather since Jason King was in town in 1972. But if you can see past the night-club surroundings and the pretentious musings on the enormous menu you'll get to the food, which is really the point of the place. The French cooking is modern without being showy and meticulous without being fussy. There are nods to Lyon and several dishes are designed for two. Prices are not exactly accessible, especially those on the wine list, but the food brings something different to the London dining scene and the service is well-organised and refreshingly starch-free.

First Course
- Watermelon gazpacho, avocado and langoustines.
- Duck foie gras 'au torchon'.

Main Course
- Rib of milk fed veal with girolles, spinach and potato gnocchi.
- Pike mousseline, frogs legs and garlic nougatine.

Dessert
- White peach soufflé.
- Fried apricots with rosemary on Breton sablé.

Bibendum

E6

French 🍴🍴🍴

Michelin House, 81 Fulham Rd ✉ SW3 6RD
⊖ South Kensington
▶ Plan XI
✆ (020) 7581 5817
Closed 25-26 December and 1 January
Fax (020) 7823 7925
e-mail reservations@bibendum.co.uk **www**.bibendum.co.uk

Menu £30 (lunch and Sunday dinner) – Carte £41/60

A/C
🍴
☀
VISA
MC
AE
①

Dine with the Editor of the Michelin Guide here and he'll go all misty eyed as he remembers when part of the restaurant was once his office. This extraordinarily imaginative building, opened in 1911 and designed by a Michelin employee, anticipated the art deco movement of the 1920s, with its ceramic tiles and stained glass windows, and remained our UK HQ until the mid 1980s. Named after the Michelin Man, Bibendum proved an instant hit as a restaurant by combining all the elements of style, design, service and carefully prepared food. Today, it remains a favourite by continuing to offer dependably good cooking that, appropriately enough, still retains that French connection, along with professional service and surroundings that never fail to impress.

One-O-One

F4

Seafood 🍴🍴🍴

at Sheraton Park Tower Hotel, 101 Knightsbridge ✉ SW1X 7RN
⊖ Knightsbridge
▶ Plan XI
✆ (020) 7290 7101 **Fax** (020) 7235 6196
www.onetoonerestaurant.com

Menu £19/30 (lunch) – Carte £19/69

A/C
☀
VISA
MC
AE
①

A big refurbishment in 2007 not only saw a new and improved decorative style for this spacious restaurant on the ground floor of the Sheraton Park Tower hotel, but also coincided with a change of concept for the food presentation. The Brittany-born chef still focuses primarily on seafood, especially Norwegian, but those who prefer a lighter and more flexible style of eating can now order 'petit plats'- four or five of these should be sufficient. However, traditionalists can still order the standard size. The room is certainly comfortable and has been broken up a little; the service remains sufficiently dutiful. The unremittingly anodyne background music, though, hints at a loss of nerve on someone's part.

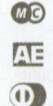

Fifth Floor

Modern European

F4

at Harvey Nichols,
Knightsbridge ✉ SW1X 7RJ
✆ (020) 7235 5250
Fax (0870) 1916 019
e-mail reception@harveynicols.com **www**.harveynichols.com

⊖ Knightsbridge
▶ **Plan XI**
Closed Christmas and Sunday dinner

Menu £20/40 – Carte £29/47

Those weak-willed in the face of shopping opportunities can bypass the department store by taking the express lift to the Fifth Floor, but even there one might find it hard to avoid the epicurean treats of the food hall or the similarly arresting sirens in the bar. The restaurant was made-over in 2007 and its pod-like shape and coloured lighting give it a space-age chicness. Table size is generous but the room retains a sense of intimacy. The menu is modern European with the focus on France. The kitchen has a delicate touch and there are occasional flashes of originality. The Market Menu at lunch is good value and the wine list is an impressive work, with particular emphasis on French and dessert wines, as well as champagne.

Chutney Mary

Indian

D8

535 King's Rd ✉ SW10 0SZ
✆ (020) 7351 3113 **Fax** (020) 7351 7694
e-mail chutneymary@realindianfood.com
www.realindianfood

⊖ Fulham Broadway
▶ **Plan XI**
Dinner only

Carte £34/45

Chutney Mary is one of the senior members of the Indian restaurant fraternity but that doesn't mean it has rested on its laurels. A few years back it was given a head-to-toe revamp which modernised what was already a very comfortable place. The large conservatory is still there but now the room is fringed with storm-lamps and the mood is altogether more seductive and sophisticated. 1840s etchings of Indian life combine with mirrors to add a touch of glamour and the young team provide service that is both conscientious and attentive. The menu is as interesting as it has always been, with good quality seasonal ingredients and strong presentation. The well chosen wine list challenges those who think only a Kingfisher beer can accompany an Indian meal.

Bombay Brasserie

D6

Indian XXX

Courtfield Rd ✉ SW7 4QH
✆ (020) 7370 4040 **Fax** (020) 7835 1669
e-mail bombay1brasserie@aol.com
www.bombaybrasserielondon.com

⊖ Gloucester Road
► **Plan XI**
Closed 25-26 December
– buffet lunch

Menu £19 (weekday lunch buffet) – Carte £42/52

A/C ◷ ☼ VISA MC AE ①

Bombay Brasserie opened its doors in 1982 and its neon sign and doorman have become established local features. It was one of the first restaurants to prove to Londoners that Indian food merits glamorous surroundings just as much as any other cuisine and succeeds so well in its task that you'll never be able to look flock wallpaper in the eye again. The vast, perpetually busy, dining room is divided into two: the main room with its striking mural of Bombay life and the conservatory extension. A whole army of staff all know exactly what to do and do so with aplomb. Influences from across India feature, from Kerala to Mughlai, and this includes seafood dishes from Goa and fragrant Parsi fare. The lunchtime buffet is a veritable institution.

Awana

F6

Malaysian XXX

85 Sloane Ave ✉ SW3 3DX
✆ (020) 7584 8880
Fax (020) 7584 6188
e-mail info@awana.co.uk **www**.awana.co.uk

⊖ South Kensington
► **Plan XI**
Closed 25-26 December and 1 January
– booking essential

Menu £15 (lunch)/40 – Carte £26/43

A/C ☼ VISA MC AE ①

Eddie Lim, the owner, has over 70 restaurants around the world so clearly knows what he's doing. Awana is no exception; a charming welcome and endearing service are the norm, the food is fresh and invigorating and the room comfortable, particularly the stylish bar. If you sit at the satay bar for the house speciality then ensure you chat to the chef who's a font of information about Malaysian cuisine. Curries, grills and stir-fries are the mainstays of the main menu; the curries are almost soup-like with their sauces so make sure you order plenty of roti canai, the wonderful bread; the grills include whole sea bass or rack of lamb, while the stir-fries will make us realise the inadequacies of what we all knock up these days at home.

IN HOC SIGNO VINCES
RAMOS PINTO
PORTO 10 ANOS
ENVELHECIDO EM CASCO
QUINTA DE ERVAMOIRA

NEW Michelin Tourist Guides: expand your holiday horizons

Great Britain

Plan Discover Explore

Now ALL in small format

Spain · French Alps · Brittany

All **TOURIST GUIDES £14.99**

- New cover
- New layout
- New information
- New smaller format

MICHELIN
A better way forward

Toto's

F5

Italian XXX

Walton House, Walton St
✉ SW3 2JH
✆ (020) 7589 0075 **Fax** (020) 7581 9668

⊖ Knightsbridge
▶ **Plan XI**

Closed 3 days Christmas
– booking essential at dinner

Menu £27 (lunch) – Carte £49/54

Any restaurant this busy but without a website, still including a cover charge and beyond the jurisdiction of the fashion police, must be doing something right. Walton House is home to Toto's, with the entrance on the cobbled Lennox Garden Mews. It is old-fashioned in the best sense of the word: you'll feel genuinely looked after. The ground floor is where the action is but tables on the balcony offer more privacy. Despite the smart surroundings, the Italian food is decidedly earthy and rustic. Freshness and consistency are the hallmarks of the kitchen and there's a simplicity and honesty to the cooking. The handmade pasta is a strength and those daunted by a middle course can merely ask for a reduced portion.

Aquasia

D8

International XXX

at Wyndham Grand Hotel,
Chelsea Harbour ✉ SW10 0XG
✆ (020) 7300 8443
www.wyndhamlondon.com

⊖ Fulham Broadway
▶ **Plan XI**

Carte £34/47

The all-suite Wyndham Grand Hotel may not be the most accessible place in London if you haven't got a limo but have lunch on the sun deck of their restaurant Aquasia, overlooking the yachts of Chelsea Harbour, and you'll think you've landed in the Med. The room is shaped like an ocean liner and is all very fresh and light in tone, with a wall of windows that open out on warm days. Most of the tables have a view, although some prefer to gaze inward in case any of the hotel's more famous guests wander in. As the name implies, the cooking blends Mediterranean ingredients with Asian aromatics and techniques to create appealingly refined dishes. On Sundays the Champagne brunches have become very popular, helped no doubt by the offer of unlimited champagne.

Rasoi

F6

Indian

10 Lincoln St ⊠ SW3 2TS
✆ (020) 7225 1881
Fax (020) 7581 0220
e-mail info@rasoirestaurant.co.uk
www.rasoirestaurant.co.uk

⊖ Sloane Square
▶ **Plan XI**
Closed 25-26 December,
Saturday lunch, and Sunday

Menu £26 (lunch) – Carte £55/80

One assumes all sorts of activities go on behind the elegant façades of Chelsea's Georgian townhouses but running a successful and innovative Indian restaurant must be one of the more unexpected. Bombay-born chef owner Vineet Bhatia may now have business concerns all over the world but his Rasoi remains his pride and joy. Ring the bell and the next instant you'll find yourself in an appealingly exotic atmosphere, thanks to the aroma, the warm lighting and the collection of Indian artefacts. They have taken a few tables out of the ground floor dining room, while upstairs is now used exclusively for private parties. Locals can still drop in for a classic curry but it is in the main menu where you'll find Vineet's inventiveness. He has always been strong on artistic presentation but it is never at the expense of flavour: his spicing is controlled and balanced. Vegetarians are well looked after and he's constantly striving to find the best ingredients. The mix of nationalities doing the service can sometimes make for a variable experience but they do all share the owner's enthusiasm.

First Course
- Mustard-infused chicken tikka with milk fritter and chilli chutney.
- Scallops with chilli and cauliflower and onion relish.

Main Course
- Lamb shank and morels, with saffron mash, rosemary naan.
- Spiced lobster jus, curry leaf, broccoli khichdi, spiced cocoa powder.

Dessert
- Rose petal sandwich with saffron baked yoghurt, fruits of the forest jelly.
- Saffron poached pear, dried fruits, saffron ice cream.

Daphne's

Italian XX

E6

112 Draycott Ave
✉ SW3 3AE
☏ (020) 7589 4257 **Fax** (020) 7225 2766
e-mail reservations@daphnes-restaurant.co.uk
www.daphnes-restaurant.co.uk

⊖ South Kensington
▶ **Plan XI**
Closed 25-26 December
– booking essential

Menu £17 (lunch) – Carte £33/49

Its fortunes may have been mixed since opening in the '60s but today Daphne's is an unequivocally constant blink on the fashionista's radar screen. Lunch is full of ladies weighed down with bags from a hard morning's 'Imeldaring' at Jimmy Choo, while dinner is populated with the tanned and buffed figures of the entertainment world - this is not the place to go when you're not looking your best. Where the restaurant surprises is in the care and accuracy of the Italian cooking - the kitchen knows what's in season and what goes with what - and the diligence of the service. The front room is where to be seen but if it's privacy you're after then it's best at the back, with there's a retractable roof for summer and a fireplace in winter.

Racine

French XX

E5

239 Brompton Rd
✉ SW3 2EP
☏ (020) 7584 4477 **Fax** (020) 7584 4900

⊖ South Kensington
▶ **Plan XI**
Closed 25 December

Menu £20 (lunch) – Carte £31/47

It's all change again at the top. Now it is Henry Harris who is back running the kitchen and the show in general, and Eric Garnier, his erstwhile partner, who has left. However, Racine has such a loyal following that it virtually runs itself – or gives that impression. Most other elements remain unchanged and that authentic French brasserie feel couldn't be more bedded in: the brown leather now has a real lived-in look, the wood has darkened and the mirrors have gone a smoky opaque. There are good value menus for lunch and early dinner and from the à la carte you can expect a comprehensive selection of bourgeois classics, from tête de veau to steak tartare and crème caramel, although the 14½ % service charge can push up the final bill.

Nozomi

Japanese XX

15 Beauchamp Pl ⊠ SW3 1NQ — ⊖ Knightsbridge
✆ (020) 7838 1500 **Fax** (020) 7838 1001 ▶ **Plan XI**
e-mail marios@nozomi.co.uk www.nozomi.co.uk   Closed Sunday

Carte £50/80

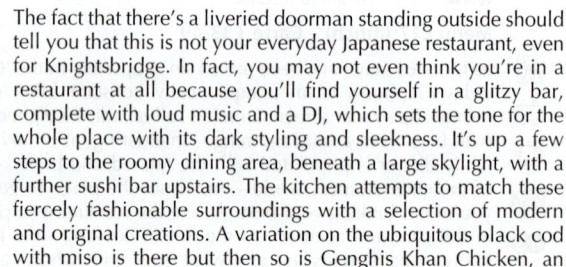

The fact that there's a liveried doorman standing outside should tell you that this is not your everyday Japanese restaurant, even for Knightsbridge. In fact, you may not even think you're in a restaurant at all because you'll find yourself in a glitzy bar, complete with loud music and a DJ, which sets the tone for the whole place with its dark styling and sleekness. It's up a few steps to the roomy dining area, beneath a large skylight, with a further sushi bar upstairs. The kitchen attempts to match these fiercely fashionable surroundings with a selection of modern and original creations. A variation on the ubiquitous black cod with miso is there but then so is Genghis Khan Chicken, an altogether more threatening sounding dish.

Bluebird

British XX

350 King's Rd ⊠ SW3 5UU — ⊖ Sloane Square
✆ (020) 7559 1000 **Fax** (020) 7559 1115 ▶ **Plan XI**
e-mail enquiries@bluebird-restaurant.co.uk
www.bluebird-restaurant.com

Menu £19 – Carte £32/52

Bluebird is a giant brasserie housed in a former garage built in 1923, which was where Malcolm Campbell's famous Bluebird cars were made. The noise of revving engines has now been replaced by the sound of clinking cutlery but, with nearly 200 seats to fill, this place does need to be busy to get going. Its decoration was given a subtle refreshment in 2007 and the bar remains something of a destination in its own right. The kitchen does its bit to champion British produce. The menu offers quite a range, from pies to pasta, but your best bet is to head for the inherently British offerings like Herdwick lamb, Cromer crab or Yorkshire grouse, where the quality of the produce really shines through.

Poissonnerie de l'Avenue

French XX

E6

82 Sloane Ave ⊠ SW3 3DZ
⌀ (020) 7589 2457
Fax (020) 7581 3360
e-mail peterr@poissoneire.co.uk
www.poissonneriedelavenue.co.uk

⊖ South Kensington
▶ **Plan XI**
Closed 24-26 December and Sunday

Menu £24 (lunch) – Carte £29/45

A/C ⌂ VISA MC AE ⓪

Poissonnerie de l'Avenue is a trusty Chelsea institution with a loyal band of followers. Refreshingly unmoved by the dictates of fashion, the restaurant comes divided into three classically decorated rooms with wood panelling, seafaring-themed oil paintings and a decidedly grown-up atmosphere. The regulars prefer the newer far room. As the name suggests, it is all about fish here, whether that's the confident and robust Mediterranean-inspired main courses or the new season oysters one can enjoy in the bar. The fish is supremely fresh, exceptionally well sourced and comes unmasked in flavour and undisguised in presentation. Enough to make one almost forget the 15% service charge on top of a cover charge.

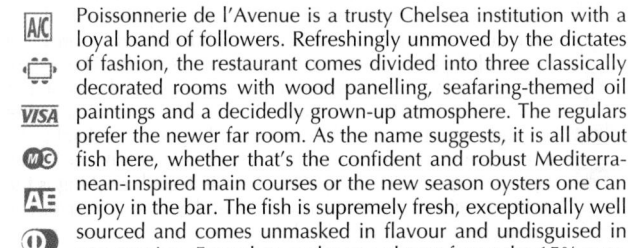

Le Cercle

French XX

F6

1 Wilbraham Pl ⊠ SW1X 9AE
⌀ (020) 7901 9999
Fax (020) 7901 9111
e-mail info@lecercle.co.uk
www.lecercle.co.uk

⊖ Sloane Square
▶ **Plan XI**
Closed Christmas - New Year, Sunday, Monday and Bank Holidays

Menu £15 (lunch) – Carte £18/31

A/C VISA MC AE

It was originally going to be a swimming pool hence the unusual basement layout; the somewhat repetitive procedures on arrival highlight some of the logistical problems. But don't miss the seductive little bar halfway down the stairs, from where you can survey the scene; there's another, louder one around a fireplace. As this is an offshoot of Club Gascon, expect appealing tasting plates that are still bigger than your average tapas. The 'terroir' French cooking means flavours are distinctive and dishes satisfyingly rich. The wine list focuses on Bordeaux and Alsace and wines are paired with the dishes. Staff are a patient and clued-up lot. As many regard this as more of a winter destination, look out for tempting summer promotions.

Le Colombier

French ✕✕

E6

145 Dovehouse St ⊖ South Kensington
✉ SW3 6LB ▶ Plan XI
☏ (020) 7351 1155 **Fax** (020) 7351 5124
e-mail lecolombier1998@aol.com **www**.lecolombier-sw3.co.uk

Menu £16/19 – Carte £30/40

It's a French restaurant in Chelsea but could equally be a Chelsea restaurant in France. The loyalty and regularity of attendance shown by those in the neighbourhood ensures that there's always that cheery atmosphere of familiarity. The restaurant, with a large covered terrace/conservatory at the front, has more than a little feel of a brasserie. It's also quite sizeable but manages to retain a certain intimacy, helped considerably by the presence of the experienced owner who will never knowingly let a face go unrecognised. Classic French cooking is the order of the day and it's hearty, stout and generous in size. The munificence of the set price lunch menu is enough in itself to make regulars of us all.

Caraffini

Italian ✕✕

F6

61-63 Lower Sloane St ⊖ Sloane Square
✉ SW1W 8DH ▶ Plan XI
☏ (020) 7259 0235 Closed 25 December, Easter, Sunday and Bank
Fax (020) 7259 0236 Holidays – booking essential
e-mail info@caraffini.co.uk **www**.caraffini.co.uk

Carte £27/38

One doesn't have to look far to see why Paolo Caraffini's restaurant is always so busy: it has a wonderfully genial host, smooth service, reliably good Italian food and a highly hospitable atmosphere. Just watching the number of regulars Paolo greets as friends, from Chelsea art dealers to King's Road shoppers, will make you want to become a part of the club. Warm and cosy in winter, bright and sunny in summer with pavement tables for alfresco dining, this really is a place for all seasons. Daily specials supplement the already balanced menu that covers many regions of Italy and any requests to veer off-menu are satisfied without fuss or fanfare. Caraffini is proof that good hospitality is very much alive and kicking.

L'Etranger

Innovative XX

D5

36 Gloucester Rd ⊠ SW7 4QT
☏ (020) 7584 1118
Fax (020) 7584 8886
e-mail etranger@etranger.co.uk
www.circagroupltd.co.uk

⊖ Gloucester Road
▶ **Plan XI**
Closed 25-26 December and Saturday lunch
– booking essential

Menu £20 (lunch) – Carte £31/86

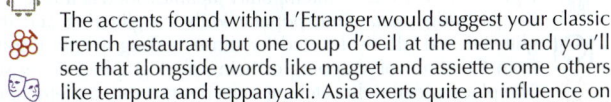

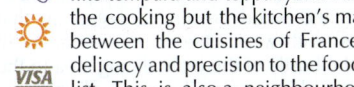

The accents found within L'Etranger would suggest your classic French restaurant but one coup d'oeil at the menu and you'll see that alongside words like magret and assiette come others like tempura and teppanyaki. Asia exerts quite an influence on the cooking but the kitchen's main selling point is a marriage between the cuisines of France and Japan. So you'll find a delicacy and precision to the food as well as an impressive wine list. This is also a neighbourhood restaurant whose band of sophisticated regulars are a loyal bunch. Their reward is a menu section marked 'favourites' - popular dishes that the chef dare not take off, such as his own take on black cod with miso. The lighting is moody, the music a little loungey and the vibe, friendly.

Langan's Coq d'Or

Traditional XX

C6

254-260 Old Brompton Rd
⊠ SW5 9HR
☏ (020) 7259 2599 **Fax** (020) 7370 7735
e-mail admin@langansrestaurant.co.uk
www.langansrestaurants.co.uk

⊖ Earl's Court
▶ **Plan XI**
Closed 25-26 December

Menu £24 – Carte approx. £28

The celebrated restaurateur Peter Langan may no longer be with us, but Richard Shepherd has created a restaurant of which his friend would no doubt have approved. He has also named it in honour of the original moniker of Langan's in Stratton Street. It is almost two restaurants in one: the glass enclosed front section goes by the name of the 'bar and grill', is more informal in style and opens out onto the street in summer, while beyond is the main restaurant, whose walls are filled with a huge collection of artwork. The menu is a no-nonsense celebration of the best of British combined with what Europe can offer. So, expect bangers and mash alongside rack of lamb. For the incurably louche, breakfast is served until early evening.

Zuma

F5

Japanese ✗✗

5 Raphael St ✉ SW7 1DL ⊖ Knightsbridge
✆ (020) 7584 1010 **Fax** (020) 7584 5005 ▶ **Plan XII**
e-mail info@zumarestaurant.com Closed 25 December and 1 January
www.zumarestaurant.com

Carte approx. £26

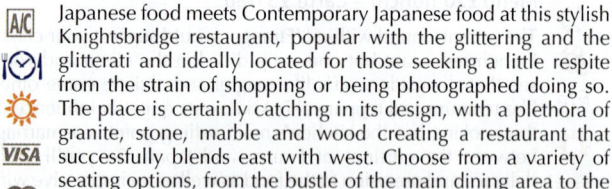

Japanese food meets Contemporary Japanese food at this stylish Knightsbridge restaurant, popular with the glittering and the glitterati and ideally located for those seeking a little respite from the strain of shopping or being photographed doing so. The place is certainly catching in its design, with a plethora of granite, stone, marble and wood creating a restaurant that successfully blends east with west. Choose from a variety of seating options, from the bustle of the main dining area to the theatre afforded by the sushi counter. The menu offers up an intriguing mix of the traditional with the ultra modern, all expertly crafted and delicately presented. Lovers of sake will find over thirty varieties available.

Mr Chow

F4

Chinese ✗✗

151 Knightsbridge ✉ SW1X 7PA ⊖ Knightsbridge
✆ (020) 7589 7347 **Fax** (020) 7584 5780 ▶ **Plan XII**
e-mail mrchowuk@aol.com Closed 24-26 December and 1 January
www.mrchow.com

Menu £27/38 – Carte dinner £39/48

Chinese food, Italian waiters, swish surroundings, steep prices and immaculately coiffured regulars; it's an unusual mix that clearly works because Mr Chow celebrated its fortieth birthday in 2008. Even if you're not recognisable, you'll get a friendly welcome and the champagne chariot will be wheeled towards you. The laminated menu is long but clearly divided between sections entitled 'from the sea', 'from the land' and 'from the sky'; chickens will be pleased to find themselves in this last category. The cooking is far better than you expect, with genuine care shown. The desserts are thoroughly European and come on a trolley, with tarts the speciality. Your final bill won't be clearly itemised but this doesn't seem to bother anyone.

Papillon

F6

French

96 Draycott Ave ✉ SW3 3AD
✆ (020) 7225 2555
Fax (020) 7225 2554
e-mail info@papillonchelsea.co.uk www.papillonchelsea.co.uk

⊖ South Kensington
▶ **Plan XI**
Closed 24-26 December and 1 January

Menu £17 (lunch) s – Carte £33/51 s

Ask for one of the large round tables by the French windows that open onto the pavement patio for that authentic brasserie experience. Papillon is the genuine French article: the mirrors, lamps and animated conversations are all there. The kitchen, too, makes its mark on classic regional recipes: snails with garlic, steak tartare and Mediterranean fish soup can be followed by roast turbot with truffle sauce, saddle of lamb with Lyonnaise potato or Chateaubriand Rossini. There are also plenty of thoughtfully-created salads for those who prefer to keep things light – this is Chelsea, after all. The wine list is also mainly Gallic, with Italy and Spain getting a little look-in. Lunch and early evening see a keenly-priced menu.

Pasha

D5

Moroccan

1 Gloucester Rd ✉ SW7 4PP
✆ (020) 7589 7969
Fax (020) 7581 9996
e-mail info@pasha-restaurant.co.uk www.pasha-restaurant.co.uk

⊖ Gloucester Road
▶ **Plan XI**
Closed 24-25 December and 1 January

Menu £15/37 – Carte £24/42

Now under the same ownership as Levant restaurant, Pasha has been recharged and refreshed and now represents a fun night out. The ground floor is given over to the atmospheric cocktail lounge bar, with the exotic scent of hookah pipes and joss-sticks in the air. Downstairs, low tables are strewn with rose petals, light from lanterns and candles bounces off the mosaic floor, while the cushions and rich colours add to the seductive feel. As does the belly-dancer. Moroccan home-style cooking is the feature here, with sharing the key. Lunch is a simpler affair but in the evenings try one of the 'feast' menus. The main menu is divided into tagines, couscous or grills but don't forget Morocco offers good seafood as well as meats.

Cambio de Tercio

Spanish ✗✗

D6

163 Old Brompton Rd ⊖ Gloucester Road
✉ SW5 0LJ ▶ **Plan XI**
✆ (020) 7244 8970 **Fax** (020) 7373 2359 Closed 2 weeks Christmas
e-mail alusa@btconnect.com **www**.cambiodetercio.co.uk

Carte £27/39

In summer this Spanish restaurant spills out onto the street but still the best tables are right at the back in a cosy little glass-roofed section. The menu is appealing and authentic and the choice extensive. Starters are divided into hot and cold, followed by four meat and four fish dishes which also come in a choice of size, so your best bet is to come with friends and share a load. Spain's proud culinary heritage is there for all to see: Galecian octopus, Serrano and Iberico hams, Manchego cheese, Valencian rice, Segovian suckling pig and crema Catalan all make you wonder why there are not more Spanish restaurants around. Mustard coloured walls and bright Matador paintings complete the scene. The young owners also have a tapas bar across the road.

Khan's of Kensington

Indian ✗✗

E6

3 Harrington Rd ✉ SW7 3ES ⊖ South Kensington
✆ (020) 7584 4114 **Fax** (020) 7581 2900 ▶ **Plan XI**
e-mail info@khansofkensington.co.uk Closed 25 December
www.khansofkensington.co.uk

Menu £9/17 – Carte £18/29

Virtually opposite South Kensington tube, Khan's of Kensington has been a local feature for quite a few years now and the locals have been resolute in their loyalty. It's really quite contemporary inside and the modern Warhol-esque pictures take you a little by surprise. The size is near perfect: big enough to generate an atmosphere but small enough to create a certain intimacy. The downstairs tables and chairs have been removed and the space has been turned into a comfortable lounge bar. The menu provides a more modern and, consequently, more interesting selection of dishes, all of which are carefully prepared to a good standard with the emphasis on the North West frontier. A takeaway service is also available.

Pellicano

F6

Italian XX

19-21 Elystan St ⊠ SW3 3NT
☏ (020) 7589 3718
Fax (020) 7584 1789
e-mail pellicano@btconnect.com **www**.pellicanorestaurant.co.uk

⊖ South Kensington
▶ **Plan XI**
Closed Christmas and New Year

Menu £20 (lunch) – Carte £25/41

This is another one of those neighbourhood Chelsea restaurants that makes you wonder why your street doesn't look like this. Unless, of course, this is your street. The large blue canopy, with half a dozen tables nestled beneath, highlights the location of this popular local Italian. It has a fresh feel to the interior, with its warm yellows and blues, and the clever use of mirrors makes the place seem bigger than it is. The pelican motif is evident in some of the lively artwork. It is from Sardinia that the kitchen takes its influence, which is evident as soon as the terrific basket of assorted breads arrives. From the pecorino cheese to the culurgiones (ravioli), the flavours are as bright and aromatic as the island itself.

Chelsea Brasserie

F6

Modern European XX

at The Sloane Square Hotel,
7-12 Sloane Sq. ⊠ SW1W 8EG
☏ (020) 7881 5999
e-mail robert@chelsea-brasserie.co.uk
www.sloanesquarehotel.co.uk

⊖ Sloane Square
▶ **Plan XI**
Closed 25 December

Carte £24/42

Due to local demand, they've added a bar to the Chelsea Brasserie and those locals have clearly taken to the place, which is hardly surprising as it's in a great spot. The frequently changing, seasonal menu has something to suit all times of days and all moods; it is mostly modern European in its influence but there can be an occasional Asian note. The pre-theatre menu comes in at an appealing price and there are pavement tables for coffees, salads or a variety of blended juices. Inside, it's a roomy affair, not without some style and nicely kitted out with contemporary art and striking green lamps. It forms part of the Sloane Square Hotel, although you wouldn't actually be aware of this when you're inside.

Painted Heron

Indian XX

112 Cheyne Walk
SW10 0DJ
✆ (020) 7351 5232 **Fax** (020) 7351 5313
www.thepaintedheron.com

⊖ Gloucester Road
▶ **Plan XI**
Closed 25 December,
1 January and Saturday lunch

Menu £32 – Carte £33/40

There is hardly a single house on Cheyne Walk without a blue plaque commemorating the literary and artistic talent of a past resident, but one wonders how many of the current occupiers realise they've also got a place like The Painted Heron on their doorstep. The restaurant is immaculately laid out, with pillars dividing it in into cosier areas. The simple, fresh décor is enlivened by some contemporary paintings. Stylish leather chairs and neatly dressed tables complete the picture of an undeniably smart neighbourhood Indian restaurant. The menu is printed daily according to what fresh produce is available and the cooking exhibits an understanding of those ingredients and a degree of originality in their preparation.

Vama

Indian XX

438 King's Rd ⊠ SW10 0LJ
✆ (020) 7565 8500
Fax (020) 7565 8501
e-mail vamakingsroad@tiffinbites.com
www.vama.co.uk

⊖ Sloane Square
▶ **Plan XI**
Closed 25-26 December and
1 January – booking essential
– dinner only and
lunch Saturday-Sunday

Menu £12 (lunch) – Carte £35/45 s

The Northwest Frontier and the Punjab provide inspiration for the cooking at Vama, so vegetarians will find that they have an equal number of dishes to choose from as the carnivores and that there will be an assortment of authentic breads to soak up the creamy sauces. The brightly lit façade provides a welcoming beacon, particularly on a winter's evening, while inside the place is divided into three. The first section is where the action seems to be; the second area is a narrow tent-like space and this leads into the rear conservatory, ideal for those after a little more intimacy. Teak carvings, oil paintings, Indian stone and pretty crockery all add to the Indian feel and help create very pleasant surroundings.

Carpaccio

Italian ✗✗

E6

4 Sydney St ✉ SW3 6PP
✆ (020) 7352 3435
Fax (020) 7622 8304
e-mail carpacciorest@aol.com
www.carpacciorestaurant.co.uk

⊖ South Kensington
▶ **Plan XI**
closed 25 December, Easter, last 2 weeks August,
Sunday and Bank Holidays

Carte £23/35

This long, narrow restaurant may be within a pretty Georgian house and fringed with chocolate coloured seating, but the decorative features are more from the testosterone school of interior design – walls come with stills from James Bond films and the owner has displayed his fondness for Formula 1 by hanging the full fibre glass cockpit of an Ayrton Senna racing car. In this age when every chef is trying to do something different, it can sometimes be reassuring to find a kitchen sticking to the classics. As the name implies, carpaccio is the house speciality with beef, tuna and assorted fish given the treatment. Elsewhere on the menu you'll find familiar but nonetheless carefully prepared Italian classics.

Eight over Eight

Asian ✗✗

E7

392 King's Rd ✉ SW3 5UZ
✆ (020) 7349 9934
Fax (020) 7351 5157
www.rickerrestaurants.com

⊖ Gloucester Road
▶ **Plan XI**
Closed 25 December,
1 January and lunch Sunday

Carte £27/43

What was once the Man in the Moon pub is now a fiercely fashionable pan-Asian restaurant, proving that the King's Road is not all high street chains and baby shops and can still cut it with the fashionistas. The menu has a fairly wide remit to cover much of South East Asia with Chinese, Japanese, Malaysian, Korean and Thai influences all featuring and most dishes designed for sharing. Don't hesitate to ask for help from the charming, and alarmingly attractive, staff. The room is all moody and cool, with a slick bar at the front and the restaurant at the back. Chocolate coloured leather seating and two shades of oak on the walls contrast with the delicate silk parasol styled lamps. Try not to covet the booths too openly.

Good Earth

E5

Chinese 🍴🍴

233 Brompton Rd ✉ SW3 2EP
☎ (020) 7584 3658 **Fax** (020) 7823 8769
e-mail goodearthgroup@aol.com
www.goodearthgroup.co.uk

◎ Knightsbridge
▶ **Plan XI**
Closed 22-31 December

Menu £14/30 – Carte £24/50

Restaurants, boutiques, shops and salons have all come and gone on Brompton Road but good old Good Earth has outlasted them all, and just keeps on doing its thing. This longevity can be put down to a number of factors: it has been impervious to fashion, its standards are reliable and it gives the punters what they want. The welcome is guaranteed to be polite and the staff all know what they're doing and do it well. Spread over the ground floor and basement, it wouldn't necessarily win any design awards but the atmosphere is never less than convivial. The menu is large without being worryingly vast and performs a clever balancing trick of offering dishes of recognisable popularity alongside others of a more unusual bent.

The Botanist

F6

Modern European 🍴🍴

7 Sloane Square ✉ SW1W 8EE
☎ (020) 7730 0077 **Fax** (020) 7730 7177
e-mail info@thebotanistonsloanesquare.com
www.thebotanistonsloanesquare.com

◎ Sloane Square
▶ **Plan XI**

Carte £26/43

Tom and Ed Martin have found themselves another great spot to woo both the drink-after-work crowd and the local dining market. Getting through those drinkers can be a bit of a bunfight but you'll be rewarded by a sleek and swish restaurant that occupies the other half of this corner establishment; try to sit near the back, next to the botanical backdrop. It's open from early breakfast until late dinner and the menus are modern European in their influence and tone; the kitchen has the confidence to eschew over-embellishment and flavours are true and distinctive. On a summer's night the windows open up all around, creating a very pleasant atmosphere. Service captures the mood but not at the expense of attentiveness.

Marco

Traditional

Stamford Bridge, Fulham Rd
✉ SW6 1HS
☏ (020) 7915 2929
Fax (020) 7915 2931
e-mail info@marcorestaurant.co.uk **www**.marcorestaurant.co.uk

⊖ Fulham Broadway
▶ **Plan XVIII**
Closed Sunday and Monday – dinner only

Carte £34/59

A section of Manchester United fans was once derided as being prawn sandwich eaters; London expectations being what they are, at Chelsea's ground you get a restaurant from Marco Pierre White. Some will inevitably cry foul and shed a tear for football's working class roots; others will cheer for this evidence of our growing culinary maturity. Both sides, though, should applaud the menu, which offers British classics and 'bloke' food galore, from classically prepared liver and bacon to fish and chips and rib-eyes with assorted accompaniments. This being a polyglot club means other nationalities are also represented, in this case a bit of Italy and France, and more sophisticated fare such as foie gras terrine or duck confit is also available.

Foxtrot Oscar

Traditional

79 Royal Hospital Rd
✉ SW3 4HN
☏ (020) 7349 9595 **Fax** (020) 7592 1603
e-mail foxtrotoscar@gordonramsay.com **www**.gordonramsay.com

⊖ Sloane Square
▶ **Plan XI**
Booking essential

Carte £20/30

This Chelsea institution was created by Michael Proudlock nearly 30 years when he returned from New York with tales of burgers and eggs Benedict. Years later Gordon Ramsay and his chefs from up the road became regulars and so he jumped at the change of buying it in 2007. Fast forward to the present and even though it's part of the Ramsay empire, Michael is still there, greeting his regulars. It's taken a couple of goes but they're steadily getting the feel of the place and the style of service right. Meanwhile, the kitchen effortlessly captures the essence of comfort food for which the restaurant is known. Expect pies, cassoulet and coq au vin alongside fishcakes and potted duck. And they still do a pretty good burger and eggs Benedict.

Tom's Kitchen

E6 French

27 Cale St ✉ SW3 3QP ⊖ South Kensington
☎ (020) 7349 0202 ▶ **Plan XI**
Fax (020) 7823 3652 Closed 25 Decmeber and 1 January
e-mail info@tomskitchen.co.uk www.tomskitchen.co.uk

Carte £29/51

The Tom is Tom Aikens and this is a simpler but immeasurably worthy addendum to his eponymous restaurant around the corner. What was previously The Blenheim pub now has an industrial-lite feel, with eating on the ground floor, a bar on the second and private dining at the top. Once you've found the right door to get in you'll be welcomed by an enthusiastic team and those without reservations are steered to the counter. Open from breakfast to very late, the menu offers uncomplicated but carefully prepared comfort food. French is the main influence, with such classics as steak tartare and confit of duck, but Britain supplies the majority of the ingredients as well as the occasional dish, while Italy turns up too with the odd risotto or panna cotta.

Manicomio

F6 Italian

85 Duke of York Sq, King's Rd ⊖ Sloane Square
✉ SW3 4LY ▶ **Plan XI**
☎ (020) 7730 3366 Closed 25-26 December and 1 January
Fax (020) 7730 3377
www.manicomio.co.uk

Carte £28/41

With the Saatchi Gallery next door, Manicomio has really hit the jackpot: the King's Road looks to be on the rise again and Duke of York Square could turn out to be one of its most fashionable quarters. The restaurant has bedded in nicely – another branch has opened in The City – and its terrace is deservedly popular on warm days. The deli occupies one half; the restaurant the other, and the cooking is Italian and wholesome. The pasta dishes are a meal in themselves and the kitchen keeps flavours natural and dishes simple and reliable. Service never loses its sense of fun, even when creaking slightly under the pressure of being busy. The restaurant has a warm and relaxed feel with exposed brick walls, modern artwork and a bar on one side.

Aubaine

E6

French

260-262 Brompton Rd
✉ SW3 2AS
☏ (020) 7052 0100 **Fax** (020) 7052 0622
e-mail info@aubaine.co.uk www.aubaine.co.uk

⊖ South Kensington
▶ Plan XI

Carte £22/44

Whether it's a croissant, croque monsieur or coq au vin, Aubaine is among the increasing number of operations of a more fluid nature which recognise that we don't always want to eat three courses at 1pm. Describing itself as a 'boulangerie, patisserie and restaurant', it opens early morning until late at night and offers a comprehensive choice of French specialities to satisfy all appetites at all times, with the location making it especially busy during shopping hours. The breads are baked here and the 'shop' section does a roaring trade. The dining area fuses country and city; dressers, flowers and distressed wooden tables are juxtaposed with the modernity of exposed air-con vents and it all opens out onto the pavement in summer.

Bangkok

E6

Thai

9 Bute St ✉ SW7 3EY
☏ (020) 7584 8529
www.bangkokrestaurant.co.uk

⊖ South Kensington
▶ Plan XI

Closed Christmas-New Year, Sunday and Bank Holidays

Carte £20/28

Bangkok was the first Thai restaurant to open in London and is now not too far from celebrating its fortieth birthday. The same owner is still here and can often be seen at the stove. Dishes may sound rather simple on the menu but the cooking is skilfully executed and the flavours are clear, fresh and nicely balanced. Don't let the smart canopied façade raise your expectations too high: this is not the most comfortable restaurant around. Basic tables and chairs are close together and on the walls hang simple photographs of Thai life. But the open kitchen gives diners something to look at and there's always a sociable atmosphere. Everyone appears to leave feeling sated and, more unusually these days, with wallets free of burn holes.

Bibendum Oyster Bar

Seafood

E6

Michelin House, 81 Fulham Rd ✉ SW3 6RD
☏ (020) 7823 7925
Fax (020) 7823 7148
e-mail reservations@bibendum.co.uk **www**.bibendum.co.uk

⊖ South Kensington
▶ **Plan XI**
Closed 25-26 December and 1 January – bookings not accepted

Carte £25/35

As an alternative to the more formal restaurant upstairs, Bibendum Oyster Bar provides relaxed surroundings in which to enjoy a variety of seafood. It is also just the sort of place we encounter on holiday in France and then ask why we don't have anything like it at home. The speciality is, as the name suggests, oysters but the plateau de fruits de mer must come a close second. There are also salads, daily specials and plenty of other seafood on the extensive menu. The tiled walls and mosaic floor add to the appeal and the atmosphere is generally relaxed. Service from the young team can be a little hit and miss. If you haven't had your fill, you can stock up on more at Bibendum Crustacea, with its counter on the old garage forecourt.

The Admiral Codrington

Gastropub

F6

17 Mossop St ✉ SW3 2LY
☏ (020) 7581 0005 **Fax** (020) 7589 2452
e-mail admiral-codrington@333holdingsltd.com
www.theadmiralcodrington.com

⊖ South Kensington
▶ **Plan XI**
Closed 24-27 December

Carte £25/32

The personnel running the place may change occasionally but the local reputation of 'The Cod' remains largely unchanged. Lunch can be had in the bar or the restaurant but in the evenings the locals descend and drinkers rule so the serving of food is restricted to the dining room. This in turn becomes something of a haven of relative peace (which presumably explains the curious appearance of a cover charge). The retractable roof remains an appealing feature as does the booth seating for larger parties. The perennial favourites are never removed from the menu, like crispy squid and the fishcakes, and it's generally a pleasing mix of British and European classics, from fish pie to veal Holstein via assorted pasta dishes and a fish of the day.

Chelsea Ram

Gastropub

D8

32 Burnaby St ⊠ SW10 0PL
✆ (020) 7351 4008
e-mail bookings@chelsearam.co.uk

⊖ Fulham Broadway
▶ **Plan XI**

Carte £20/27

This stalwart of the London dining scene remains as popular as ever; book or arrive early for lunch as they only have 17 tables and they get snapped up quickly, particularly the two by the fire. There's full table service and whilst it all chills out a little at dinner, timings from the kitchen are generally spot-on. Comforting classics and honest home-cooking is how the chef describes his food: homemade soup comes with crusty bread, lamb chops with bubble and squeak, sausages with mash and rib-eye with dauphinoise potatoes; there are pies and casseroles and even some mean snacks to accompany a pint. You can also get a proper pudding, not a dessert, and these could include sticky banana or a crumble.

Swag and Tails

Gastropub

E5

10-11 Fairholt St, Knightsbridge
⊠ SW7 1EG
✆ (020) 7584 6926
Fax (020) 7581 9935
e-mail theswag@swagandtails.com **www**.swagandtails.com

⊖ Knightsbridge
▶ **Plan XI**
Closed Christmas-New Year, Saturday,
Sunday and Bank Holidays

Carte £22/32

The Swag and Tails is one of the prettier pubs around, with its hanging baskets, log fire, panelling and those swagged and tailed drapes. The dining area is at the rear with a conservatory extension. The kitchen clearly knows its customers and gives them a balanced selection combining modern, Mediterranean-influenced cooking while still satisfying those who just want a decent steak sandwich. There's also a degree of sophistication in that the liver comes with pancetta and the duck is accompanied by pistachios; they also throw in the occasional Asian twist in the form of duck pancakes or spring rolls. Plates of charcuterie or Caesar salads are there for those with lighter appetites. Most of the wine comes in at around £20 a bottle.

Builders Arms

Gastropub

E6

13 Britten St ✉ SW3 3TY
✆ (020) 7349 9040
e-mail buildersarms@geronimo-inns.co.uk
www.geronimo-inns.co.uk

⊖ South Kensington
▶ **Plan XI**
Closed 25-26 December
– bookings not accepted

Carte £20/35

A/C ☼ VISA MC AE

They don't take bookings and no orders for food can be placed until 7.15pm, by which time the place is absolutely jumping with locals, so knowing when to arrive is anyone's guess. But at 7.15 precisely the service swings into action like a minor military operation and thereafter is surprisingly helpful and polite. Beyond the bar, those early swarms congregate noisily on sofas, while diners tend to head for the stripped pine tables on the other side. Slightly less frenetic is the glass-roofed area at the back. Food here mixes gutsy, classic pub cooking with contemporary European dishes, and pies and fish and chips sit happily on the menu alongside salt and pepper squid with chilli dip, or steak with marrow.

The Pig's Ear

Gastropub

E7

35 Old Church St ✉ SW3 5BS
✆ (020) 7352 2908
Fax (020) 7352 9321
e-mail thepigsear@hotmail.co.uk **www**.thepigsear.co.uk

⊖ Sloane Square
▶ **Plan XI**
Closed 10 days Christmas to New Year

Carte £30/50

☼ VISA MC AE

This foodie pub off the King's Road, with its board games and newspapers, is a great spot for whiling away a weekend hour or three. The owners' love of cinema and music is evident in the plethora of posters and photos; a jug of Bloody Mary sits proudly on the bar and bottles of Bréton cider are served alongside the beers and wines. It can feel as if all of Chelsea has come out to play, so book ahead for the panelled dining room, or alternatively, ask if you can commandeer the Blue Room – a cosy, curtained off area with a real fire. The menu is modern British meets the Med, with dishes like beef marrow, lamb stew and dumplings, or Cornish crab Thermidor. Charcuterie is a staple and the great bread comes from The Flour Station in Battersea.

The Phoenix

F6

Gastropub

23 Smith St ✉ SW3 4EE
☏ (020) 7730 9182
e-mail thephoenix@geronimo-inns.co.uk
www.geronimo-inns.co.uk

⊖ Sloane Square
▶ **Plan XI**
Closed 25-26 December

Carte £15/25

The Phoenix may be part of an ever-expanding group of pubs but you'd never know it. It's a rather chic little number, close enough to the King's Road to be a useful pit-stop but also something of a local destination. The largest part of the pub is taken over by those very civilised locals, relaxing in the squashy sofas, enjoying a Welsh rarebit with their drinks. But work your way through to the back and you'll find the dining room, refurbished in 2008, where the murmur from the bar reminds you you're still in a pub. The food is tasty and satisfying, whether that's eggs Benedict, Portland crab on toast or steak and hand-cut chips which arrive in sweet enamel pie dishes. The seasonal specials on the blackboard get snapped up quickly.

The Cross Keys

E7

Gastropub

1 Lawrence St ✉ SW3 5NB
☏ (020) 7349 9111
Fax (020) 7349 9333
e-mail xkeys.nicole@hotmail.co.uk **www**.thexkeys.net

⊖ South Kensington
▶ **Plan XI**
Closed 24-25 December, 1 January,
Bank Holidays

Carte £25/30

This may be a pub with a history dating back well over 200 years, but the interior owes more to today's sense of irony and fun. The bar offers plenty of elbow room and its own menu but beyond is the glass-roofed dining room which comes complete with little statues, its own tree and an eye-catching frieze of garden implements. The kitchen is more conventional in its approach than the surroundings would suggest, with food that is modern in style but robust in flavour and influences are kept largely within old Europe, so expect to find alluring sounding dishes like smoked duck with glazed figs, wild mushroom tart with pesto, lamb cutlets, coq au vin and poached pear in red wine. There are also blackboard specials to supplement the menus.

Lots Road Pub & Dining Room

Gastropub

D8

114 Lots Rd ⊠ SW10 0RJ
✆ (020) 7352 6645 **Fax** (020) 7376 4975
e-mail lotsroad@foodandfuel.co.uk
www.lotsroadpub.com

⊖ Fulham Broadway
▶ **Plan XI**

Carte £20/26

The high windows of this corner building give the impression that it is empty; in reality, the reverse is nearly always true. What keeps the punters, if the Chelsea set could ever be called punters, coming back time and again are the earthy pub dishes such as tasty hamburgers, lamb shanks and belly pork offered on a daily-changing menu, plus the sort of heart-warming puddings that all pubs should do. The sign reads, 'You haven't lived until you've tried our sticky toffee pud,' and its popularity bears witness. Diligent and friendly young staff stay on the move between table and open kitchen. It calls itself a 'bar and dining room' so drinkers are made welcome and Thursday evenings see regular wine tastings, with bar snacks laid on.

Your opinions are important for us: please write and let us know about your discoveries and experiences – good or bad!

C. Barrely / MICHELIN

Kensington · North Kensington · Notting Hill

It was the choking air of 17C London that helped put **Kensington** on the map: the little village lying to the west of the city became the favoured retreat of the asthmatic King William III who had Sir Christopher Wren build **Kensington Palace** for him. Where the king leads, the titled follow, and the area soon became a fashionable location for the rich. For over 300 years, it's had no problem holding onto its cachet, though a stroll down Kensington High Street is these days a more egalitarian odyssey than some more upmarket residents might approve of.

The shops here mix the everyday with the flamboyant, but for a real taste of the exotic you have to take the lift to the top of the Art Deco Barkers building and arrive at the Kensington Roof Gardens, which are open to all as long as they're not in use for a corporate bash. The gardens are now over seventy years old, yet still remain a 'charming secret'. Those who do make it up to the sixth floor discover a delightful woodland garden and gurgling stream, complete with pools, bridges and trees. There are flamingos, too, adding a dash of vibrant colour.

Back down on earth, Kensington boasts another hidden attraction in **Leighton House** on its western boundaries. The Victorian redbrick façade looks a bit forbidding as you make your approach, but step inside and things take a dramatic turn, courtesy of the extraordinary Arab Hall, with its oriental mosaics and tinkling fountain creating a scene like something from *The Arabian Knights.* Elsewhere in the building, the Pre-Raphaelite paintings of Lord Leighton, Burne-Jones and Alma-Tadema are much to the fore. Mind you, famous names have always had a hankering for W8, with a particular preponderance to dally in enchanting **Kensington Square,** where there are almost as many blue plaques as buildings upon which to secure them. William Thackeray, John Stuart Mill and Edward Burne-Jones were all residents.

One of the London's most enjoyable green retreats is **Holland Park,** just north of the High Street. It boasts the 400 year-old Holland House, which is a fashionable focal point for summer-time al fresco theatre and opera. Holland Walk runs along the eastern fringe of the park, and provides a lovely sojourn down to the shops; at the Kyoto Garden, koi carp reach hungrily for the surface of their pool, while elsewhere peacocks strut around as if they own the place.

Another world beckons just north of here – the seedy-cum-glitzy environs of **Notting Hill.** The main drag itself, Notting Hill Gate, is little more than a one-dimensional thoroughfare only enlivened by second hand record shops, but to its south are charming cottages with pastel shades in leafy streets, while to the north the appealing **Pembridge Road** evolves into the boutiques of Westbourne Grove. Most people heading in this direction are making for the legendary Portobello Road market – particularly on Saturdays, which are manic. The market stretches on for more than a mile, with a chameleon-like ability to change colour and character on the way: there are antiques at the Notting Hill end, followed further up by food stalls, and then designer and vintage clothes as you reach the Westway. Those who don't fancy the madding crowds of the market can nip into the Electric Cinema and watch a movie in supreme comfort: it boasts two-seater sofas and leather armchairs. Nearby there are another two film-houses putting the hip into the Hill – the Gate, and the Coronet, widely recognised as one of London's most charming 'locals'.

Hidden in a mews just north of **Westbourne Grove** is a fascinating destination: the Museum of Brands, Packaging and Advertising, which does pretty much what it says on the label. It's both nostalgic and evocative, featuring thousands of items like childhood toys, teenage magazines…and HP sauce bottles.

Kensington, North Kensington and Notting Hill
(Plan XIII)

The Ledbury 🌸

French

127 Ledbury Rd ✉ W11 2AQ
📞 (020) 7792 9090
Fax (020) 7792 9191
e-mail info@theledbury.com
www.theledbury.com

🚇 **Notting Hill Gate**
Closed 24-26 December and
August Bank Holiday

Menu £60 (dinner) – Carte lunch £38/50

An assortment of visiting Australians have decided over the years to make London home, from retired sportsmen to political advisers, acclaimed actors to social commentators; even the odd backpacker has been known to stay. Now chefs can be added to that list and among them is the talented Brett Graham. He has been running the kitchen at The Ledbury since it opened in 2005, having perfected his craft at its sister restaurant, The Square. His cooking exudes confidence; his dishes all display both an inherent understanding of flavours and a real appreciation of how differing textures can inform a dish. The improving quality of this country's produce is also evident on the menu, from the fish landed at Looe to the use of wild herbs. The lunch menu is good value, especially as it often features a full dish from the à la carte rather than just a dumbed-down version. The room is sleek and comfortable, with the atmosphere lightened by the genuine neighbourhood feel. The service is confident and quite detailed but also comes with personality.

First Course
- Flame-grilled mackerel with a mackerel tartare, avocado and shiso.
- Roast scallops, liquorice, fennel and roasting juices.

Main Course
- Breast and confit of pigeon, sweetcorn, almond and girolles.
- Roast cod with leeks, potato gnocchi, truffle emulsion.

Dessert
- Date and vanilla tart with cardamom and orange ice cream.
- Pavé of chocolate, sunflower seeds and basil.

Belvedere

French

B4

Holland House, off Abbotsbury Rd
✉ W8 6LU
✆ (020) 7602 1238 **Fax** (020) 7610 4382
e-mail info@belvedererestaurant.co.uk
www.belvedererestaurant.co.uk

↔ Holland Park
Closed 26 December,
1 January and Sunday dinner

Menu £18/25 (lunch) – Carte £28/53

Built in 17C as the summer ballroom to the Jacobean Holland House, The Belvedere sits in a stunning position in Holland Park. It's hard to believe you're still in London but check the location first as signposts within the park are a little elusive. The ground floor is the more glittery, with mirrors, glass balls and a small bar area. Upstairs is more traditional in style and leads out onto the charming terrace which is well worth booking in summer. Service remains decidedly formal. The menu covers all bases from eggs Benedict to even the occasional Thai, but it's worth sticking to the more classical, French influenced dishes as these are kitchen's strength. Produce is well sourced and dishes nicely balanced. France dominates the wine list.

Min Jiang

Chinese

D4

at Royal Garden Hotel,
10th Floor, 2-24 Kensington High St
✉ W8 4PT
✆ (020) 7361 1988 **Fax** (020) 7361 1987
e-mail reservations@minjiang.co.uk www.minjiang.co.uk

↔ High Street Kensington
▶ **Plan XIII**

Carte £30/50

Restaurants with views are rare in London so it's no surprise that this Chinese restaurant, which opened in July 2008 on the 10th floor of the Royal Garden Hotel, makes the most of its position overlooking Kensington Palace and Gardens. Named after the Min River of Sichuan, an area which influences the menu, it's an offshoot from the original in the group's Singapore hotel. The lunchtime dim sum is done particularly well, while the speciality of the à la carte is the Beijing duck which is roasted in a wood fired oven. The presence of lobster, abalone and shark fin can somewhat distort the prices of the appealing menu. The room is a long, stylish one, with vases influenced by the Ming Dynasty and photos of assorted Chinese scenes.

Launceston Place

D5

Modern European 🍴🍴🍴

1a Launceston Pl ✉ W8 5RL
📞 (020) 7937 6912
Fax (020) 7938 2412
e-mail lpr-res@danddlondon.com
www.launcestonplace-restaurant.co.uk

⊖ Gloucester Road
Closed Christmas and
New Year and Monday lunch

Menu £24/38 – Carte £35/48

A/C

VISA
MC
AE
DC

Now under the ownership of D&D restaurants, Launceston Place has been resuscitated, reinvigorated and relaunched. The walls may be darker, the lighting moodier and the ambition more evident but the best thing it that the appealing neighbourhood feel has not been lost, even with service that takes itself seriously. Tristan Welch, who previously worked with Marcus Wareing, is the confident young chef at the helm and his cooking is original but also well grounded and balanced. He's also a keen champion of home-grown produce: about 80% of the ingredients come from within the British Isles and he's planning to increase this figure further. The Tasting Menu is priced not far north of the à la carte and showcases his talent well.

Notting Hill Brasserie

B3

French 🍴🍴

92 Kensington Park Rd
✉ W11 2PN
📞 (020) 7229 4481 **Fax** (020) 7221 1246
e-mail enquiries@nottinghillbrasserie.com
www.nottinghillbrasserie.com

⊖ Notting Hill Gate
Closed Bank Holidays and
lunch Monday and Tuesday

Menu £23/30 – Carte £40/48

A/C

🎵

VISA
MC
AE

The lighting is flatteringly dim and there's always a good smattering of locals but this restaurant, housed within an Edwardian townhouse, is hardly what one expects from somewhere calling itself a brasserie. It's got a large bar, where the jazz musos perch themselves each evening and the dining room is divided up between smaller rooms, each with their own individual character and this adds to the intimacy. Service is a real strength and the staff are all generally clued-up. The menu reads very well, with each dish headlined by the single main component and influences stretch across the Mediterranean. When those dishes arrive they look very appealing, although flavours can sometimes be a little timid.

Zaika

Indian

D4

1 Kensington High St
W8 5NP
⌀ (020) 7795 6533 **Fax** (020) 7937 8854
e-mail info@zaika-restaurant.co.uk **www**.zaika-restaurant.co.uk

⊖ High Street Kensington
Closed Saturday lunch, Christmas,
New Year and Bank Holidays

Menu £20 (lunch) – Carte £29/43

Chef Sanjay Dwivedi is making his mark here at Zaika and choosing from his menu can take time as there are plenty of things on it that sound different and interesting. His judicious use of spicing ensures that the main ingredient of each dish is never overwhelmed and while his cooking has a refined and sophisticated quality that's a far cry from most Indian restaurants, those dishes still arrive in generous proportions. To see what the kitchen can really do, try one of the tasting menus. Perhaps to disguise its previous incarnation as a bank, the room has been decorated in a theatrical and flamboyant way, with plenty of drapes and lots of colour. The bar is a fun spot for drinks and service is unobtrusive and efficient.

Clarke's

Modern European

C4

124 Kensington Church St
W8 4BH
⌀ (020) 7221 9225 **Fax** (020) 7229 4564
e-mail restaurant@sallyclarke.com **www**.sallyclarke.com

⊖ Notting Hill Gate
Closed 2 weeks Christmas
- New Year and Bank Holidays

Menu £47 (dinner) – Carte lunch approx. £29

Sally Clarke spent a few years in California and those who know Alice Waters' Chez Panisse will recognise the concept: crisp, seasonal produce, a minimal amount of interference from the kitchen and clean, fresh flavours. As the restaurant approaches its quarter of a century it's clear that it doesn't have to be warm and sunny outside to appreciate this type of cooking. The only significant change happened a few years back when customers were given a choice at dinner: for many years there had been a set menu with no alternative. The downstairs is a good spot to watch the kitchen in action; upstairs is more intimate. The long-standing manager keeps things rolling along nicely and knows his regulars. There's bounty galore in the shop next door.

Babylon

Modern European 𝄪

C4

at The Roof Gardens,
99 Kensington High St
(entrance on Derry St) ✉ W8 5SA
☏ (020) 7368 3993 **Fax** (020) 7368 3995
e-mail babylon@roofgardens.virgin.co.uk **www**.roofgardens.com

⊖ High Street Kensington
Closed Christmas-New Year and Sunday dinner

Menu £20 (lunch) – Carte £39/55

The challenge is to find the entrance which is secreted on the right as you walk down Derry Street; then it's the lift up to the 7th floor and suddenly you're surrounded by trees. There's no doubting that this is quite a spot and while the gardens just below may not be 'hanging' they are an understandably appealing place for a party. The restaurant is a long, narrow affair whose contemporary décor reflects the leafy outdoors and the terrace takes some beating in summer. Influences on the menu remain largely within Europe and the cooking shows a degree of perkiness and ambition. The lunch time set menu is priced to appeal to local businesses while the à la carte can get a little expensive. The wine list plants its flag firmly in the New World.

Edera

Italian 𝄪

B4

148 Holland Park Ave ✉ W11 4UE
☏ (020) 7221 6090 **Fax** (020) 7313 9700

⊖ Holland Park
Closed Bank Holidays

Carte £32/49

No restaurant can survive without the support of regulars and few restaurants demonstrate the importance of customer loyalty more than Edera. In an area not overburdened with exciting choices, Edera maintains decent numbers by focusing its attentions on its regulars. The room may not have too much character but the atmosphere is local and congenial. Meanwhile, the kitchen does what all good Italians do: it uses superior ingredients, eschews fads and doesn't crowd the plate. There is a subtle Sardinian element to the menu here – you'll find malloreddus pasta, the bottarga comes as carpaccio or with spaghetti and there's often suckling pig available at weekends – while the desserts display an appealing lightness of touch.

E&O

B2

Asian XX

14 Blenheim Crescent
✉ W11 1NN
✆ (020) 7229 5454
Fax (020) 7229 5522
e-mail eando@rickerrestaurants.com
www.rickerrestaurants.com

⊖ Ladbroke Grove
Closed Christmas,
New Year and August Bank Holiday

Carte £31/42

Once you've sidestepped the full-on bar of this Notting Hill favourite, a step from Portobello Road, you'll find yourself in a moodily sophisticated restaurant packed with the beautiful and the hopeful. The room is understatedly urbane, with slatted walls, large circular lamps and leather banquettes, while noise levels are at the party end of the auditory index. Waiting staff are obliging, pleasant and often among the prettiest people in the room. E&O stands for Eastern and Oriental and the menu journeys across numerous Asian countries, dividing itself into assorted headings which include dim sum, salads, tempura, curries and roasts. Individual dishes vary in size and price, so sharing, as in life, is often the best option.

Whits

C5

Modern European XX

21 Abingdon Rd
✉ W8 6AH
✆ (020) 7938 1122
Fax (020) 7937 6121
e-mail eva@whits.co.uk
www.whits.co.uk

⊖ High Street Kensington
Closed Christmas - New Year, Easter,
Saturday lunch, Sunday dinner and Monday
– dinner only

Menu £19/24 – Carte £29/37

Privately-owned restaurants with a couple at the helm are becoming something of a rarity but there is a certain kind of service one only gets from an owner of a restaurant; it is usually a combination of concern, confidence, pride and sincerity. Eva at Whits is a case in point – she's one of life's natural hosts who puts all customers at ease and the relaxed atmosphere is the restaurant's great strength. Her partner Steve's cooking certainly doesn't pull any punches; combinations are tried and tested, techniques are classic and flavours bold and upfront. The presentation on the plate is somewhat elaborate but diners all leave eminently satisfied, thanks to some generous portioning. There's a good value set menu alongside the à la carte.

11 Abingdon Road

C5

Mediterranean ✖✖

11 Abingdon Rd
✉ W8 6AH
✆ (020) 7937 0120
e-mail eleven@abingdonroad.co.uk
www.abingdonroad.co.uk

⊖ High Street Kensington
Closed Bank Holidays

Carte £26/33

A/C
☀
VISA
MC
AE

Opened late in 2005 and sister restaurant to Sonny's and The Phoenix, 11 Abingdon Road is already attracting quite a following who are helped along, no doubt, by not having to look up the street name and number first. The stylish façade is reflected in the contemporary feel of the clean white lines and lighting of the interior which add to the general feeling of spaciousness. The owners' own art collection adorns the walls and the tables are set close together, adding to the atmosphere and general buzz. The Mediterranean provides most of the influence in the kitchen, with bright, vibrant colours and fresh, clean flavours. There is a good value set menu available at lunchtimes and early evenings.

Timo

B5

Italian ✖✖

343 Kensington High St
✉ W8 6NW
✆ (020) 7603 3888 **Fax** (020) 7603 8111
e-mail timorestaurant@fsmail.net
www.timorestaurant.net

⊖ High Street Kensington
Closed 25 December,
Sunday and Bank Holidays

Menu £14 (lunch) – Carte dinner £28/44

A/C
🕗
VISA
MC
AE

At the Olympia end of Kensington High Street sits this warm and inviting Italian restaurant. The colours of cream and beige, matched with summery paintings of garden landscapes, lend a sunny feel, whatever the season outside. The tables are as smartly dressed as the waiters, who provide conscientious service and the suited owner does the rounds and knows his regulars. The set menu comes divided into the typically Italian four courses, although the impressive looking bread basket will test your powers of self-restraint. Daily specials to supplement the menu are temptingly described and the desserts merit particular investigation. This is a solidly reliable neighbourhood restaurant which sensibly doesn't try to reinvent anything.

Memories of China

B5

Chinese ✗✗

353 Kensington High St
✉ W8 6NW
☏ (020) 7603 6951 **Fax** (020) 7603 0848
www.memories-of-china.co.uk

⊖ High Street Kensington
Closed Christmas-New Year
– booking essential

Carte £25/50

A/C ☀ VISA MC AE

Memories of China is a well established Chinese restaurant which pulls in both the locals, many of whom will never have a bad word said about the place, and those staying in one of the surrounding hotels. As such, it's always busy so it's well worth coming secure in the knowledge that you've made a reservation. The menu, rather like the room, is relatively compact and keeps things on the straight and narrow by focusing on classic Cantonese and Sichuan cooking. Set menus are available for groups or those who prefer others to make their decisions for them. The glass façade of this corner restaurant chimes with the bright and modern décor of the interior with Chinese themed murals and calligraphy.

L Restaurant & Bar

C5

Spanish ✗✗

2 Abingdon Rd
✉ W8 6AF
☏ (020) 7795 6969 **Fax** (020) 7795 6699
e-mail info@l-restaurant.co.uk www.l-restaurant.co.uk

⊖ High Street Kensington
Closed 25 December and Monday lunch

Menu £16 (lunch) – Carte £26/36

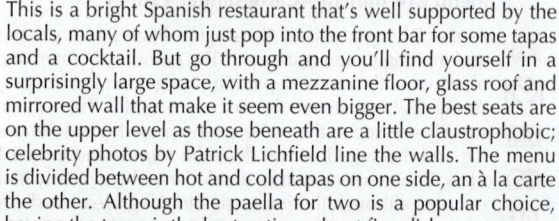

A/C 🛗 ☀ VISA MC AE

This is a bright Spanish restaurant that's well supported by the locals, many of whom just pop into the front bar for some tapas and a cocktail. But go through and you'll find yourself in a surprisingly large space, with a mezzanine floor, glass roof and mirrored wall that make it seem even bigger. The best seats are on the upper level as those beneath are a little claustrophobic; celebrity photos by Patrick Lichfield line the walls. The menu is divided between hot and cold tapas on one side, an à la carte the other. Although the paella for two is a popular choice, having the tapas is the best option; about five dishes per person should suffice. Occasional live music helps the atmosphere along, as does the reasonably priced wine list.

Kensington Place

Modern European

C3

201 Kensington Church St
⊠ W8 7LX
☏ (020) 7727 3184 **Fax** (020) 7792 9388
e-mail kprreservations@danddlondon.com
www.kensingtonplace-restaurant.co.uk

⊖ Notting Hill Gate
Closed Christmas and 1 January
– booking essential

Menu £20/25 – Carte £22/46

When Kensington Place opened in 1987, it broke the mould by showing Londoners that good food could be served in a relaxed style and for that we should all be grateful. Now, some twenty or so years later it is gearing up for its new incarnation as something of an elder statesman and is under the new ownership of D&D. Rowley Leigh may also have left but the new kitchen is not reinventing any wheels. The cooking remains unfussy, seasonal and decently proportioned. Classics like foie gras with a sweet corn pancake and scallops with pea purée remain and accompaniments to the main courses are well chosen. The wine list is lengthy and listed by grape variety and style. The acoustics are still terrible but the atmosphere remains great.

Bumpkin

Modern European

C2

209 Westbourne Park Rd
⊠ W11 1EA
☏ (020) 7243 9818 **Fax** (020) 7229 1826
www.bumpkinuk.com

⊖ Westbourne Park
Closed 25-26 December and 1 January
– dinner only

Carte £27/40

The aim was to create a clubby place with a wholesome, homespun feel and for that they chose a derelict pub with a dubious past. It works, largely because they have eschewed the gastropub in favour of creating something a little different. The ground floor is a brasserie with an appealing menu of light bites, pots, pies and grills with satisfying dishes ranging from macaroni cheese to liver and bacon. Those wanting something equally gutsy, but slightly more refined, can head to the first floor restaurant for dishes such as osso bucco or wild sea bass. Both kitchens share an emphasis on seasoning, sourcing and buying organic where possible. The other floors are taken up with private dining and whisky tasting.

Malabar

Indian

C3

27 Uxbridge St ⊠ W8 7TQ
⌀ (020) 7727 8800
e-mail feedback@malabar-restaurant.co.uk
www.malabar-restaurant.co.uk

⊖ Notting Hill Gate
Closed 23-27 December
– buffet lunch Sunday

Menu £23 – Carte £21/28 s

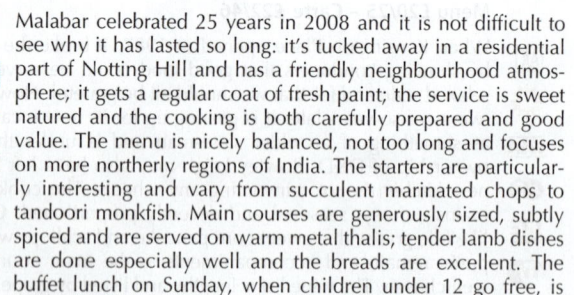

Malabar celebrated 25 years in 2008 and it is not difficult to see why it has lasted so long: it's tucked away in a residential part of Notting Hill and has a friendly neighbourhood atmosphere; it gets a regular coat of fresh paint; the service is sweet natured and the cooking is both carefully prepared and good value. The menu is nicely balanced, not too long and focuses on more northerly regions of India. The starters are particularly interesting and vary from succulent marinated chops to tandoori monkfish. Main courses are generously sized, subtly spiced and are served on warm metal thalis; tender lamb dishes are done especially well and the breads are excellent. The buffet lunch on Sunday, when children under 12 go free, is terrific value.

Cibo

Italian

A5

3 Russell Gdns
⊠ W14 8EZ
⌀ (020) 7371 6271
Fax (020) 7602 1371
e-mail ciborestaurant@aol.com **www**.ciborestaurant.net

⊖ Kensington Olympia
Closed Christmas-New Year,
Saturday lunch and Sunday dinner

Carte £25/39

Behind the rather elegant façade lies this personable and intimate Italian restaurant. Cibo has established itself over the years as something of a local landmark in this smart residential area, due to the mix of refreshingly unabashed and eclectic décor, reliably good Italian food and amiable service. The menu leans towards seafood and the portion size is on the generous side. The wide variety of breads on offer merit full investigation as do the pasta specials. The place is usually full of locals whose loyalty is such that they appear to exert an influence over the menu content; you're also likely to see one of two local celebrities on any given night. Cibo is one of the best reasons for living in Holland Park.

Notting Grill

B2

Beef specialities

123A Clarendon Rd ✉ W11 4JG
✆ (020) 7229 1500
Fax (020) 7229 8889
e-mail nottinggrill@awtrestaurants.com **www**.awt.com

⊖ Holland Park
Closed 25-26 December and
Monday-Friday lunch except December

Menu £19 (dinner) – Carte approx. £30

From the outside it still looks like the pub it once was, but inside it's gone all soft and spongy. Cushions are everywhere and a mix of pictures, rich colours and exposed brick all give it a warm, rustic yet welcoming feel. It's certainly worth staying downstairs as the room upstairs can't compete on atmosphere and personality. 'Well Bred, Well Fed and Well Hung' proclaims the menu, referring not to the owner, Antony Worrall Thompson, but to the speciality of the house - their well sourced steaks and grilled meats, which explains the dubious pun in the name. Comfort food is very much the order of the day and lovers of the old classics will find much to stir nostalgic thoughts, although those more of the present are not forgotten.

Wódka

D5

Polish

12 St Albans Grove
✉ W8 5PN
✆ (020) 7937 6513
Fax (020) 7937 8621
e-mail info@wodka.co.uk **www**.wodka.co.uk

⊖ High Street Kensington
Closed 25-26 December, 1 January,
Easter Sunday, Monday lunch and
Saturday lunch

Menu £15 (lunch) – Carte £29/34

Come to Wódka to celebrate all things Eastern European. Housed in what was once the dairy to Kensington Palace, the décor inside is industrial-lite, where warmth and intimacy soften the sharper edges of the tough minimalism. The robust flavours and classic dishes of Polish and Eastern European cooking are all here, from blinis to pierogi and golabki (stuffed cabbage) to Bigos (Polish Hunters stew). Those who prefer dishes in a lighter, more modern style will find that they haven't been forgotten. The restaurant has been run by an exclusively Polish team from a time when that was considered a novelty. With a variety of vodkas available, all served directly from the freezer, no one leaves without their heart a little warmer. Na Zdrowie!

The Fat Badger

B1

Gastropub

310 Portobello Road
W10 5TA
⌀ (020) 8969 4500 **Fax** (020) 8969 6714
e-mail rupert@thefatbadger.com **www**.thefatbadger.com

⊖ Ladbroke Grove.
Closed 25-26 December

Menu £15 – Carte £30/50

What was once The Caernarvon Castle appears to be another pub makeover with the old sofas, church seats and wood floors, but those chandeliers and that intriguing wallpaper hint at something a little different. Sure enough, one glance at the menu reveals that there is nothing gastropub-formulaic about the cooking. The chef's philosophy is British and seasonal, with a waste-not-want-not approach to butchery. Whole beasts are delivered to the kitchen and they are not afraid of offering unfamiliar cuts; the menu is constantly changing to reflect what the suppliers deem worthy and vegetables reflect what's in season. This is real and earthy cooking. Breakfast and brunch menus also reveal that this is a kitchen with imagination and integrity.

Good food without spending a fortune? Look out for the Bib Gourmand 😊.

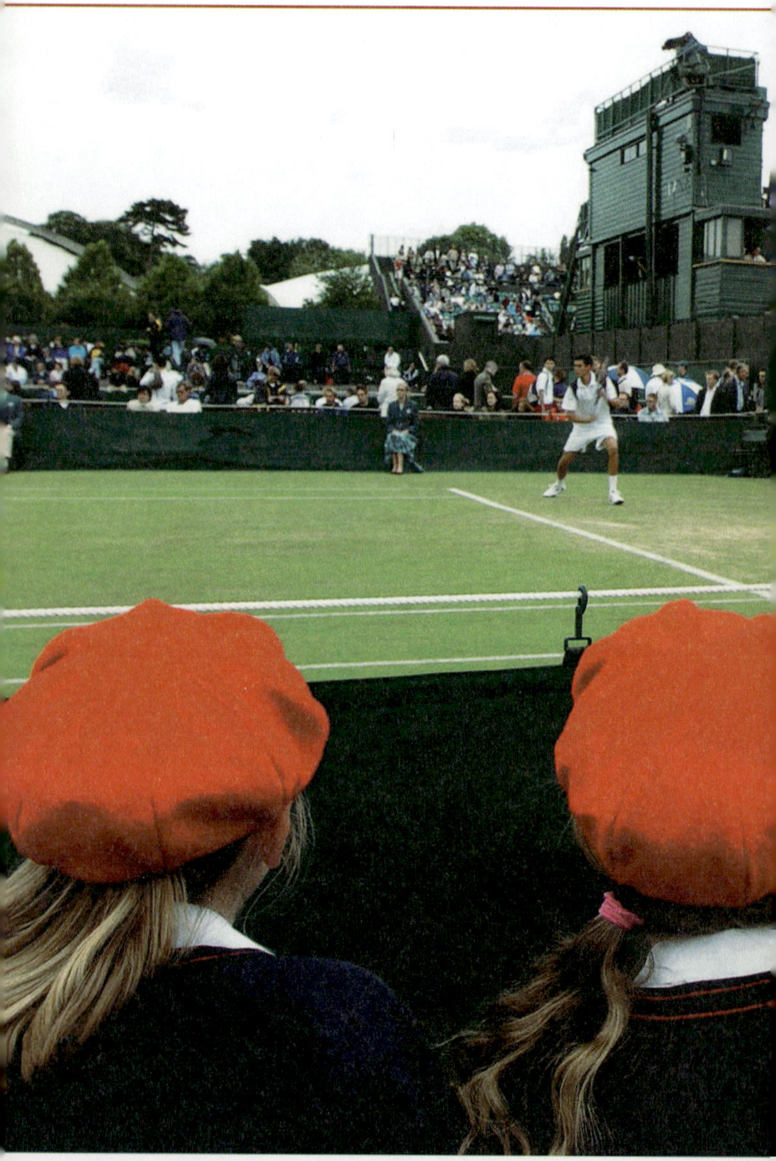

Greater London

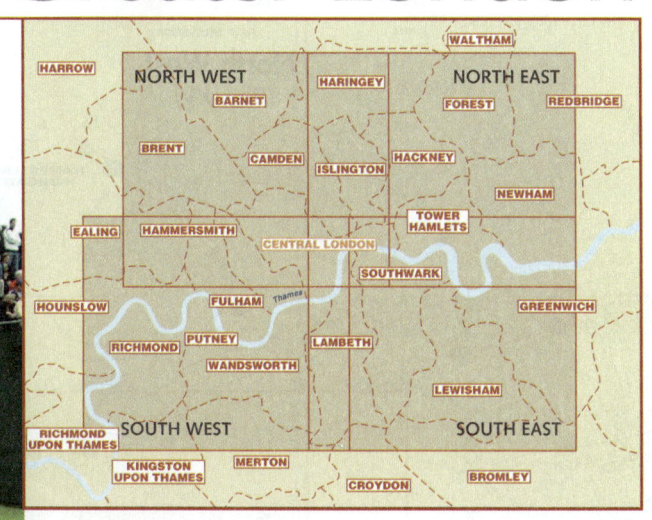

- ▶ North-West — **268**
- ▶ North-East — **286**
- ▶ South-East — **304**
- ▶ South-West — **316**

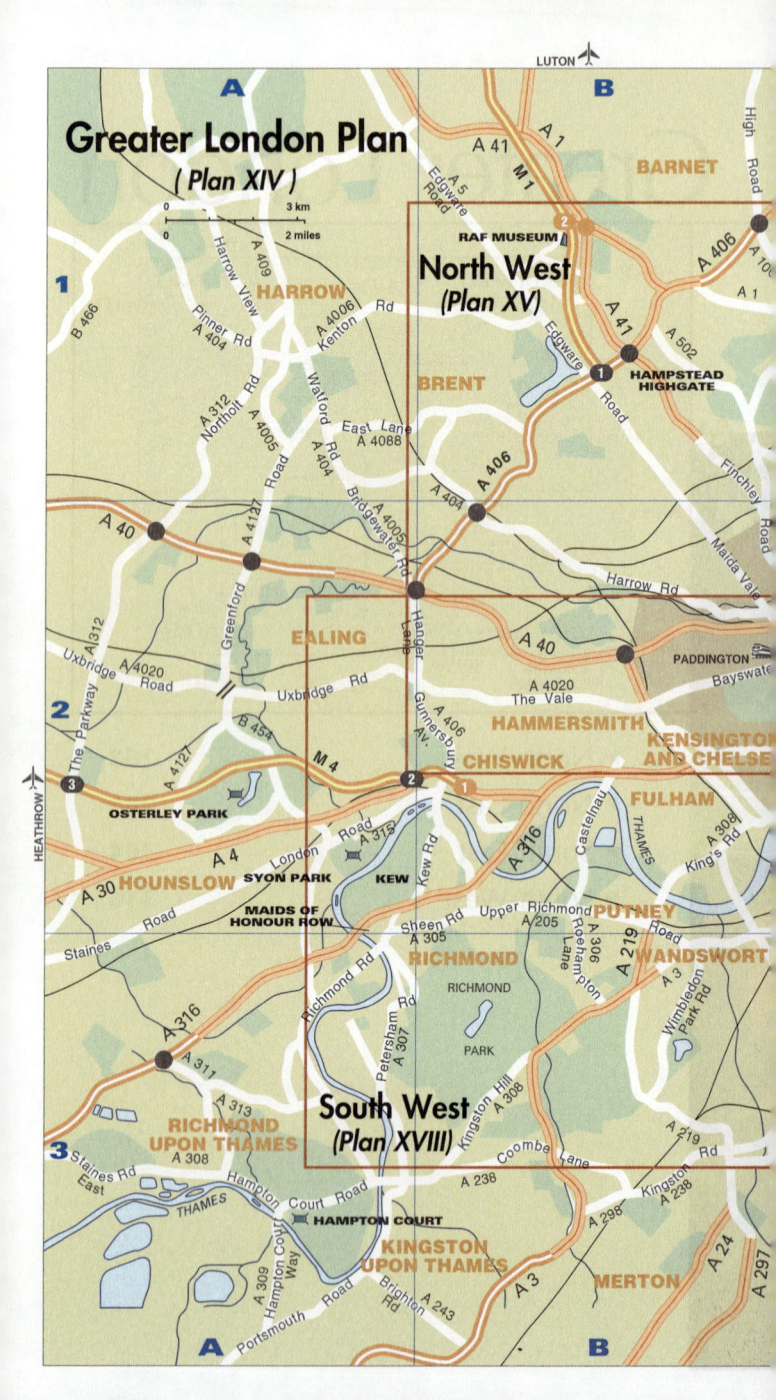

Greater London Plan
(Plan XIV)

North West *(Plan XV)*

South West *(Plan XVIII)*

STANSTED
GATWICK
North East
(Plan XVI)
Central London
(Plan I - XIII)
South East
(Plan XVII)
WALTHAM FOREST
HARINGEY
HACKNEY
ISLINGTON
CAMDEN
TOWER HAMLETS
NEWHAM
BATTERSEA
SOUTHWARK
LAMBETH
LEWISHAM
GREENWICH
BROMLEY
CROYDON
CANARY WHARF
LONDON CITY AIRPORT
THE O2
MILLENNIUM DOME
THAMES BARRIER
ISLE OF DOGS
ST KATHARINE'S DOCK
LIVERPOOL STREET
KING'S CROSS
EUSTON
WATERLOO
THAMES
A 406
A 10
M 11
A 104
A 503
A 12
A 13
A 2
A 20
A 21
Forest Road
Woodford New Rd
Lea Bridge Road
Leytonstone Rd
Romford Road
Aldersbrook Road
High St North
Commercial Rd
Aspen Way
Silvertown Way
Lower Rd
Evelyn St
Old Kent Rd
Trafalgar Rd
Shooters Hill Road
Peckham Rd
Lewisham Way
Lee High Rd
Brownhill Rd
Stanstead Rd
Bromley Rd
Southend Lane
Lordship Lane
Dulwich Common
Sydenham Hill
Church Rd
Anerley Rd
Widmore Rd
Bromley Common
Links Way
White Horse Rd
London Road
Croydon Rd
Tooting Bec Road
Norwood Rd
Brixton Rd
Clapham Rd
Camden Rd
Holloway Road
Archway Rd
Seven Sisters Road
Green Lanes
Kingsland Road
Mare St
Upper Clapton Rd
Academy Rd

North-West London

Heading north from London Zoo and Regent's Park the green baton is passed to two of the city's most popular and well-known locations: Hampstead Heath and Highgate Wood. In close proximity, they offer a favoured pair of lungs to travellers emerging from the murky depths of the Northern Line. Two centuries ago, they would have been just another part of the area's undeveloped high ground and pastureland, but since the building boom of the nineteenth century, both have become prized assets in this part of the metropolis.

People came to seek shelter in **Hampstead** in times of plague, and it's retained its bucolic air to this day. Famous names have always enjoyed its charms: Constable and Keats rested their brush and pen here, while the sculptors Henry Moore and Barbara Hepworth were residents in more recent times. Many are drawn to such delightful places as Church Row, which boasts a lovely Georgian Terrace. You know you're up high because the thoroughfares bear names like Holly Mount and Mount Vernon. The Heath is full of rolling woodlands and meadows; it's a great place for rambling, particularly to the crest of **Parliament Hill** and its superb city views. There are three bathing ponds here, one mixed, and one each for male and female swimmers, while up on the heath's northern fringes, **Kenwood House,** along with its famous al fresco summer concerts, also boasts great art by the likes of Vermeer and Rembrandt. And besides all that, there's an ivy tunnel leading to a terrace with idyllic pond views.

Highgate Wood is an ancient woodland and conservation area, containing a leafy walk that meanders enchantingly along a former railway line to **Crouch End,** home to a band of thespians. Down the road at Highgate Cemetery, the likes of Karl Marx, George Eliot, Christina Rossetti and Michael Faraday rest in a great entanglement of breathtaking Victorian over-decoration. The cemetery is still in use – most recent notable to be buried here is Alexander Litvinenko, the Russian dissident.

Next door you'll find **Waterlow Park,** another fine green space, which, apart from its super views, also includes decorative ponds on three levels. Lauderdale House is here, too, a 16C pile which is now an arts centre; more famously, Charles II handed over its keys to Nell Gwynn for her to use as her North London residence. Head back south from here, and **Primrose Hill** continues the theme of glorious green space: its surrounding terraces are populated by media darlings, while its vertiginous mass is another to boast a famously enviable vista.

Of a different hue altogether is **Camden Town** with its buzzy edge, courtesy of a renowned indie music scene, goths, punks, and six earthy markets selling everything from tat to exotica. Charles Dickens grew up here, and he was none too complimentary; the area still relishes its seamy underside. A scenic route out is the **Regent's Canal,** which cuts its way through the market and ambles to the east and west of the city. Up the road, the legendary Roundhouse re-opened its arty front doors in 2006, expanding further the wide range of Camden's alt scene.

One of the music world's most legendary destinations, the **Abbey Road** studios, is also in this area and, yes, it's possible to join other tourists making their way over that zebra crossing. Not far away, in Maresfield Gardens, stands a very different kind of attraction. The Freud Museum is one of the very few buildings in London to have two blue plaques. It was home to Sigmund during the last year of his life and it's where he lived with his daughter Anna (her plaque commemorates her work in child psychiatry). Inside, there's a fabulous library and his working desk. But the pivotal part of the whole house is in another corner of the study – the psychiatrist's couch!

Greater London: North West

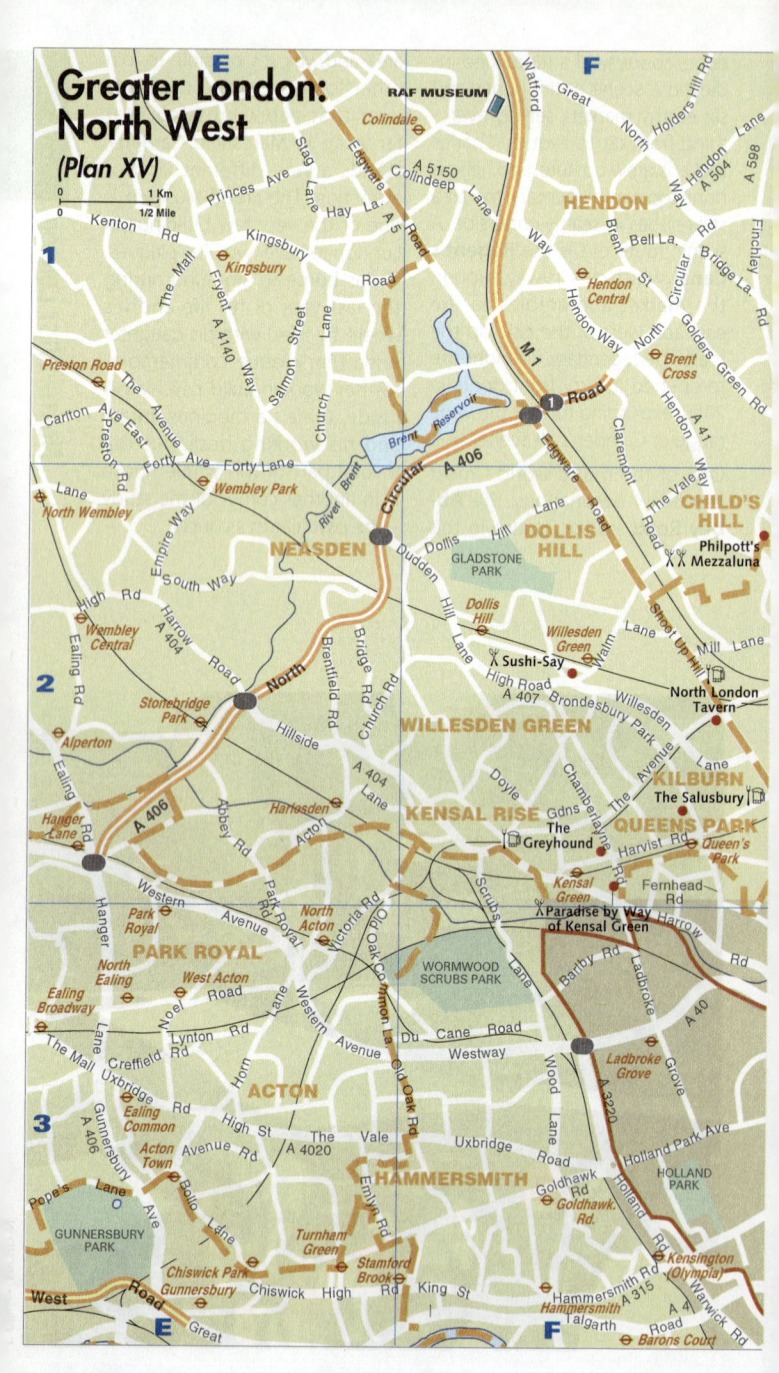

(Plan XV)

0 — 1 Km
0 — 1/2 Mile

270

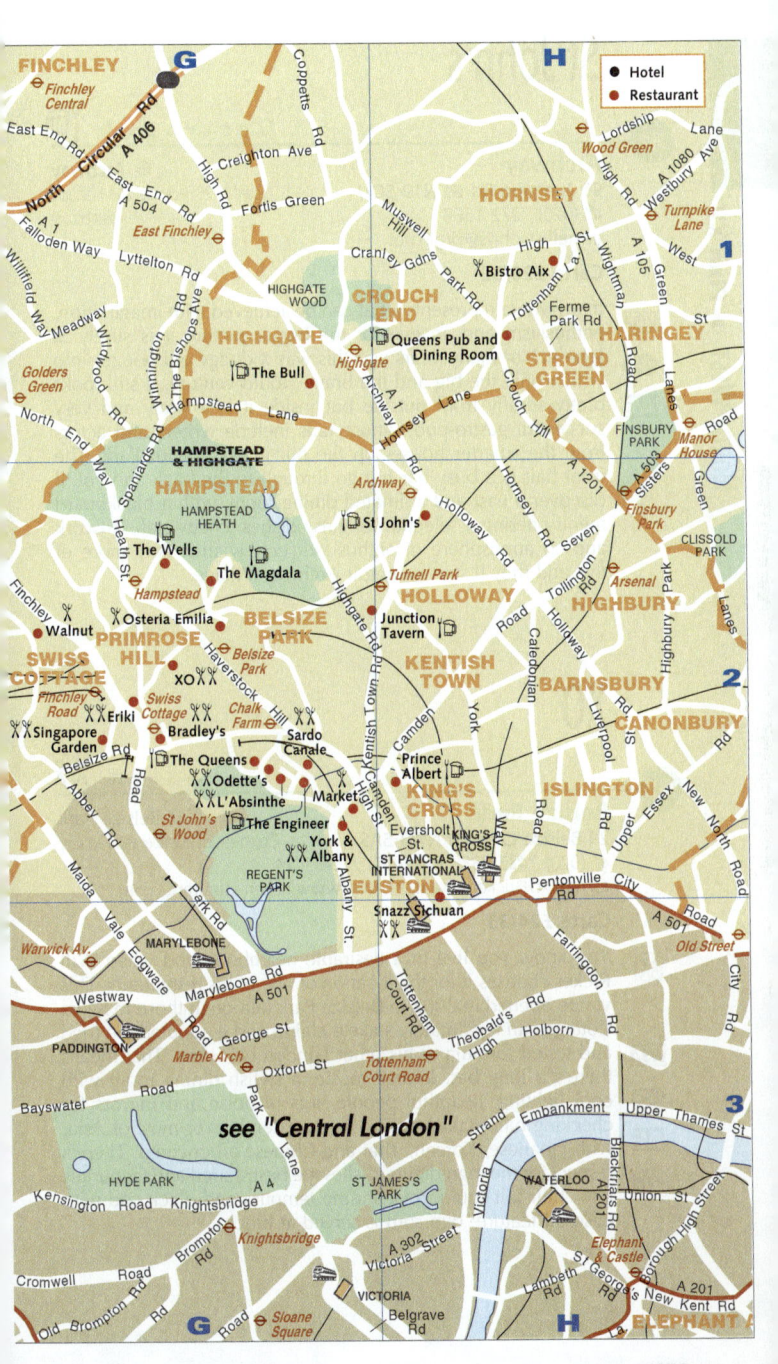

North London Map

Legend:
- ● Hotel
- ● Restaurant

Areas
- FINCHLEY
- HORNSEY
- HIGHGATE
- CROUCH END
- HARINGEY
- STROUD GREEN
- HAMPSTEAD & HIGHGATE
- HAMPSTEAD
- FINSBURY PARK
- CLISSOLD PARK
- HIGHBURY
- HOLLOWAY
- BELSIZE PARK
- KENTISH TOWN
- BARNSBURY
- CANONBURY
- SWISS COTTAGE
- PRIMROSE HILL
- CHALK FARM
- KING'S CROSS
- ISLINGTON
- ST JOHN'S WOOD
- REGENT'S PARK
- EUSTON
- MARYLEBONE
- PADDINGTON
- HYDE PARK
- ST JAMES'S PARK
- VICTORIA
- WATERLOO
- ELEPHANT & CASTLE

Restaurants and Hotels
- Bistro Aix
- Queens Pub and Dining Room
- The Bull
- St John's
- The Wells
- The Magdala
- Osteria Emilia
- Walnut
- Tufnell Park
- Junction Tavern
- XO
- Eriki
- Swiss Cottage
- Singapore Garden
- Bradley's
- Sardo
- Canale
- The Queens
- Odette's
- L'Absinthe
- Prince Albert
- The Engineer
- York & Albany
- Snazz Sichuan

Major Roads
- North Circular Road A406
- East End Rd A504
- A1 Falloden Way
- A1 Archway
- A1201
- A503 Seven Sisters Road
- A105
- A1080 Westbury Ave
- A501 Marylebone Rd
- A501 Pentonville Rd / City Rd
- A302 Victoria Street
- A201
- A4 Knightsbridge
- Westway
- Old Street
- Tottenham Court Road
- Oxford St
- Strand
- Upper Thames St
- New Kent Road

see "Central London"

271

St John's

Gastropub

H2

Archway
91 Junction Rd ✉ N19 5QU
☏ (020) 7272 1587
e-mail st.johns@virgin.net

⊖ Archway
Closed 25-26 December and 1 January
– dinner only

Carte £20/32

VISA
MC
AE

If anywhere represents what can be achieved with imagination, enthusiasm and an eye for the bigger picture it is surely St John's. Not many years ago this was a dodgy old boozer into which only the big and the brave would venture. It still looks pretty scruffy from outside but inside it is a lively and very successful gastro-pub, whose fans include writers and actors from the smarter houses up the hill in Dartmouth Park. The front half is a busy bar but go through to the back and you'll discover a vast and animated dining room, with a blackboard menu offering a selection of gutsy dishes, chatty staff, artwork and an atmosphere of enthusiastic conviviality. Any more of this and they'll start calling it Archway Village.

XO

Asian XX

G2

Belsize Park
29 Belsize Lane ✉ NW3 5AS
☏ (020) 7433 0888 **Fax** (020) 7794 3474
e-mail xo@rickerrestaurant.com **www**.rickerrestaurants.com

⊖ Belsize Park
Closed 25-26 December and 1 January

Carte £24/33

A/C
☼
VISA
MC
AE
D

You know you live in a desirable neighbourhood when Will Ricker chooses it for the location of one of his restaurants. This venue opened in 2007 in Belsize Park (although those in Swiss Cottage can legitimately stake a claim) and it adopted the tried and tested formula of his other London branches. That means there's a long bar, lounge music, a stylish dining room with cool lighting, beautiful people, lots of noise and mirrors for checking hair/make-up. The menu extends over most of Asia, with Japanese, Korean, Thai and Chinese all covered. There's respect for the ingredients, dishes are best shared and favourites like chilli-salt squid, rock shrimp tempura and black cod with miso all feature; dim sum is served at lunch.

Osteria Emilia

Italian

G2

Belsize Park
85b Fleet Road ✉ NW3 2QY
☏ (020) 7433 3317
e-mail info@oe.com

⊖ Belsize Park
Closed Sunday,
Saturday lunch and Monday lunch

Carte £24/36

A/C
VISA
MC
AE

The Giacobazzi family have run the deli across the road for 18 years so when they opened this Italian restaurant in April 2008 there was plenty of goodwill in the neighbourhood. They hail originally from near Bologna and so the name refers to the region of Emilia-Romagna, the 'bread basket' of Italy and it is this area which informs the menu. The kitchen not only eschews the usual generic Italian fare but is also unafraid of doing things differently: expect ravioli stuffed with sea bass or saltimbocca made with rabbit rather than veal; the grilled polenta is a good way to start things off. The 44 seater restaurant is spread over two floors (ask for upstairs) and its white, bright, paired-down simplicity works well.

York & Albany

Modern European

G2

Camden Town
127-129 Parkway ✉ NW1 7PS
☏ (020) 7388 3344
e-mail y&a@gordonramsay.com **www**.gordonramsay.com

⊖ Camden Town
Booking essential

Carte £26/33

For his first hotel, Gordon Ramsay has taken a virtually derelict 1820s John Nash-designed coaching house and has turned it into a contemporary space with ten bedrooms that is, apart from a proliferation of suited managers, refreshing informal. As expected, the restaurant is the focal point of the operation and comes under the aegis of Angela Hartnett. The kitchen, which is on view from the lower level of the restaurant, eschews luxury ingredients in favour of more straightforward, comforting classics, such as pumpkin risotto, fish stew and treacle pudding, but all prepared with the care and deftness one would expect. There are pizzas and assorted snacks in the roomy front bar and a deli in the old stables next door.

Market 😊

British 🍴

G2

Camden Town   ⊖ Camden Town
43 Parkway ✉ NW1 7PN   Closed Christmas-New Year, Sunday dinner and
✆ (020) 7267 9700   Bank Holidays – booking essential
e-mail primrose.gourmet@btconnect.com
www.marketrestaurant.co.uk

Menu £15 (lunch) – Carte £20/30

Naming a restaurant in Camden 'Market' may open up all manner of "who's on first base?" confusion but the mere fact that a decent restaurant has opened here at last is cause for celebration. The pared-down look of exposed brick walls, zinc-toped tables and old school chairs works well but it is in the cooking where the appeal lies. While there may be the occasional pasta, the best thing about the daily-changing menu is the Britishness of it all. Pre-starter nibbles, like the glorious mutton dripping on toast, hint at what's to follow. Start with salt beef salad or devilled kidneys follow up with lemon sole, Barnsley chop or a chicken and ham pie and you can finish with a treacle sponge or pear crumble. The prices are pretty decent too.

Prince Albert

Gastropub 🍺

H2

Camden Town   ⊖ Camden Town
163 Royal College St   Closed 25-26 December – booking essential
✉ NW1 0SG
✆ (020) 7485 0270 **Fax** (020) 7713 5994
e-mail info@princealbertcamden.com
www.princealbertcamden.com

Menu £17/22 – Carte £23/33

Albert had only been Prince Consort for three years when this pub opened in 1843. In 1863 work began down the road on St. Pancras and it seems appropriate that the reopening of this Gothic Victorian masterpiece has coincided with the rebirth of the pub. The Prince Albert has kept much of its character but now comes with an appealing neighbourhood feel. The simpler lunch menu is served throughout the pub but in the evening the upstairs restaurant gets it own menu. Decent olives and homemade soda bread are on hand while choosing from a selection of satisfyingly filling dishes, where traceability is given every respect. The wine list is on the back of the menu and offers over a dozen labels by the glass and plenty of choice for under £20.

Philpott's Mezzaluna

Italian influences ✗✗

F2

Child's Hill
424 Finchley Rd ✉ NW2 2HY
✆ (020) 7794 0455 **Fax** (020) 7794 0452
www.philpotts-mezzaluna.com

Closed 25-26 December, 1 January,
Saturday lunch and Monday

Menu £20/28

A/C
VISA
MC

Madonna, Robert De Niro, Marlon Brando – all Italian, without actually being Italian. Fittingly, their pictures adorn the walls of this inviting looking trattoria because the place may be owned and run by a couple of English blokes but it feels sufficiently Italian to do the job. The food is tasty and unpretentious and the menu comes at a price that reminds you, should you need reminding, that you're not in the West End - this part of Finchley Road is pretty dreary. Unusually, the more ambitious dishes are often more successful than the simpler ones and influences can occasionally come from beyond Italy's borders. It has a fiercely local clientele and the place feels slightly old fashioned – but in a good way.

Bistro Aix

French ✗

H1

Crouch End
54 Topsfield Parade, Tottenham Lane ✉ N8 8PT
✆ (020) 8340 6346 **Fax** (020) 8348 7236
e-mail bistroaix@hotmail.co.uk **www**.bistroaix.co.uk

Closed Monday – dinner only

Menu £15 – Carte £19/35

VISA
MC
AE
◐

The location may be Crouch End, the chef owner may be American but for a couple of hours this little bistro will whisk you off to the verdant French countryside. The high ceiling, mustard coloured walls, dressers, plants and mirrors all add to that rustic feel, while two specially commissioned paintings of cooks and pastoral scenes tell you this is a place run by, and for, those with a genuine love of food. Francophiles will find plenty of contentment in the vast majority of the menu, which features all the favourites from classic onion soup or seared foie gras to steak frites or rack of lamb, but there are other dishes whose origins owe more to Italian cooking. Look out for the good value weekday set menu.

The Queens Pub and Dining Room

Gastropub

H1
Crouch End
26 Broadway Parade ✉ N8 9DE
☏ (020) 8340 2031
e-mail queens@foodandfuel.co.uk **www**.thequeenscrouchend.co.uk

Carte £15/28

This classic Victorian pub, with its mahogany panelling and ornate plasterwork, was once known more for the fighting than the food but the 2006 makeover ensures that now the closest thing here to an episode of Eastenders is the occasional presence of a cast member. The menu changes daily and food is served all day. It's a confident kitchen, offering a mix of modern British with plenty of Mediterranean influence so the sausages that come with the mash may include Toulouse as well as wild boar, and apple crumble might arrive with pistachio ice cream. There's a cocktail of the week and an accessible wine list with plenty available by the glass or carafe; non-drinkers are not ignored either – there's homemade lemonade to stir childhood memories in many.

Snazz Sichuan

Chinese

H2
Euston ⊖ Euston
37 Chalton St ✉ NW1 1JD
☏ (020) 7388 0808
www.newchinaclub.co.uk

Menu £19/39 – Carte £10/50

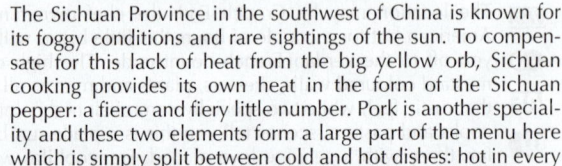

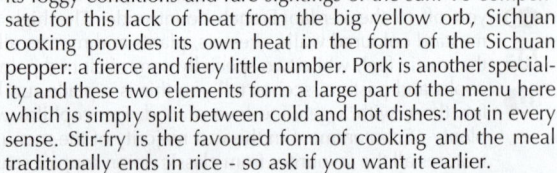

The Sichuan Province in the southwest of China is known for its foggy conditions and rare sightings of the sun. To compensate for this lack of heat from the big yellow orb, Sichuan cooking provides its own heat in the form of the Sichuan pepper: a fierce and fiery little number. Pork is another speciality and these two elements form a large part of the menu here which is simply split between cold and hot dishes: hot in every sense. Stir-fry is the favoured form of cooking and the meal traditionally ends in rice - so ask if you want it earlier.

Window seats are the best, loudness and laughter are positively encouraged and the restaurant virtually doubles as the Sichuan tourist board as it also houses a gallery and traditional tea room.

The Wells

Gastropub 🍺

G2

Hampstead
30 Well Walk ✉ NW3 1BX
📞 (020) 7794 3785 **Fax** (020) 7794 6817
e-mail info@thewellshampstead.co.uk
www.thewellshampstead.co.uk

⊖ Hampstead
Closed 1 January

Carte £25/35

Owned by Beth Coventry, sister of restaurant critic Fay Maschler, The Wells lies somewhere in between a restaurant and a pub. But whatever you consider it to be, one thing for sure is that it's in a grand old spot and adds to the mystery of why there are not more places to eat in Hampstead. The ground floor is the pubbier part, with a well chosen menu of the sort of dishes that go well with beer, but it can be a bit of a bunfight, especially in summer and at weekends. Upstairs is an altogether more composed affair but one that still has considerable charm. Muscular gastropub staples like lamb shank or calves liver with onion gravy sit alongside dishes whose flavours are more Asian in origin, while others exhibit Italian roots.

The Magdala

Gastropub 🍺

G2

Hampstead
2A South Hill Park ✉ NW3 2SB
📞 (020) 7435 2503 **Fax** (020) 7435 6167
e-mail themagdala@hotmail.co.uk **www**.the-magdala.com

⊖ Belsize Park
Closed 25 December

Carte £18/26

The Magdala has its place in history as it was outside this pub where Ruth Ellis, the last woman to be hanged in Britain, shot her paramour in 1955. To its credit, the pub doesn't let this episode define it but instead concentrates on its community feel, general air of friendliness and decent food. The owner worked here for several years before buying it in 2007 and she certainly keeps her eye on the ball. The concise but balanced menu keeps its heart and influences mostly within the British Isles. There are also interesting snacks and sharing plates, like antipasti, on the supplementary blackboard. Wisely, no great risks are taken in preparation; this is about decent pub food. The menu lengthens at weekends when the upstairs room comes into play.

The Bull

Gastropub

G1

Highgate
13 North Hill ✉ N6 4AB
📞 (0845) 456 5033
Fax (0845) 456 5034
e-mail info@inthebull.biz www.themeredithgroup.co.uk

Menu £18 (lunch) – Carte £28/35

⊖ Highgate
Closed 26 December, 1 January and Monday lunch except Bank Holidays

If the first thing you notice is a drinks trolley then you know you're not in your, or anyone else's, local boozer. It's all about the food here, which is modern European with a dominant French gene running through it. Dishes are seasonally pertinent and the construction, ingredients and execution are aimed more at the 'serious' end of the dining pub scale, although there is a good value lunch menu available. The home-baked breads are excellent. Those who have a boat they wish to push out will find their task aided by the wine list, which does also offer plenty of affordable bottles. Weekends welcome a more family atmosphere, where brunch is offered. The room is bright, service is on the ball and Thursday night is music night.

Paradise by way of Kensal Green

Gastropub

F2

Kensal Green
19 Kilburn Lane ✉ W10 4AE
📞 (020) 8969 0098
Fax (020) 8969 8830
www.theparadise.co.uk

Carte £23/30

⊖ Kensal Green
Closed 25-26 December,
1 January and lunch Monday-Friday

"For there is good news yet to hear and fine things to be seen / before we go to Paradise by way of Kensal Green", so ended a poem by G.K Chesterton, writer, philosopher, theologian and vegetarian-loather. The pub reminds us that there's more to the local area than a cemetery. It's appealingly bohemian, with mismatched furniture, Murano chandeliers, old portraits and even the odd birdcage. Burlesque shows, comedy and live music all happen upstairs. The bar menu ranges from Welsh rarebit to plates of charcuterie but the main menu appears in the evening in the restaurant. Mostly British ingredients come with enduring partners, like asparagus with butter, York ham with Cumberland sauce and lemon sole with Jersey Royals. Portions are man-sized.

The Greyhound

Gastropub

F2

Kensal Green
64-66 Chamberlayne Road
✉ NW10 3JJ
☏ (020) 8969 8080 **Fax** (020) 8969 8081
e-mail thegreyhound@needtoeat.co.uk

⊖ Kensal Green
Closed 25 December and 1 January

Menu £18 – Carte £20/25

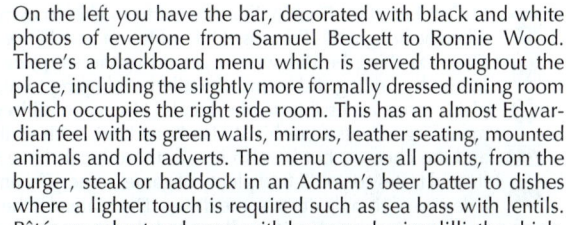

On the left you have the bar, decorated with black and white photos of everyone from Samuel Beckett to Ronnie Wood. There's a blackboard menu which is served throughout the place, including the slightly more formally dressed dining room which occupies the right side room. This has an almost Edwardian feel with its green walls, mirrors, leather seating, mounted animals and old adverts. The menu covers all points, from the burger, steak or haddock in an Adnam's beer batter to dishes where a lighter touch is required such as sea bass with lentils. Pâtés are robust and come with homemade piccalilli, the chicken is free range, fish comes daily from Cornwall and vegetarians are well looked after (if they can avert their eyes from the taxidermy).

North London Tavern

Gastropub

F2

Kilburn
375 Kilburn High Rd ✉ NW6 7QB
☏ (020) 7625 6634 **Fax** (020) 7372 2723
e-mail northlondontavern@realpubs.co.uk **www**.realpubs.co.uk

⊖ Kilburn
Closed 25 December

Carte £23/27

The dining room is separated from the bar by a red curtain and glass panelling and, like the bar, it can quickly fill up. Old church seats, mismatched tables, high ceilings and chandeliers add a little gothic character. Lunch is a simpler affair in the bar but at dinner the printed menu, which is rather needlessly repeated verbatim on a large blackboard, offers a comprehensive selection of gastropub greatest hits, from belly pork to rib-eye, tuna niçoise to apple crumble, plus a couple of veggie options. The crusty bread is terrific and each dish arrives fully garnished and appetisingly presented on big white plates. There's a whole roast beast at weekends and the wine list keeps things mostly under £20.

Odette's

Modern European ✖✖

G2

Primrose Hill
⊖ Chalk Farm
130 Regent's Park Rd ✉ NW1 8XL — Closed Christmas,
✆ (020) 7586 8569 **Fax** (020) 7586 8362 — Sunday dinner and Monday
e-mail info@odettesprimrosehill.com
www.odettesprimrosehill.com

Menu £22 (lunch) – Carte approx. £40

In October 2008 Bryn Williams went from chef to owner-chef when he bought this Primrose Hill institution from Vince Power. The next thing he did was to get rid of the set price dinner menu; by pricing dishes individually he's hoping to make the place more accessible to the locals. His menu still contains many ingredients from his Welsh homeland, such as the beef and the cheeses, but he also knows those locals have sophisticated tastes so you'll find plenty of game, some offal and quite a degree of complexity to some dishes. Decoratively, the restaurant remains awash with yellow and there's a nice enclosed terrace at the back. Service could do with replacing some of that formality with a little more personality.

Sardo Canale

Italian ✖✖

G2

Primrose Hill
⊖ Chalk Farm
42 Gloucester Ave ✉ NW1 8JD — Closed Christmas and Sunday lunch
✆ (020) 7722 2800 **Fax** (020) 7722 0802
e-mail info@sardocanale.com **www.**sardocanale.com

Carte £25/32

It may be beside Regent's Canal but the gates and security camera spoil the image somewhat. That being said, this good-looking restaurant beneath a red-brick building is still a bright spot in which to spend a summer's evening and is not bad either for the other seasons. It comes divided into different areas; the most interesting being the vaulted brick section which was once a canal access tunnel. This being the sister to Sardo in Bloomsbury means Sardinian specialities, from golden hued spaghetti alla bottarga to pastas like malloreddus, culurgiones and fregola. The cooking is nicely balanced and has a zingy freshness to it. The wine list is fairly priced and promotes exploration of Vermentino and other Sardinian wines.

L'Absinthe

French

G2 | **Primrose Hill**
40 Chalcot Road ✉ NW18LS
📞 (020) 7483 4848

⊖ Chalk Farm
Closed Christmas, August and Monday

Carte £21/32

A/C
🍴
☀
VISA
MC
AE

40 Chalcot Road has long been Primrose Hill's Bermuda Triangle: many restaurants have tried this corner and all have failed. The new owner gave many years of his life to Marco Pierre White as a manager so who would begrudge him success with his own place, especially when he's clearly so passionate? He's created your classic French bistro, right down to the Belle Epoque posters, tightly packed little tables and cries of bonjour! The menu also ticks all the right boxes, from onion soup and steak frites, Lyonnais salad to duck confit. The place is jumping, lunch is a steal and the exclusively French wine list comes with a commendable pricing structure, with corkage charged on the retail price. Whisper it, but maybe this time…

The Queens

Gastropub

G2 | **Primrose Hill**
49 Regent's Park Rd ✉ NW1 8XD
📞 (020) 7586 0408 **Fax** (020) 7586 5677
e-mail thequeens@geronimo-inns.co.uk
www.geronimo-inns.co.uk

⊖ Chalk Farm
Closed 25 December

Carte £18/29

VISA
AE

The Queens will have a place in the annals of gastropub history, as it was one of the pioneers in bringing decent food into an environment hitherto resistant to change and proved that a local with good food was not a contradiction. Its location on the main drag and alongside the Hill is clearly another attraction and the balcony terrace is a sought after summer spot. The whole place was stripped down and done up in 2006. The narrow bar remains an established local meeting point, with the footie on the TV on the corner, but head upstairs and you'll find a warm and welcoming dining room. Here, gutsy gastropub staples are on offer; main courses come with a good choice of side dishes and there's a daily special for two to share.

The Engineer

Gastropub

G2

Primrose Hill
65 Gloucester Ave ✉ NW1 8JH
✆ (020) 7722 0950 **Fax** (020) 7483 0592
e-mail info@the-engineer.com **www**.the-engineer.com

⊖ Chalk Farm
Closed 25-28 December

Carte £30/60

The Engineer has been doing its gastropubbery since the early '90s and can show all those johnny-come-latelys a thing or two. Its success is down to a number of factors, not least the enviably attractive surroundings of Primrose Hill. But it also understands what people want from a pub menu. That means plenty of interesting dishes like Moroccan lamb or the more eclectic miso marinated cod but also reassuringly satisfying favourites like a sirloin steak with béarnaise sauce and fabulous 'baker fries' or a cheeseburger. The kitchen is flexible and clearly takes pride in its work. It's open all day, the dining room spills out onto the delightful terrace and staff prove that looking good and being friendly are not mutually exclusive.

The Salusbury

Gastropub

F2

Queens Park
50-52 Salusbury Road ✉ NW6 6NN
✆ (020) 7328 3286
e-mail thesalusbury@london.com

Closed 25 December, 1 January and
Monday lunch except Bank Holidays

Carte £22/29

Salusbury Road is becoming quite a foodie quarter. There's a Sunday farmers' market up the road, plenty of local cafés and The Salusbury Pub & Dining Room, complete with its own food store a couple of doors down. It's divided down the middle and is half pub, half dining room although you have to fight through the former to get to the latter. The style is pleasantly higgledy and the occasional shared table contributes to the bonhomie. The cooking, though, is more restaurant than pub and comes with a distinct Italian accent. Quality bread and olive oil set things off and the various pasta dishes come as either starters or mains. Flavours are pronounced, ingredients good and portions generous. It's also well worth leaving trouser space for dessert.

Bradley's

Modern European ✗✗

Swiss Cottage
25 Winchester Rd ✉ NW3 3NR
☏ (020) 7722 3457 **Fax** (020) 7435 1392
e-mail bradleysnw3@btinternet.com www.bradleysnw3.co.uk

⊖ Swiss Cottage
Closed 1 week Christmas and Sunday dinner

Menu £17/23 – Carte £30/36

Bradley's has matured nicely over the years and the rejuvenated Hampstead Theatre has given it an extra shot in the arm. The cooking is uncomplicated and nimble; it's grounded in France but with ingredients from across the British Isles, whether that's crab from Dorset, beef from Orkney or a daily fish delivery from Looe. The fixed price menu, run alongside the more extensive à la carte, represents excellent value, as does the wine list which offers the majority of bottles under £30. Service is well marshalled by the owner and the kitchen dispatches dishes promptly, which is sensible when the theatre crowd form a major part of the business. The room is light and open, although sound can bounce around a little.

Eriki

Indian ✗✗

Swiss Cottage
4-6 Northways Parade, Finchley Rd ✉ NW3 5EN
☏ (020) 7722 0606 **Fax** (020) 7722 8866
e-mail info@eriki.co.uk www.eriki.co.uk

⊖ Swiss Cottage
Closed 24-25 December, 1 January, lunch Saturday and Bank Holidays

Carte £28/30

You'll see it just at the moment you realise you're in the wrong lane. Eriki's location may not be the greatest, bang on the permanently busy Finchley Road, but once seated all is calm and the traffic outside gets quickly forgotten. The decoration certainly helps in this regard - the vivid red and orange walls, carved wooden screens and smart table settings make the room smart yet unstuffy and the cutlery, imported from Rajasthan, is certainly original. Furthermore, the conscientious and obliging waiters, all in smart tunics, ensure that everyone is attended to. The menu takes diners on a culinary trail around India and the carefully prepared dishes come with a level of refinement usually associated with more expensive establishments.

Singapore Garden

Asian ✕✕

Swiss Cottage
83 Fairfax Road ✉ NW6 4DY
📞 (020) 7328 5314 **Fax** (020) 7624 0656
www.singaporegarden.co.uk

⊖ Swiss Cottage
Closed 5 days Christmas

Menu £20/29 – Carte £26/46

Singapore Garden has been a stalwart of Swiss Cottage for many a year but a relatively recent refurbishment and relaunch has widened its appeal even further. The room is now bright and smart, although the tables for two are set very close together. Service has an endearing enthusiasm. The menu is the usual lengthy affair but just ignore the more generic dishes and head to the back page for the Singaporean and Malaysian specialities, for here is where the kitchen's expertise lies. These dishes are supplemented by a list of seasonal specials. So, whether you start with some roti canai with curry, try a laksa, a ho jien omelette or a vibrant rojak, you'll find cooking full of zingy freshness and vitality.

Junction Tavern

Gastropub 🍺

Tufnell Park
101 Fortess Rd ✉ NW5 1AG
📞 (020) 7485 9400 **Fax** (020) 7485 9401
www.junctiontavern.co.uk

⊖ Tufnell Park
Closed 24-26 December and 1 January

Carte £22/30

With its brass cock glinting in the sun, you can't miss The Junction, and nor would you want to. Just as impressive inside, it's painted ox blood red, with rich wood panelling. There's a conservatory, dining room and terrace as well as the bar, so plenty of space to accommodate the youthful regulars. The choice on the daily-changing menu is as eclectic as the range of cookbooks propped up at one end of the open kitchen. Wholesome and bold, choices might include wild mushroom and spinach crepes or dukkah crusted tofu - and the chunky chips deserve a special mention. An ale pub at heart, the weekly-changing selection boasts a menu all of its own and enthusiasts gather several times a year for a beer festival.

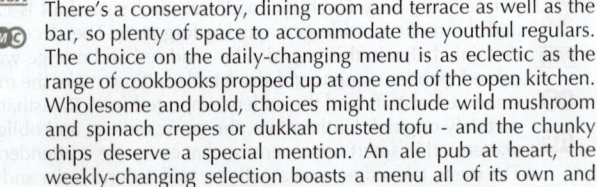

Walnut

G2

Traditional ✖

West Hampstead
280 West End Lane
✉ NW6 1LJ
☏ (020) 7794 7772
e-mail info@walnutwalnut.com **www**.walnutwalnut.com

Menu £24/35

⊖ West Hampstead
Closed 1 week Christmas and
1 week late August – dinner only

[A/C] VISA MC AE ⓪

West Hampstead may have plenty of coffee and snack emporia but Walnut is its proper restaurant, having successfully established itself on a corner site where many failed before. The place has a relaxed informality, with 70% of the customers being regulars; it's bursting at the seams at weekends so a discount is offered to encourage weekday dining. The imperturbable chef-owner is on view in the raised open kitchen and his menu reveals his classical training. A choice of around 10 main courses keeps everyone happy; there are no unusual flavour combinations and his specialities are game and fish. He not only uses seasonal British produce but also works closely with Sustain, the 'alliance for better food and farming.'

Sushi-Say

F2

Japanese ✖

Willesden Green
33B Walm Lane ✉ NW2 5SH
☏ (020) 8459 2971
Fax (020) 8907 3229

Menu £10/21 – Carte £15/40

⊖ Willesden Green
Closed 25-26 December, 1 January,
2 weeks August, Monday and Tuesday
following Bank Holiday Monday – dinner only
and lunch Saturday and Sunday

VISA MC

It's been given a little makeover and now the tinted windows make it look really quite inviting. Sushi-Say is an authentic neighbourhood Japanese restaurant and the perfect antidote to those restaurants that deem Japanese food ripe for reinterpretation. This is all about tradition and the care taken in the preparation of the dishes is clear.

The layout remains the same: the owner stands, complete with his head band, behind his sushi counter and this is the favoured spot of the regulars and, as the name suggests, the house speciality. Otherwise, it's through to the simply furnished little dining room. There's a surprisingly large number of staff and plenty of set menus which deliver a good all round experience.

NORTH-WEST ▶ Plan XV

North-East London

If northwest London is renowned for its leafy acres, then the area to its immediate east has a more urban, brick-built appeal. Which has meant, over the last decade or so, a wholesale rebranding exercise for some of its traditionally shady localities. A generation ago it would have been beyond the remit of even the most inventive estate agent to sell the charms of Islington, Hackney or Bethnal Green. But then along came Damien Hirst, Tracey Emin et al, and before you could say 'cow in formaldehyde' the area's cachet had rocketed.

Shoreditch and **Hoxton** are the pivotal points of the region's hip makeover. Their cobbled brick streets and shabby industrial remnants were like heavenly manna to the artists and designers who started to colonise the old warehouses twenty years ago. A fashionable crowd soon followed in their footsteps, and nowadays the area around **Hoxton Square** positively teems with clubs, bars and galleries. Latest must-see space is the year-old Rivington Place, a terrific gallery that highlights visual arts from around the world. Nearby are Deluxe (digital installations), AOP (photographic shows) and Hales (Spencer Tunick's acres of gooseflesh... etc).

Before the area was ever trendy, there was the Geffrye Museum. A short stroll up Hoxton's **Kingsland Road**, it's a jewel of a place, set in elegant 18C almshouses, and depicting English middle-class interiors from 1600 to the present day. Right behind it is St. Mary's Secret Garden, a little oasis that manages to include much diversity including a separate woodland and herb area, all in less than an acre. At the southern end of the area, in Folgate Street, Dennis Severs' House is an original Huguenot home that recreates 18 and 19C life in an original way – cooking smells linger, hearth and candles burn, giving you the impression the owners have only just left the place. Upstairs the beds remain unmade: did a certain local artist pick up any ideas here?

When the Regent's Canal was built in the early 19C, **Islington's** fortunes nose-dived, for it was accompanied by the arrival of slums and over-crowding. But the once-idyllic village managed to hold onto its Georgian squares and handsome Victorian terraces through the rough times, and when these were gentrified a few years ago, the area ushered in a revival. **Camden Passage** has long been famed for its quirky antique emporiums, while the slinky Business Design Centre is a flagship of the modern Islington. Cultural icons established themselves around the Upper Street area and these have gone from strength to strength. The **Almeida** Theatre has a habit of hitting the production jackpot with its history of world premieres, while the King's Head has earned itself a reputation for raucous scene-stealing; set up in the seventies, it's also London's very first theatre-pub. Nearby, the Screen on the Green boasts a wonderful old-fashioned neon billboard.

Even in the 'bad old days', Islington drew in famous names, and at Regency smart **Canonbury Square** are the one-time homes of Evelyn Waugh (no.17A) and George Orwell (no.27). These days it houses the Estorick Collection of Modern Italian Art; come here to see fine futuristic paintings in a Georgian villa. To put the history of the area in a proper context, head to St. John Street, south of the City Road, where the Islington Museum's shiny new headquarters tells the story of a colourful and multi-layered past.

Further up the A10, you come to **Dalston,** a bit like the Islington of old but with the buzzy Ridley Road market and a vibrant all-night scene including the blistering Vortex Jazz Club just off Kingsland Road. A little further north is **Stoke Newington,** referred to, a bit unkindly, as the poor man's Islington. Its pride and joy is Church Street, which not only features some characterful bookshops and eye-catching boutiques, but also lays claim to Abney Park Cemetery, an enchanting old place with a wildlife-rich nature reserve.

Greater London: North East
(Plan XVI)

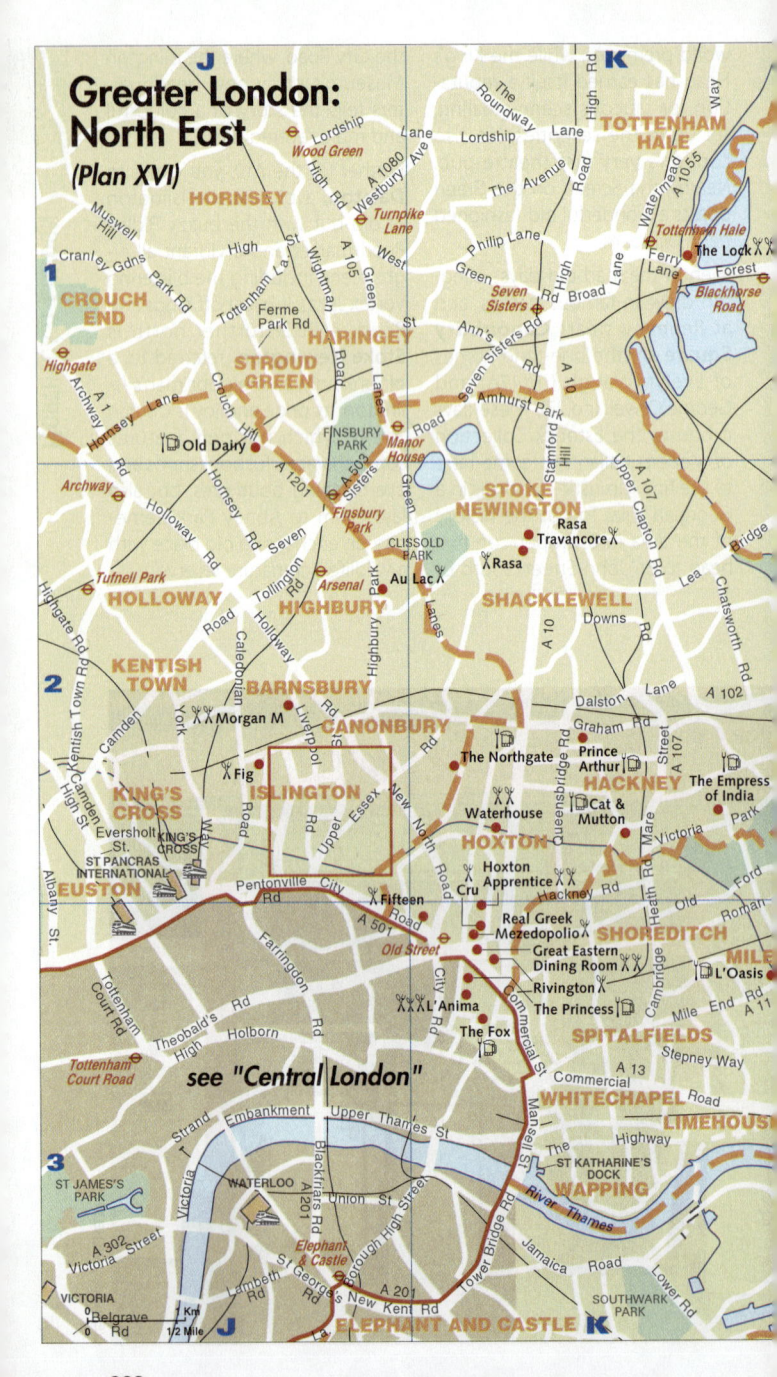

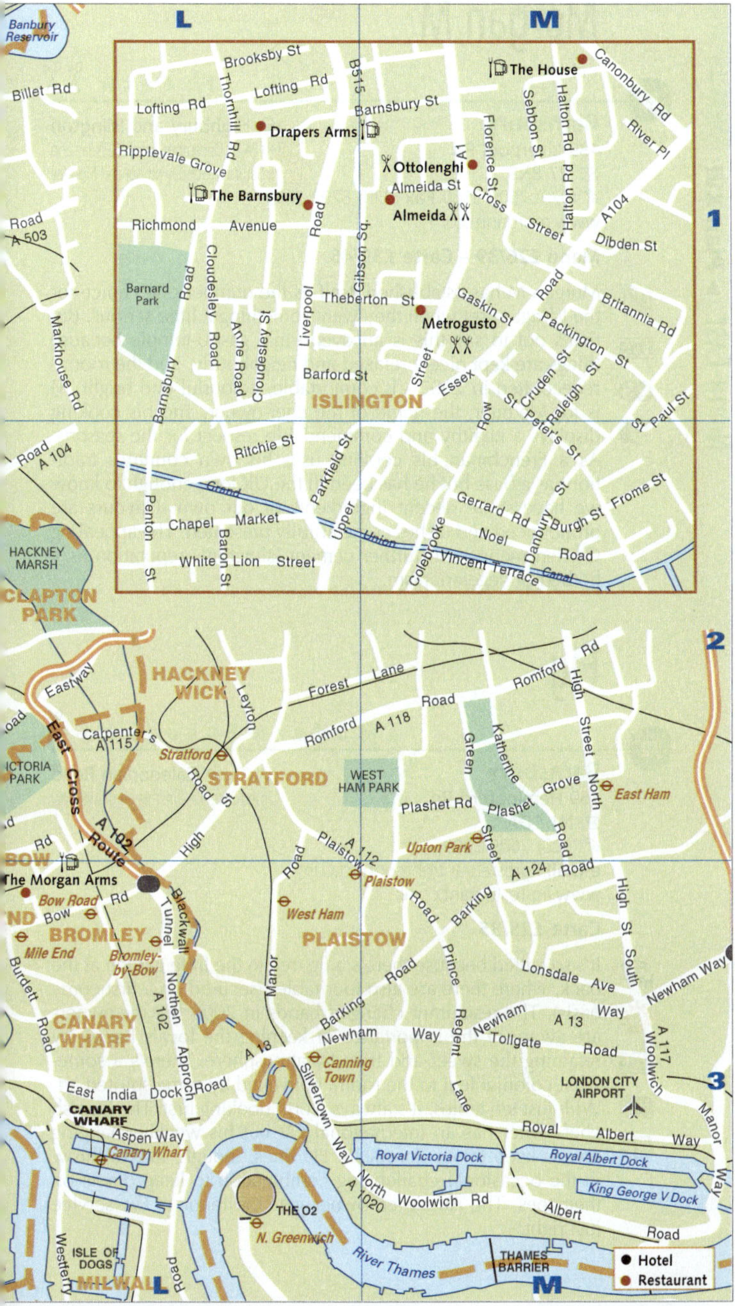
L
M
1
2
3
Banbury Reservoir
Billet Rd
Road A 503
Markhouse Rd
Road A 104
HACKNEY MARSH
CLAPTON PARK
Brooksby St
Lofting Rd
Thornhill Rd
Drapers Arms
Ripplevale Grove
The Barnsbury
Richmond Avenue
Barnard Park
Barnsbury Road
Cloudesley Road
Anne Road
Cloudesley St
Liverpool Road
Gibson Sq.
B515
Barnsbury St
Ottolenghi
Almeida St
Almeida
A1
Florence St
Cross Street
The House
Sebbon St
Halton Rd
Canonbury Rd
River Pl
A104
Dibden St
Theberton St
Metrogusto
Gaskin St
Essex Road
Packington St
Britannia Rd
Barford St
Street
ISLINGTON
Row
St Peter's St
Cruden St
Raleigh St
St Paul St
Ritchie St
Parkfield St
Grand Union Canal
Upper
Gerrard Rd
Danbury St
Burgh St
Frome St
Penton St
Chapel Market
Baron St
White Lion Street
Colebrooke
Noel Road
Vincent Terrace
HACKNEY WICK
Eastway
East Cross Route
Carpenter's A 115
Leyton
Stratford
Road
STRATFORD
Forest Lane
Romford Road
A 118
Romford Rd
High Street North
WEST HAM PARK
Green
Katherine
Plashet Rd
Plashet Grove
Road
East Ham
ICTORIA PARK
High St
A 102
Rd
BOW
The Morgan Arms
Bow Road
Bow Rd
Blackwall Tunnel Northern Approach
A 102
BROMLEY
Mile End
Bromley-by-Bow
Road
Plaistow A 112
Plaistow
West Ham
PLAISTOW
Upton Park
Street
A 124 Road
Barking
Prince Regent Lane
High St South
Lonsdale Ave
Newham Way
Burdett Road
CANARY WHARF
Manor Road
Barking Road
Newham Way
A 13
Tollgate Road
A 117 Woolwich
A 13
Canning Town
East India Dock Road
Silvertown Way
LONDON CITY AIRPORT
Manor Way
CANARY WHARF
Aspen Way
Canary Wharf
Royal Albert Way
Royal Victoria Dock
Royal Albert Dock
King George V Dock
North Woolwich Rd
A 1020
Albert Road
THE O2
N. Greenwich
River Thames
THAMES BARRIER
ISLE OF DOGS
MILWALL
Westferry
Road
Hotel
Restaurant

Morgan M

French ✕✕

J2

Barnsbury
489 Liverpool Rd
✉ N7 8NS
✆ (020) 7609 3560 **Fax** (020) 8292 5699
www.morganm.com

⊖ Highbury and Islington
Closed 24-30 December, lunch Tuesday and Saturday, Sunday dinner and Monday

Menu £26/39 – Carte £39/45

Morgan M has established itself as the number one choice for the Islington set when they want something a little serious. But that's not to say this is an overformal gastro-temple because things are kept nicely relaxed and neighbourly, and the room - redecorated in 2007 - is comfortable, colourful and bright. M is for Meunier, the name of the chef-owner, and his cooking displays a healthy and commendable respect for the seasons. As a Frenchman, his cooking uses his own country's traditions as a base but he has been in the UK long enough to know we have some decent ingredients of our own. Flavours are pronounced and dishes come artfully presented. The appealing Garden menus will further cement Islington's reputation as a hotbed of vegetarianism.

Fig

Modern European ✕

J2

Barnsbury
169 Hemingford Rd
✉ N1 1DA
✆ (020) 7609 3009
e-mail figrestaurant@btconnect.com
www.fig-restaurant.co.uk

⊖ Caledonian Road
Closed 2 weeks Christmas – dinner only

Carte £25/35

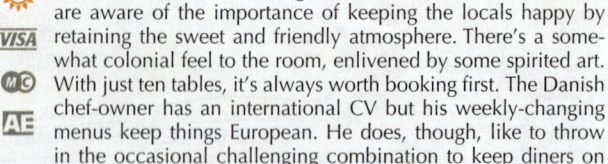

It's so called because there's a fig tree in the little garden at the back, where there are also four tables (secured on a first come basis). The restaurant changed hands in 2006 but the owners are aware of the importance of keeping the locals happy by retaining the sweet and friendly atmosphere. There's a somewhat colonial feel to the room, enlivened by some spirited art. With just ten tables, it's always worth booking first. The Danish chef-owner has an international CV but his weekly-changing menus keep things European. He does, though, like to throw in the occasional challenging combination to keep diners on their toes. The Aussie co-owner gets the tenor of the service just right.

The Morgan Arms

Gastropub

L3

Bow
43 Morgan St ✉ E3 5AA
✆ (020) 8980 6389
e-mail themorgan@geronimo-inns.co.uk
www.geronimo-inns.co.uk

⊖ Bow Road.
Closed 24-26 December, 1 January
— bookings not accepted

Carte £20/31

The eponymous Mr Morgan owned all the land around these parts in the 1800s and he would, no doubt, be flattered to see this characterful pub in what is now a smart residential area. Shabby chic is the order of the day, with an appealing mismatch of furniture, although the partially separated dining room is marginally quieter than the raucous bar. The menu is always appealing and constantly evolving. Regular trips to Billingsgate are in evidence and the kitchen is not afraid of offering different things like pig's cheeks or oxtail ravioli; there's even a helpful glossary to explain some of the more unusual ingredients. This is robust, filling and full-on cooking, entirely appropriate for what was formerly a spit and sawdust boozer.

The House

Gastropub

M1

Canonbury
63-69 Canonbury Rd
✉ N1 2DG
✆ (020) 7704 7410 **Fax** (020) 7704 9388
e-mail info@inthehouse.biz
www.themeredithgroup.co.uk

⊖ Highbury and Islington
Closed 24-26 December and Monday lunch

Menu £18 (lunch) – Carte £26/35

When Islingtonians arrange to meet you back at 'the house', more than likely they mean at this coolly sophisticated pub, tucked away in a residential part of the borough. It effortlessly combines a laid back vibe at the bar, which adjoins a triangular shaped terrace at the front, with a more urbane atmosphere found in the nattily attired dining room. Just reading the menu provides evidence that The House has loftier culinary ambitions than many a gastropub. Indeed, a number of the kitchen's carefully composed dishes would not look out of place in restaurants sporting a much higher brow and a more prosperous postcode. Pleasingly, it also remembers its roots and still knows how to do a decent shepherd's pie.

The Empress of India

Gastropub

Hackney
130 Lauriston Road, Victoria Park
✉ E9 7LH
✆ (020) 8533 5123 **Fax** (020) 7404 2250
e-mail info@theempressofindia.com **www**.theempressofindia.com

⊖ Mile End
Closed 25-26 December

Menu £25 – Carte £19/33

The building dates from the 1880s and has enjoyed various past incarnations as a nightclub and a floristry training school. Now a smart, open plan pub with the emphasis firmly on dining, it's brightly lit with high ceilings, mosaic flooring, red leather banquettes and eye-catching murals picturing Indian scenes. The seasonally-evolving menu is classically based with some Mediterranean influences, and blends the robust with the more refined. The patrons use rare breeds for their meats and poultry, and these can often be temptingly seen and smelt cooking on the rotisserie. It's also open all day, with the Empress Afternoon tea accompanied by an interesting selection of leaf teas. Kids have their own menu that they can colour in.

Cat & Mutton

Gastropub

Hackney
76 Broadway Market ✉ E8 4QJ
✆ (020) 7254 5599
Fax (020) 7254 2797
e-mail catandmutton@yahoo.co.uk **www**.catandmutton.co.uk

⊖ Bethnal Green
Closed 25-26 December, 1 January,
Sunday dinner and Monday lunch

Menu £15 (weekday dinner) – Carte £21/33

The Cat and Mutton is your typical early Victorian corner pub with a bona fide London feel; it is a drinking pub that does decent food, rather than vice versa. It can take a hammering with the after-work crowd and has a rough and ready vibe, with exposed brick walls and a resolute lack of decorative embellishment. Such uncompromising surroundings make it an unlikely spot in which to find decent food but that's exactly what The Cat and Mutton delivers, although it's still not the place for that romantic dinner à deux. The blackboard offers around five choices per course, which could include anything from chilli squid to a decent steak. Using some ingredients garnered from the local market, the cooking is full-bodied and satisfying.

Prince Arthur

K2

Gastropub

Hackney — Bethnal Green
95 Forest Road — E8 3BH
(020) 7249 9996 **Fax** (020) 7249 7074
e-mail info@theprincearthurlondonfields.com
www.theprincearthurlondonfields.com

Carte £20/27

The Prince Arthur is less gastropub, more your favourite little local serving proper pub grub. Much of the old character remains but the owners, brothers Tom & Ed Martin, have added some ironic touches, from stuffed animals to a collection of saucy seaside postcards. It's also for locals, with the occasional corduroyed Martin Amis enthusiast thrown in. The menu is appealingly unaffected. Soup comes with crusty bread, prawns by the pint and there are pub classics like cottage pie. Desserts should really be written as 'puddings' as they are of the weigh-you-down-but-make-you-feel-good variety. That being said, the deep-fried jam sandwich with carnation milk ice cream appears to be more of an attention-grabber than a culinary breakthrough.

Au Lac

J2

Vietnamese

Highbury — Arsenal
82 Highbury Park — N5 2XE   Dinner only
(020) 7704 9187 **Fax** (020) 7704 9187

Carte £8/21

On a busy road boasting a number of dining options, several of them Vietnamese and some of questionable quality, Au Lac manages to stand out from the crowd and pull in plenty of regulars. Its draw is perhaps not in its decoration, which has a simple but curiously comforting modesty about it, but in the tangy Vietnamese cooking and the extensive choice available. The brothers who run the place are eager to please and the charming nature of the staff helps guide those unfamiliar with the zesty delicacies. Vegetarians will find many appealing dishes and there are set menus available for larger parties. Perhaps best of all, the generous pricing allows for unabashed experimentation and unselfish sharing.

Great Eastern Dining Room

Asian ✕✕

K3

Hoxton
54 Great Eastern St ⌧ EC2A 3QR
☏ (020) 7613 4545 **Fax** (020) 7613 4137
e-mail greateastern@rickerrestaurants.com
www.rickerrestaurants.com

⊖ Old Street
Closed Saturday lunch and Sunday

Menu £30/45 – Carte £23/29

Will Ricker's flourishing group of hip restaurants came into its own here in Great Eastern Street and coincided with Hoxton's own emergence onto the fashion radar. The format here is similar to the others in the group: the bar, given equal billing as the restaurant, occupies most of the front section and it's usually so packed a sardine would think twice. The noise spills into the restaurant, adding a lively vibe to the place. It's all great fun. The kitchen's influences spill across South East Asia, with dim sum, curries, roasts and tempura all carefully prepared. Helpfully, the reverse of the menu carries a glossary of Asian culinary terms. The serving team are a sassy and well-informed bunch.

Water House

Italian influences ✕✕

K2

Hoxton
10 Orsman Road ⌧ N1 5QJ
☏ (020) 7033 0123
e-mail eat@waterhouserestaurant.co.uk
www.waterhouserestaurant

⊖ Essex Road Station
Closed Sunday dinner

Carte £23/36

Acorn House's eco-friendly credentials reaped plenty of interest and the charitable trust behind it has now opened a second project, Water House. The ambitions here are even greater, for the restaurant not only harnesses renewable power, thanks to its canalside location, but also seeks practical ways of reducing its carbon footprint. Moreover, it trains local people, aims to help regenerate a hitherto unfashionable part of town and play a part in local life to boot. These virtuous goals would count for little if the cooking was not so satisfying. It is Italian in influence and style; the menu is refreshingly succinct and seasonal; ingredients are not mucked about with; flavours are natural and the prices are fair.

Fifteen London

K3

Italian

Hoxton
13 Westland Pl ✉ N1 7LP
✆ (0871) 3301 515 **Fax** (020) 7251 2749
www.fifteen.net

⊖ Old Street
Closed 25-26 December and 1 January

Menu £30 (weekday lunch)/60 – Carte £39/44

This is the original branch of Jamie Oliver's charitable 'Fifteen' restaurants and it's already on its seventh intake of trainees. Their programme lasts for 18 months, where they receive schooling in all departments of the restaurant while being closely monitored by the experienced full-time staff. There are two operations here: the buzzy ground floor trattoria and a slightly more formal basement restaurant. The Italian cooking bears the unmistakeable signature of Jamie Oliver and the students are clearly being taught that most valuable of lessons: buy the best quality, seasonal ingredients and don't mess them about too much. This laudable project makes worrying about the occasional lapse seem somewhat mean spirited.

Hoxton Apprentice

K2

Modern European

Hoxton
16 Hoxton Sq ✉ N1 6NT
✆ (020) 7749 2828
e-mail info@hoxtonapprentice.com **www**.hoxtonapprentice.com

⊖ Old Street
Closed Monday

Menu £13 (lunch) – Carte £18/31

Despite the severe parking restrictions, Hoxton Square has become quite a dining quarter and Hoxton Apprentice stands out from others for two reasons. Firstly, it was set up by a charity, Training for Life, to give opportunities to the unemployed or homeless with all the profits going back into the charity and, secondly, the cooking is rather good. This is not merely a restaurant for the community minded - the restaurant stands up in its own right. The apprentices work alongside pros and the kitchen uses decent, seasonal ingredients; the wine is competitively priced and the service is both conscientious and considerate. Housed in a former Victorian school, the room retains a relaxed and easy feel, with French windows opening out onto the terrace.

Real Greek Mezedopolio

Greek ✗

K3

Hoxton — Old Street
15 Hoxton Market ⊠ N1 6HG — Closed 25-26 December and 1 January
℘ (020) 7739 8212 **Fax** (020) 7739 4910 — bookings not accepted
e-mail hoxton@therealgreek.com **www**.therealgreek.co.uk

Carte £15/20

What were previously two distinct neighbouring restaurants, the Real Greek and Mezedopolio, are now one, which focuses on providing a very relaxed environment, where the emphasis is on an unstructured, shared eating experience. The menu is divided between cold and hot meze, souvlaki and large plates for 'sharers', which could be fish, meat or vegetarian, and it's all very fresh and healthy. The idea is to chat, drink and order a few plates – like barrel-aged feta, flatbread, grilled kalamari or loukaniko sausage – then have a few more drinks, followed by more chat and more ordering. It's all housed within a 1913 Christian Mission, with the large marble bar the best place to sit if you're just in for a quick bite after work.

Almeida

French ✗✗

M1

Islington — Angel
30 Almeida St ⊠ N1 1AD
℘ (020) 7354 4777 **Fax** (020) 7354 2777
e-mail sharonw@danddlondon.com
www.almeida-restaurant.co.uk

Menu £18/29 – Carte £18/30

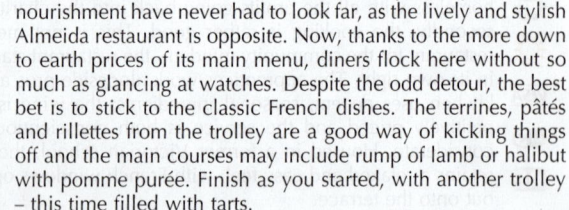

Described by Jonathan Miller as "the most interesting theatrical space in London", The Almeida Theatre continues to attract audiences from afar. Those in search of pre or post theatre nourishment have never had to look far, as the lively and stylish Almeida restaurant is opposite. Now, thanks to the more down to earth prices of its main menu, diners flock here without so much as glancing at watches. Despite the odd detour, the best bet is to stick to the classic French dishes. The terrines, pâtés and rillettes from the trolley are a good way of kicking things off and the main courses may include rump of lamb or halibut with pomme purée. Finish as you started, with another trolley – this time filled with tarts.

Metrogusto 😊

M1

Italian 🍴🍴

Islington
13 Theberton St ✉ N1 0QY
📞 (020) 7226 9400
Fax (020) 7226 9400
e-mail ambroianeselli@btconnect.com **www**.metrogusto.co.uk

↔ Angel
Closed 25-26 December – dinner only

Menu £19 (dinner) – Carte £24/36

A/C
🎭
VISA
MC
AE

Just looking in the window tells you that this is no ordinary Italian restaurant. One rarely sees interesting artwork in local restaurants - maybe some chefs feel threatened by the presence of someone else's creativity - but Metrogusto shows that having interesting pieces of art can, at the very least, provide diners with a conversation piece. The menu, too, shows an unwillingness to merely go with the flow and offers four courses of carefully prepared dishes, where the vitality of the ingredients is very much to the fore and where hints of originality are subtle and well judged. The pricing structure sensibly allows those who have come for an occasion or for a simple, quick bite to do so without breaking the bank.

Ottolenghi

M1

International 🍴

Islington
287 Upper St ✉ N1 2TZ
📞 (020) 7288 1454 **Fax** (020) 7704 1456
e-mail upper@ottolenghi.co.uk **www**.ottolenghi.co.uk

↔ Highbury and Islington
Closed 25-26 December,
1 January and Sunday dinner

Menu £15 (lunch) – Carte £24/45

A/C
VISA
MC
AE
①

Ottolenghi provides further evidence of the current trend for more spontaneous dining and less structured menus. A hugely appealing display of tempting pastries, unusual salads and mouth-watering desserts greet you as you enter. Behind this, one finds the restaurant, decorated as white as celestial purity, where two long communal tables dominate. Waiting staff will explain the 'concept' which involves ordering an assortment of small dishes, some of which display certain Mediterranean leanings while others may exhibit subtle Eastern spicing. The breads and puddings are particularly good. Takeaway is a large part of the business and lunch is an altogether simpler affair, with mostly salads and quiches.

The Drapers Arms

Gastropub

L1

Islington
44 Barnsbury St
✉ N1 1ER
✆ (020) 7619 0348 **Fax** (020) 7619 0413
e-mail info@thedrapersarms.co.uk **www**.thedrapersarms.co.uk

⊖ Highbury and Islington
Closed 24-27 December,

Carte £22/28

This battleship grey Victorian pub in an oasis of leafy residential splendour must be good, because all the access streets have speed humps. Its secret appears to be in its sincerity – it just feels like a proper pub, albeit one with decent food. Granted, there's a more formal dining room upstairs, but the same menu is served throughout, so stay downstairs for the banter in the bar, decorated with assorted drapery-themed photos. Dishes are British in their frankness or Mediterranean in their inclination, so choose between chips and couscous, steak and risotto, and Eton mess and crème brûlée. The catch of the day can be three different fish, flavours are pronounced and natural, and dishes are heartening in their lack of pretension.

The Northgate

Gastropub

K2

Islington
113 Southgate Rd ✉ N1 3JS
✆ (020) 7359 7392 **Fax** (020) 7359 7393
e-mail thenorthgate@hotmail.co.uk

⊖ Old Street
Closed 25-26 December,
and 1 January – dinner only and
lunch Saturday and Sunday

Carte £20/30

The Northgate is a large, square Victorian pub located on a corner of, paradoxically, Southgate Road. It may look fairly unremarkable from the outside but it was one of the first of many Islington pubs to blossom into a gastropub. There's an honesty about the place which engenders a relaxed and welcoming vibe, even when it is full-on busy, which appears to be most evenings. The front section comes decked out with the gastropub uniform of mismatched furniture, modern art and a large central bar. There's a separate dining room at the back with a skylight and the terrace is a big draw. From the blackboard menu comes liberally sized plates of satisfying wholesome gastropub staples, like tiger prawns and lamb shank.

The Barnsbury

L1

Gastropub

Islington
209-211 Liverpool Rd
✉ N1 1LX
✆ (020) 7607 5519 **Fax** (020) 7607 3256
e-mail info@thebarnsbury.co.uk www.thebarnsbury.co.uk

⊖ Highbury and Islington
Closed 25-26 December, 1 January

Carte £35/45

It may have been spruced up a few years back but The Barnsbury is still your proper local. Hence, you'll find it on down-to-earth Liverpool Road rather than glossier Upper Street which runs parallel. The more traditional features of restored wood panelling and a large central counter contrast with contemporary touches, such as the chandeliers made from crystal wine glasses and the regularly changing local artwork. It's all very relaxed and the young staff are helpful and competent. The owner, an acolyte of the Conran empire, clearly knows what he is doing. The menu will satisfy the appetites of both those who like to see recognisable British ingredients, as well as those who prefer more of an Italian connection to their food.

L'Oasis

K3

Gastropub

Mile End
237 Mile End Rd ✉ E1 4AA
✆ (020) 7702 7051 **Fax** (020) 7265 9850
e-mail info@loasisstepney.co.uk www.loasisstepney.co.uk

⊖ Stepney Green
Closed Monday and Bank Holidays

Carte £20/33

Fully confident in his chef's abilities, the owner of the pub formerly known as The Three Crowns decided that the new name L'Oasis would perfectly reflect its role in the culinary desert that is Stepney Green. Although it looks more like a bar than a modern dining pub, the inside is cavernous and bright, with original features including a delightful ornamental Victorian ceiling and decorative glazed tiles. Upstairs, a bright yellow function room copes with any overflow, service is friendly and efficient and food delivery is prompt even when they are busy. Concise menus offer hearty, rustic cooking with influences from all over the world, and what dishes may lack in finesse, they more than make up for in flavour and size.

L'Anima

Italian XXX

K3

Shoreditch
1 Snowden Street ⊠ EC2 2DA
☎ (0207) 422 7000 **Fax** (0207) 422 7077
e-mail enquiries@lanima.co.uk **www**.lanima.co.uk

⊖ Liverpool St
Closed Saturday, Sunday,
Christmas and Bank Holidays

Menu £24 (lunch) – Carte £34/51

VISA
MC
AE

It clearly cost a considerable amount of money to look this understated. Designed by architect Claudio Silverstrin, the dining room of L'Anima (Italian for 'the soul') is a thing of real beauty. The high ceiling and wall of glass lets light flood in but rough-cut brown stone cuts through the brightness of the whiteness, while the limestone, leather and marble add to the luxury. The menu comes with a helpful glossary of Italian culinary terms and is also positioned at the extravagant end of things but then one can see the quality of ingredients on the plate. The influences come from Sardinia and southern parts, from Puglia down to Sicily and dishes come packed with flavour. Those who can't get enough can also come for breakfast.

Rivington

British X

K3

Shoreditch
28-30 Rivington St ⊠ EC2A 3DZ
☎ (020) 7729 7053
e-mail shoreditch@rivingtongrill.co.uk **www**.rivingtongrill.co.uk

⊖ Old Street
Closed 25-26 December

Carte £21/39

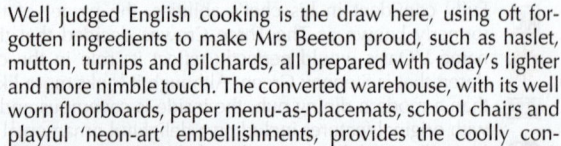

A/C
☼
VISA
MC
AE

Well judged English cooking is the draw here, using oft forgotten ingredients to make Mrs Beeton proud, such as haslet, mutton, turnips and pilchards, all prepared with today's lighter and more nimble touch. The converted warehouse, with its well worn floorboards, paper menu-as-placemats, school chairs and playful 'neon-art' embellishments, provides the coolly contemporary backdrop for this everyman fare. It even attracts all manner of customer, from business-type to local - even the odd hoodie has been known to venture over the threshold. Serving staff all have their skates on, particularly at lunch when delivery from the kitchen is swift, but those in even more of a hurry can grab something from the next door deli.

The Princess

Gastropub

K3

Shoreditch
76-78 Paul St ✉ EC2A 4NE
☎ (020) 7729 9270
e-mail princesspub@gmail.com

⊖ Old Street
Closed 24 December-1 January and Bank Holidays

Carte £25/30

How exactly did a dodgy old boozer full of villains turn into a gastropub run by antipodeans? Social historians can explain but we should just be grateful that it did, as The Princess now ticks all the right boxes. The downstairs remains loyal to its Victorian roots, except with better food, but ascend the spiral staircase and you'll find yourself in an unexpectedly stylish dining room. A little art deco, oil paintings, floral wallpaper, mirrors and a fireplace all set the tone. The kitchen is skilled at producing flavoursome and robust dishes of assorted influences, but with a pronounced seasonality. The name of the place is not, sadly, in honour of East End vernacular but is a shortened version of the original, The Princess Royal.

The Fox

Gastropub

K3

Shoreditch
28 Paul St ✉ EC2A 4LB
☎ (020) 7729 5708
e-mail thefoxpublichouse@thefoxpublichouse.com
www.thefoxpublichouse.com

⊖ Old Street
Closed one week Christmas to New Year
– booking essential

Carte £19/25

Friday lunchtime and it'll be like a rugby scrum at the bar, but head upstairs for the contrasting serenity of the first floor dining room, where you'll also find a delightful roof terrace. Four choices per course form the set menu, although there's no pressure exerted to have the full three-courser. Dish descriptions are refreshingly concise and this no-nonsense simplicity is reflected in the rustic cooking with specialities of either a British or Mediterranean persuasion. The dining room boasts an appealingly thrown-together quality and, in between their constant sprints up and down the stairs from the kitchen, the waiting staff pitch the tone of service perfectly.

Rasa

K2 | Indian 🍴

Stoke Newington
55 Stoke Newington Church St
✉ N16 0AR
✆ (020) 7249 0344 **Fax** (020) 7637 0224
www.rasarestaurants.com

Closed 24-26 December, and 1 January – booking essential – dinner only

Menu £16 – Carte £9/13

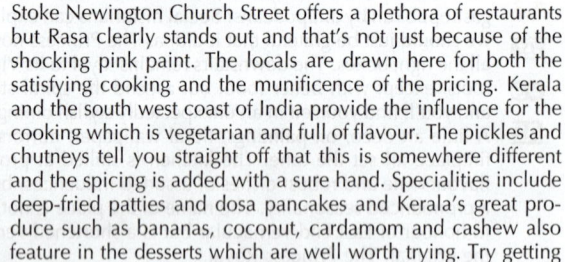

A/C · ☀ · VISA · MC · AE

Stoke Newington Church Street offers a plethora of restaurants but Rasa clearly stands out and that's not just because of the shocking pink paint. The locals are drawn here for both the satisfying cooking and the munificence of the pricing. Kerala and the south west coast of India provide the influence for the cooking which is vegetarian and full of flavour. The pickles and chutneys tell you straight off that this is somewhere different and the spicing is added with a sure hand. Specialities include deep-fried patties and dosa pancakes and Kerala's great produce such as bananas, coconut, cardamom and cashew also feature in the desserts which are well worth trying. Try getting a table in the back as it offers a little more room.

Rasa Travancore

K2 | Indian 🍴

Stoke Newington
56 Stoke Newington Church St
✉ N16 0NB
✆ (020) 7249 1340
www.rasarestaurants.com

Closed 23-30 December – dinner only

Carte approx. £12

A/C · ☀ · VISA · MC · AE · ◐

Virtually opposite Rasa is its sister Rasa Travancore. It also offers specialities from the Kerala region of India, but this time carnivores are catered for as it celebrates the unique cooking found within the Christian Syrian communities. Meat and fish play a large part and the menu offers a balanced selection, from steamed prawns to chicken stews and lamb curries. Despite having a basement kitchen, the dishes arrive piping hot and portions are in manageable sizes, so be sure to try some of the pre-meal snacks. Ornamentation within the two dining rooms is relatively limited but the delightful and charming service more than compensates. Everyone involved in the restaurant hails from Kerala and they're all rightly proud of their cuisine.

The Old Dairy

Gastropub

Stroud Green — Closed 25 December
1-3 Crouch Hill ✉ N4 4AP
✆ (020) 7263 3337 **Fax** (020) 7561 1851
e-mail theolddairy@realpubs.co.uk www.realpubs.co.uk

Carte £20/25

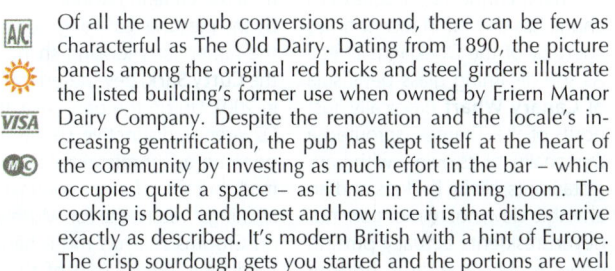

Of all the new pub conversions around, there can be few as characterful as The Old Dairy. Dating from 1890, the picture panels among the original red bricks and steel girders illustrate the listed building's former use when owned by Friern Manor Dairy Company. Despite the renovation and the locale's increasing gentrification, the pub has kept itself at the heart of the community by investing as much effort in the bar – which occupies quite a space – as it has in the dining room. The cooking is bold and honest and how nice it is that dishes arrive exactly as described. It's modern British with a hint of Europe. The crisp sourdough gets you started and the portions are well judged and confidently flavoured. Weekend brunches are a real hit.

The Lock

Mediterranean

Tottenham — ⊖ Tottenham Hale
Heron House, Hale Wharf, — Closed Monday
Ferry Lane ✉ N17 9NF
✆ (020) 8885 2829 **Fax** (020) 8885 1618
e-mail thelock06@btconnect.com www.thelockrestaurant.com

Menu £19 – Carte £20/33

Full marks to The Lock for opening in Tottenham and doing their bit for the regeneration of this part of London. It's in the big yellow industrial looking building on your left as you approach from the west and, while the address may hint at a rather charming lock-side setting, the Norfolk Broads it ain't. It is, though, a very sweetly run place, with two keen young owners. The room's quite spacious, with a bar and sofas on one side and the restaurant, with its mismatched tables and chairs, on the other. With much of the produce coming from Walthamstow market, the open kitchen offers up a menu of French and Italian influences, with the odd idiosyncratic twist, and several vegetarian choices.

South-East London

Once considered not only the wrong side of the tracks, but also most definitely the wrong side of the river, London's southeastern chunk has thrived in recent times courtesy of the Docklands Effect. As the gleaming glass peninsula of **Canary Wharf** (ironically, just north of the Thames) sprouted a personality of its own – with bars, restaurants, slinky bridges and an enviable view, not to mention moneyed residents actually putting down roots – the city's bottom right hand zone began to achieve destination status on a par with other parts of London. You only have to stroll around the glossy and quite vast **Limehouse Basin** – a slick marina that was once a hard-grafting East End dock – to really see what's happened here.

Not that the area hasn't always boasted some true gems in the capital's treasure chest. **Greenwich,** with fabulous views across the water to the docklands from its delightfully sloping park, has long been a favourite of kings and queens: Henry VIII and Elizabeth I resided here. The village itself bustles along with its market and plush picturehouse, but most visitors make their way to the standout attractions, of which there are many. The **Royal Observatory** and the Meridian Line draw stargazers and hemisphere striders in equal number, while the palatial Old Royal Naval College is a star turn for lovers of Wren, who designed it as London's answer to Versailles. On the northern edge of Greenwich Park, the **National Maritime Museum** has three floors of sea-faring wonders; down by the pier, the real thing exists in the rather sorry-looking shape of the **Cutty Sark,** devastated by fire in 2007. Up on the peninsula, the O2 Arena's distinctive shape has become an unmistakable landmark, but if you fancy a contrast to all things watery, the Fan Museum on Crooms Hill has more hand-held fans (over 3,000 of them) than anywhere else on earth. Strolling south from Greenwich park you reach **Blackheath,** an alluring suburban village, whose most striking feature is the towering All Saints' Church, standing proud away from the chic shops and restaurants.

Of slightly less spectacular charms, but a real crowd-pleaser nevertheless, is **Dulwich Village,** hidden deeper in the southeastern enclaves. It's a leafy oasis in this part of the world, with a delightful park that boasts at its western end, next to the original buildings of the old public school, the Dulwich Picture Gallery. This will soon reach its 200th birthday, and its pedigree is evident in works by the likes of Rembrandt, Rubens, Van Dyck and Canaletto. Half an hour's walk away across the park is the brilliant Horniman Museum, full of natural history and world culture delights – as well as a massive aquarium that seems to take up much of southeast London.

A bit further east along the South Circular, there's the unexpected gem of Eltham Palace, originally the childhood home of Henry VIII with a magnificent (and still visible) Great Hall. What makes it unique is the adjacent Art Deco mansion built for millionaires in the 1930s in Ocean Liner style. It's the closest you'll ever get to a setting fit for hog roast and champagne. Heading back towards London, a lifestyle of bubbly and banquets has never really been **Peckham**'s thing, but it boasts a couple of corkers in the shape of the South London Gallery with its zeitgeist-setting art shows, and the Peckham Library, a giant inverted 'L' that after a decade still looks like a lot of fun to go into.

Back in the luxury flat-lands of the **Docklands, Wapping** has become an interesting port of call, its new-build architecture mixing in with a still Dickensian feel, in the shape of glowering Victorian warehouses and Wapping New Stairs, where the bodies of pirates were hanged from a gibbet until seven tides had showered their limp bodies. You can catch a fascinating history of the whole area in the nearby Museum in Docklands.

Greater London: South East
(Plan XVII)

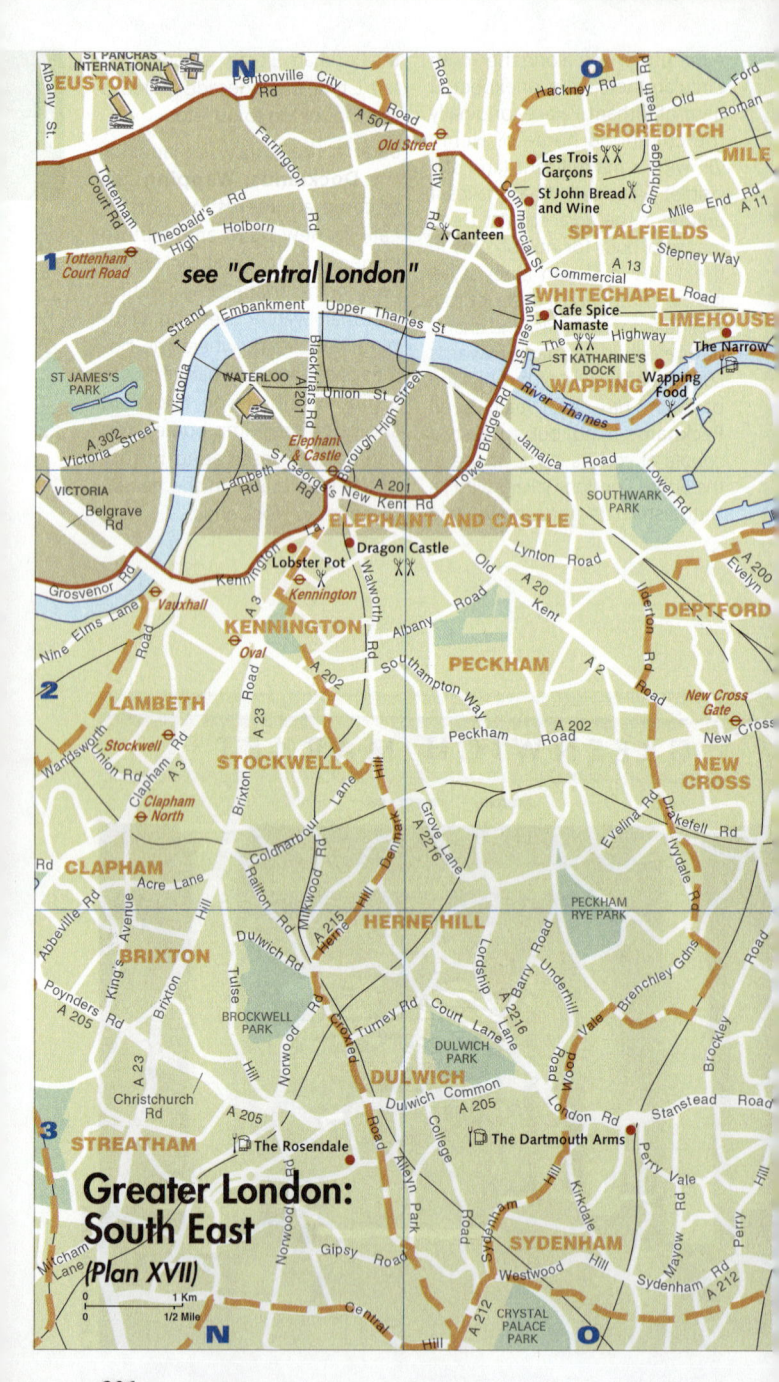

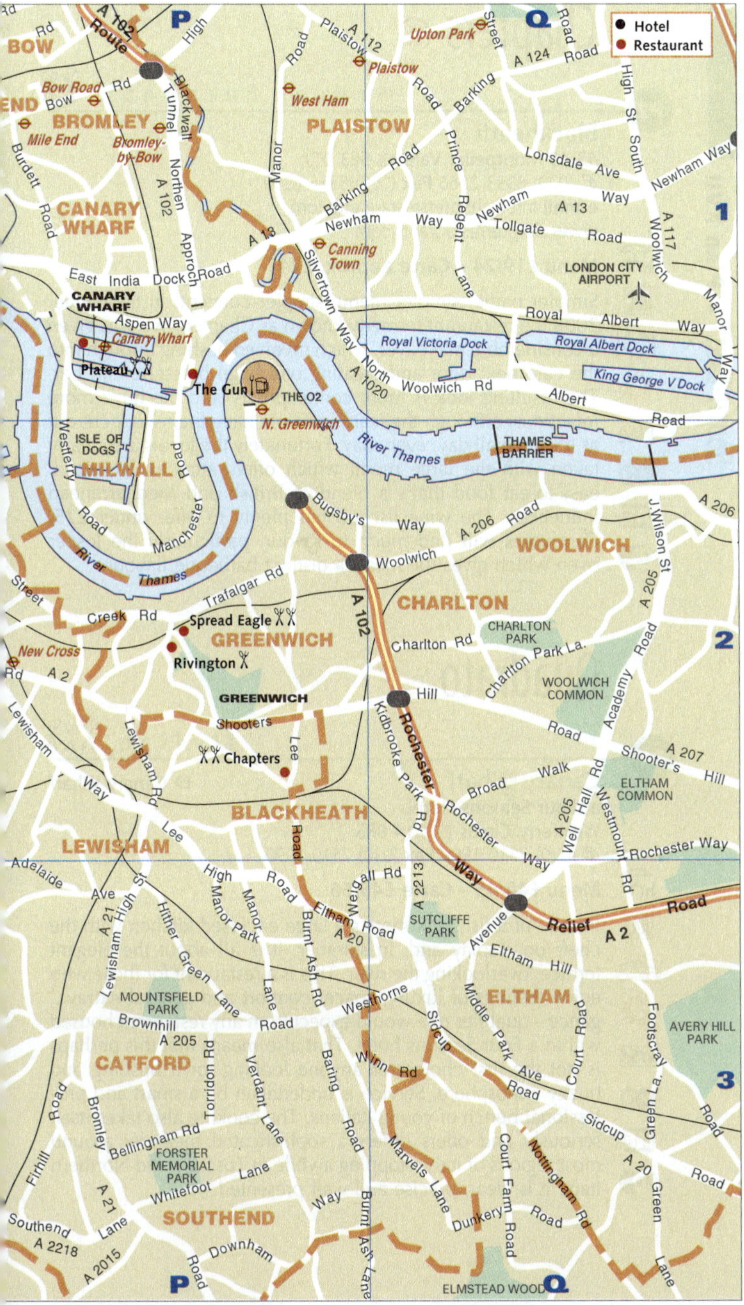
Hotel
Restaurant
P
Q
1
2
3
BOW
BROMLEY
Bow Road
Bow Rd
Mile End
Bromley-by-Bow
CANARY WHARF
PLAISTOW
Plaistow
Upton Park
West Ham
Canning Town
A 102 Route
Blackwall Tunnel Northern Approach
A 102
Burdett Road
Manor Road
Plaistow Road
Prince Regent Lane
Barking Road
A 112
A 124
Lonsdale Ave
High St South
Newham Way
Newham Way
A 13
Tollgate Road
A 117 Woolwich
Manor Way
LONDON CITY AIRPORT
East India Dock Road
Silvertown Way
North Woolwich Rd
A 1020
Royal Albert Way
Royal Victoria Dock
Royal Albert Dock
King George V Dock
Albert Road
Aspen Way
Canary Wharf
Plateau
The Gun
THE O2
N. Greenwich
River Thames
THAMES BARRIER
ISLE OF DOGS
MILWALL
Westferry Road
Manchester Road
Bugsby's Way
A 206 Road
Woolwich
WOOLWICH
A 206
J. Wilson St
A 205
CHARLTON
Trafalgar Rd
Creek Rd
Spread Eagle
Rivington
GREENWICH
GREENWICH
New Cross
A 2
Street
Charlton Rd
CHARLTON PARK
Charlton Park La.
WOOLWICH COMMON
Academy Road
Hill
Shooters Hill Road
Shooter's Hill
A 207
Kidbrooke Park Rd
Rochester Way
Rochester Way
Lewisham Way
Lewisham Rd
Chapters
Lee
Broad Walk
ELTHAM COMMON
Well Hall Rd
Westmount Rd
Rochester Way
BLACKHEATH
Road
LEWISHAM
Lee High Road
Adelaide Ave
A 21
Lewisham High St
Hither Green Lane
Manor Park
Manor Lane
Burnt Ash Rd
Weigall Rd
Eltham Road
A 20
A 2213
SUTCLIFFE PARK
Avenue
Relief Road
A 2
Eltham Hill
ELTHAM
MOUNTSFIELD PARK
Brownhill Road
A 205
Westhorne
Sidcup
Winn Rd
Middle Park Ave
Court Road
Footscray Road
AVERY HILL PARK
CATFORD
Torridon Rd
Verdant Lane
Baring Road
Marvels Lane
Sidcup Road
Green La.
Firhill Road
Bromley Road
Bellingham Rd
FORSTER MEMORIAL PARK
Whitefoot Lane
A 21
Southend Lane
A 2218
A 2015
SOUTHEND
Downham Way
Burnt Ash Lane
Dunkery Road
Court Farm Road
Nottingham Rd
A 20
Green Lane
ELMSTEAD WOOD

Chapters

Blackheath

Modern European XX

43-45 Montpelier Vale ⊠ SE3 0TJ
☎ (020) 8333 2666 **Fax** (020) 8355 8399
e-mail info@chaptersrestaurants.com
www.chapterrestaurants.com

Menu £19/24 – Carte approx. £24

Simpler name, simpler menu, simpler concept. In September 2008 the restaurant formerly known as Chapter Two was given a considerable makeover, which involved bashing through into the café next door and creating one large brasserie and bar. The resulting look is more contemporary and the buzz more infectious, although the team certainly have their work cut out as it's open all day, every day. Fortunately the locals are clearly taken with the large menu which offers attractively priced, easy-to-eat food that's a blend of British and Mediterranean influences. The wine list too has plenty to offer under £25. Carnivores will find much to savour, particularly the Josper oven which gives the meats a distinct barbeque flavour.

Quadrato

Canary Wharf

Italian XXX

⊖ Canary Wharf

at Four Seasons Hotel,
Westferry Circus ⊠ E14 8RS
☎ (020) 7510 1999 **Fax** (020) 7510 1998

Menu £40/45 – Carte £45/56

Instead of a fish tank there's a large enclosed kitchen with the chefs on display and, in summer, it is all about the elegant terrace, overlooking the river. This is a restaurant for those who enjoy feelings of luxury, space, comfort and general extravagance – qualities one would expect from any restaurant housed within a Four Seasons hotel. That also means that this perhaps is not the first choice for anyone looking for a bustling and buzzy atmosphere. Service is undertaken by a smart and professional bunch of young Italians. The cooking also takes itself seriously and offers diners a sophisticated meander around most regions of Italy, stopping awhile in Tuscany and Northern Italy. It is clear, precise and well presented.

Plateau

Modern European ✗✗

P1

Canary Wharf　　　　　　　　　⊖ Canary Wharf
(4th floor) Canada Place, Canada　　Closed 25-26 December, 1 January,
Square ✉ E14 5ER　　　　　　　　Sunday and Bank Holidays
✆ (020) 7715 7100 **Fax** (020) 7715 7110
e-mail plateaureservations@danddlondon.com
www.plateaurestaurant.com

Menu £35 – Carte £21/35

London's own Masters of the Universe gather here at Plateau, the closest thing London has to the Manhattan skyline. It's certainly an impressive open-plan space and the dramatic glass walls and ceilings make the surrounding monolithic office blocks look strangely appealing. The striking 1970s retro design also seems to fit perfectly. There are two choices: the Grill where, as the name suggests, the choice is from rotisserie meats and classic grilled dishes, or the more formal restaurant beyond with its more comfortable surroundings. Here, the range is more eclectic and dishes are constructed with more global influences. They also come in ample sizes, though, so ignore the enthusiastic selling of the side dishes.

The Gun

Gastropub

P1

Canary Wharf　　　　　　　　⊖ Blackwall (DLR)
27 Coldharbour ✉ E14 9NS　　　　Closed 25-26 December
✆ (020) 7515 5222
e-mail info@thegundocklands.com **www**.thegundocklands.com

Carte £27/32

This is a thoughtfully restored 18C pub with a long connection to the river and was where Lord Nelson conducted his trysts with Lady Emma Hamilton. But sit on the terrace or in the back with the locals and the views are of the O2 Arena. The concise menu is a balanced selection of European based dishes, prepared with a light yet assured touch. Fish is a key component of the blackboard daily specials and comes from Billingsgate, no further than a hefty cast away. Those side dishes can push up the final bill and there are plenty of temptations on the wine list, but this is a pub for those who know their food. There are jazz nights on Sundays; news that will attract and repel in equal measure but bite the bullet and get down to The Gun.

Dragon Castle

Chinese

N2

Elephant and Castle
114 Walworth Rd
✉ SE17 1JL
✆ (020) 7277 3388
e-mail dragoncastle@hotmail.com **www**.dragoncastle.eu

⊖ Elephant and Castle
Closed 25-26 December

Carte £15/30

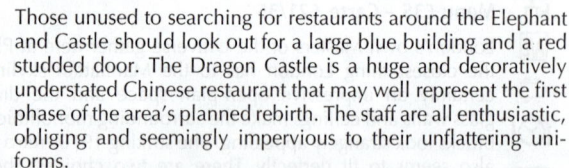

Those unused to searching for restaurants around the Elephant and Castle should look out for a large blue building and a red studded door. The Dragon Castle is a huge and decoratively understated Chinese restaurant that may well represent the first phase of the area's planned rebirth. The staff are all enthusiastic, obliging and seemingly impervious to their unflattering uniforms.

The cooking is Cantonese and, if you're a little more adventurous and want something different from the usual crowd pleasers, then go for what the Chinese clientele are having. This way you'll find yourself with very generously sized plates of authentic and enticing specialities, such as eel or hotpots of pork. The daytime dim sum is proving very popular.

The Dartmouth Arms

Gastropub

O3

Forest Hill
7 Dartmouth Road ✉ SE23 3HN
✆ (020) 8488 3117 **Fax** (020) 7771 7230
e-mail info@thedartmoutharms.com
www.thedartmoutharms.com

Closed 25-26 December, 1 January

Menu £15/18 – Carte £23/31

The Dartmouth Arms' position opposite Forest Hill train station meant that this was once the sort of pub whose main selling point was as somewhere to dive into for a swift one on the way home. Since its makeover in 2004 it is now the sort of place in which to spend the evening. The couple running the show know what their customers want and the menu offers an appealing mix of dishes. Many have more of a restaurant pedigree than your average pub grub, but there's commendable Britishness in evidence here, as well as a healthy regard for seasonality. So expect to see Barnsley chops, asparagus, samphire and Jersey Royals at certain times of the year. There's also some invention so you'll find the black pudding in a risotto and crab beignets with chilli jam.

Spread Eagle

French ✕✕

P2

Greenwich
1-2 Stockwell St ✉ SE10 9FN
☎ (020) 8853 2333 **Fax** (020) 8293 1024
www.spreadeaglerestaurant.co.uk

⊖ Greenwich (DLR)
Closed 1 January

Menu £20/31 s – Carte £21/41 s

[A/C] [☼] [VISA] [MC] [D]

Forming part of a 17th century coaching inn, the Spread Eagle in its current incarnation has been part of the Greenwich dining scene since 1966 and, in that time, has remained proudly impervious to changing design and decorative tastes. There are a number of different sitting areas, the best being the two semi-private booths on the ground floor, but the more able-bodied should try upstairs, via the original spiral staircase. On a winter's night the place really comes into its own with its log fire, panelling, antiques and dim lighting all adding to the well-mannered atmosphere. The kitchen attempts a modern interpretation of rustic French cooking and offers tasting menus, one of which is vegetarian, accompanied by chosen wines.

Rivington

British ✕

P2

Greenwich
178 Greenwich High Rd
✉ SE10 8NN
☎ (020) 8293 9270
e-mail office@rivingtongrill.co.uk **www**.rivingtongrill.co.uk

⊖ Greenwich (DLR)
Closed 25-26 December, Monday, lunch Tuesday and Wednesday

Carte £21/39

[A/C] [☼] [VISA] [MC] [AE]

It's open from breakfast until late and the menu changes every two weeks so they can introduce seasonal specials; the 'on toast' section is a local favourite and includes Welsh rarebit and devilled kidneys. Steaks are from Scotland; the prosperous can upgrade their fish and chips to lobster and chips and the puds are rich and satisfying. The wine list is sensibly priced and includes beers and Somerset brandies. It's spread over two floors, with the ground floor being the more casual, and attracts a younger, hipper crowd than the Shoreditch branch. It also has more of a local feel and gets swamped with look-alikes whenever there's a pop siren playing the O2 arena. Tables of up to four people can get a discount at the next door cinema.

Lobster Pot

French

N2

Kennington
3 Kennington Lane ✉ SE11 4RG
✆ (020) 7582 5556
www.lobsterpotrestaurant.co.uk

⊖ Kennington
Closed 2 weeks Christmas,
Sunday and Monday

Menu £22/40 – Carte £34/45

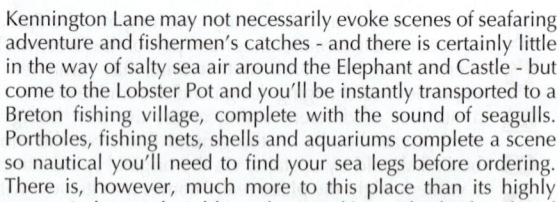

Kennington Lane may not necessarily evoke scenes of seafaring adventure and fishermen's catches - and there is certainly little in the way of salty sea air around the Elephant and Castle - but come to the Lobster Pot and you'll be instantly transported to a Breton fishing village, complete with the sound of seagulls. Portholes, fishing nets, shells and aquariums complete a scene so nautical you'll need to find your sea legs before ordering. There is, however, much more to this place than its highly eccentric but undeniably endearing décor. The husband and wife team know what they're doing and serve authentic and expertly timed French accented seafood, supplemented by daily specials depending on the day's catch.

The Narrow 😊

Gastropub

O1

Limehouse
Narrow Street ✉ E14 8DP
✆ (020) 7592 7950 **Fax** (020) 7265 9503
e-mail thenarrow@gordonramsay.com **www**.gordonramsay.com

⊖ Limehouse (DLR)
Booking essential

Carte £35/45

If anything proved that the Gordon Ramsay group had the right infrastructure, it was the opening of the Narrow: it may have been his first foray into the world of the gastropub but it also appeared to be an instant success. It certainly helped starting with a handsome pub in a great spot – a Grade II listed former dockmaster's house on the river. But the real experience is there on the plate; you'll find potted crabs, sardines on toast, salt beef, monkfish and chips and proper puddings, not fancy desserts. The kitchen knows what it's doing and what's more, the prices are competitive, although too many of the tempting but individually priced side dishes can push up the final bill.

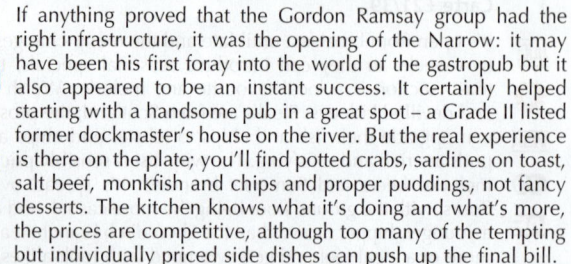

Les Trois Garcons

French

Spitalfields
1 Club Row ✉ E1 6JX
✆ (020) 7613 1924
Fax (020) 7012 1236
e-mail info@lestroisgarcons.com **www**.lestroisgarcons.com

⊖ Shoreditch
Closed 2 weeks late August - early September, Christmas-New Year and Sunday — dinner only

Menu £50 – Carte £36/51

The surrounding streets may be somewhat drab but the three friends (hence the name) who own this former pub are also antique dealers, hence the eccentric and exuberant decoration that resembles a theatrical props department. There are stuffed animals, beads, handbags and assorted objets d'art; heavy velvet curtains ensure that the lighting is dim and atmospheric. The kitchen, on the other hand, uses fairly classical French cooking techniques and flavour combinations, although the majority of ingredients are British. The menus change seasonally and presentation on the plate is neat and appetising. The early-in-the-week set menu is good value; the à la carte somewhat expensive. Service can occasionally veer from the efficient to the over-confident.

Canteen

British

Spitalfields
2 Crispin Pl ✉ E1 6DW
✆ (07957) 2164 44
e-mail lisa.ispani@canteen.co.uk **www**.canteen.co.uk

⊖ Liverpool Street
Closed 25 December

Carte approx. £23

Canteens are beginning to appear in various locations around London but this glass enclosed cube, juxtaposed next to the old Spitalfield market, was the prototype and it's easy to understand why they are proliferating. It has an all-day menu, shared refectory tables and well priced, decidedly British food. Whether it's a morning bacon sarnie, a lunchtime pie or an evening stew, there's something for everyone and every appetite. The daily roasts and fish are favourites but all flavours are natural and all produce conscientiously sourced.

If you're a team of four you may snag one of the outer tables with cushioned seats. Otherwise, just hunker down with your fellow man and rediscover some classics.

St John Bread and Wine

British

O1

Spitalfields
94-96 Commercial St ✉ E1 6LZ
☏ (020) 7251 0848 **Fax** (020) 7247 8924
e-mail reservations@stjohnbreadandwine.com
www.stjohnbreadandwine.com

↔ Shoreditch
Closed Christmas-New Year and Bank Holidays

Carte £23/27

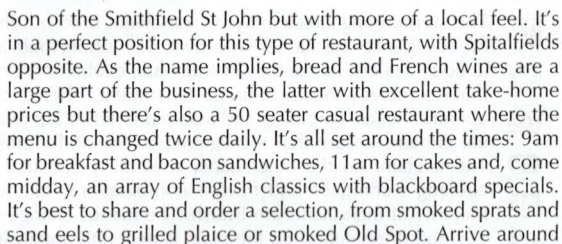

Son of the Smithfield St John but with more of a local feel. It's in a perfect position for this type of restaurant, with Spitalfields opposite. As the name implies, bread and French wines are a large part of the business, the latter with excellent take-home prices but there's also a 50 seater casual restaurant where the menu is changed twice daily. It's all set around the times: 9am for breakfast and bacon sandwiches, 11am for cakes and, come midday, an array of English classics with blackboard specials. It's best to share and order a selection, from smoked sprats and sand eels to grilled plaice or smoked Old Spot. Arrive around 7pm for the roast just out of the oven and, for dessert, try some warm Madeleines or British cheeses.

Wapping Food

Modern European

O1

Wapping
Wapping Wall ✉ E1W 3SG
☏ (020) 7680 2080
www.thewappingproject.com

↔ Wapping
Closed Christmas-New Year, Sunday dinner and Bank Holidays

Carte £25/45

For some reason industrial spaces make great backdrops to restaurants and this Victorian former hydraulic power station, which was used to light up the West End theatres, is certainly no exception. Opened in 2000, you can not only sit amongst the abandoned machinery but you're also surrounded by monthly-changing art exhibitions. The owner is an Aussie and her wine list is an exclusively Australian affair, while the cooking is equally unfussy and straightforward. The kitchen rightly relies on the quality of the produce to carry the dish, to which they add some Mediterranean or occasionally Asian touches. The serving team are a friendly bunch and they all know the answers to any questions relating to the history of the place.

The Rosendale

N3

Gastropub

West Dulwich
65 Rosendale Rd
✉ SE21 8EZ
✆ (020) 8670 0812 **Fax** (020) 8671 9008
e-mail dine@therosendale.co.uk www.therosendale.co.uk

⊖ West Dulwich (rail)
Closed 1 January

Menu £20 (lunch) – Carte £20/28

Included among the many things that stand out about The Rosendale are that they make their own butter as well as their own bread and have a wine list that is remarkable in its breadth, depth and affordability. This vast former coaching inn dates from the 1820s and has a soaring ceiling and plenty of original features. There are two menus - the front bar has a grill menu, with more of your typical pub food. Go through to the dining room at the back and the menu there is of a more ambitious nature. It can appear even more complicated on the plate but there is no denying the quality of the ingredients and sourcing is clearly taken seriously. Fish is delivered daily from Cornwall; they hang their own meat and smoke their own fish.

Cafe Spice Namaste

O1

Indian

Whitechapel
16 Prescot St ✉ E1 8AZ
✆ (020) 7488 9242
Fax (020) 7481 0508
e-mail info@cafespice.co.uk www.cafespice.co.uk

⊖ Tower Hill
Closed Christmas-New Year,
Saturday lunch, Sunday and Bank Holidays

Menu £30 – Carte £23/29

This red brick Victorian building was once a magistrate's court. That information hardly prepares you for the sheer vivaciousness of the interior. Cyrus Todiwala's vibrant and ebullient restaurant has been going strong now for over a decade, having been at the vanguard of the new wave of Indian restaurants. It comes divided into two large, high-ceilinged rooms separated by the bar. If there is a colour that hasn't been used in the fabrics or on the walls it's because it hasn't yet been created. Don't be surprised to see game and other classic British ingredients on the menu - the cooking here has moments of real innovation. All dishes come fragrantly spiced and nicely balanced, but look out for the Parsee specialities.

South-West London

Meandering like a silver snake, **The Thames** coils serenely through south-west London, adding definition to the area's much-heralded middle-class enclaves and leafy suburbs. It's the focal point to the annual **university boat race** from **Putney** to **Mortlake,** and it serves as the giant glass pond attractively backing countless bank-side pubs. This area has long been regarded as the cosy bourgeois side of town, though within its postcode prowls the lively and eclectic **Brixton,** whose buzzing street markets and lauded music venues such as the Academy and the Fridge add an urban lustre and vibrant edge.

In most people's minds, though, south-west London finds its true colours in the beautiful terrace view from the top of **Richmond Hill,** as the river bends majestically through the meadows below. Or in the smart **Wimbledon Village,** its independent boutiques ranged prettily along its own hill, with the open spaces of the Common for a back garden. Or, again, in the Italianate architecture that makes **Chiswick House** and grounds a little corner of the Mediterranean close to the Great West Road.

Green space is almost as prolific in this zone as the streets of Victorian and Edwardian villas. **Richmond Park** is the largest royal park in the whole of London and teems with kite flyers, cyclists and deer – though not necessarily in that order. From here, round a southerly bend in the river, delightful grounds surround **Ham House,** which is all set for its 400th birthday in 2010; celebrations should be good, but maybe not as excessive as during the seventeenth century when it was home to Restoration court life. Head slightly north to **Kew Gardens** and its world famous 300 acres can now be viewed from above – the treetop walkway, opened in 2008, takes you 60 feet up to offer some breath-taking views. Just across the river from here is another from the historical hit-list: **Syon Park,** which boasts water meadows still grazed by cattle, giving it a distinctly rural aspect. Syon House is considered one of architect Robert Adam's finest works; it certainly appealed to Queen Victoria, who spent much of her young life here. Up the road in bourgeoning Brentford, two unique museums bring in hordes of the curious: the Musical Museum includes a huge Wurlitzer theatre organ (get lucky and watch it being played), while almost next door, the Kew Bridge Steam Museum shows off all things steamy on a grand scale, including massive beam engines which pumped London's water for over a century.

Hammersmith may be known for its bustling Broadway and flyover, but five minutes' walk from here is the Upper Mall, which has iconic riverside pubs and Kelmscott House, the last home of artistic visionary William Morris: down in the basement and coach house are impressive memorabilia related to his life plus changing exhibitions of designs and drawings. From here, it's just a quick jaunt across **Hammersmith Bridge** and down the arrow-straight Castelnau to the Wetland Centre in Barnes, which for nearly ten years has lured wildlife to within screeching distance of the West End. **Barnes** has always revelled in its village-like identity – it juts up like an isolated peninsula into the Thames and boasts yummy boutiques and well-known restaurants. The Bulls Head pub in Lonsdale Road has featured some of the best jazz in London for half a century.

In a more easterly direction, the urbanised areas of **Clapham** and **Battersea** have re-established themselves as desirable places to live over the last decade. **Clapham Common** is considered prime southwest London turf, to the extent that its summer music festivals are highly prized. It's ringed by good pubs and restaurants, too. Battersea used to be famous for its funfair, but now the peace pagoda in the park lends it a more serene light. And if you're after serenity on a hot day, then a cool dip in the wondrous **Tooting** Lido is just the thing.

Greater London: South West
(Plan XVIII)

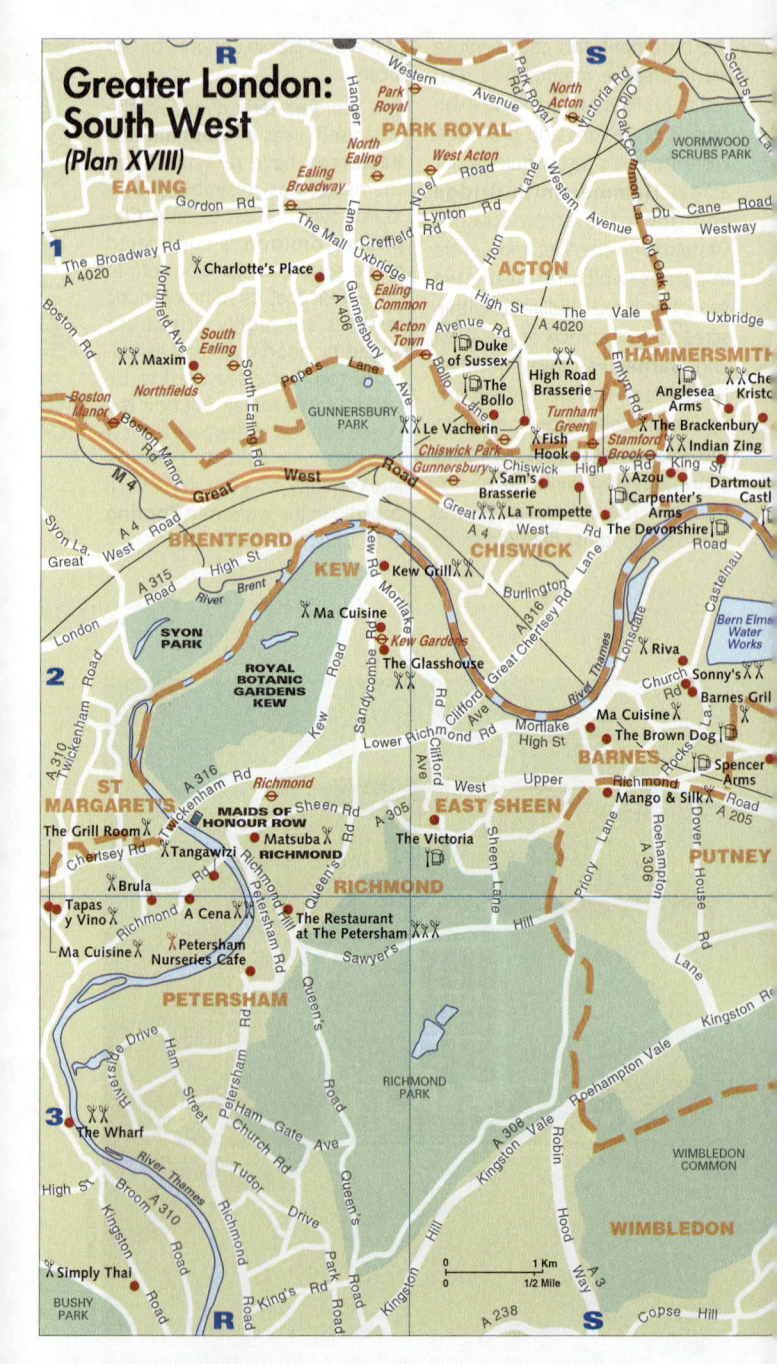

319

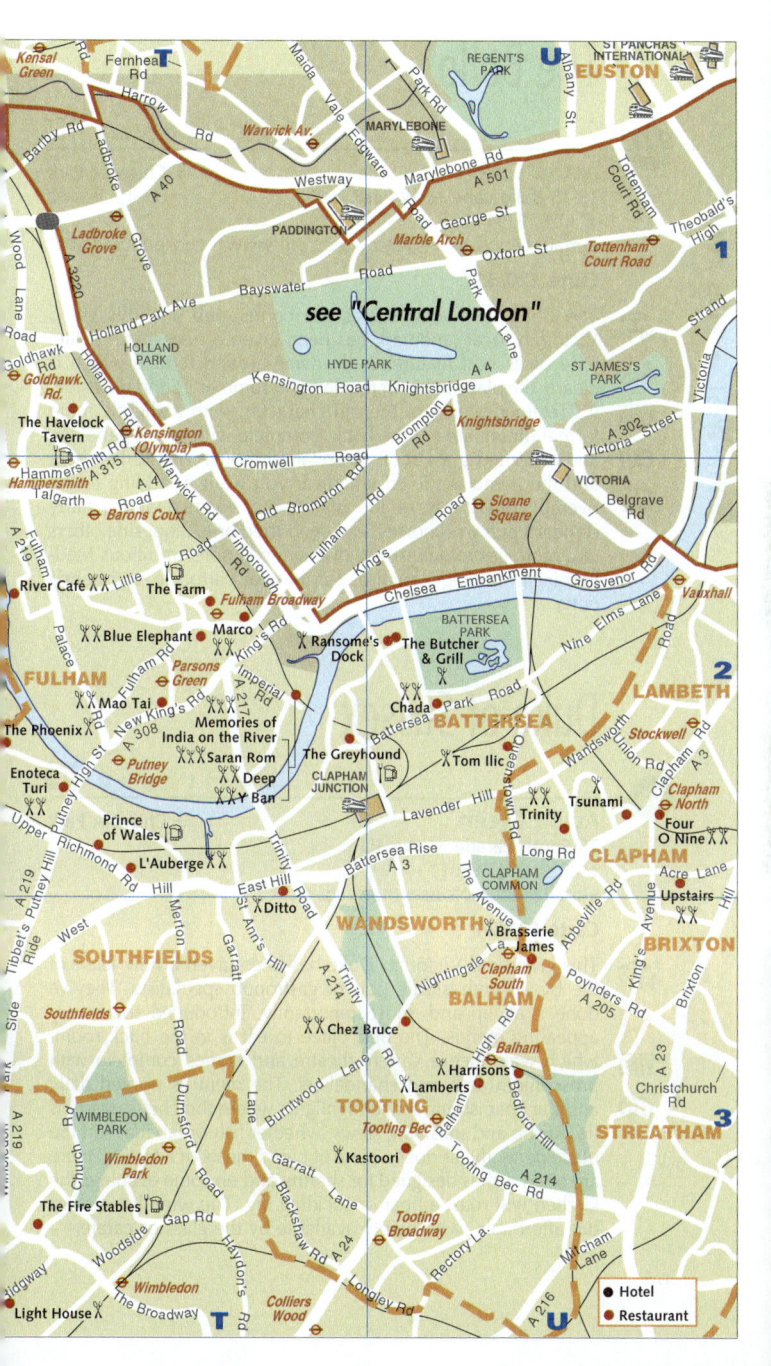

The Bollo

S1

Gastropub

Acton Green
13-15 Bollo Lane ✉ W4 5LR
📞 (020) 8994 6037
e-mail thebollohouse@btconnect.com **www**.thebollohouse.co.uk

⊖ Chiswick Park
Closed 25 December

Carte £20/35

The Bollo is a large, handsome corner pub and this grand Victorian local landmark has been given a new lease of life. One of its best features is the wrap-around terrace which is clearly the place to be for that languid summer's Sunday. Inside, it's retained plenty of the old character, with a slightly more formal dining area at the back, complete with wood panelling and a domed glass roof. Hospitality, though, is the key here and the menu is served wherever you want it, adding to the overall conviviality of the place. That menu features fairly standard pub workhorses, like deep-fried brie, alongside others of a more gastro nature and displaying a more ambitious Mediterranean heritage, such as sea bass al cartoccio and panna cotta.

Duke of Sussex

S1

Gastropub

Acton Green
75 South Parade ✉ W4 5LF
📞 (020) 8742 8801
e-mail thedukeofsussex@realpubs.co.uk

⊖ Chiswick Park

Carte £21/24

This grand old Victorian Duke has been given a new lease of life by an enthusiastic pair of gastropub specialists. They've done it all up and, most importantly, introduced some very appealing menus. The best place to eat is in the back room, which was once a variety theatre and comes complete with proscenium arch and chandeliers. The menu is printed daily and the Spanish influence highlights where the chef's passions lie. Rustic and satisfying stews, whether fish or fabada, suit the place perfectly, as does a plate of cured meats or a tortilla; there are often dishes designed for sharing and on some evenings the kitchen will roast a boar or suckling pig. The wine list is short but affordable, with plenty available by the glass or carafe.

Tierce Majeure

Reserve de la Comtesse
Second Vin du Château
Pichon Longueville Comtesse de Lalande

Chateau Pichon Longueville
Comtesse de Lalande
Grand Cru Classé en 1855 - Pauillac

Chateau Bernadotte
Haut Médoc

33250 Pauillac - France - Tel. 33 (0)5 56 59 19 40 - Fax. 33 (0)5 56 59 29 78

WWW.PICHON-LALANDE.COM

- → Discover the best restaurant ?
- → Find the nearest hotel ?
- → Find your bearings using our maps and guides ?
- → Understand the symbols used in the guide...

Follow the red Bibs !

Advice on restaurants from **Chef Bib**.

Tips and advice from **Clever Bib** on finding your way around the guide and on the road.

Advice on hotels from **Bellboy Bib**.

Harrison's

Mediterranean

U3

Balham
15-19 Bedford Hill ✉ SW12 9EX
✆ (020) 8675 6900 **Fax** (020) 8673 3965
e-mail info@harrisonsbalham.co.uk **www**.harrisonsbalham.co.uk

⊖ Balham

Menu £16/18 (lunch midweek) – Carte £26/36

Following the success of Sam's Brasserie in Chiswick, owner Sam Harrison took over what was Soho House Bar and Grill and turned it into another all-day brasserie. It provides a lesson for all neighbourhood restaurants in the importance of being a focal point for the local community: it is open from breakfast until late and is as welcoming to those just in for a coffee as those wanting a three course meal. The food is uncomplicated, fresh and satisfying, whether that's a cheeseburger, tuna Niçoise, Cumberland sausages or a fishcake. Brunch is served at weekends; they offer a kids' menu as well as a good value weekday set menu, and there's a decent wine selection. It's hardly surprisingly the locals have embraced the place.

Lamberts

Traditional

U3

Balham
2 Station Parade ✉ SW12 9AZ
✆ (020) 8675 2233
e-mail bookings@lambertsrestaurant.com
www.lambertsrestaurant.com

⊖ Balham
Closed Sunday and Monday
– dinner only

Menu £20 (midweek) – Carte £28/35

Balham is less 'gateway to the south', more the 'new Notting Hill' according to some locals. If that's the case then it needs better restaurants, so Lamberts' arrival is timely. The aim of the eponymous owner Joe was to offer simple cooking in a relaxed environment, yet with a degree of comfort and style and all at an affordable price - in other words, just the sort of place we'd all like in our own High streets. The à la carte menu is usually set for the month, with additions and subtractions according to the seasons. The cooking is quite classical, with the occasional modern touch by way of presentation. They offer a daily fish dish, their Sunday roast beef has established quite a following and portions are on the satisfying side.

Brasserie James

Modern European

U3

Balham
47 Balham Hill ⊠ SW12 9DR
☏ (020) 8772 0057
e-mail info@brasseriejames.com **www**.brasseriejames.com

⊖ Clapham South
Closed 24 December - 4 January

Menu £14 (lunch) – Carte £19/32

If you have the courage to open your own restaurant, especially in times of economic anxiety, then no one will begrudge your naming it eponymously. Craig James is a former chef in the Conran/D&D empire and he has brought his experience to bear in the more relaxed environs of a neighbourhood joint. It's on a site previously home to a Pakistani restaurant that was itself quite a local institution and he's given it a top-to-toe revamp. There's something for everyone on the menu, from seasonal oysters and the popular moules à la crème, to daily fish from the market, quality meats, pasta and good old fashioned puds. There are good value set price menus, brunch at weekends and sensibly priced wines by the bottle, glass or carafe.

Sonny's

Modern European

S2

Barnes
94 Church Rd ⊠ SW13 0DQ
☏ (020) 8748 0393 **Fax** (020) 8748 2698
e-mail manager@sonnys.co.uk **www**.sonnys.co.uk

Closed Sunday dinner and Bank Holidays

Menu £16/22 – Carte £26/34

From the outside one would be virtually unaware of the scale of the operation within – Sonny's was clearly constructed by the same people who brought us the Tardis. It's really several operations in one: you have a small but well-stocked deli at the front, the front part of the restaurant which doubles as a daytime café and the main restaurant itself. However, at dinner it all becomes one. As well as a keenly priced and nicely balanced set menu, there is a decent choice of easy-to-eat dishes whose influences are kept within Europe – expect the likes of steak tartare, soufflés, sea bass with fennel, peppered tuna and assorted summer and winter salads. There are also plenty of interesting wines available by the glass.

Riva

Italian

S2

Barnes
169 Church Rd ✉ SW13 9HR
✆ (020) 8748 0434 **Fax** (020) 8748 0434

Closed last 2 weeks August, 1 week Christmas,
Saturday lunch and Bank Holidays

Carte £32/44

Apparently the menus outside keep getting stolen but, as this is Barnes, it probably just means the local villains are after some new recipes. What they will find themselves with is a collection of rustic, satisfying and comforting Italian dishes, with a nod towards more northerly parts and plenty of pasta. What they will miss is the highly personable owner within, describing the half dozen daily specials which are usually the popular choice. Few proprietors exert as much influence on their establishments as Andrea Riva and his charm and personality ensure that the place is so full of regulars that you feel you've gate-crashed a private party. Many will let him choose the wine or sometimes even the whole meal.

Barnes Grill

Beef specialities

S2

Barnes
2-3 Rocks Lane ✉ SW13 0DB
✆ (020) 8878 4488

Closed 25-26 December
– booking essential – dinner only

e-mail barnesgrill@awtrestaurants.com **www**.awtrestaurants.com

Carte £26/42

There are a number of rather affluent suburbs around the edges of London wholly devoid of decent restaurants. Barnes is not one of them because here the locals have always been very supportive of any local endeavours and it only takes one good restaurant to succeed for others to follow. Barnes Grill is a relative new boy but comes with an established format which was developed in Notting Hill and Kew and comes courtesy of Antony Worrall Thompson, TV chef and champion restaurant-opener. That format is relatively simple: bright and casual surroundings with a few eye-catching decorative touches and a generally relaxed atmosphere coupled with an appealing menu of classic British dishes, with the emphasis on well hung steaks.

Ma Cuisine 🐕

French

S2

Barnes
7 White Hart Lane ✉ SW13 0PX
📞 (020) 8878 4092
e-mail info@macuisinebarnes.co.uk **www**.macuisinebarnes.co.uk

Menu £16 (lunch) – Carte £21/29

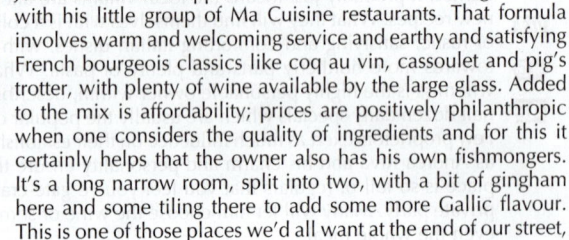

John McClements appears to have hit on a winning formula with his little group of Ma Cuisine restaurants. That formula involves warm and welcoming service and earthy and satisfying French bourgeois classics like coq au vin, cassoulet and pig's trotter, with plenty of wine available by the large glass. Added to the mix is affordability; prices are positively philanthropic when one considers the quality of ingredients and for this it certainly helps that the owner also has his own fishmongers. It's a long narrow room, split into two, with a bit of gingham here and some tiling there to add some more Gallic flavour. This is one of those places we'd all want at the end of our street, for casual local dining.

The Brown Dog 🐕

Gastropub

S2

Barnes
28 Cross Street ✉ SW13 0AP
📞 (020) 8392 2200 **Fax** (020) 8392 2200
www.thebrowndog.co.uk

Closed 25-26 December and 1 January

Carte £22/33

Tucked away down a veritable labyrinth of residential streets, you may feel you need a ball of string to help find your way back from The Brown Dog but the locals can count themselves lucky. The décor is charming - cast iron fireplaces and antique furniture, eclectic artwork, and space age lamps. Set around a horseshoe bar, seating is split into snug lounge and separate dining area. The daily-changing, seasonal menu mixes traditional with modern to produce moreish dishes like winter fish stew, lamb shank with root veg or cauliflower soup with truffle oil. Why the Brown Dog? Well, when a Geordie claims, "I'm taking the dog for a walk," what he really means is, "I'm off down the pub for a bottle of Newcastle Brown Ale." So now you know.

Chada

U2 Thai XX

Battersea Closed Sunday and Bank Holidays
208-210 Battersea Park Rd ✉ SW11 4ND — dinner only
✆ (020) 7622 2209 **Fax** (020) 7924 2791
e-mail enquiry@chadathai.com **www.**chadathai.com

Carte £21/37

It may have been around for over twenty years but Chada has been given a makeover and looks positively resplendent, although there isn't much in the way of competition along Battersea Park Road these days. It may never be the busiest restaurant around but the welcome is always warm, the service polite and endearing and the Thai cooking satisfying and keenly priced. The menu is still a very long affair but it's easy to navigate. Several dishes, such as tom kha soup and phad prik, are available with a choice of meat, prawn or vegetables. Flavours are clean and fresh, and efforts are made to make dishes look appetising. There are plans afoot to simplify the choice and introduce some fish dishes.

Ransome's Dock

U2 Modern European X

Battersea Closed Christmas, August Bank Holiday and
35-37 Parkgate Rd ✉ SW11 4NP Sunday dinner
✆ (020) 7223 1611 **Fax** (020) 7924 2614
e-mail chef@ransomesdock.co.uk **www.**ransomesdock.co.uk

Carte £25/38

It may never have had a full river view but these days Ransome's Dock, a converted warehouse, is somewhat dwarfed by the new apartment buildings that hug the south side of the river. Inside, though, still has a freshness and something of a 'by the sea' feel. The real clues to the owner's great passion are in the wine-themed prints: his wine list is thoughtful, extensive, reasonably priced and ripe for exploration. It also provides easy matches for the food, where ingredients are thoughtfully paired, like foie gras rillettes with caper berries; or altogether more classic and down to earth, such as liver and bacon with bubble and squeak. Name-checked suppliers ensure those ingredients are fresh and seasonal.

Tom Ilić

Traditional 🍴

U2

Battersea
123 Queenstown Rd
✉ SW8 3RH
☎ (020) 7622 0555
e-mail info@tomilic.com
www.tomilic.com

Closed 1 week August, 1 week Christmas, Tuesday lunch, Saturday lunch, Sunday dinner and Monday – booking essential

Menu £15 (lunch) – Carte dinner £24/29

A/C · VISA · MC · AE

Serbian Tom Ilic came to the UK 20 years ago, took a job as a dish washer before a planned career in engineering, developed an interest in food and now has his own restaurant. Formerly occupied by The Food Room, the site he has chosen is an unpretentious, neighbourly place with closely set tables and a semi-open kitchen. It's also in an area of Battersea that's played host to a few famous restaurants in its day. His menu is written in a refreshingly straightforward way. There's plenty of offal featured as well as lots of pork, something of a beloved national dish for Serbs. Flavours are far from shy but his cooking also displays a certain graft and clear respect for the ingredients; prices are kept realistic.

The Butcher & Grill

Traditional 🍴

U2

Battersea
39-41 Parkgate Rd ✉ SW11 4NP
☎ (020) 7924 3999 **Fax** (020) 7223 7977
e-mail info@thebutcherandgrill.com **www**.thebutcherandgrill.com

Closed 26 December and Sunday dinner

Menu £15 (midweek lunch) – Carte £21/42

Terrace · A/C · Booking advisable · VISA · MC · AE

The name really says everything - this is all about carnivores and all about meat. What better way is there of providing customers with provenance assurance than by having your own butcher's shop, complete with a Master Butcher, forming part of your restaurant? Simply pick your meat of choice, get it grilled to your liking, decide what 'stuff on the side' you want and tuck in with your Rambo hunting knife. Even the napkins are man-sized tea towels. A converted warehouse provides just the right surroundings for this clever concept, with everything exposed and spread over two levels. Prices are kept realistic, while the atmosphere is contagiously enthusiastic. There is one fish dish available for those who came by accident.

The Greyhound at Battersea

T2

Gastropub 🍺

Battersea

136 Battersea High St ✉ SW11 3JR
✆ (020) 7978 7021 **Fax** (020) 7978 0599
e-mail eddie@savpubs.com
www.thegreyhoundatbattersea.co.uk

Closed 24 December - 1 January,
Sunday dinner and Monday

Menu £21 (lunch)/31 – Carte £21/33

This is anything but your average local - this is a real foodie pub, with prices to reflect the ambition and endeavour. The current chef is Italian and although there may be the odd ravioli or gnocchi dish, the menu stays true to the pub's philosophy of supporting artisanal producers and sourcing top quality meats like Herdwick Mutton, Black Pig pork and Galloway beef. Dishes come presented as straightforwardly as they are described and flavours are clean and distinct. The Aussie owner has also used his past experience as a sommelier to good effect: the wine list is interesting yet accessible and there are plenty of unfamiliar wines as well as a good selection by the glass. The pub itself has a contemporary yet welcoming feel.

Upstairs 😊

U2

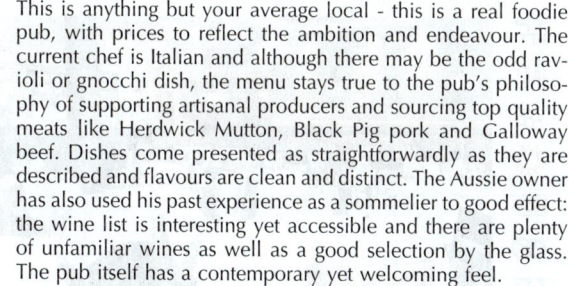

Modern European 🍴🍴

Brixton

89b Acre Lane ✉ SW2 5TN
✆ (020) 7733 8855
www.upstairslondon.com

⊖ **Clapham North**
Closed 18-31 August, 22 December - 4 January,
Sunday and Monday – dinner only

Menu £25/35

Look out for the Opus Coffee shop because upstairs is Upstairs but the only clue is a non-descript door and entry buzzer. Once you're in and up the narrow stairs you'll find a bar on the first floor and the restaurant on the second. It's a cosy affair with seating for 26; turquoise is the favoured colour and there's plenty of natural light. The menu comes on a single sheet of A4; there are three starters, mains and desserts at a set price, although there are usually also a couple of supplements. The cooking is neat, accurate and things are kept simple. The style is a mix of French and English so alongside the potted shrimps may be a foie gras parfait and you could follow the Guinea fowl with apple crumble or chocolate millefeuille.

SOUTH-WEST ▶ Plan XVIII

La Trompette ❀

French XXX

S2

Chiswick
5-7 Devonshire Rd ✉ W4 2EU
✆ (020) 8747 1836 **Fax** (020) 8995 8097
e-mail reception@latrompette.co.uk
www.latrompette.co.uk

⊖ **Turnham Green**
Closed 24-27 December and 1 January
– booking essential

Menu £24/38

The buzz of the place hits you immediately, especially on a summer's day when the full-length windows are open at the front. La Trompette shares many of the characteristics of its sibling, Chez Bruce, not least a welcoming and unpretentious atmosphere. Half the room will be suited and booted, the other half after-work-casual and this adds to the relaxing, local feel. The menu is a balanced and appealing mix of French-influenced fare; the kitchen sensibly avoids anything too audacious and instead focuses on harmonious combinations of flavours and seasonally pertinent produce. Lunch represents pretty decent value but it is the early evening menu, which offers slightly pared down dishes from the main dinner menu at a terrific price, that is the real draw and ensures that the restaurant is already pretty busy shortly after 6.30pm. This is the sort of restaurant where everyone will feel at home, thanks to the personable and confident team out front and the carefully prepared but fulfilling food.

First Course
- Foie gras and chicken liver parfait with brioche.
- Crispy goujons of plaice with tartare sauce.

Main Course
- Red mullet with shrimp risotto, grilled fennel and samphire.
- Slow cooked shoulder of lamb with mashed potatoes and baby vegetables.

Dessert
- Panna cotta with strawberries and biscotti.
- Peach and almond tart with raspberry sauce and Jersey cream.

High Road Brasserie

S2

Traditional 🍴🍴

Chiswick
162 Chiswick High Rd
✉ W4 1PR
✆ (020) 8742 7474
www.highroadhouse.co.uk

⊖ Turnham Green

Carte £34/38

They've certainly nailed that brasserie look, with the mirrors, pewter-topped tables, leather seats and tiled flooring. And they also have the necessary hustle and bustle you'd expect; it takes some pretty fierce weather to deter anyone from the pavement terrace. The appeal continues with the menu which blends the classics with the more contemporary. There's a tempting array of dishes available throughout the day, from small plates of hummus to assorted salads; dressed crab to gnocchi and rib-eye to lemon sole. It all starts from breakfast and, at times, service can be a little frenzied but also comes with a degree of charm. Chances are, there will be someone bearing down on your table the moment you get up to leave.

Le Vacherin

S1

French 🍴🍴

Chiswick
76-77 South Par. ✉ W4 5LF
✆ (020) 8742 2121
Fax (020) 8742 0799
e-mail info@levacherin.co.uk **www**.levacherin.co.uk

⊖ Chiswick Park
Closed 1-2 January,
Monday lunch and Bank Holidays

Carte £26/45

There's something very comforting and reassuring about the two words 'French' and 'Brasserie'. They usually mean satisfying food, efficient service and a convivial atmosphere and Le Vacherin is no exception. It has the leather banquettes, the belle époque prints and, most importantly, the classic menu. Appropriately enough, Vacherin appears as the house speciality when it is baked with almonds and truffles but it always pops up in the desserts in a subtly flavoured ice cream which demonstrates the chef patron's lightness of touch. All the favourites are there on the menu, from snails to cassoulet, steak tartare to côte de boeuf, while the all-French wine list is considered and balanced and offers several wines by the carafe.

Sam's Brasserie

Mediterranean

S2

Chiswick
11 Barley Mow Passage
✉ W4 4PH
☏ (020) 8987 0555 **Fax** (020) 8987 7389
e-mail info@samsbrasserie.co.uk www.samsbrasserie.co.uk

⊖ Turnham Green
Closed 25-26 December

Menu £15 (lunch) – Carte £25/32

A/C ☼ VISA MC AE

Sam and his brasserie continue to pull in the crowds, thanks to a combination of lively surroundings and appealing menus to suit everyone. The Barley Mow Centre was once a paper mill and this semi-industrial space provides the ideal backdrop for this busy restaurant, where the locals can just drop in at any time. Noise levels are at the party end of the spectrum and the staff keep things moving along nicely. There are all sorts of menus available, from Brunch and Early Evening deals to something for the kids, and the kitchen knows what brasserie food is all about. That means satisfying and easy-to-eat dishes for whatever hour, such as omelettes and bowls of pasta or more adventurous offerings like sea bass with sauce *vierge* or shin of veal.

Fish Hook

Seafood

S1

Chiswick
6-8 Elliott Rd ✉ W4 1PE
☏ (020) 8742 0766 **Fax** (020) 8742 3374
e-mail info@fishhook.co.uk www.fishhook.co.uk

⊖ Turnham Green
Closed 25 December

Menu £15 (lunch) – Carte £35/49

A/C ☼ VISA MC AE

The clue is in the name - this is all about good seafood, cooked precisely. The chef owner sources most of his fish from around the British Isles, and in particular Cornwall where he gets his lobster, haddock and mackerel. His cooking is confident and his influences mostly classical, although he does drop in the occasional Asian note, such as a soft shell crab tempura. The lunch menu is very good value and carnivores are offered more than just token dishes. The wine list is short but considered and the service relaxed but attentive. The simply decorated room, with its quite tightly packed tables, bears a few scars from its popularity but it's the convivial atmosphere and what's going on in the open-plan kitchen that draws in the locals.

The Devonshire

S2

Gastropub

Chiswick
126 Devonshire Rd
✉ W4 2JJ
✆ (020) 7592 7962 **Fax** (020) 7592 1603
e-mail thedevonshire@gordonramsay.com
www.gordonramsay.com

⊖ Turnham Green
Closed 23 December-3 January and Monday

Menu £17 (lunch)/19 – Carte £25/28

The Devonshire joined Gordon Ramsay's burgeoning pub portfolio at the end of 2007 and, like The Narrow, enjoyed almost immediate success. The striking Edwardian façade is matched by the characterful oak panelling and polished floor in the bar and here you can enjoy such egalitarian treats as scotch eggs or pots of pickled cockles. For more structured eating, head for the neatly laid-out restaurant with its concise and good value menu with its daily-changing specials. You'll find an appealing mix of pub classics alongside other dishes that are more West End in their pedigree. There's an 'on toast' selection, which could include herring roes, as well as weekly-changing soups and assorted pies. Service is young and attentive.

Four O Nine

U2

Modern European

Clapham
entrance on Landor Rd, 409
Clapham Rd ✉ SW9 9BT
✆ (020) 7737 0722
e-mail reservations@fouronine.co.uk **www**.fouronine.co.uk

⊖ Clapham North
Closed 25-27 December and 1 January
– dinner only

Carte £31/38

If anyone's watching you from their car on Clapham Road they'll see you ring the bell before being let in and think something nefarious is afoot. However, the shabby staircase and secretive entrance pay dividends by somehow adding to the intimacy of this surprisingly smart first floor restaurant. The chef is an acolyte of Chez Bruce and his set menus share the philosophy of crisp, appetisingly presented food, free from unnecessary over-elaboration and with natural flavours to the fore. The influences are predominantly French but occasionally there are dishes or ingredients derived from over the Italian border such as a linguini, risotto or some excellent prosciutto. The wine list is less predictable than many.

Trinity

Innovative ✕✕

U2

Clapham
4 The Polygon ✉ SW4 0JG
✆ (020) 7622 1199 **Fax** (020) 7622 1166
e-mail dine@trinityrestaurant.co.uk **www**.trinityrestaurant.co.uk

⊖ Clapham Common
Closed 25-26 December,
1 January and Monday lunch

Menu £20 (lunch) – Carte dinner £31/42

A/C ☀

Judging by the scarcity of empty tables, Clapham gastronauts are rather taken with Trinity. It's a light and bright room, with a modern feel and a real sense of place; service is well meaning and avoids being too ceremonial, while the chef has always enjoyed a good local reputation. His menu is appealingly laid out; each dish is titled by the three main components such as Squid-Skate-Chorizo, with the supporting cast of ingredients listed below. There's plenty of originality, the plates are artfully presented and, despite a slight tendency to over-elaborate, his know-how, gathered by working in some serious places, is apparent. A lighter menu is available at lunch, while the atmosphere remains appealingly local and relaxed.

Tsunami

Japanese ✕

U2

Clapham
Unit 3, 5-7 Voltaire Rd
✉ SW4 6DQ
✆ (020) 7978 1610 **Fax** (020) 7978 1591
www.tsunamijapaneserestaurant.co.uk

⊖ Clapham North
Closed 25-26 December and Easter
– dinner only and Saturday-Sunday lunch

Carte approx. £30

A/C VISA MC AE

The restaurant certainly doesn't make life easy for itself as we all now understand the name and the location is on the uninspiring side but, thanks to this Japanese restaurant's coolly minimalist interior, once inside, this things will be quickly forgotten. Tsunami attracts a younger clientele and proves that one doesn't have to be in the West End to sample good food in stylish surroundings. While the menu will easily satisfy the more traditionally minded, it is those willing to try the more exotic specialities and original combinations who will get most out of the experience. Indeed, the knowledgeable staff positively encourage you to try something different. Dishes arrive from the kitchen as and when they are ready, so sharing is encouraged.

Maxim

Chinese ✕✕

R1

Ealing
153-155 Northfield Ave
✉ W13 9QT
✆ (020) 8567 1719 **Fax** (020) 8932 0717

⊖ Northfields
Closed 25-28 December and Sunday lunch

Menu £15/20 – Carte £18/30

A/C
VISA
MC
AE

Loyalty is a two-way street which is why you'll find Mr Chow doing the rounds in his restaurant, greeting his guests and keeping them happy. Those guests include a high proportion of regulars who have made Maxim a local favourite for over thirty years. The service is never less than attentive and the suited managers are all equally personable. The restaurant itself is also more comfortable than the norm and is broken up into different areas, with splashes of colour coming from the huge vases and dragon costume. Mrs Chow runs the kitchen with the same level of reliable enthusiasm. You'll find all the favourites as well as specialities from Peking and the best bet is to go for one of the four good value set menus.

Charlotte's Place

Modern European ✕

R1

Ealing
16 St Matthew's Rd ✉ W5 3JT
✆ (020) 8567 7541
e-mail restaurant@charlottes.co.uk **www**.charlottes.co.uk

⊖ Ealing Common
Closed 1-2 January,
26-30 December and lunch Monday

Menu £15 (lunch) – Carte £24/32

VISA
MC

Charlotte may have long gone but the restaurant still exudes the feel of a friendly, neighbourhood restaurant. Ealing's most noted feature, the Common, is right outside the door and the large windows and mirrors ensure there's plenty of light. The ground floor seats twenty and is more fun than the somewhat soulless basement area which is used as an overflow or for larger parties. The menu combines modern Euro food, like sea bass with crushed new potatoes, with brasserie classics such as Caesar salad and fishcakes. British and Irish cheeses are a feature and there's a good value set menu for lunch and early-in-the-week dinners. The wine list is largely Old World and what it lacks in depth it more than makes up in its affordability.

Mango & Silk

Indian

S2

East Sheen
199 Upper Richmond Rd West
SW14 4QT
(020) 8876 6220
www.mangoandsilk.co.uk

Closed Monday – dinner only and lunch Saturday and Sunday

Carte £14/16

VISA
MC
AE

Mango and Silk welcomes you to "the mystic and exotica of classic Indian dining in a serene and peaceful surrounding" and you can't argue with that. Owner Radhika Jerath is a natural and charming hostess but, more importantly, she has persuaded Udit Sarkhel back to the stove. His reputation was sealed from the day he opened his eponymous restaurant in Southfields and his menu provides an exhilarating culinary tour of India. His cooking displays a lightness of touch, expert spicing and a respect for ingredients; the Hyderabadi Chicken Sixers are a speciality. That window on the kitchen works both ways: he likes to see his customers enjoying themselves. The prices are terrific and those are his paintings on the wall.

The Victoria

Gastropub

S2

East Sheen
10 West Temple Sheen   SW14 7RT
(020) 8876 4238 **Fax** (020) 8878 3464
e-mail bookings@thevictoria.net **www**.thevictoria.net

Closed 24-27 December

Carte £22/38

VISA
MC
AE

Paul Merrett has been lured away from the bright lights of TV cookery shows to take over this popular neighbourhood pub, virtually concealed in a leafy residential street. It comes divided into two main areas: the relaxed bar and the conservatory restaurant with its wood-burning stove, although the same menu is available throughout. Sourcing of quality ingredients is clearly a top priority and, while the menu descriptions can make dishes sound quite ambitious, the cooking is earthy and satisfying and flavours well matched. 21 day aged Devon beef comes served on a wooden board and there's a large outside terrace with a rotisserie for the summer. It has a warm and buzzy atmosphere and the place feels as though it's in good hands.

Saran Rom

T2

Thai XXX

Fulham ⊖ Fulham Broadway
The Boulevard, Imperial
Wharf, Townmead Rd
✉ SW6 2UB
☎ (020) 7751 3111
e-mail river@blueelephant.com **www**.blueelephant.com/river

Menu £39 – Carte £42/43

Saran Rom was taken over by the Blue Elephant group early in 2008 so is now in safe hands. Imperial Wharf's restaurants have not exactly been overflowing with customers: a lack of a direct tube link hasn't helped, but then neither has having main courses in the £23plus region. This is still a pleasant spot, based on a Thai Royal summer palace, with a terrific riverside terrace. The series of dining rooms are built around the central area; the top floor is now only used on special occasions. Service is engaging and staff eager to please. Most of the ingredients come directly from Thailand; the menu is not overly long and has a slight seafood bias. Cooking shows care and craft and most go for the balanced Royal Thai Banquet menu.

Memories of India on the River

T2

Indian XXX

Fulham ⊖ Fulham Broadway
7 The Boulevard, Imperial   Closed 25 December
Wharf ✉ SW6 2UB
☎ (020) 7736 0077 **Fax** (020) 7731 5222
www.memoriesofindiaontheriver.co.uk

Menu £25 (lunch) – Carte £32/43

No restaurant development is complete without Indian representation and so it is that, in among all the matching façades on the boulevard of Imperial Wharf, one finds Memories of India. It occupies the same amount of square footage as its neighbours. A love of white emulsion paint has been thoughtfully balanced by colourful silks and large pictures of spice baskets, and the room is certainly light and open in its feel. Larger parties should try for one of the four booths beneath the central palm tree. There's ample choice on the menu, with the nucleus exhibiting a fair degree of originality and impressive presentation, although those who prefer more familiar dishes are not forgotten. A takeaway service is available for locals.

Yi-Ban

Chinese ✕✕

T2

Fulham
The Boulevard, Imperial
Wharf ✉ SW6 2UB
✆ (020) 7731 6606 **Fax** (020) 7731 7584
www.yi-ban.co.uk

⊖ Fulham Broadway
Closed Sunday – dinner only

Menu £15, £45 – Carte £30/60

A/C
VISA
MC
AE
◐

Yi-Ban completes the roll call of international cuisines found at Imperial Wharf by offering Chinese cooking. The decorative style is seductively nocturnal - appropriate as the restaurant does not open at lunchtime - with billowing sheer drapes, moody lighting and dark, polished tables. The menu comes clearly laid out and covers a number of bases by offering contemporary dishes alongside more traditional specialities and, curiously, some Japanese sushi. Efforts are made with the presentation, portion size is creditably generous and service comes courtesy of a young team in traditionally inspired outfits. It's divided into three main areas: a smart cocktail bar, a grill and sushi counter and the main dining area.

Deep

Seafood ✕✕

T2

Fulham
The Boulevard, Imperial
Wharf ✉ SW6 2UB
✆ (020) 7736 3337
Fax (020) 7736 7578
e-mail info@deeplondon.co.uk www.deeplondon.co.uk

⊖ Fulham Broadway
Closed 2 weeks Christmas - New Year,
1 week August, Monday, Sunday dinner,
Saturday lunch and Bank Holidays

Menu £20 – Carte £25/43

🌂
A/C
VISA
MC
AE

Apart from pavement terraces clouded with exhaust fumes, the choice of where to eat on a summer's day is not altogether overwhelming. Fortunately, Deep is at hand. It not only has a great terrace but also offers river views from its spot on this revived riverside wharf. Inside it's all very slick and contemporary, with immaculate napery and comfortable armchairs making it all a relaxing experience. It is also very big, which is presumably why it was used as the setting for Gordon Ramsay's 'F Word' TV programme. The bar is quite an attraction. It has its own terrace and the UK's largest selection of Aquavit. Seafood is the speciality of the house and comes with a delicate Scandinavian touch, reflecting the owners' nationality.

Blue Elephant

Thai ✕✕

T2

Fulham
4-6 Fulham Broadway
✉ SW6 1AA
✆ (020) 7385 6595 **Fax** (020) 7386 7665
e-mail london@blueelephant.com **www**.blueelephant.com

⊖ Fulham Broadway
Closed Christmas and Saturday lunch
– booking essential

Menu £15/35 – Carte £30/50

A/C
😊
☀
VISA
MC
AE
◐

There are now Blue Elephants stretching from Dubai to Moscow but the Fulham branch has had a twenty year head start and is still as busy as ever. The façade gives nothing away but, then again, no façade could do justice to what's going on inside. It's a cross between a tropical forest and a film-set with a decent budget. There are plants and flowers, water gardens, streams, bridges, barges and pergolas. No, really, it's a jungle in there. Fortunately, they realise that the surroundings won't distract the diners forever and put just as much effort into the cooking. Those relatively unfamiliar with Thai could do worse than head for the Royal Banquet menu, while the main menu offers an intriguing mix of the familiar and the more original.

Mao Tai

Chinese ✕✕

T2

Fulham
58 New Kings Rd, Parsons Green
✉ SW6 4LS
✆ (020) 7731 2520
e-mail mark.maotai@googlemail.com **www**.maotai.co.uk

⊖ Parsons Green
Closed 24-25 December
– dinner only

Carte £33/47

A/C
VISA
MC
AE
◐

Apart from the hint in the name, there is little to suggest, to the casual observer, that this is a Chinese restaurant - the plush new cocktail bar is a stylish and popular spot while the main dining room, split between two levels, is a moodily lit affair. Mao Tai does appear to have been invigorated by its new image, both in the enthusiastic service and in the cooking. An appealing dim sum menu is served until 8pm, while the à la carte offers a comprehensive mix of modern and more traditional dishes, with a subtle nod towards more fiery Sichuan specialities; it's also unafraid of throwing in the occasional Thai or even Japanese influence. The beef is particularly tender and there's a fresh zing to the seafood dishes.

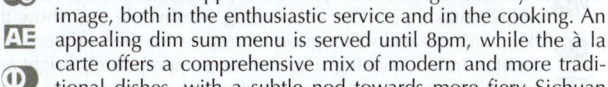

The Farm

Gastropub

T2

Fulham
18 Farm Lane ✉ SW6 1PP
☏ (020) 7381 3331
e-mail info@thefarmfulham.co.uk **www.**thefarmfulham.co.uk

⊖ Fulham Broadway
Closed 25 December

Menu £25/29 – Carte £25/40

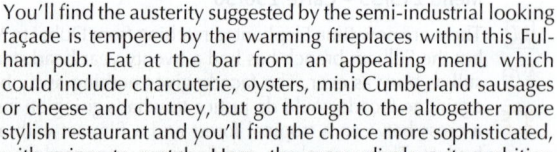

You'll find the austerity suggested by the semi-industrial looking façade is tempered by the warming fireplaces within this Fulham pub. Eat at the bar from an appealing menu which could include charcuterie, oysters, mini Cumberland sausages or cheese and chutney, but go through to the altogether more stylish restaurant and you'll find the choice more sophisticated, with prices to match. Here, the menu displays its ambition through dishes such as black pudding with foie gras or sea bass with sauce vierge but there are also more traditionally British dishes such as smoked salmon and Dover sole. The strength of the kitchen, however, lies in the astute sourcing and preparation of the meat dishes, particularly the very tender beef.

Indian Zing

Indian

S1

Hammersmith
236 King St ✉ W6 0RF
☏ (020) 8748 5959 **Fax** (020) 8748 2332
e-mail indianzing@aol.com **www.**indianzing.co.uk

⊖ Ravenscourt Park

Menu £15/22 – Carte £22/36

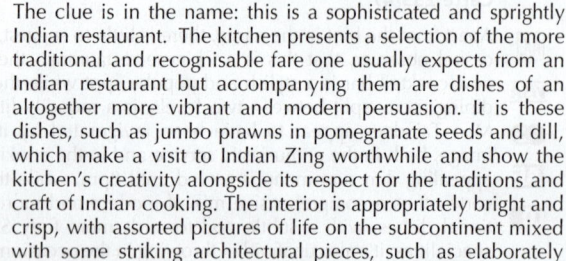

The clue is in the name: this is a sophisticated and sprightly Indian restaurant. The kitchen presents a selection of the more traditional and recognisable fare one usually expects from an Indian restaurant but accompanying them are dishes of an altogether more vibrant and modern persuasion. It is these dishes, such as jumbo prawns in pomegranate seeds and dill, which make a visit to Indian Zing worthwhile and show the kitchen's creativity alongside its respect for the traditions and craft of Indian cooking. The interior is appropriately bright and crisp, with assorted pictures of life on the subcontinent mixed with some striking architectural pieces, such as elaborately carved doors. The service is thoughtful and efficient.

River Café ✤

T2   Italian ××

Hammersmith
Thames Wharf, Rainville Rd
✉ W6 9HA
✆ (020) 7386 4200
Fax (020) 7386 4201
e-mail info@rivercafe.co.uk www.rivercafe.co.uk

⊖ Barons Court
Closed Christmas-New Year,
Bank Holidays and Sunday dinner
– booking essential

Carte £42/56

The River Café was closed for a period in 2008 while they made some alterations: the kitchen is now much more open-plan; a feature has been made of the wood-fired oven and a mightily impressive glass enclosed cheese-room, which doubles as a private dining room, has been created. The restaurant has also grown by three tables but otherwise the most important news is that no other changes have occurred and all the ingredients that made the restaurant what it is are still there. Those who believe in the existence of some sort of Michelin orthodoxy in the awarding of stars always conveniently fail to mention the River Café: here is a restaurant that's far from formal, with service that is never too ceremonial, in a room with plenty of bustle. That star is awarded for the quality of the cooking which, in this case, avoids pointless elaboration and instead focuses on the quality and seasonal freshness of the ingredients. It is earthy, full in flavour and eminently satisfying. Drop in during the afternoon and you'll se the kitchen writing that evening's menu.

First Course
- Wood-roasted sardines, pine nuts, chilli and olives.
- Tagliatelli with girolles, thyme and parmesan.

Main Course
- Wild sea bass, dried porcini, fennel and salsa verde.
- Char-grilled leg of lamb with basil, tomatoes and peppers.

Dessert
- Apricot and almond tart.
- Panna cotta with grappa and raspberries.

SOUTH-WEST ▶ Plan XVIII

Chez Kristof

French

S1

Hammersmith
111 Hammersmith Grove, Brook Green ✉ W6 0NQ
✆ (020) 8741 1177
e-mail info@chezkristof.co.uk www.chezkristof.co.uk

⊖ Hammersmith
Closed Christmas

Menu £18 – Carte £23/30

The French windows open out onto a pleasant summer terrace, while in winter the interior is inviting and romantically lit. Chez Kristof comes from the same stable as Baltic and Wodka but looks more to the west, rather than the east, for its culinary influences. This includes a sizeable amount of French input, both on the menu and from the staff. The menu is printed daily and there is a good value lunch menu with dishes extracted from the dinner à la carte. The large tart Tatin is something of a speciality. There's a deli attached, which comes with its own menu which is ideal for those after a quick snack. The restaurant can get pretty frantic at weekends but the pace during the week is altogether gentler.

The Brackenbury

Modern European

S1

Hammersmith
129-131 Brackenbury Rd
✉ W6 0BQ
✆ (020) 8748 0107 **Fax** (020) 8748 6159
e-mail info@thebrackenbury.com www.thebrackenbury.co.uk

⊖ Ravenscourt Park
Closed 25-26 December, 1 January,
Saturday lunch and Sunday dinner

Menu £15/18 – Carte £25/34

Local estate agents may still insist on calling the area Brackenbury Village but, for most of us, it's just the place we looked up in the A-Z to find The Brackenbury restaurant all those years ago. It may have changed hands a couple of times over the years but for many it remains a firm favourite and is still the type of place we'd all like on our own street. It's simply furnished but adequately comfy and comes divided into two rooms with a bold colour scheme. There's a popular heated terrace at the front. The daily changing menu focuses on primary ingredients, in dishes ranging from the modern and eclectic to more traditional European and British. It still gets busy and the lively atmosphere remains one of the attractions.

Azou

North African

S2

Hammersmith
375 King St ✉ W6 9NJ
✆ (020) 8563 7266 **Fax** (020) 8741 1425
e-mail info@azou.co.uk **www**.azou.co.uk

⊖ Stamford Brook
Closed 25 December, Bank Holidays and lunch Saturday and Sunday

Carte £17/25

A/C
VISA
MC
AE

Morocco, Tunisia and Algeria are the main countries whose cooking features most at this sweet little neighbourhood restaurant, although other North African and Middle Eastern influences occasionally find themselves on the menu. The husband and wife team run a cosy little place with only ten tables and the room is simply but decoratively furnished with draped silks and Moroccan lanterns. Specialities of the house include brik, rich tagines and assorted couscous dishes which will all satisfy the heartiest of appetites. It is certainly worth leaving room to sample the gloriously sweet pastries, especially when accompanied by mint tea, although they do also offer a well chosen selection of wines and beers.

Anglesea Arms

Gastropub

S1

Hammersmith
35 Wingate Rd ✉ W6 0UR
✆ (020) 8749 1291 **Fax** (020) 8749 1254
e-mail anglesea.events@gmail.com **www**.angleseaarms.co.uk

⊖ Ravenscourt Park
Closed 23-27 December
– bookings not accepted

Carte £15/35

If, for some reason, you need another excuse to visit a pub then just remember that they can always provide a little local history. The Marquess of Anglesea was Wellington's Number Two at Waterloo, where he lost his leg, and many of the surrounding streets are named after the Duke. The pub dates back to 1909 and the builders responsible for the charming properties in those streets were housed in the pub. What The Marquess would have made of seeing French classics like Beef Bourguignon on the menu doesn't bear considering. That menu often changes twice daily and the cooking is gutsy, wholesome and satisfying. Eat in either the glass-roofed restaurant with the open kitchen or the dark panelled bar. Good wine by the glass selection.

The Havelock Tavern

Gastropub

T1

Hammersmith
57 Masbro Rd, Brook
Green ✉ W14 0LS
✆ (020) 7603 5374
e-mail info@thehavelocktavern.co.uk
www.thehavelocktavern.co.uk

⊖ Kensington Olympia
Closed 25 December – bookings not accepted

Carte £19/28

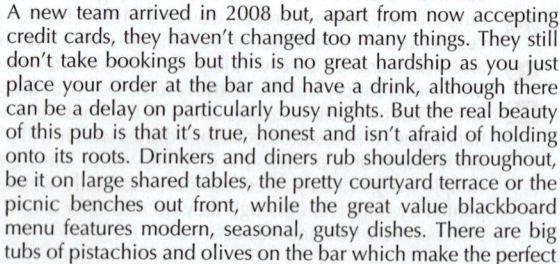

A new team arrived in 2008 but, apart from now accepting credit cards, they haven't changed too many things. They still don't take bookings but this is no great hardship as you just place your order at the bar and have a drink, although there can be a delay on particularly busy nights. But the real beauty of this pub is that it's true, honest and isn't afraid of holding onto its roots. Drinkers and diners rub shoulders throughout, be it on large shared tables, the pretty courtyard terrace or the picnic benches out front, while the great value blackboard menu features modern, seasonal, gutsy dishes. There are big tubs of pistachios and olives on the bar which make the perfect intro, and heart-warming desserts as great finales.

Carpenter's Arms

Gastropub

S2

Hammersmith
91 Black Lion Lane ✉ W6 9BG
✆ (020) 8741 8386 **Fax** (020) 8741 6437
e-mail info@carpentersarms-info

⊖ Stamford Brook
Closed 25 December and 1 January
– booking essential

Carte £22/35

Pubs come in all sorts of shapes, sizes and guises; the Carpenter's Arms is from the 'doesn't actually look much like a pub' school of pub. It has changed name a few times over the years and even spent time as a French brasserie but now, under the same ownership as Chelsea's Pig's Ear, it has found its niche. Decoratively, it's as understated as the exterior but there's lots of natural light and a small rear terrace. The cooking continues this theme of unpretentiousness; dishes are a mix of stout British produce like liver, eel, rabbit or duck, enlivened by more worldly accompaniments such as gnocchi or ricotta and the seasonal vegetables are a major strength. Expect the food to arrive in generous dimensions – this is, after all, a pub. Really.

The Dartmouth Castle

Gastropub

S1

Hammersmith

26 Glenthorne Road ✉ W6 0LS
📞 (020) 8748 3614 **Fax** (020) 8748 3619
e-mail dartmouth.castle@btconnect.com
www.thedartmouthcastle.co.uk

⊖ Hammersmith
Closed 24 December to 1 January, first Monday in August

Carte £18/27

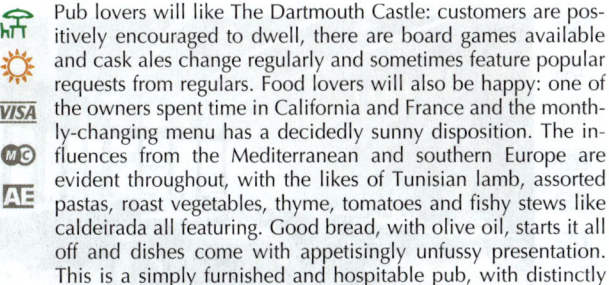

Pub lovers will like The Dartmouth Castle: customers are positively encouraged to dwell, there are board games available and cask ales change regularly and sometimes feature popular requests from regulars. Food lovers will also be happy: one of the owners spent time in California and France and the monthly-changing menu has a decidedly sunny disposition. The influences from the Mediterranean and southern Europe are evident throughout, with the likes of Tunisian lamb, assorted pastas, roast vegetables, thyme, tomatoes and fishy stews like caldeirada all featuring. Good bread, with olive oil, starts it all off and dishes come with appetisingly unfussy presentation. This is a simply furnished and hospitable pub, with distinctly pleasing food.

Kew Grill

Beef specialities ✕✕

S2

Kew

10b Kew Green ✉ TW9 3BH
📞 (020) 8948 4433 **Fax** (020) 8605 3532
e-mail kewgrill@awtrestaurants.com **www**.awtrestaurants.com

⊖ Kew Gardens
Closed 24-26 December and Monday lunch
– booking essential

Menu £15 (lunch) – Carte approx. £31

Busy, relaxed and fun are the hallmarks of these Antony Worrall Thompson neighbourhood joints specialising in meats. Top quality steaks come with a choice of a sauce or butter; there are daily specials like shepherd's pie or duck confit and even a section dedicated to AWT's pork. There are seasonal dishes like haunch of venison; fish-eaters and veggies are catered for and children aren't forgotten either. The cooking is heart-warming and unfussy, the aged beef really is excellent and the puds will finish you off. The concise wine list is helpfully divided by price, under £20, under £30 etc. It's all done in quite a narrow room with something of a country feel; the friendly staff help the atmosphere along nicely.

The Glasshouse ✿

Modern European

R2

Kew　　　　　　　　　　　　　⊖ Kew Gardens
14 Station Parade ✉ TW9 3PZ　　Closed 24-26 December and 1 January
☏ (020) 8940 6777 **Fax** (020) 8940 3833
e-mail info@glasshouserestaurant.co.uk
www.glasshouserestaurant.co.uk

Menu £36/48

Ok, so the Victorian train station may dominate somewhat but giving Kew's delightful marketplace the thoroughly prosaic name of 'Station Parade' shows a distinct lack imagination at the Civic Centre: anywhere else in Europe and this would be the Plaza, Piazza or Place de Something. Under a canopy of trees you'll find The Glasshouse and one of the reasons why locals don't have to catch one of those trains heading east to get themselves a good meal. The decoration is much like the food: a lot of work has gone into making it appear quite simple. Chef Anthony Boyd understands the principle that good cooking is often more about what you leave off the plate: his food is true to the seasons and there are never too many flavours on the plate battling it out for supremacy. France provides most of the influence but there are also Mediterranean elements. A simple steak and chips will use Longhorn beef; the more elaborate Assiette of Pork is a local favourite and there are always good cheeses. Desserts are fruity and comfortingly traditional.

First Course
- Spaghetti of rabbit, girolles, tarragon and parmesan.
- Shrimp and avocado cocktail, rosemary crostini.

Main Course
- Sea bass and king prawn with fennel purée.
- Confit of rabbit, celeriac, carrot and capers.

Dessert
- Peaches with rice pudding Chantilly.
- Blood orange and pistachio trifle.

344

Ma Cuisine 😊

French

R2

Kew — Kew Gardens

The Old Post Office,
9 Station Approach — TW9 3QB
📞 (020) 8332 1923
e-mail info@macuisinekew.co.uk **www**.macuisinekew.co.uk

Menu £16 (lunch) – Carte £21/29

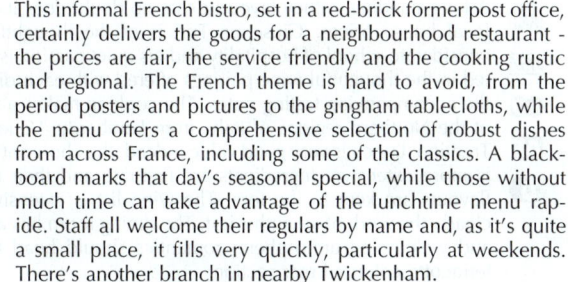

This informal French bistro, set in a red-brick former post office, certainly delivers the goods for a neighbourhood restaurant - the prices are fair, the service friendly and the cooking rustic and regional. The French theme is hard to avoid, from the period posters and pictures to the gingham tablecloths, while the menu offers a comprehensive selection of robust dishes from across France, including some of the classics. A blackboard marks that day's seasonal special, while those without much time can take advantage of the lunchtime menu rapide. Staff all welcome their regulars by name and, as it's quite a small place, it fills very quickly, particularly at weekends. There's another branch in nearby Twickenham.

L'Auberge

French

T2

Putney

22 Upper Richmond Rd
— SW15 2RX
📞 (020) 8874 3593
www.ardillys.com

Closed 2 weeks Summer, 1 week Winter, Sunday and Monday – dinner only

Menu £17 – Carte £24/31

This is what those of a certain maturity would call a 'proper' restaurant - it's run by a husband and wife team, provides authentic and traditionally prepared French cuisine and is decorated in a rustic and homely style which makes the countryside feel that little bit closer. The L shaped dining room comes with yellow walls of heavily textured artex, tiled flooring and even Edith Piaf makes the odd appearance on the soundtrack to add to the Gallic character. The owners provide service that is reassuringly gracious and warm hearted while the menu is decidedly old fashioned but in the very best sense. Just make sure you leave room for a dessert, the speciality of the house, as the chef-owner originally trained as a patissier.

Enoteca Turi

Italian

T2

Putney
28 Putney High St ⊠ SW15 1SQ
☏ (020) 8785 4449
Fax (020) 8780 5409
e-mail enoteca@tiscali.co.uk www.enotecaturi.com

⊖ Putney Bridge
Closed 25-26 December, 1 January,
Sunday and lunch Bank Holidays

Menu £18 (lunch) – Carte £31/39

A long-standing Putney favourite that no doubt does its bit for local house prices. Giuseppe Turi is of the thoughtful and considerate school of hospitality and his quiet passion is reflected in the thoughtful wine pairings offered with each dish and the accompanying tasting notes. The cooking makes a feature of the Northern regions of Italy, from Lombardy, Veneto and Trentino. Lunch is very good value indeed; the choice at dinner is more extensive. Ingredients are first-rate and their natural flavours are kept to the fore. The wine list is extensive and clearly the work of an enthusiast. The dining room has a warm and welcoming atmosphere; romantics should head for the terracotta coloured rear section.

The Phoenix

Italian influences

T2

Putney
Pentlow St ⊠ SW15 1LY
☏ (020) 8780 3131 **Fax** (020) 8780 1114
e-mail thephoenix@sonnys.co.uk www.sonnys.co.uk

Closed Bank Holidays

Menu £16 (lunch) – Carte £19/35

Just look out for the twinkling lights wrapped round the shrubs in front. Monthly-changing art for sale adorns the white walls of the two adjoining rooms, while in summer the charming terrace has a screen to hide the traffic but, sadly, not the noise. There's a great value set menu, although it's not available on Friday and Saturday nights. Like the tower in Pisa, the menu has Italian leanings; there's lots of flavour and a certain perkiness to the cooking. This being a neighbourhood restaurant means you can just pop in for a plate of San Daniele ham with figs, a bowl of risotto or rabbit with porcini mushrooms. There are also contributions from Blighty, like potted shrimps or apple crumble; over fifteen wines are available by the glass.

The Spencer Arms

S2

Gastropub

Putney
237 Lower Richmond Road
SW15 1HJ
(020) 8788 0640 **Fax** (020) 8788 2216
e-mail info@thespencerarms.co.uk **www**.thespencerarms.co.uk

⊖ East Putney.
Closed 25 December, 1 January

Carte £22/32

A/C
☼
VISA
MC

This Victorian pub sits on the edge of Putney Common and is close to the river which is exactly where you'd want to find a gastropub. It even has a pavement terrace for summer days. Etched glass and a lick of paint have brightened the exterior, while the inside has been sympathetically updated and divided in two. On your left as you enter is an area with leather sofas, a fireplace and plenty of books and games, while on the other side you'll find a rustic bar-cum-restaurant, with the ubiquitous hardwood floor, pine scrubbed tables and mix and match chairs. The semi open-plan kitchen delivers a well-balanced menu of dishes that are as hearty as they are heart-warming, from a blackboard menu which focuses on seasonality and changes daily.

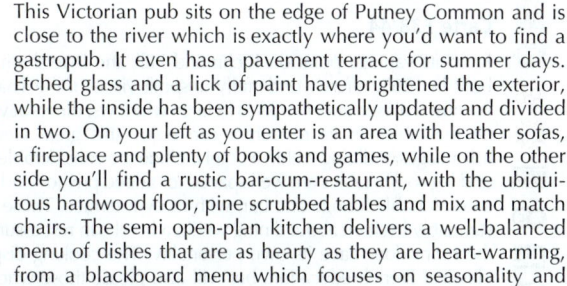

Prince of Wales

T2

Gastropub

Putney
138 Upper Richmond Rd
SW15 2SP
(020) 8788 1552 **Fax** (020) 8180 0191
e-mail info@princeofwalesputney.co.uk
www.princeofwalesputney.co.uk

⊖ East Putney
Closed 25-26 December

Carte £22/30

☼
VISA
MC

Those who decry the rise of the gastropub should have tried The Prince of Wales in its past: such was its reputation that it earned the nickname 'The Prince of Darkness'. Now it's a thoroughly civilised spot, thanks to its Scottish owner whose ambition was to create a 'country pub in the city'. The dining room at the back in the best place to sit as it has the feel of a billiard room in a Scottish Baronial hall complete with stuffed animals and deer antlers. This gives some clues as to the cooking: it is robust and British, with game featuring strongly. The kitchen tends to buy the whole beast so expect prime cuts, offal, then stews, pies, terrines and parfaits and there are often dishes for two such as cassoulet or a roast leg of venison.

The Restaurant at The Petersham

R3

French 𝕏𝕏𝕏

Richmond
at Petersham Hotel,
Nightingale Lane ✉ TW10 6UZ
✆ (020) 8939 1084 **Fax** (020) 8939 1002
e-mail restaurant@petershamhotel.co.uk www.petershamhotel.co.uk

Closed 25-26 December

Carte £38/44

From its vantage point on Richmond Hill, the Petersham Hotel, built in 1865, offers wonderfully unspoilt vistas of the Thames at its most majestic and, thanks to its large windows, diners at virtually all the tables in its restaurant can enjoy this great view. The advantages of dining within a hotel include the considerable elbow and leg-room: tables are well spaced for added privacy and there's a comfortable lounge and bar, with its own terrace. Those understandably hesitant about dining within a hotel can rest assured that the room does have its own personality. The cooking displays a classical French education, but will also please those who prefer their culinary ambitions to be a little closer to home.

Matsuba

R2

Japanese 𝕏

Richmond
10 Red Lion St ✉ TW9 1RW
✆ (020) 8605 3513
e-mail matsuba10@hotmail.com www.matsuba.co.uk

Closed 25-26 December, 1 January and Sunday

Menu £35/45 – Carte approx. £35

The sleek and contemporary interior of this Japanese restaurant on the High Street, with its panelled walls, polished tables and high-backed leather chairs, provides a perfectly comfortable environment in which to enjoy their delicately prepared specialities. However, with only eight tables in the restaurant, those without reservations may find themselves having to wait. It's family run which adds to the relaxed and friendly mood. A small counter is also on hand from where an impressive selection of sushi and sashimi is offered. Lunchtime visitors will find particularly good value Bento Boxes in assorted variations, as well as various 'rice bowl' options which come with appetiser, soup, pickles and fruit.

Petersham Nurseries Café

R3

Italian influences

Richmond
Closed Monday – lunch only
Church Lane (off Petersham Rd) ✉ TW10 7AG
✆ (020) 8605 3627
e-mail cafe@petershamnurseries.com
www.petershamnurseries.com

Carte £36/48

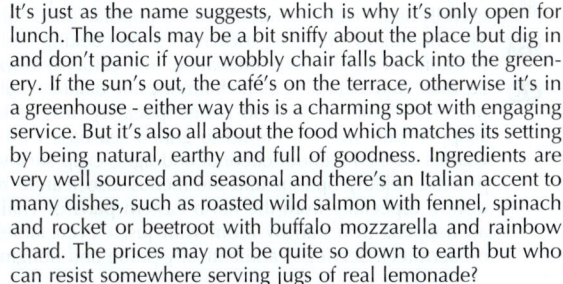

It's just as the name suggests, which is why it's only open for lunch. The locals may be a bit sniffy about the place but dig in and don't panic if your wobbly chair falls back into the greenery. If the sun's out, the café's on the terrace, otherwise it's in a greenhouse - either way this is a charming spot with engaging service. But it's also all about the food which matches its setting by being natural, earthy and full of goodness. Ingredients are very well sourced and seasonal and there's an Italian accent to many dishes, such as roasted wild salmon with fennel, spinach and rocket or beetroot with buffalo mozzarella and rainbow chard. The prices may not be quite so down to earth but who can resist somewhere serving jugs of real lemonade?

The Wharf

R3

Modern European

Teddington
Closed Monday and Bank Holidays
22 Manor Rd ✉ TW11 8BG
✆ (020) 8977 6333 **Fax** (020) 8977 9444
e-mail team@thewharfteddington.com
www.thewharfteddington.com

Menu £16 (lunch) – Carte £28/40

The Wharf is a delightful converted boathouse on the banks of the Thames, overlooking Teddington Lock, and reminds us how little we sometimes make of this great river. On warm summer days the whole place becomes one vast terrace and many will leave a July lunch wishing they had a little something to navigate towards the landing stage next time. Weekends and Twickenham match days are naturally the busy periods and the upstairs floor is ideal for private parties. Those coming during the weekdays are rewarded with keenly priced menus. The chef-owner, a protégé of Anton Mosimann, offers modern European cuisine, coupled with some Asian touches. Waiting staff catch the mood with their competence and courtesy.

Simply Thai

Thai

R3

Teddington
196 Kingston Rd ✉ TW11 9JD
℘ (020) 8943 9747

Closed Easter Sunday, 25 December and Sunday lunch – booking essential at lunch

e-mail simplythai1@yahoo.co.uk **www**.simplythai-restaurant.co.uk

Menu £17 – Carte £20/26

Disguised by a fairly unremarkable façade, Simply Thai is a friendly little Thai restaurant with a popular local following. The thoroughly engaging owner does the cooking and credits her aunt for her culinary education. She certainly displays an absolute understanding of the harmony and balance that underpins Thai cooking; seafood is her speciality, from crispy red snapper with sweet tamarind to grilled sea bass with ginger. Curries cooked without coconut and light, crisp stir-fry dishes provide healthy options and the menus also feature regional dishes, especially from the north eastern parts of Thailand. It all happens in a narrow room with just eleven tables but a modern feel. Service is authentically polite and obliging.

Kastoori

Indian

U3

Tooting
188 Upper Tooting Rd
✉ SW17 7EJ
℘ (020) 8767 7027

⊖ Tooting Bec
Closed 25-26 December and lunch Monday and Tuesday

Carte £14/18

Proof that one should never judge a restaurant by its appearance comes in the form of Kastoori. An unremarkable façade is matched by a fairly modest interior, but this is all about the owners, the Thanki family, celebrating their East African and Gujarati heritage through their cooking, and the pride they have in their restaurant is obvious to everyone. All dishes here are vegetarian and prepared to order; if a certain vegetable is unavailable then the dish isn't on. The cooking is assured, vibrant and invigorating – Kastoori means 'fragrant'- but it is also philanthropically priced, hence a need to book at weekends. They even make their own garam masala to a secret recipe involving the roasting of over 24 spices.

A Cena

R3

Italian ✖✖

Twickenham
418 Richmond Rd ✉ TW1 2EB
☏ (020) 8288 0108
Fax (020) 8940 5346
www.acena.co.uk

⊖ Richmond
Closed Christmas,
Sunday dinner and Monday lunch

Carte £20/37

A/C
VISA
MC
AE

Just as Italy is now an established participant in the Six Nations Rugby, so it is appropriate that an Italian restaurant, A Cena, has built a reputation among the assorted dining options available in the vicinity of Twickenham, home of English rugby. Italian for 'to eat', A Cena succeeds by combining flavoursome cooking, a well chosen all-Italian wine list, grown-up service and calming, stress-free surroundings. Decorated with church pew style chairs and scrubbed floorboards, with large mirrors adding to the feel of light and space, the room also benefits from having a stylish bar offering an extensive cocktail list to those making it more of an occasion. Odds on an English restaurant opening in Rome remain long.

Brula 😊

R3

Modern European ✖

Twickenham
43 Crown Rd, St Margarets ✉ TW1 3EJ
☏ (020) 8892 0602 **Fax** (020) 8892 7727
e-mail lawrence@brula.co.uk www.brula.co.uk

Closed 1 week Christmas
– booking essential

Menu £20/29 – Carte £20/36

VISA
MC
AE

There have been a few changes at Brula: for starters, they've reverted back to the original name and dropped the word 'bistrot'; it's had a lick of paint and some new fabrics but still has that comfortable French feel; and thirdly, the menu has changed somewhat. Prices are per course rather than dish and the cooking is not as fiercely French as before: now you'll find influences from other European countries, from Blighty to Italy, and a more polished edge to the cooking. However, those who prefer all things Gallic will still find much to savour, especially with the cheeses and the wine list. Staff interact well with the customers, most of whom appear to be local dwellers and regular attendees who know a bargain when they see one.

Ma Cuisine 😊

R3 | French 🍴

Twickenham — Closed 1 January and Sunday
6 Whitton Rd ✉ TW1 1BJ
✆ (020) 8607 9849
e-mail info@macuisinetw1.co.uk **www**.macuisinetw1.co.uk

Menu £16 (lunch) – Carte £21/29

VISA
MC

Londoners have always appreciated that dining out should be part of every day living. This does, in turn, call for plenty of affordable restaurants and here Ma Cuisine fits the bill nicely. By keeping prices low, it has proved a real local draw and makes us wish we had one of these at the end of our street. For starters, it's a bistro, with the sort of informality that makes dining out a relaxing, stress-busting experience. Secondly, it serves reassuringly rustic and recognisable French classics like onion soup, coq au vin and lemon tart. The French theme continues in the decoration, in the posters and the music, gingham table covers and plenty of cries of "bon appétit" from the staff. You get all this without breaking the banque.

The Grill Room

R3 | Beef specialities 🍴

Twickenham — Closed Sunday dinner
2 Whitton Rd ✉ TW1 1BJ
✆ (020) 8891 0803
e-mail johnmac21@aol.com **www**.thegrillroomtw1.co.uk

Carte £19/33

A/C
VISA
MC
AE

Owner John McClements has tried a few different concepts on this site and The Grill Room is his latest. Sandwiched between two of his other restaurants, he's gone for a classic steakhouse this time, with cuts sourced from across the British Isles, ranging from 7oz fillet to 14oz T-bone, and all hung on the premises for between 32 and 42 days. They come with a choice of sauce and chunky chips. Other grilled dishes are as British as the starters and range from Arbroath Smokies to Lancashire hot pot but the steaks are the stars of the show. If you're not full by pudding, then you certainly will be afterwards, as they include crumbles and sundaes. Try reserving one of the booths which occupy one side of the room.

ViaMichelin

Click...make your choice, Click...place your booking!

HOTEL BOOKING AT
www.ViaMichelin.com

Plan your route on-line with ViaMichelin to make the most of all your trips. You can compare routes, select your stops at recommended restaurants and learn more about any not-to-be-missed tourist sites along your route. And...for peace of mind, you can check real-time availability in 60,000 hotels across Europe (independents and chains). Simply specify your preferences (parking, restaurant, etc) and place your booking on-line.

- ■ *No booking fee*
- ■ *No cancellation fee*
- ■ *No credit card fee*
- ■ *Best available prices*
- ■ *The option to filter and select hotels from The Michelin Guide*

MICHELIN
A better way forward

Add variety to your journey with Michelin maps and guides.

Michelin maps and guides allow you to choose the best routes for your journey.

Discover our latest selection of star ranked sites and the most scenic routes with the Michelin green guide.

With the MICHELIN guide, experience the best places in every price range.

www.michelin.co.uk

MICHELIN
A better way forward

Tangawizi

Indian

R2

Twickenham
406 Richmond Rd, Richmond Bridge
✉ TW1 2EB
📞 (020) 8891 3737 **Fax** (020) 8891 3737
e-mail tangawizi_richmond@hotmail.com **www**.tangawizi.co.uk

⊖ Richmond
Closed 25 December
– dinner only

Carte £14/28

A/C
☀
VISA
MC
AE

Rich in colour and vitality, Tangawizi - meaning 'ginger' in Swahili – is another in the new breed of Indian restaurants. That means thoughtful design with clever use of silks and saris, attentive and elegant staff but, above all, cooking that is original, fresh and carefully prepared. North India provides much of the influence and although the à la carte menu offers plenty of 'safe' options, there are gems such as the roasted then stir-fried 'liptey' chicken. Diners should, however, head for the 'specials' section where the ambition of the kitchen is more evident. Lamb is another house speciality and is marinated to ensure it arrives extremely tender. For cooking this good, the prices are more than fair.

Tapas y Vino

Mediterranean

R3

Twickenham
111 London Rd ✉ TW1 1EE
📞 (020) 8892 5417
e-mail info@tapasyvino.co.uk **www**.tapasyvino.co.uk

Closed Sunday, Monday and
restricted opening July-August

Menu £20 (dinner) – Carte £15/20

VISA
MC

The name almost says it all – the only thing missing is mention of the low prices. This is a couple of doors down from Ma Cuisine and under the same ownership; it's simply done out in a pseudo Spanish style, but what's attracting the locals is the carefully judged and satisfying tapas. Not exclusively Spanish tapas, however - the influences stretch across the Med, taking in Morocco and Greece. The menu divides itself into traditional hot, cold and speciality tapas and this final section is where you find the interesting stuff, like tagine, snails with Jabugo ham, roast suckling pig or morcilla black puddings with quince. Unless you've come straight from the rugby ground, four plates per person should be sufficient.

Chez Bruce

French

Wandsworth — Tooting Bec
2 Bellevue Rd ⊠ SW17 7EG
Closed 24-26 December, January and first 2 weeks February – booking essential
✆ (020) 8672 0114
Fax (020) 8767 6648
e-mail enquiries@chezbruce.co.uk **www**.chezbruce.co.uk

Menu £26/40

Chez Bruce

Good restaurants have a certain rhythm to their bustle and this comes from both sides understanding the other. The customers at Chez Bruce expect satisfying, uncomplicated and flavoursome food and the chefs and waiters deliver it in relaxed but fun and animated surroundings. Bruce Poole describes his cooking as "regional French with some Mediterranean overtones". On the plate, this means winning combinations of ingredients, a refreshing lack of over-elaboration and total confidence in those ingredients delivering their natural flavours. The daily changing, set price menu will usually feature some roasted or grilled fish; offal; rich beef dishes; a vegetarian option; imaginative salads and game in season. Cheese is certainly worth taking as an extra course and the wine list is constantly being revised: it currently has quite a large Austrian section as they feel that the style of wine goes well with the food here. That basket of palmiers at the end of the meal has become a very popular tradition.

First Course
- Foie gras and chicken liver parfait with brioche.
- Rabbit charcuterie, endive salad, lentils, bacon and prunes.

Main Course
- Fillet of bream, risotto nero, squid and provençale vegetables.
- Côte de boeuf, hand-cut chips, béarnaise sauce.

Dessert
- Roast spiced pineapple, pain d'épice, coconut sorbet.
- Crème brûlée.

Light House

International

T3

Wimbledon
75-77 Ridgway ✉ SW19 4ST
✆ (020) 8944 6338 **Fax** (020) 8946 4440
e-mail info@lighthousewimbledon.com
www.lighthousewimbledon.com

⊖ Wimbledon
Closed 25-26 December, 1 January,
Easter Day and Sunday dinner

Menu £17 (midweek lunch) – Carte £23/33

VISA
MC
AE

Those expecting a tall, tubular building with a light on the top will be disappointed. The name refers to the time when this was a shop selling lights and light fittings. Nowadays it provides an illuminating insight into our more adventurous dining habits by offering cooking unfettered by national boundaries. On any one day you may find influences ranging from a bit of Italian, Greek or Tunisian to the odd Asian twist. The fact that it seems to work speaks volumes for the quality of the ingredients. The pricing is also eminently sensible, especially for the set lunch menu. The restaurant itself is a relatively simple affair, with plenty of light wood, a semi-open kitchen and a roomy bar area. The atmosphere is one of contented bonhomie.

The Fire Stables

Gastropub

T3

Wimbledon
27-29 Church Rd ✉ SW19 5DQ
✆ (020) 8946 3197 **Fax** (020) 8946 1101
e-mail thefirestables@youngs.co.uk
www.firestableswimbledon.co.uk

⊖ Wimbledon

Menu £16/25 – Carte £20/30

A/C
☼
VISA
MC
AE
DC

This may have originally been where the horses to pull the old fire engines were stabled but nowadays it calls itself a 'pub and dining room' and is modish in style without being threateningly trendy. It is also the nearest place to eat when leaving the well-known local tennis courts. Whatever it is, it seems to work. You'll find a separate bar area with its own snackier menu and a long dining room at the back overlooking the garden. Lunch times appear popular with mothers and their young children, while noise levels become more boisterously adult in the evenings. The menu covers all bases, from Caesar salads and burgers to more adventurous choices such as game in season and rack of lamb. Puddings are full-bodied and satisfying.

Where to **stay**

Alphabetical list of Hotels

Hotel	Page
Andaz Liverpool Street	369
Aster House	404
B + B Belgravia	406
The Berkeley	362
Blakes	379
Brown's	370
The Cadogan	385
Capital	373
Charlotte Street	374
Claridge's	361
The Connaught	363
Covent Garden	377
Dorchester	358
Dorset Square	393
Draycott	383
Dukes	380
Durrants	392
Egerton House	394
The Gore	396
The Goring	366
The Halkin	375
Hart House	407
Haymarket	372
Hazlitt's	401
The Hempel	381
InterContinental	365
K + K George	395
Knightsbridge	388
Knightsbridge Green	399
The Lanesborough	364
The Levin	389
Mandarin Oriental Hyde Park	359
Mayflower	405
The Metropolitan	384
The Milestone	378
Miller's	402
Number Sixteen	391
One Aldwych	367
The Pelham	387
The Ritz	360
The Rockwell	398
The Rookery	400
Sanderson	382
Sofitel St James London	371
St Martins Lane	386
The Soho	368
Stafford	376
Twenty Nevern Square	403
22 Jermyn Street	397
The Zetter	390

Dorchester

G4

Park Lane ✉ W1K 1QA ⊖ Hyde Park Corner
✆ (020) 7629 8888 **Fax** (020) 7629 8080
e-mail info@thedorchester.com **www**.thedorchester.com

200 rm – ♦£335/699 ♦♦£652/828, ⌐ £25.50 – 49 suites

Alain Ducasse at The Dorchester and China Tang
(See restaurant listing)

The Dorchester has always been one of the agenda-setters when it comes to luxury living and it continues to set the standard. The most recent development is the new roof-top suites, with their sleek and contemporary interior design, full butler service and fantastic outdoor spaces which have taken the concept of a suite to a new level. The spa is gradually being updated and the ever-popular Promenade, open from 7am until the wee small hours, has now been blended into the lobby more. But this programme of constant renewal and refurbishments is not done at the expense of tradition: the majority of bedrooms retain a classic British look, with exceptional detail and are impeccably kept. You can still get a great Martini or Bellini from Giuliano, who has been a mainstay of the bar for over 20 years; and classic roast beef in The Grill, which announces itself with its exuberant decoration of tartans and dancing Highlanders. Chinese food in stylish surroundings is found at China Tang while late 2007 saw the arrival of a London outpost of the Alain Ducasse global empire.

Mandarin Oriental Hyde Park

66 Knightsbridge ✉ SW1X 7LA ⊖ Knightsbridge
✆ (020) 7235 2000 **Fax** (020) 7235 2001
e-mail molon-dine@mohg.com
www.mandarinoriental.com/london

173 rm – ♦£452/652 ♦♦£593/652, ⌑£29 – 25 suites
Foliage *(See restaurant listing)*

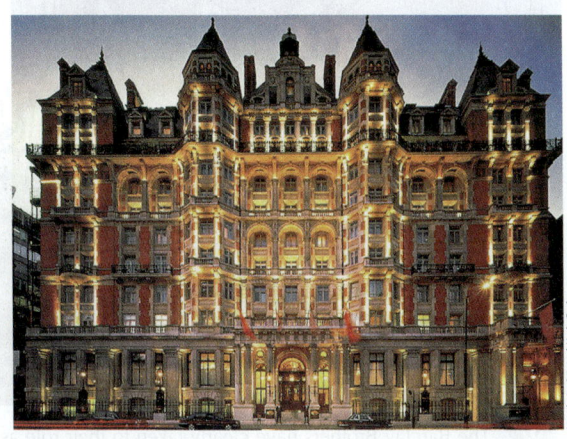

The vast building site next door where the serviced apartments are being added may not be doing the original 1889 façade any favours but the hotel is certainly doing its best to make its guests as unaware of it as possible. This remains one of the smartest hotels around and few can boast that they have Hyde Park as a back garden. Most of the suites face the park, with 'The Royal' and 'Hyde Park' being the top two. The bedrooms come in two styles – the beige and blue or the red and gold – and all the services and details one expects from the Mandarin Oriental name are there. An on-going refurbishment means that every month some rooms are taken out of circulation to have their carpets changed and their surfaces buffed. The rooms have a palpable sense of Britishness, although the vast TVs are slightly at odds with the softness of the decoration. Along with a smart spa, there are two restaurants: the Park is the more informal of the two and has a wide ranging menu, while Foliage's culinary ambitions are loftier.

The Ritz

150 Piccadilly ✉ **W1J 9BR** ⊖ **Green Park**
📞 (020) 7493 8181 **Fax** (020) 7493 2687
e-mail enquire@theritzlondon.com **www**.theritzlondon.com

116 rm – †£294/552 ††£458/552, ⌑ £30 – **17 suites**
🍴 **The Ritz Restaurant** *(See restaurant listing)*

The Barclay Brothers have clearly taken to their role as custodians of this historic hotel, built in 1906 in the style of a French chateau, with Louis XVI furnishings: their vast investment has not only ensured the hotel keeps its place as one of the country's finest but that it also upholds the traditions of César Ritz himself. The Ritz is also still a name that conjures up images of luxury and extravagance: such is the popularity of its celebrated Afternoon Tea, served in the grand surroundings of the Palm Court, that the hotel has redefined the word "afternoon" to mean something beginning at 11.30am and finishing at 9pm. Until the next bedroom development, the William Kent House remains the latest addition to the hotel and it houses some of the most lavish reception rooms one would wish for and has its own team of staff. The Ritz Restaurant is an historically opulent affair. Antique furniture, gold leaf, period features and rich and exquisite fabrics ensure that bedrooms are as sumptuous as they are comfortable.

Claridge's

G3

Brook St ✉ W1K 4HR ⊖ Bond Street
📞 (020) 7629 8860 **Fax** (020) 7499 2210
e-mail guest@claridges.co.uk **www**.claridges.co.uk
143 rm – †£576/658 ††£776, ☐ £28 – **60 suites**
🍴 **Gordon Ramsay at Claridge's** *(See restaurant listing)*

Claridge's, as we know it, was built in 1898 but there has been a hotel at this site since 1812: Mr & Mrs Claridge had run it in the 1850s and were responsible for establishing its reputation. That reputation remains today and the hotel's two most celebrated features are still its art deco styling and close links with the Royal family. But the hotel continues to evolve: the Fumoir Bar has now become the Lalique Bar, where all the cocktails are served in Lalique glass; Claridge's Bar, re-designed by David Collins while retaining its art deco feel, now attracts a younger, hipper crowd. Few places can match The Foyer, with its resident harpist, as a spot for afternoon tea. Gordon Ramsay continues to have responsibility for the large restaurant; the cooking is accomplished and the room a grand affair. All arriving guests are offered champagne and those whose journeys have been particularly stressful can take a seat in the lift. Lord Linley has restyled the suites and all rooms have call boxes to summon a member of staff, of which there are 400 - which represents two per room.

The Berkeley

G4

Wilton Pl ✉ SW1X 7RL ⊖ Knightsbridge
✆ (020) 7235 6000 **Fax** (020) 7235 4330
e-mail info@the-berkeley.co.uk www.the-berkeley.co.uk

189 rm – ♦£552/658 ♦♦£658, ⌑ £26 – **25 suites**

Marcus Wareing at The Berkeley *(See restaurant listing)*

The Berkeley's image is getting more fashionable by the day: The Blue Bar is as cool as the name and decoration suggest and on the other side of the lobby you'll find The Caramel Room whose target audience is obvious when you consider that tea is called "Prêt-à-Portea" and biscuits are fashioned on handbags. The spacious Boxwood Café, with its own street entrance, offers informal dining while Marcus Wareing has now left the Gordon Ramsay stable and the next chapter of this luxury restaurant has begun. The most unique area of the hotel must be the 7th floor, with its roof-top pool, vast treatment rooms and personal training services which should satisfy the most slavishly health-conscious traveller. By using a number of different designers, bedrooms have both a sense of individualism and personality; the most recent have softer, calmer colours and a lighter, more contemporary feel while the classic rooms are richer, thanks to their deeper, more intense colours. All the rooms are immaculately kept and several of the suites have their own balcony.

The Connaught

Carlos Place ✉ W1K 2AL   ⊖ Bond Street
✆ (020) 7499 7070 **Fax** (020) 7495 3262
e-mail info@theconnaught.co.uk **www**.the-connaught.co.uk
95 rm – ♦£387/717 ♦♦£434/717, ☕ £28 – **27 suites**
🍴 **Hélène Darroze at The Connaught**
(See restaurant listing)

2008 saw the much anticipated reopening of The Connaught, following a £70million renovation and restoration programme. This wasn't just about updating the air-conditioning, plumbing and wiring - this was about restoring and cementing the hotel's position as one of the finest around. The bedrooms have been fully updated in style and technology, without compromising that thoroughly British feel. Antiques have been restored; every door remade in mahogany and new artwork hung. They have also introduced personal butlers. Through using different designers for separate parts of the hotel, there is no dominant signature except a respect for the hotel's heritage. The Coburg Bar, named in honour of the hotel's original name, evokes that former spirit; The Connaught Bar is the more contemporary space. The Gallery is an informal alternative to the main restaurant which is now under the auspices of celebrated French chef, Hélène Darroze. Those who always felt that the best thing about The Connaught was its staff will be pleased to see many recognisable faces.

The Lanesborough

G4

Hyde Park Corner ⊖ Hyde Park Corner
✉ SW1X 7TA
✆ (020) 7259 5599 **Fax** (020) 7259 5606
e-mail info@lanesborough.com **www**.lanesborough.com

86 rm – †£441/582 ††£582/675, ⌑ £30 **– 9 suites**

Although it was built in 1733 as Viscount Lanesborough's country house it never became so and was better known as a hospital, before being converted into a hotel in 1991. Being on Hyde Park means it gets a fresh coat of paint regularly but it's inside where that luxury is most apparent, with the designers looking to the rich and decorative Regency period for inspiration. What also impress are the technological advances that mean the TVs are all touch-pad controlled and landline calls to the USA and Europe are complimentary. 350 members of staff, including butlers on each floor, mean that the hotel enjoys one of the highest staff to guest ratios. The Library has a vast selection of whiskies and cognacs (and the same pianist since the hotel's opening). The most recent change has been the opening of the Adam Tihany designed Italian restaurant, Apsleys. The conservatory roof remains but it is now a chic and opulent space, although the cooking is somewhat incongruously rustic. The Garden Room was created for the benefit of cigar smokers.

InterContinental

G4

1 Hamilton Place, Park Lane ⊖ Hyde Park Corner
✉ W1J 7QY
✆ (020) 7409 3131 **Fax** (020) 7493 3476
e-mail london@ihg.com **www.**london.intercontinental.com
399 rm – †£282/388 ††£282/388, ⌐ £27 – **48 suites**
Theo Randall *(See restaurant listing)*

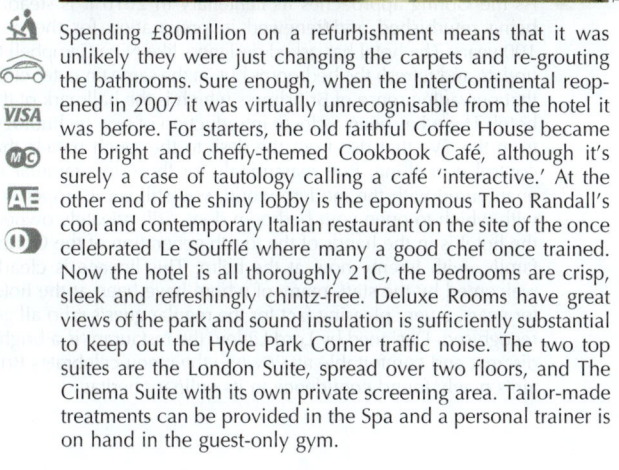

Spending £80million on a refurbishment means that it was unlikely they were just changing the carpets and re-grouting the bathrooms. Sure enough, when the InterContinental reopened in 2007 it was virtually unrecognisable from the hotel it was before. For starters, the old faithful Coffee House became the bright and cheffy-themed Cookbook Café, although it's surely a case of tautology calling a café 'interactive.' At the other end of the shiny lobby is the eponymous Theo Randall's cool and contemporary Italian restaurant on the site of the once celebrated Le Soufflé where many a good chef once trained. Now the hotel is all thoroughly 21C, the bedrooms are crisp, sleek and refreshingly chintz-free. Deluxe Rooms have great views of the park and sound insulation is sufficiently substantial to keep out the Hyde Park Corner traffic noise. The two top suites are the London Suite, spread over two floors, and The Cinema Suite with its own private screening area. Tailor-made treatments can be provided in the Spa and a personal trainer is on hand in the guest-only gym.

The Goring

H5

15 Beeston Pl, Grosvenor Gdns ⊖ Victoria
✉ SW1W 0JW
☏ (020) 7396 9000 **Fax** (020) 7834 4393
e-mail reception@goringhotel.co.uk www.goringhotel.co.uk

65 rm – †£234/388 ††£246/717, ⊑ £24 – 6 suites

As the Goring approaches its centenary in 2010 it is steadily being refurbished and renewed in preparation for the next 100 years. The hotel has asked designers like Nina Campbell to update and refresh the bedrooms but, at the same time, to retain that pervading sense of Britishness which is the hallmark of the hotel. There has been a clever introduction of new technology, from the TVs that rise from the desk to the touch panels that control everything. But, reassuringly for those less familiar or enamoured with the modern world, you still get a proper key with which to open your bedroom door. Still privately owned, the hotel is in the hands of the fourth generation of the Goring family, with Jeremy now at the helm. This lineage is clearly welcomed by the staff, many of whom have been at the hotel for years, a very pleasing fact for the regular guests who all get recognised. Designed by Lord Linley, the restaurant is a bright, discreet and comfortable affair while the menu celebrates Britain's newly-found confidence in its culinary heritage.

One Aldwych

1 Aldwych ✉ WC2B 4RH　　　　　　　　　　⊖ Temple
✆ (020) 7300 1000 **Fax** (020) 7300 1001
e-mail sales@onealdwych.com **www**.onealdwych.com

96 rm – ♦£223/447 ♦♦£223/447, ☕ £24.75 – 9 suites
🍴 **Axis** *(See restaurant listing)*

In 2008 One Aldwych celebrated ten years as one of London's more fashionable addresses. Not only is the location still just so but the contemporary styling within this converted 19C bank and former home to the Morning Post remains fresh and vibrant. There are over 400 pieces of artwork and sculpture scattered throughout the hotel and they start in the enormous lobby which doubles as a bar – a concept that may sound strange but one that works surprisingly well. The bedrooms are very comfortable, with an unfussy and discreet style but one still exuding plenty of warmth. Expect to find all the extras and more. There are two restaurants - Indigo is on the mezzanine level, looking down on the lobby bar, and is the place for salads and lighter fare. Axis has more of a personality as a stand-alone restaurant with its own bar and more ambitious cooking. The leisure facilities have to be good to compete with the attractions outside the front door - and they certainly are. Staff are enthusiastic and committed.

The Soho

4 Richmond Mews — Tottenham Court Road
W1D 3DH
(020) 7559 3000 **Fax** (020) 7559 3003
e-mail soho@firmdale.com www.sohohotel.com

89 rm – †£329 ††£411, ⌒£18.50 – 2 suites

Amazing what you can do with an old NCP car park, imagination, and an eye for detail and design; the ten foot bronze cat by the entrance tells you this is no ordinary hotel. For one thing, it proves that style need not compromise comfort and that size does sometimes matter - the bedrooms here are more than large and the Penthouse and Soho suites are both handsome and vast. Modern art and sculptures are found throughout the rooms and no detail has been overlooked in their design. 'Refuel' is half bar, half restaurant, with an enormous mural paying ironic homage to this site's former life. The menu treads a sunny path through warmer climes and offers something for everyone. The adjoining bar will be a welcoming sight after a long day, as will the two sitting rooms which both have a soothing and relaxed quality about them. The young staff are confident and knowledgeable about their hotel. Even with Soho just outside the door and a youthful clientele, the bedrooms somehow manage to be relatively quiet.

Andaz Liverpool Street

Liverpool St ✉ EC2M 7QN ⊖ Liverpool Street
☏ (020) 7961 1234 **Fax** (020) 7961 1235
e-mail info.londonliv@andaz.com
www.london.liverpoolstreet.andaz.com

264 rm ⌑ – ♦£428/511 ♦♦£605 – 3 suites

The fact that the reception is now called 'the Living Space' and staff are all 'guest-serving and without title' alerts you to the fact that this is a new 'concept' hotel which, in this case, appears to be the challenging job of creating a luxury hotel with an informal feel. The 'Andaz' brand belongs to Hyatt and this is the prototype before its export to the US. However, this hotel is not entirely new to design as it was originally owned by Sir Terence Conran and called The Great Eastern. A recent refurbishment has added warmth to the bedrooms, while the number of restaurants offering everything from seafood and Japanese to British and European, ensures that there is something for everyone. Through all the talk of 'empowering guests to define their own experience' there is one particularly good development: the transparent and uniform pricing policy means the room charge includes everything from breakfast to laundry. The best thing about the place, though, is still the old Masonic Lodge used for comedy nights.

Brown's

H3 🏨

Albemarle St ✉ W1S 4BP ⊖ Green Park
☏ (020) 7493 6020 **Fax** (020) 7493 9381
e-mail reservations.browns@roccofortecollection.com
www.roccofortecollection.com

105 rm – †£415/575 ††£540/725, ☕ £27 – 12 suites

Opened in 1837 by James Brown, Lord Byron's butler, Brown's has a long and distinguished history and has been the favoured hotel of many a visiting dignitary: it was here that Alexander Graham Bell first demonstrated his telephone and The Kipling Suite is just one named after a former guest. It reopened in 2005 after a full face-lift, with Olga Polizzi personally overseeing the design and her blending of the traditional with the modern works well. The bedrooms have personality and reflect the character of the hotel, albeit with all of today's required gadgetry. One thing that has remained constant is the popularity of the afternoon teas – the selling point, apart from the pianist, is that the waiter replenishes all stands and pots without extra charge. The wood-panelled restaurant has taken longer to bed in and now goes by the name of The Albemarle; the menu features British comfort food. The Donovan Bar is probably the hotel's best feature and celebrates the British photographer Terence Donovan – the only change here recently is that the nibbles are less Spanish, more British.

Sofitel St James London

14

6 Waterloo Pl ✉ SW1Y 4AN ⊖ Piccadilly Circus
✆ (020) 7747 2200 **Fax** (020) 7747 2210
e-mail H3144@accor.com **www**.sofitelstjames.com

179 rm – †£382/441 ††£441/400, ☕ £21 – 6 suites
Brasserie Roux *(See restaurant listing)*

Sofitel St James London

VISA AE

The Accor hotel company offers all sorts of accommodation around the world and Sofitel is their brand that covers the luxury end of the market. Furthermore, this is the area where the company has been spending time and money on improving still further. The Sofitel St James opened in 2002 and is a in a grand position overlooking Waterloo Place. It is housed within the Grade II listed former HQ of the Cox and Kings Company, built in 1923 when it merged with a bank (which became Lloyd's Bank). It is now a hotel that's managed the task of appearing quite contemporary to those who like things shiny and new and sufficiently conservative to those who like things to be done properly. They have also taken good care of the basic but important aspects like soundproofing and double-glazing. The bedrooms all have a certain style and logic to their décor and come in assorted categories. The Brasserie is a large French affair and those for whom afternoon tea is a prerequisite of a London visit should get along to the Rose Lounge.

Haymarket

14

1 Suffolk Place ✉ SW1Y 4BP ⊖ Piccadilly Circus
☏ (020) 7470 4000 **Fax** (020) 7470 4004
e-mail haymarket@firmdale.com **www**.haymarkethotel.com

47 rm – ♦£294 ♦♦£382, ☕ £18.50 **– 3 suites**

This most recent hotel from Tim & Kit Kemp is a stylish, hip place, refreshingly free from any bland corporate appurtenances. They converted a grand John Nash Regency building that had been a gentleman's club and office before being gutted by a fire. Art and an eclectic collection of furniture now run through it; the lobby, conservatory and library of the ground floor are immaculately dressed and set the tone for the hotel. Individually styled bedrooms come with dressed mannequins - the motif of the Kemp's hotels – and custom-made furniture. They are all bright and calming with a subtle English feel. For extra quietness ask for one overlooking the inner decked courtyard. The location couldn't be better for those coming 'up west': theatre-land is literally just outside – indeed, the hotel adjoins the Haymarket theatre – and is a short stroll away from all that London offers. If that isn't enough, there's a very cool swimming pool downstairs. Brumus is the restaurant – named in honour of the owner's hound - and offers easy Italian food in spacious surroundings.

Capital

F5

22-24 Basil St ⊠ SW3 1AT ⊖ Knightsbridge
☏ (020) 7589 5171 **Fax** (020) 7225 0011
e-mail reservations@capitalhotel.co.uk www.capitalhotel.co.uk

49 rm – †£253/335 ††£345/523, ⌑ £18.50

🍴 **The Capital Restaurant** *(See restaurant listing)*

The way to stay on top of your game is to constantly strive for improvement. The Capital is certainly one of London's most British hotels but its position as one of its most luxurious is down to the team who run it and it no doubt helps that it's been under the same family ownership since 1971. Sure, it has all the other components one would expect: the atmosphere is discreet, bedrooms are immaculately kept and the roll-call of designers includes Ralph Lauren and Nina Campbell. But the hotel's great strength is in the service: the staff all appear suitably proud of their hotel and no one entering the small lobby can do so without being acknowledged. The hotel is also continually striving to add more services, from a hair and beauty butler to arranging a jogging partner for those who need a little motivation going around the park. No persuasion should be needed to dine at The Capital's acclaimed restaurant on the ground floor, while the serious shopper will find the hotel's location hard to beat.

Charlotte Street

15 Charlotte St ✉ W1T 1RJ ⊖ Goodge Street
☏ (020) 7806 2000 **Fax** (020) 7806 2002
e-mail charlotte@firmdale.com www.charlottestreethotel.co.uk

48 rm – †£259/294 ††£364, ⌑ £19 **– 4 suites**
🍴 ● **Oscar** (See restaurant listing)

It's not just the location, within strolling distance of Soho, or that the hotel has its own private screening room that attract the media types, film industry sorts and arty souls who have made this hotel their own, but the stimulating way in which it has been decorated and the prevailing vibe. This one-time dental warehouse has been deftly transformed into a very chic hotel and proves that comfort and design can be equal bed fellows and that something good has come from British dentistry. Using a combination of abstract art, sculpture and paintings from artists of the neighbouring Bloomsbury set, the hotel manages to be also quite English in tone. The drawing rooms are tranquil, stress-free areas, in contrast to the bustle of the bar and Oscar restaurant. Dotted among the bedrooms are one-off pieces of furniture combined with top drawer fabrics and fittings, all supported by a maintenance programme of virtually constant refurbishment. Staff all appear to be enthusiastic and confident. The loft and penthouse suites will stir emotions of envy and desire or, if you've got one, glee.

The Halkin

5 Halkin St ✉ SW1X 7DJ   ⊖ Hyde Park Corner
✆ (020) 7333 1000 **Fax** (020) 7333 1100
e-mail res@halkin.como.bz www.halkin.como.bz

35 rm – ♦£458 ♦♦£458, ☕ £26 – 6 suites
🍴 **Nahm** (See restaurant listing)

The Halkin was one of the first places in London to call itself a 'townhouse hotel' before any of us really knew what that meant. It recognised that design and aesthetics were as important as the number of TV channels on offer and that fewer rooms ensured more personal service and a more intimate atmosphere. Today, through constant refurbishment and refreshment, it remains one of the city's most chic addresses, offering understated English elegance matched with Italian design flair, while effortlessly complementing the very charming Georgian surroundings of Belgravia. You know you're somewhere pretty glamorous when even the staff are wearing Giorgio Armani. The lobby is a relatively discreet affair, with gossamer drapes dividing it from the bar. Nahm, also on the ground floor, offers artful Thai cuisine. The accommodation, spread over five floors, offers guests all the latest hi-tech facilities at the tap of a touch-pad. Rooms are uncluttered and unfussy, with white the predominant colour, and the bathrooms are very luxurious.

Stafford

H4

16-18 St James's Pl ✉ SW1A 1NJ ⊖ Green Park
☏ (020) 7493 0111 **Fax** (020) 7493 7121
e-mail information@thestaffordhotel.co.uk
www.thestaffordhotel.co.uk

73 rm – ♦£353/494 ♦♦£623/682, ⌑£24 **– 32 suites**

Those for whom only a Penthouse Suite will ever do may never have considered The Stafford but their new suites in the Mews House, a converted office block in the rear courtyard of the hotel, are pretty impressive and the top floor suite has its own roof terrace. Those in the more traditional Carriage House are also very comfortable: The Guv'nor's Suite is, ironically, a stylish affair spread over two floors but the jarring name is wholly at odds with what is a rather genteel and very English hotel. As with many traditional hotels in London, it has an American Bar where men are required to wear a jacket. It may have been extended but the impressive collection of ties, helmets and pictures means it has lost none of its character. The restaurant is all quite formal and the cooking keeps thing quite British: they still have the daily special on the trolley, be it York ham or Sirloin of beef. The feel of the hotel may be of a country house in the city, although it does have a very well connected concierge team if you want to take advantage of London life.

Covent Garden

13

10 Monmouth St ✉ WC2H 9HB   ⊖ Covent Garden
✆ (020) 7806 1000 **Fax** (020) 7806 1100
e-mail covent@firmdale.com **www**.coventgardenhotel.co.uk

56 rm – †£264/323 ††£376, ☕£19.50 – **2 suites**

A perfectly symmetrical row of pencils and a bowl of shiny red apples on the reception desk tell you that this is a hotel which takes design seriously. It takes comfort, individuality and service equally seriously and that is why this is such a charming place to stay. Formerly a French hospital - the words 'Nouvel hopital et dispensaire francais' are etched into the brickwork – the hotel makes 'Englishness' the central tenet of its decorative style. Mannequins, embroidered fabrics, the antique juxtaposed with the new and strong colours give the rooms personality and warmth; an ongoing refurbishment programme and exemplary housekeeping ensures it all stays tip-top. The restaurant, Brasserie Max, has been extended but has kept its intimacy and sense of neighbourhood. The menu is pretty global in its reach but also keeps things fairly light. Where the residents are most fortunate is in having exclusive use of the sitting room and library; delightful and surprisingly restful wood-panelled rooms on the first floor. There is also a private screening room, now with a drinks licence.

BLOOMSBURY ▶ Plan VI

The Milestone

D4

1-2 Kensington Court ⊖ High Street Kensington
✉ W8 5DL
✆ (020) 7917 1000 **Fax** (020) 7917 1010
e-mail bookms@rchmail.com **www**.milestonehotel.com

57 rm – ♥£276/311 ♥♥£370/405, ⌑ £25 **– 6 suites**

The Milestone proves that it is the service, not the space, which makes a hotel. With 100 members of staff for 57 bedrooms, it's odds-on you'll be well looked after; the hotel prides itself on keeping records of the whims and preferences of their regulars. Plenty of thought has gone into the design and decoration of the bedrooms which are undergoing a refurbishment. It's in the detail where you notice the extra effort: there's a little gift with the turn-down service and the bathrobes are seasonally adjusted so one gets a lighter robe in summer. The suites display greater levels of whimsy than the standard rooms – just check out the art deco inspired Mistinguett Suite, named in honour of the celebrated music hall entertainer, while Johnny Weissmuller would feel more at home in The Safari Suite. The sitting room is a comfy place, with a jaunty looking Noel Coward hanging above the fireplace. The Jockey bar is so named as this was where the horses were stabled in the days when this Victorian building was a private house. The dining room is an intimate, wood-panelled affair.

Blakes

33 Roland Gdns ✉ SW7 3PF ⊖ Gloucester Road
✆ (020) 7370 6701 **Fax** (020) 7373 0442
e-mail blakes@blakeshotels.com **www**.blakeshotels.com

40 rm – ♦£176/311 ♦♦£382/441, ☕£25 – 8 suites

Before they applied to hotels like Blakes, words like "daring" and "dramatic" were only used to describe the more eccentric of guest when the poor loves had nowhere to stay that really understood them. The opening by Anouska Hempel of Blakes in 1981 not only provided London with its first strikingly theatrical hotel, but it also blazed a trail in hotel design in which all subsequent boutique hotels and townhouses were to follow. The lobby sets the tone with oriental boxes, bamboo, birdcages and idiosyncratic little design touches, which all tell you this is no ordinary hotel. The Chinese room and bar which adjoin the basement restaurant have become popular nightspots and this fusion of east meets west continues in the blend of specialities on the menu. But it is in the bedrooms where the uniqueness and sheer individuality is most evident. Stencils, shutters, prints, period furniture, ethereal drapes and trompe d'oeils make every room a true original. Many hotels boast of not having two rooms alike, but few can really claim to boast of differences as conspicuous as Blakes.

Dukes

H4

35 St James's Pl ⌧ SW1A 1NY ⊖ Green Park
✆ (020) 7491 4840 **Fax** (020) 7493 1264
e-mail bookings@dukeshotel.com **www**.dukeshotel.com

83 rm – ♂£282/376 ♂♀£323/417, ⌑ £22 – 7 suites

Dukes celebrated its centenary in 2008 by undertaking one of those refurbishments that costs a fortune but manages to ensure that the feel and atmosphere of the original remain largely unchanged. That feel is a very British one, as befits a hotel that was once part of the Royal Estate and apparently used to accommodate members of the Royal Family. It's in a great spot, hidden away on a narrow lane, and is surprisingly quiet for a Central London hotel. Dukes Bar remains famous for its martinis so it comes as no surprise to learn that Ian Fleming was a regular visitor and the line "shaken, not stirred" came to life here. The understated dining room downstairs prepares fresh and seasonal British cooking and the good value Sunday roast is a popular local event. Bedrooms have the elegant feel of a contemporary country house but now come with all the electronic gadgetry, while the pretty little drawing room overlooks an enclosed Zen-inspired garden. Service, meanwhile, remains old school in the best sense and is discreet and keen.

The Hempel

31-35 Craven Hill Gdns ✉ W2 3EA ⊖ Queensway
✆ (020) 7298 9000 **Fax** (020) 7402 4666 Closed 24-28 December
e-mail hotel@the-hempel.co.uk www.the-hempel.co.uk

46 rm – †£210/304 ††£210/304, ⊑ £21.50 – 4 suites

Anyone whose idea of a hotel is a trouser-press, a kettle and those little capsules of UHT milk will just not get The Hempel, for here is a hotel all about aesthetics, symmetry and style. Designed by Anouska Hempel and now owned by a publicity-shy Irish family, the hotel was like nowhere else when it opened over a decade ago. All monochrome and minimalist, anyone wishing for privacy needed only to wear white and they would disappear, chameleon-like, into the surroundings. Today, the place remains just as crisp and uncluttered as ever but things have been softened up somewhat with the addition of a little splash of colour here and the occasional spot of whimsy there. I-Thai as a restaurant concept has finally reached the end of its lifespan and there are plans afoot for a new concept. But it's the bedrooms that are the main event here. They are idiosyncratic, chic and original. Room 107 must have one of the highest ceilings in London, there's a suspended bed in 110 and those who like black should ask for 405.

Sanderson

H2

50 Berners St ✉ W1T 3NG ⊖ Oxford Circus
✆ (020) 7300 1400 **Fax** (020) 7300 1401
e-mail sanderson@morganshotelgroup.com
www.morganshotelgroup.com

150 rm – ♦£282/423 ♦♦£282/423, ☑ £25

Oil paintings of pastoral scenes hang in all the bedrooms - the difference is that at The Sanderson they hang on the ceiling. Welcome to the world of Philippe Starck. The celebrated French designer's touch is evident everywhere, reflecting his love of the playful, the whimsy, the clean and the uncluttered. The dream-like style of the lobby alone sets the tone for this most fashionable hotel, which takes its name from the building's previous incarnation as HQ of the famous wallpaper company. The Purple Bar is as exclusive as it gets and uses fabrics of every shade of purple to create a theatrical and mysterious vibe. In contrast, the Long Bar rejoices in light and freshness. Suka is the restaurant, with Malaysian dishes designed for sharing. Agua offers some serious pampering, while those who prefer more active therapy should head to the billiard room, with its striking John Piper stained glass. Modernity and originality continue in the bedrooms which come with glass enclosed bathrooms, sleigh beds, bright white walls and sheer drapes.

Draycott

F6

26 Cadogan Gdns ✉ SW3 2RP ⊖ Sloane Square
✆ (020) 7730 6466 **Fax** (020) 7730 0236
e-mail reservations@draycotthotel.com **www**.draycotthotel.com

31 rm – ♦£158/183 ♦♦£233/370, ⛌ £21.95 – **4 suites**

Three Edwardian houses were knocked together to create The Draycott but you can't see the join and the place has a cosy and intimate feel. The focus is still very much the charming sitting room: not only does it overlook the gardens at the back but here you'll find a well-stocked honesty bar, complimentary tea offered at 4pm, champagne at 6pm and hot chocolate at 9.30pm. If that still isn't enough liquid refreshment there's always room service. As for the bedrooms, they are all boldly decorated in an unabashed Edwardian style and fittingly named after a theatrical great, be it Gielgud or Coward; their photographs and biographies are placed in the rooms too. Six of the rooms have fireplaces and there's plenty of antique furniture around, along with the more useful stuff like CD and DVD players. Not many hotels these days put guest's names on the door and each has a visitor's book so you can try to guess who made that mark on the carpet. Breakfast is served in the incongruously named 'Peter O'Toole Breakfast Room.'

CHELSEA ▶ Plan XI

The Metropolitan

G4

Old Park Lane ⊠ W1K 1LB ⊖ Hyde Park Corner
(020) 7447 1000 **Fax** (020) 7447 1100
e-mail res.lon@metropolitan.como.bz www.metropolitan.como.bz

147 rm – £763 £763, £26 **– 3 suites**

Nobu *(See restaurant listing)*

The Metropolitan celebrated its tenth birthday in 2007 and it's as busy now as it ever was. Much of its popularity comes down to its perceived exclusiveness: after 9pm the surprisingly compact but perennially fashionable Met Bar is open only to hotel guests, members or those "on the list," which usually includes celebrities with something to plug feigning displeasure at being snapped on the way out. Meanwhile, on the first floor, is Nobu: proof that restaurants within hotels can be a life and personality of their own. The bedrooms on the park side still offer relaxing pastoral vistas but the City views shouldn't be ignored as they take in the rooftops and, much like many of the guests, come alive at night. The palette is neutral, the wood practical and the light natural but this is a hotel that set the understated-style agenda a few years back and now the opposition are beginning to fight back, especially in the field of guest gadgetry. The challenge for The Metropolitan is keeping up with those expectations.

The Cadogan

75 Sloane St ✉ SW1X 9SG ⊖ Knightsbridge
✆ (020) 7235 7141 **Fax** (020) 7245 0994
e-mail info@thesteingroup.com **www**.cadogan.com

63 rm – ♦£300/347 ♦♦£347, ⌑£24 – **2 suites**

The Cadogan's light redecoration has added an elegant but slightly more contemporary look, although the Edwardian feel is still very much in evidence, particularly for those talking afternoon tea in the wood panelled drawing room. The updating has also been done in a way that's respectful of the hotel's history and The Cadogan certainly has history, thanks to its two most renowned former residents, Oscar Wilde and Lillie Langtry, former royal mistress. The restaurant is named in her honour and the menu is appropriately English in its demeanour but with the addition of some continental vim. Bedrooms further reflect the character of the house. Room 118 witnessed the arrest of Oscar Wilde in 1895 while for the full, pink, Lillie Langtry experience try Room 109. Edward VII's Room 111 is for those after a more masculine room. The hotel appeals to a refined and well-mannered group who have remained very loyal over the years. The neighbours aren't too bad either, with the likes of Prada, Jimmy Choo, Versace and Armani just a few of the local boutiques.

St Martins Lane

13

45 St Martin's Lane
WC2N 4HX
(020) 7300 5500 **Fax** (020) 7300 5501
e-mail stmartinslane@morganshotelgroup.com
www.morganshotelgroup.com

⊖ Charing Cross

202 rm – ♦£253/370 ♦♦£253/370, ☐ £25 – 2 suites

To the uninitiated this still looks like a 1960s office block and the hotel doesn't bother with anything as crass as a sign but, then again, St Martins Lane is not like most hotels. For starters, Philippe Starck's design of the modern juxtaposed with the baroque reinvents the concept of a lobby. Secondly, the noise of enthusiastic and alarmingly youthful punters gives the place energy and sheen. All boxes are ticked for a cool and contemporary hotel: the fiercely trendy Light Bar, with its weekend DJ and air of exclusivity and the 'concept' restaurant, in this case Asia de Cuba, which fuses the zest and gracefulness of Asia with fiery and muscular Latin America. The bedrooms continue the theme of style and design. Floor to ceiling windows ensure light streams into all the rooms which are painted in sheer white. As most of the guests have mastered the art of wearing dark glasses inside this is not a problem, although the colour of the lighting can be changed to match a mood. Staff have that insouciance which comes with looking good.

The Pelham

E6

15 Cromwell Pl ✉ SW7 2LA   ⊖ South Kensington
✆ (020) 7589 8288 **Fax** (020) 7584 8444
e-mail reservations@pelhamhotel.co.uk **www**.pelhamhotel.co.uk

51 rm – †£212/235 ††£341, ☕ £17.50 – 1 suite

The Pelham is now owned by the same team who have The Gore. This is a charming and individual townhouse, decorated in that quintessential English country house style. The two drawing rooms both have fireplaces and are delightful; one has original pine panelling the other mahogany lined bookcases. Downstairs you'll find Kemps, the cosy restaurant decorated with original works of art which becomes a very romantic spot in the evenings. The menu offers a satisfying selection of dishes with either a British or Mediterranean bent. All the bedrooms are individually decorated and continue the theme of a country house in the city. Those on the first and second floors benefit from higher ceilings and many share some of the original features of the house. Mod cons are discreetly blended into the decoration to ensure that the modern traveller has all the facilities they require, without the feeling of sleeping in an office. South Kensington tube station is literally across the road so, if the plethora of attractions nearby is not enough, reaching those around the city could not be easier.

SOUTH KENSINGTON ▶ Plan XI

Knightsbridge

F5

10 Beaufort Gdns ✉ SW3 1PT　　　⊖ Knightsbridge
✆ (020) 7584 6300 **Fax** (020) 7584 6355
e-mail knightsbridge@firmdale.com **www**.knightsbridgehotel.com

44 rm – ♦£200/247 ♦♦£345/405, ⌇£17.50

The peaceful and leafy surroundings of Beaufort Gardens provide much needed sanctuary from the retail madness that is Knightsbridge and Brompton Road and, within this tree-lined square, you'll find the Knightsbridge Hotel. The assorted works by British artists, from Carol Sinclair's slate stack to Peter Clark's dog collages, tell you this is a hotel with an eye for design - not too much of a surprise as it belongs to the Firmdale group of hotels. It opened in 2002, from a row of converted Victorian terrace houses, but has already been refreshed and refurbished. The Library Room not only has real books but a great honesty bar that includes everything from ice cream to champagne. The style in the bedrooms is contemporary English and all have individual character and wonderfully coordinated decoration. The Knightsbridge Suite stretches along the front of the house and comes with its own balcony. There's no restaurant but there's a comprehensive room service menu and considerable choice for breakfast.

The Levin

28 Basil St ✉ SW3 1AS   ⊖ Knightsbridge
✆ (020) 7589 6286 **Fax** (020) 7823 7826
e-mail reservations@thelevinhotel.co.uk **www**.thelevinhotel.co.uk

12 rm – ♔♕**£300/535**, ☕ **£16.50**

The Capital may be their more famous hotel but a few doors down you'll find the Levin family's other jewel, called - and why not? - The Levin. The standards that have made The Capital what it is are also evident here, namely attention to every detail and seriously high levels of luxury. It takes the 1930s as its decorative inspiration which works very well, and with only twelve sleek and stylish bedrooms, it certainly falls into the 'boutique' class of hotel. The first thing you come across is the striking 18 metre chandelier but the second thing you notice is a collection of Penguin classics which further underlines the proper Britishness of the whole affair. The clientele, meanwhile, are clearly the sort whose idea of a corner shop is Harrods as the mini-bars in the bedrooms are stocked exclusively with champagne. Le Metro is the relaxed brasserie with a menu of reassuringly familiar European and British classics; the wine list features some selections from the Levin family vineyard in the Loire Valley.

The Zetter

K1

St John's Square, 86-88 Clerkenwell Rd
✉ EC1M 5RJ
☏ (020) 7324 4444 **Fax** (020) 7324 4456
e-mail info@thezetter.com **www**.thezetter.com

⊖ Farringdon

59 rm – ♦£194 ♦♦£194, ☕£16.50

The Zetter ticks all the boxes for a contemporary hotel: it's a converted Victorian warehouse in a hitherto neglected area of the city that's now having its time and is environmentally aware, with spring water bottled from its building's own well. Its laid-back restaurant with a menu of mainly Mediterranean influence is a popular place for weekend brunches; it has understated bedrooms offering everything from a huge array of music tracks to classic Penguin paperbacks and, to appreciate all these things, it attracts a clientele who know their wiis from their wi-fis. But what makes the place more than just another hip hotel is its friendly and hospitable staff who understand that the principles of hospitality remain the same, regardless of whether the hotel is trendy or traditional, and that coolness need not equate to aloofness. The restaurant has personality and really comes into its own on sunny days, thanks to its large windows overlooking St John's Square, and the whole hotel has a definable sense of time and place.

Number Sixteen

E6

16 Sumner Pl ⊠ SW7 3EG ⊖ South Kensington
✆ (020) 7589 5232 **Fax** (020) 7584 8615
e-mail sixteen@firmdale.com www.numbersixteenhotel.co.uk
42 rm – ♦£141/235 ♦♦£317, ☕£17.50

Actually, it's numbers 14 – 17 but whose counting? Anyway, Number Sixteen is a snappier name. The hotel is made up of four lustrously bright white houses in a mid Victorian terrace, located in a very charming street with all the museums, shops and restaurants you'll need within walking distance. Unlike many a recent conversion from private house to intimate hotel, this one has ensured that everyone has plenty of room. On the ground floor there are two delightful drawing rooms, overlooking Sumner Place and decorated with interesting modern British artwork. The conservatory breakfast room leads out into a pretty private garden, which is surprisingly large given the South Kensington location, and indeed four of the bedrooms open out onto this very restful space. All the bedrooms combine a sense of Englishness with a modern freshness and vitality. Roberts radios are in all the rooms, along with granite bathrooms and top of the range fabrics and the housekeeping department is clearly on top of its game.

SOUTH KENSINGTON ▶ Plan XI

Durrants

G2

26-32 George St ✉ W1H 5BJ ⊖ Bond Street
✆ (020) 7935 8131 **Fax** (020) 7487 3510
e-mail enquiries@durrantshotel.co.uk **www**.durrantshotel.co.uk

89 rm – †£125 ††£175, ⌑ £14.50 – 3 suites

Durrants may be one of London's more traditional, privately owned hotels but that doesn't mean it is resting on any laurels. Having a separate breakfast room to the main dining room had always seemed something of an extravagance and this room has now been turned into a lounge area, as private parties had started to encroach on the existing sitting rooms and, commendably, the hotel was concerned about its staying guests. The bars have been given a little spruce up as well, although the muskets are still there for those who like some weaponry with their whisky. The clubby dining room still offers the likes of Dover Sole and a carving trolley but there are now some lighter, more Mediterranean dishes for the youngsters. The bedrooms are the final piece of the operation being brought up to date. The refurbishment is nothing too outrageous so there'll be no scaring of the horses. Instead, the rooms are being brightened and lightened, while retaining that very sense of Englishness that makes the hotel what it is.

Dorset Square

F1

39-40 Dorset Sq ✉ NW1 6QN ⊖ Marylebone
📞 (020) 7723 7874 **Fax** (020) 7724 3328 Closed 1 week Christmas
e-mail reservations@dorsetsquare.co.uk www.dorsetsquare.co.uk
37 rm – ♦£165/282 ♦♦£206/329, ⌑£14.50

It's a pretty Regency house and the square opposite was where Thomas Lord laid out his ground in 1787, before it moved up the road in 1814 to what is now Lord's. His memory lives on in the hotel in subtle little ways – the room keys come with little cricket balls attached and the occasional MCC member can be spotted during the summer months. For those sadly impervious to the charms of a game that lasts five days and usually ends in a draw, there is still much to appreciate in the hotel, not least it's proximity to the centre but without the bustle and noise. There's a charming drawing room with an honesty bar and the Potting Shed restaurant downstairs is as delightful as the name suggests. Here you'll find a menu offering a balanced selection of modern European food, with the occasional live jazz accompaniment and another cricketing reminder in the form of a large mural. The bedrooms reflect the age of the house which means a mix of sizes and some sloping lintels; they all share fine country style fabrics and bags of charm.

Egerton House

F5

17-19 Egerton Terrace ⊖ South Kensington
✉ SW3 2BX
✆ (020) 7589 2412 **Fax** (020) 7584 6540
e-mail bookeg@rchmail.com **www**.egertonhousehotel.com

27 rm – ♦£300 ♦♦£370/582, ☕ £24.50 – 1 suite

Another thing that London does very well is the Townhouse Hotel. They come in various shapes and standards and degrees of style and personality, but it is in their running where the standards really vary. The Red Carnation group may have refurbished Egerton House from top to bottom, blending the classic with the modern and making great use of what is quite limited space, but ultimately it is the standards it sets in service that really makes it stand out. When you check in they'll feed the meter for your car, take you up to the room and offer you a complimentary welcoming drink in the little cocktail bar; later they'll turn down the bed and leave an Evening Standard and some chocolates. The bedrooms are individually styled and all the extras are there, from Penhaligon toiletries to robes and slippers. The atmosphere in the hotel is discreet and peaceful. Ask for one of the quieter rooms at the back, overlooking the pretty enclosed garden. The hotel is in a great location and just a short walk away from most of the city's smartest shops.

K + K George

C6

1-15 Templeton Pl ✉ SW5 9NB ⊖ Earl's Court
✆ (020) 7598 8700 **Fax** (020) 7370 2285
e-mail hotelgeorge@kkhotels.co.uk **www**.kkhotels.com

154 rm ⌑ – ♦£259 ♦♦£294

K+K hotels are a small, privately owned chain, all of whose hotels seem to blend seamlessly into the fabric of the assorted European cities in which they are located. London is no exception, as the K+K George is set within an imposing stucco fronted and luminously white Georgian terrace and is in a useful location for both tourists and attendees of exhibition halls and trade fairs nearby.

In contrast to the period façade, the hotel's interior is colourfully contemporary in style, with clean lines and a refreshing lack of chintz. Those who struggle to lift their mood first thing in the day will appreciate the bright and comfortable breakfast room as it looks out onto the hotel's own private garden - a charming and, considering the location, surprisingly decent size and clearly the envy of surrounding houses.

A simple bistro style menu is served in the friendly and less structured surroundings of the bar while corporate guests will find all the kit they need for any homework. Bedrooms all come in relatively decent dimensions and have a certain Scandinavian feel and freshness about them.

EARL'S COURT ▶ Plan XI

The Gore

D5

190 Queen's Gate ✉ SW7 5EX ⊖ Gloucester Road
☎ (020) 7584 6601 **Fax** (020) 7589 8127
e-mail reservations@gorehotel.com **www**.gorehotel.com

50 rm – †£212/269 ††£269/520, ⊇ £16.95

The Gore may have changed hands relatively recently but the new owners understand the importance of preserving the hotel's highly individual feel. The narrow lobby and reception area is covered with a plethora of pictures and prints, many of which feature Queen Victoria which is appropriate as this part of London is so closely linked to her reign. There's a pleasant sitting room, although it is often used for photo-shoots. The adjacent wood panelled bar is quite a fashionable spot these days while the bistro is a bright and lively little number and it's proximity to the Albert Hall means that it's one of the few restaurants where it's easier to get a table at 8pm than it is at 5.30pm or 11.00pm. The menu offers an appealing selection of mostly European influences. Despite having 50 bedrooms, the atmosphere of the hotel remains intimate and the clientele relatively youthful. The rooms have been refurbished and all exude a sense of individuality. The Tudor Room has a fireplace, minstrel gallery and concealed bathroom door; The Judy Garland room has one of her old beds.

22 Jermyn Street

22 Jermyn St ✉ SW1Y 6HL ⊖ Piccadilly Circus
✆ (020) 7734 2353 **Fax** (020) 7734 0750
e-mail office@22jermyn.com **www**.22jermyn.com
5 rm – ♦£259 ♦♦£259 – 14 suites

A hotel for the man about town. Running between Regent and St James's Streets, Jermyn Street dates back to 1664 and is one of London's most celebrated, thanks to the roll call of familiar names providing all manner of sartorial finery to the well dressed gentleman. Number 22 was reconstructed at the turn of the 19C and has been in the Togna family since 1915, with Henry Togna, the current owner, responsible for transforming it into the luxury townhouse it is today. While there are no public areas to the hotel, the bedrooms are of sufficient size for this not to matter; of the 19 rooms, 14 are suites and who can complain when breakfast in bed is the only option? A full 24-hour room service menu is also available but this is a hotel for the sort of person who knows their way around town; there are innumerable dining options within walking distance and assorted hostelries within staggering distance. All the rooms are elegantly decorated, with additional sofa beds in the suites and plenty of extras, from DVD players to bathrobes.

The Rockwell

C5

181-183 Cromwell Rd ✉ SW5 0SF　　　　⊖ Earl's Court
✆ (020) 7244 2000 **Fax** (020) 7244 2001
e-mail enquiries@therockwell.com **www**.therockwell.com

40 rm – †£120/180 ††£180/200, ⊇ £12.50

The Rockwell brings a little contemporary styling to the less glamorous 'Australian' end of Cromwell Road. Owned by a family of builders, they have knocked together two large Victorian houses and have created a hotel with a sense of individuality and freshness. The lobby/reception is an open-plan affair with a fireplace and plenty of reading material and this leads through into the small dining room and bar which offer an easy menu of modern European staples. This, in turn, looks out over what is one of the most appealing features of the hotel – the secluded and stylishly lit south-facing garden terrace.

Bedrooms come with plenty of oak and are decorated in bold, warm colours. Flat screen TVs, mini-bars and Egyptian cotton sheets are standard features. Bathrooms are a little on the small size but more than make up for the lack of footage with the quality of the toiletries and the fittings. Room sizes vary, reflecting the age and character of the house; Garden Rooms all have their own patios and Room 107 is a quiet room with a high ceiling.

Knightsbridge Green

159 Knightsbridge ✉ SW1X 7PD ⊖ Knightsbridge
✆ (020) 7584 6274 **Fax** (020) 7225 1635 Closed 25-26 December
e-mail reservations@thekghotel.com www.thekghotel.com

16 rm – ♦£150/180 ♦♦£200/250, ☕£12 – 12 suites

If location is everything, then Knightsbridge Green has it all: it is one busy road away from the bucolic delights of Hyde Park; it's surrounded by all the swankiest department stores, shops and boutiques and is a mere taxi ride away from most major tourist attractions. The only downside is the building work going on opposite as the Mandarin Oriental builds its extension but the sound proofing is pretty decent. The hotel is spread over six floors; there's a small lounge on the ground floor, with leather sofas and frosted window to disguise the procession of buses that pass by, and a little computer room adjacent. An old fashioned lift carries you up to the rooms. Be sure to ask for one of the newly refurbished ones which come in smart blues and creams, have thick carpets and flat screen TVs. There's no separate breakfast room so it's served in the bedrooms. Knightsbridge Green feels less like a hotel, and more like you've borrowed a friend's apartment. As Boswell pointed out "it is best to have lodgings in the more airy vicinity of Hyde Park."

The Rookery

L2

12 Peters Lane, Cowcross St ⊖ Barbican
✉ EC1M 6DS
✆ (020) 7336 0931 **Fax** (020) 7336 0931
e-mail reservations@rookery.co.uk www.rookeryhotel.com

32 rm – †£206/241 ††£259/347, ⊆ £9.95 – 1 suite

The mere fact that the original opening of the hotel was delayed because the owner couldn't find quite the right chimney pots tells you that authenticity is high on the agenda here. Named after the colloquial name for the local area from a time when it had an unruly reputation, the hotel is made up of a series of Georgian houses whose former residents are honoured in the naming of the bedrooms. Its decoration remains true to these Georgian roots, not only in the antique furniture and period features but also in the colours used; all the bedrooms have either half-testers or four poster beds and bathrooms have roll top baths. Rook's Nest, the largest room, is often used for fashion shoots. However, with the addition of flat screen TVs and wireless internet access, there is no danger of the hotel becoming a twee museum piece. Breakfast is served in the bedrooms and there is just one small sitting room which leads out onto a little terrace - its mural of the owner herding some cows goes some way towards blocking out the surrounding sights of the 21C.

Hazlitt's

13

6 Frith St ✉ W1D 3JA ⊖ Tottenham Court Road
✆ (020) 7434 1771 **Fax** (020) 7439 1524 Closed 25-26 December
e-mail reservations@hazlitts.co.uk **www**.hazlittshotel.com

23 rm – ♦£206/259 ♦♦£259, ☕ £10.95 **– 1 suite**

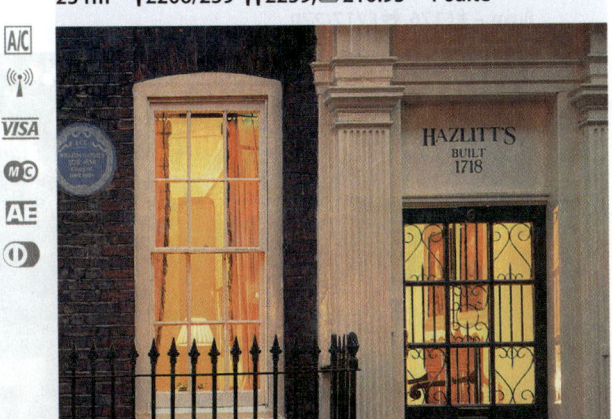

Named after the essayist and critic William Hazlitt who lived and died here in 1830, Hazlitt's is a delightfully idiosyncratic little hotel made up of three adjoining town houses dating from 1718. The 23 bedrooms are spread over three floors (there are no lifts) and are all named after writers from the 18C and 19C who were either residents or visitors to the house. Today, the hotel still attracts its fair share of writers, artists and those of a bohemian bent. Each room is full of character, with everything from wood panelling, busts and antique beds to Victorian bathroom fittings and fixtures. The Earl of Willoughby is the largest room and comes with a small sitting room. The ground floor sitting room is the only communal area and breakfast is served in the bedrooms as there's no restaurant. Being in very heart of Soho, however, means that if you can't find a restaurant here then you really shouldn't be allowed out. There are plans afoot to increase the number of bedrooms which, hopefully, will not affect the intimate atmosphere.

Miller's

C2

111A Westbourne Grove (entrance on Hereford Rd) ✉ W2 4UW
☎ (020) 7243 1024 **Fax** (020) 7243 1064
e-mail enquiries@millershotel.com **www**.millershotel.com

8 rm – ♦£176 ♦♦£217/270

⊖ Bayswater

Just look out for the red door as the only sign that tells you that this is indeed a little hotel is a discreet brass plaque. The clue lies in the name: this 18th century house is owned by Martin Miller, he of Miller's Antique Guide and his stock appears to be scattered all over the house. Ring the bell, climb the stairs and you'll find yourself in a charming drawing room chock-a-block with antiques, pictures, baubles, candles and assorted objets d'art. This is the only communal area in the hotel - and the heart of the house. It is also where breakfast is served – on a single large table. You'll find an honesty bar here as well as bowls of fruit and chocolate bars scattered around. The eight bedrooms are on the first and second floors and are all named after Romantic poets; highly appropriate as they are all quite theatrical and imaginative in their decoration. Wordsworth is big enough to let you wander; Keats is a thing of beauty and book Blake for when you want sleep to come hither. Miller's greatest selling point as a hotel is that it doesn't feel anything like a hotel.

Twenty Nevern Square

20 Nevern Sq ✉ SW5 9PD ⊖ Earl's Court
✆ (020) 7565 9555 **Fax** (020) 7565 9444
e-mail hotel@twentynevernsquare.co.uk
www.twentynevernsquare.co.uk

20 rm – ♦£85/115 ♦♦£110/150, ⊆ £9

Booking well in advance is the key here as this small but friendly hotel, with its quiet and leafy location in the typically Victorian Nevern Square, represents good value for money and gets booked up pretty quickly. The two best rooms are the Pasha and the more recently added Ottoman Suite and both have their own terrace, but all rooms are well looked after and given regular refits. Ten of the rooms overlook the gardens opposite but try to get one of the rooms on the top floor as these have more space. Hand-carved Indonesian furniture is found throughout and, together with the elaborately draped curtains, adds a hint of exoticism. You'll find gratis tea, coffee, water and a pile of daily newspapers laid on in the pleasant lounge beside the lovebirds, Mary and Joseph. Continental breakfast comes included in the room rate; it can be taken in the bedroom or the bright conservatory. The hotel's other great selling point is a genuine sense of neighbourhood one feels. Its sister hotel, the Mayflower, is around the corner.

Aster House

E6

3 Sumner Pl ✉ SW7 3EE ⊖ South Kensington
✆ (020) 7581 5888 **Fax** (020) 7584 4925
e-mail asterhouse@btinternet.com **www**.asterhouse.com

13 rm ⊃ – ♦£80/135 ♦♦£120/180

A/C
VISA
MC

R. Burr / Michelin

Sadly, but realistically, few of us will ever be able to afford to buy a huge Victorian house, spread over four floors, in the Elysian Fields known as South Kensington. So staying in a Bed and Breakfast in a delightful and typically Kensington street, with restaurants, shops and attractions all within walking distance, is a great opportunity to live the dream. Like all B&B's you get the distinct feeling you are staying in someone's house, particularly when you have to ring the doorbell to be let in. But it's not just its location where Aster House scores heavily; the house is immaculately kept, offers sizeable rooms and comes with rates that are a little more down to earth than many. Three of the thirteen rooms are classified as 'superior', including the particularly popular Garden Room which, as the name suggests, leads out onto a small garden. Breakfast is served in a very charming conservatory on the first floor which doubles as a bright and comfortable sitting room, overlooking Sumner Place and your fellow Kensington residents below.

Mayflower

C6

26-28 Trebovir Rd ✉ SW5 9NJ ⊖ Earl's Court
✆ (020) 7370 0991 **Fax** (020) 7370 0994
e-mail info@mayflower-group.co.uk **www**.mayflowerhotel.co.uk

46 rm – ♦£79/109 ♦♦£99/145, ⚏ £9

The Mayflower shares the same ownership as Twenty Nevern Square just around the corner and it too offers good value accommodation. It is also twice the size so chances of actually getting a room are somewhat greater. Some of those bedrooms can be a little tight on space but this is also reflected in the room rates. Rooms 11, 17 and 18 are the best in the house and the general decoration is a blend of the contemporary with some Asian influence; some of the rooms have jet showers and others balconies. But what makes the hotel stand out is that the owner is nearly always on the property and his enthusiasm has been passed to his staff. This may not be a glitzy West End hotel but they really do make an effort to get to know their guests and help in anyway they can. There is no restaurant, but then it doesn't need one: there are plenty of places in which to eat that are no more than a vigorous stroll away. A plentiful breakfast is provided and, on summer days, can even be taken on the small terrace.

B + B Belgravia

G6

64-66 Ebury St ✉ SW1W 9QD ⊖ Victoria
☏ (020) 7259 8570 **Fax** (020) 7259 8591
e-mail info@bb-belgravia.com **www**.bb-belgravia.com

17 rm ☕ – ♦£99/107 ♦♦£125/130

It's really more Victoria than Belgravia and is certainly a degree more stylish than your average B&B. But what is certain is that B&B Belgravia provides very good value accommodation in a central location and is just the sort of place that London needs more of. The discreet entrance and key pad entry makes you feel as though you've borrowed a friend's place while the funky lounge comes complete with a complimentary coffee machine and plenty of magazines and DVDs. Breakfast is a buffet, with eggs cooked to order; those not good in the morning may find the staff's sunny demeanour and the room's general brightness akin to a second wake-up call. Rooms are virtually identical in style: they are contemporary in tone with sleek lines, high ceilings and good amenities. 6 of the 17 rooms have baths, the rest just showers. This being Central London, the rooms on the front can get a little noisy so ask for a room overlooking the gravelled garden at the back, such as Room 12. And do the booking in plenty of time as this place is understandably popular.

Hart House

51 Gloucester Pl ⊠ W1U 8JF ⊖ Marble Arch
☏ (020) 7935 2288 **Fax** (020) 7935 8516
e-mail reservations@harthouse.co.uk **www**.harthouse.co.uk

15 rm ⊇ – ♦£75/125 ♦♦£98/135

Gloucester Place is a street made up almost entirely of large Georgian terrace houses, many of which are given over to the provision of accommodation of a budgetary nature and questionable standard. Hart House bucks the trend by proving that you can offer bedrooms that are clean, spacious and still competitively priced for those travelling on a budget or those looking for something a little less impersonal than your average overpriced city centre bed factory. Run by the same family for over thirty-five years, Hart House has its bedrooms spread over three floors where the ceilings get lower the higher you climb, reflecting the time when the house's staff had their quarters at the top of the house. Rooms on the front of the house benefit from the large windows and they're fitted with double glazing which keeps the traffic noise outside at bay, so maybe those salesmen were telling the truth after all. Four of the fifteen rooms are decently priced single rooms and there are family rooms also available. There are no communal areas except for the small basement breakfast room.

Index of maps

CENTRAL LONDON	PLAN I	30
▶ Mayfair • Soho • St James's	Plan II	34
▶ Strand • Covent Garden	Plan III	94
▶ Belgravia • Victoria	Plan IV	104
▶ Regent's Park • Marylebone	Plan V	124
▶ Bloomsbury	Plan VI	144
▶ Bayswater • Maida Vale	Plan VII	160
▶ City of London	Plan VIII	174
▶ Clerkenwell • Finsbury	Plan IX	176
▶ Southwark	Plan X	178
▶ Chelsea • Earl's Court • South Kensington	Plan XI	212
▶ Hyde Park • Knightsbridge	Plan XII	214
▶ Kensington • North Kensington • Notting Hill	Plan XIII	250
GREATER LONDON	**PLAN XIV**	**266**
▶ North-West	Plan XV	270
▶ North-East	Plan XVI	288
▶ South-East	Plan XVII	306
▶ South-West	Plan XVIII	318

Alphabetical list of Restaurants

A

Aaya	XX	81
Abeno	X	156
L'Absinthe	X	281
L'Accento	X 🍷	167
A Cena	XX	351
Acorn House	X	154
The Admiral Codrington	🍴	242
Admiralty	XX	97
Alain Ducasse at The Dorchester	XXXXX ❀❀	37
Alastair Little	XX	79
Al Duca	X 🍷	82
Alloro	XX	62
Almeida	XX	296
Amaya	XXX ❀	109
Ambassade de L'Ile	XXX ❀	221
The Ambassador	X	200
The Anchor and Hope	🍴 🍷	207
Angelus	XX	162
Anglesea Arms	🍴	341
L'Anima	XXX	300
Aquasia	XXX	225
Arbutus	X ❀	83
Archipelago	XX	150
Arturo	X	167
Asadal	XX	151
Assaggi	X ❀	166
Atami	XX	114
L'Atelier de Joël Robuchon	X ❀❀	99
Aubaine	X	241
L'Auberge	XX	345
Aubergine	XXX ❀	220
Au Lac	X	293
Aurora	X	87
Automat	X	85
L'Autre Pied	XX ❀	132
L'Aventure	XX	135
The Avenue	XX	71
Avista	XXX	58
Awana	XXX	224
Axis	XXX	95
Azou	X	341

B

Babylon	XX	255
Baltic	XX	190
Bangkok	X	241
Bank	XX	117
Barnes Grill	X	323
The Barnsbury	🍴	299
Barrafina	X	89
Bar Shu	X	87
Bedford & Strand	X	100
Bellamy's	XX	70
Belvedere	XXX	252
Benares	XXX ❀	49
Bengal Clipper	XX	185
Benja	XX 🍷	77
Bentley's (Grill)	XXX	56
Bentley's (Oyster Bar)	X	86
Bevis Marks	XX	187
Bibendum	XXX	222
Bibendum Oyster Bar	X	242
Bistro Aix	X	275
Bleeding Heart	XX	150
Bluebird	XX	228
Blue Elephant	XX	337
Blueprint Café	X	196
Boisdale	XX	116
Boisdale of Bishopgate	XX	187
The Bollo	🍴	320
Bombay Brasserie	XXX	224
Bonds	XXX	181
The Botanist	XX	238
Le Boudin Blanc	X	90
The Brackenbury	X	340
Bradley's	XX 🍷	283
Brasserie James	X	322
Brasserie Roux	XX	68
Brasserie St Jacques	XX	81
Brew Wharf	X	206
The Brown Dog	🍴 🍷	324

Brula	XÊ	351
Builders Arms	¦D	244
The Bull	¦D	278
Bumpkin	X	259
The Butcher & Grill	X	326
Butlers Wharf Chop House	X	199

C

Le Café Anglais	XX	162
The Cafe (at Sotheby's)	X	84
Cafe Boheme	X	90
Le Café du Jardin	X	100
Café Lazeez	XX	76
Cafe Spice Namaste	XXÊ	315
Caffè Caldesi	X	138
Caldesi	XX	134
Cambio de Tercio	XX	234
Camerino	XX	152
Canteen (Southbank)	X	206
Canteen (Spitalfields)	X	313
Cantina Del Ponte	X	197
Cantina Vinopolis	X	198
The Capital Restaurant	XXX✤✤	217
Le Caprice	XX	59
Caraffini	XX	230
Carpaccio	XX	237
Carpenter's Arms	¦D	342
Cat & Mutton	¦D	292
Cecconi's	XXX	51
Le Cercle	XX	229
Chada	XX	325
Chada Chada	X	139
Champor-Champor	X	204
The Chancery	XX	186
Chapters	XXÊ	308
Charlotte's Place	X	333
Chelsea Brasserie	XX	235
Chelsea Ram	¦D	243
Chez Bruce	XX✤	354
Chez Kristof	XX	340
China Tang	XXXX	36
Chinese Experience	X	86
Chisou	X	85
Chor Bizarre	XX	74
Chutney Mary	XXX	223
Cibo	X	260
Cicada	X	200

Cigala	X	153
The Cinnamon Club	XXX	111
Clarke's	XX	254
The Clerkenwell Dining Room	XX	191
Clos Maggiore	XX	97
Club Gascon	XX✤	184
The Coach & Horses	¦D	207
Cocoon	XX	74
Le Colombier	XX	230
Comptoir Gascon	XÊ	203
Il Convivio	XX	114
Coq d'Argent	XXX	182
Crazy Bear	XX	149
The Cross Keys	¦D	245

D

Daphne's	XX	227
The Dartmouth Arms	¦D	310
The Dartmouth Castle	¦D	343
Deep	XX	336
Dehesa	XÊ	89
Le Deuxième	XX	98
Devonshire Terrace	XX	191
The Devonshire House	¦D	331
Dinings	X	139
Dragon Castle	XX	310
The Drapers Arms	¦D	298
Duke of Sussex	¦D	320

E

E & O	XX	256
The Ebury	¦D	120
Edera	XX	255
Eight over Eight	XX	237
11 Abingdon Road	XX	257
Embassy	XXX	57
The Empress of India	¦D	292
The Engineer	¦D	282
Enoteca Turi	XX	346
Eriki	XX	283
L'Escargot	XXX	48
L'Etranger	XX	231

F

Fakhreldine	XX	72
The Farm	¦D	338

Restaurant		Page
The Fat Badger	🍺	262
Fifteen	X	295
Fifth Floor	XxX	223
Fig	X	290
Fino	XX	149
The Fire Stables	🍺	355
Fish Hook	X	330
Flâneur	X	155
Floridita	XX	67
Foliage	XxX ✿	218
The Forge	XX	98
Four O Nine	XX	331
The Fox	🍺	301
Foxtrot Oscar	X 😊	239
Franco's	XX	76

G

Galvin at Windows	XxxX	43
Galvin	XX 😊	130
The Garrison	🍺	209
Le Gavroche	XxxX ✿✿	39
Giaconda Dining Room	X 😊	155
The Glasshouse	XX ✿	344
Good Earth	XX	238
Gordon Ramsay	XxxX ✿✿✿	216
Gordon Ramsay at Claridge's	XxxX ✿	40
Great Eastern Dining Room	XX	294
Great Queen Street	X 😊	153
The Greenhouse	XxX ✿	44
The Greyhound	🍺	279
The Greyhound at Battersea	🍺	327
The Grill Room	X	352
The Gun	🍺	309

H

Haiku	XX	78
Hakkasan	XX ✿	148
Haozhan	XX	79
Harrison's	X	321
The Hartley		208
The Havelock Tavern	🍺 😊	342
Hélène Darroze at The Connaught	XxxX ✿	38
Hereford Road	X 😊	165
Hibiscus	XxX ✿✿	45
High Road Brasserie	XX	329
Hix Oyster and Chop House	X	202
The House	🍺	291
Hoxton Apprentice	X	295
Hush	XX	62

I

Imli	X	91
Incognico	XX	146
Indian Zing	XX	338
Inn the Park	X	84
Island	XX	165
Ivy	XxX	95

J

Jamuna	XX	163
J. Sheekey	XX	96
Junction Tavern	🍺	284

K

Kai	XxX ✿	55
Kastoori	X 😊	350
Ken Lo's Memories of China	XX	115
Kensington Place	X	259
Kenza	XX	192
Kew Grill	XX	343
Khan's of Kensington	XX	234
Kiasu	X	168
Kiku	XX	78
Konstam at the Prince Albert	X	156

L

Lamberts	X	321
Langan's Coq d'Or	XX	231
The Larder	XX	188
Latium	XxX	128
Launceston Place	XxX	253
The Ledbury	XxX ✿	251
Levant	XX	134
Light House	X	355
Lobster Pot	X	312
Locanda Locatelli	XxX ✿	127
The Lock	XX	303
Lots Road Pub and Dining Room	🍺	246

L Restaurant & Bar	XX	258
Luciano	XxX	57

M

Ma Cuisine (Barnes)	X ⊛	324
Ma Cuisine (Kew)	X ⊛	345
Ma Cuisine (Twickenham)	X ⊛	352
The Magdala	ɪD	277
Magdalen	X	201
Malabar	X ⊛	260
Mango & Silk	X ⊛	334
Mango Tree	XX	116
Manicomio (City of London)	X	240
Manicomio (Chelsea)	XX	192
Mao Tai	XX	337
Marco	XX	239
Marcus Wareing at The Berkeley	XxxX ✿✿	106
Market	X ⊛	274
Matsuba	X	348
Matsuri - High Holborn	XX	147
Matsuri - St James's	XX	71
Maxim	XX	333
Maze	XxX ✿	46
Maze Grill	XX	70
Medcalf	X ⊛	201
Memories of China	XX	258
Memsaab	XxX	335
The Mercer	XX	193
Metrogusto	XX ⊛	297
Mews of Mayfair	XX	73
Mezedopolio	X	296
Michael Moore	X	137
Min Jiang	XxX	252
Mint Leaf	XX	69
Mint Leaf Lounge	XX	194
The Modern Pantry	X ⊛	202
Momo	XX	66
Mon Plaisir	XX	146
The Morgan Arms	ɪD	291
Morgan M	XX	290
Moro	X	197
Moti Mahal	XX	151
Mr Chow	XX	232
Murano	XxX ✿	52

N

Nahm	XX ✿	113
The Narrow	ɪD ⊛	312
The National Dining Rooms	X	88
Nipa	XX	164
Nobu	XX ✿	60
Nobu Berkeley St	XX ✿	63
Norfolk Arms	ɪD	157
The Northgate	ɪD	298
North London Tavern	ɪD	279
Notting Grill	X	261
Notting Hill Brasserie	XX	253
Noura Brasserie	XX	117
Noura Central	XX	69
Nozomi	XX	228

O

L'Oasis	ɪD	299
Odette's	XX	280
Old Dairy	ɪD	303
Olivo	X	118
Olivomare	X	119
1 Lombard Street	XxX	181
One-O-One	XxX	222
The Only Running Footman	ɪD	91
Oscar	XX	129
Osteria Emilia	X	273
Osteria Stecca	XX	136
Ottolenghi	X	297
Oxo Tower	XxX	183
Oxo Tower Brasserie	X	194
Ozer	XX	133

P

Painted Heron	XX	236
The Pantechnicon Rooms	ɪD	120
Papillon	XX	233
Paradise by way of Kensal Green	ɪD	278
Pasha	XX	233
Passione	X	152
Paternoster Chop House	X	198
Patterson's	XX	59
Pearl	XxX	144
Pearl Liang	XX	164
The Peasant	ɪD	208
Pellicano	XX	235

Petersham Nurseries Café	X	349
La Petite Maison	XX	67
Philpott's Mezzaluna	XX	275
The Phoenix (Chelsea)	iD	245
The Phoenix (Putney)	X	346
Phoenix Palace	XX	135
Pied à Terre	XxX ✿✿	145
The Pig's Ear	iD	244
Plateau	XX	309
Poissonnerie de l'Avenue	XX	229
Le Pont de la Tour	XxX	182
Portal	XX	190
La Porte des Indes	XX	130
Portrait	X	88
La Poule au Pot	X	118
Prince Albert	iD	274
Prince Alfred & Formosa Dining Room	iD	169
Prince Arthur	iD	293
Prince of Wales	iD	347
The Princess	iD	301
The Providores	XX	131

Q

Quadrato	XxX	308
Quaglino's	XX	68
Quality Chop House	X	203
Queen's Head & Artichoke	iD	140
The Queens	iD	281
Queens Pub & Dining Room	iD	276
Quilon	XxX ✿	110
Quirinale	XX	112
Quo Vadis	XxX	51

R

Racine	XX	227
Ransome's Dock	X	325
Rasa	X	302
Rasa Samudra	XX	133
Rasa Travancore	X	302
Rasoi	XX ✿	226
Red Fort	XxX	56
The Restaurant at The Petersham	XxX	348
Rex Whistler	XX	115
Rhodes Twenty Four	XxX ✿	180
Rhodes W1 Brasserie	XX	129
Rhodes W1 Restaurant	XxxX ✿	126
Richard Corrigan at Lindsay House	XxX ✿	54
The Ritz Restaurant	XxXxX	36
Riva	X	323
River Café	XX ✿	339
Rivington (Greenwich)	X	311
Rivington (Shoreditch)	X	300
Roast	XX	186
Roka	XX	131
The Rosendale	iD	315
Roussillon	XxX ✿	108
Rules	XX	96

S

St Alban	XxX	48
St John	X ✿	195
St John's	iD	272
St John Bread and Wine	X	314
Sake No Hana	XxX	58
The Salt House	iD	140
Salt Yard	X ✿	154
The Salusbury	iD	282
Sam's Brasserie	X	330
Santini	XxX	111
Saran Rom	XxX	335
Sardo	XX	147
Sardo Canale	XX	280
Sartoria	XxX	50
Sauterelle	XX	185
Scott's	XxX	43
Semplice	XX ✿	64
Shepherd's	XxX	112
Silk	XX	82
Simply Thai	X	350
Singapore Garden	XX	284
Sketch (The Gallery)	XX	66
Sketch (The Lecture Room & Library)	XxxX ✿	42
Skylon	XxX	183
Smiths of Smithfield	XX	189
Snazz Sichuan	XX	276
Sonny's	XX	322
The Spencer Arms	iD	347
Spread Eagle	XX	311
The Square	XxxX ✿✿	41
Stanza	XX	77
Sumosan	XX	73

Restaurant		Page
Sushi-Say	X	285
Swag and Tails	iD	243

T

Restaurant		Page
Taman Gang	XX	65
Tamarind	XxX	50
Tangawizi	X ⊛	353
Tapas Brindisa	X	204
Tapas y Vino	X	353
Tate Modern (Restaurant)	X	196
Tatsuso	XX	188
Texture	XX	128
Theo Randall	XxX	47
The Thomas Cubitt	iD	119
Timo	XX	257
Tom's Kitchen	X	240
Tom Aikens	XxX ✿	219
Tom Ilić	X	326
Toto's	XxX	225
Trenta	XX	163
Trinity	XX	332
Les Trois Garcons	XX	313
La Trompette	XxX ✿	328
La Trouvaille	XX	75
Tsunami	X	332

U

Restaurant		Page
Umu	XxX ✿	53
Union Café	X	138
Upstairs	XX ⊛	327
Urban Turban	X	168

V

Restaurant		Page
Le Vacherin	XX	329
Vama	XX	236
Vanilla Black	XX	193
Vasco and Piero's Pavilion	XX	72
Veeraswamy	XX	75
Via Condotti	XX ⊛	65
The Victoria	iD	334
Village East	X	205
Villandry	XX	136
Vinoteca	X	199

W

Restaurant		Page
The Wallace	X	137
Walnut	X	285
Wapping Food	X	314
The Warrington	iD	170
Water House	XX	294
The Waterway	iD	169
The Well	iD	209
The Wells	iD	277
The Wharf	XX	349
The White Swan	XX	189
Whits	XX	256
Wild Honey	XX ✿	61
The Wolseley	XxX	47
Wright Brothers	X	205
Wódka	X	261

X

Restaurant		Page
XO	XX	272

Y

Restaurant		Page
Yauatcha	XX ✿	80
Yi-Ban	XX	336
York & Albany	XX	273

Z

Restaurant		Page
Zafferano	XxX ✿	107
Zaika	XX	254
Zuma	XX	232

Maps & plans

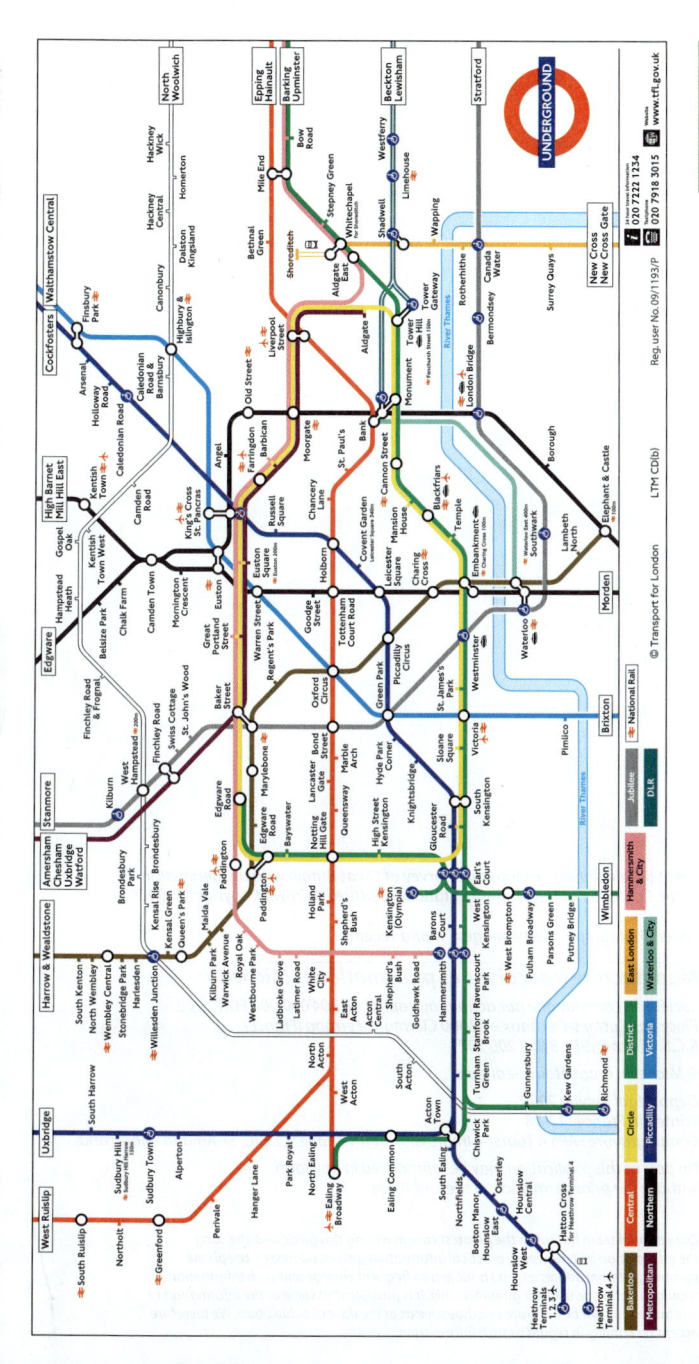

Great Britain: Based on Ordnance Survey of Great Britain with the permission of the Controller of Her Majesty's Stationery Office, © Crown Copyright 100000247.

Cover photograph : Getty Images / Maria Teijeiro

Manufacture française des pneumatiques Michelin

Société en commandite par actions au capital de 304 000 000 EUR
Place des Carmes-Déchaux – 63000 Clermont-Ferrand (France)
R.C.S. Clermont-Fd B 855 200 507

© Michelin, Propriétaires-éditeurs

Dépot légal janvier 2009
Printed in France : 12-08
Compogravure : APS à Tours – Impression et brochage : CLERC, St-Amand-Montrond

No part of this publication may be reproduced in any form without the prior permission of the publisher

Our editorial team has taken the greatest care in writing this guide and checking the information in it. However, practical information (prices, addresses, telephone numbers, internet addresses, etc) is subject to frequent change and such information should therefore be used for guidance only. It is possible that some of the information in this guide may not be accurate or exhaustive as at the date of publication. We therefore accept no liability in regard to such information.